The Last 100 Days

D0406273

The Last
100 Days

FDR at War and at Peace

David B. Woolner

BASIC BOOKS

New York

WITHDRAWN

Copyright © 2017 by David B. Woolner

Published by Basic Books, an imprint of Perseus Books, LLC, a subsidiary of Hachette Book Group, Inc.

All rights reserved. Printed in the United States of America. No part of this book may be reproduced in any manner whatsoever without written permission except in the case of brief quotations embodied in critical articles and reviews. For information, address Basic Books, 1290 Avenue of the Americas, New York, NY 10004.

Books published by Basic Books are available at special discounts for bulk purchases in the United States by corporations, institutions, and other organizations. For more information, please contact the Special Markets Department at the Perseus Books Group, 2300 Chestnut Street, Suite 200, Philadelphia, PA 19103, or call (800) 810-4145, ext. 5000, or e-mail special.markets@perseusbooks.com.

A catalog record for this book is available from the Library of Congress.

ISBN: 978-0-465-04871-7 (hardcover); ISBN: 978-0-465-09651-0 (e-book)

Library of Congress Control Number: 2017954582

LSC-C

10 9 8 7 6 5 4 3 2 1

IN MEMORIAM

Lewis B. Woolner, 1913–2016

That we shall die, we know; 'tis but the time
And drawing days out, that men stand upon.

Julius Caesar, Act III; Sc. 1

Contents

Preface

FRANKLIN DELANO ROOSEVELT IS CONSISTENTLY RANKED AS AMONG the most important and effective chief executives in American history. For most historians the two most significant aspects of his presidency remain the unprecedented nature of his response to the Great Depression and the skillful leadership he exhibited in the summer of 1940, when he made the critical decision—at great political risk—to stand behind Great Britain in the twelve perilous months following the defeat of France in June 1940.[1]

It was to meet the first of these catastrophes that FDR launched his famous "first 100 days," a period of just over three months in which Congress under FDR's leadership passed an extraordinary fifteen major pieces of legislation. Many of the provisions enacted during this frantic period—including the establishment of the Federal Deposit Insurance Corporation and the requirement for transparency in the sale of securities—are with us still. So, too, are several subsequent provisions of the "New Deal" that FDR promised the American people when he first ran for the White House, such as Social Security, unemployment insurance, and the right of workers to form unions and engage in collective bargaining. The social and economic safety net provided by these programs—which were designed, as FDR said, to lessen "the hazards and vicissitudes of life"—fundamentally changed the nature of the relationship between the American people and their government.[2]

These achievements alone are enough to render FDR among the significant of our nation's presidents. Yet he faced a growing international crisis that reached its climax less so with the German attack on Poland in

September 1939 than with the shocking collapse of the French army the next spring. The import of this second catastrophe is underappreciated by the generations of Americans who did not live through World War II. France at the time had the largest army and air force in the world, to whose strength the British army added its own. Nevertheless, the Germans were seemingly unstoppable. In response to their onslaught, many officials within the British cabinet, led by then Foreign Secretary Edward Halifax, proposed coming to terms with Hitler. In Washington the consensus among FDR's top military advisers, including his Chief of Staff, General George C. Marshall, was that Great Britain would not last much longer than France.[3]

But FDR did not agree and, despite the fact that 1940 was an election year, resolved to support Prime Minister Churchill's determination to fight on. The first manifestation of this support came in the form of an Anglo-American agreement to ship fifty mothballed US World War I destroyers to Britain, followed by secret staff talks among senior members of the British and American armed forces, an increased number of US naval patrols in the Atlantic, and, in March 1941, passage of the Lend Lease Act, which solidified America's role as "the great arsenal of democracy."[4]

As with FDR's decisive response to the economic crisis he inherited in 1933, and his response to the fall of France, the role he subsequently played in crafting the Grand Alliance that would go on to defeat the Axis is likewise viewed as one of his crowning achievements. But to FDR, winning the war was never enough. Convinced that the global economic hardship of the 1930s was what gave rise to fascism in Europe and Asia and sent the world spiraling toward war, he foresaw that the United States had to fashion a new postwar order out of the ruins of the present conflict. This conviction underlay his January 1941 articulation of the Four Freedoms and the crafting of the Atlantic Charter eight months later. In short, FDR had committed himself to the establishment of a new system of international security—as called for in the last clause of the Charter—even before the United States entered the conflict. He never lost sight of this overriding ambition and, in spite of what Frances Perkins called his "transcending preoccupation" with the day-to-day demands of the war, always considered how "each victory could be woven into a pattern of permanent peace and world organization."[5]

To a certain extent, this focus on victory and the management of the war obscured FDR's determination to use the conflict as a catalyst for the establishment of a new postwar order centered on the creation of the United Nations. There is irony in this comment, for what also makes FDR's tenure in office unique—aside from his election to four terms and the fact that he remains our only "wheelchair president"—was his willingness to hold two press conferences per week for virtually his entire tenure in office, meaning that by the time he died in April 1945 he had held a stunning 998 meetings with the press.

Still, a good deal of mystery still surrounds Franklin D. Roosevelt. We might borrow Winston Churchill's oft-quoted phrase about Russia to say that in many respects FDR remains "a riddle wrapped in a mystery inside an enigma." FDR rarely confided his innermost thoughts to his family, friends, and advisers; he also refused to take notes during meetings and insisted that the members of his cabinet and other senior officials do the same. Indeed, there were times when the president seemed to delight in being unreadable and unpredictable. He took great pleasure, for example, in the press's rampant speculation about whether or not he would run for a third term—speculation well symbolized by the papier mâché sculpture of FDR as the Egyptian Sphinx that was presented to him at the annual Gridiron Dinner of December 1939. He once told a group of astonished foreign policy experts visiting the White House that he was "a juggler. . . . I never let my right hand know what my left hand does."

The outstanding biographer of Roosevelt's early life, Geoffrey Ward, has speculated that FDR's reluctance to show emotion or reveal his inner feelings stemmed from a practice that he and his mother adopted to deal with his father's weak heart. James Roosevelt was fifty-four years old when FDR was born; as he became increasingly frail, mother and son conspired to always remain cheerful, and to avoid stress or public shows of emotion so as not to upset his delicate constitution. FDR carried this outward effervescence into adulthood, often employing it—whether consciously or not—as a mask. For confirmation of this penchant for stoicism, we need only recall how FDR and his family coped with the devastating attack of polio that left him essentially paralyzed from the waist down at the prime of his life.[6]

Emotional impenetrability has its advantages, particularly for a president. But it also has its disadvantages. It can lead to feelings of isolation and, worse still, loneliness, even for a person surrounded by a large family and dozens of aides and assistants. There is no question that by the end of 1943, the "big man," as *Time* magazine called FDR, was beginning to feel alone. By the end of 1944, the twin burdens of the presidency and the war, coupled with his growing sense of isolation, had become almost too much. FDR, in short, was exhausted, and with this exhaustion came a narrowing of his view of what was important to him, the nation, and the world.[7]

This is why a close look at the last 100 days of FDR's life and presidency is so revealing, and so significant: by focusing on FDR at a time when his reduced capacity for work meant that he had to set strict personal and public priorities, we can discern what mattered most to him. Here, we see a president and a leader shorn of the usual distractions of office, a man whose sense of duty and personal responsibility for the fate of the American people and the world bore heavily upon him as he wrestled with many of the most critical issues and events of his entire presidency: the deliberations of the Yalta conference; the near completion of the atomic bomb; how best to prosecute the closing stages of the war against Japan; a last effort to secure a homeland for the Jews in Palestine; the rising importance of Middle East oil; the transition from a wartime to a peacetime economy; concerns about Soviet behavior in Central and Eastern Europe and British behavior in Greece and other parts of the Empire; and, most important to him, the establishment of a new system of international security, which became the United Nations. All the while, he also had to tend to the domestic needs of a public weary of the demands of war and to a battlefront reeling from a surprise German counteroffensive that threatened to drive the Western Allies into the North Sea.

The following pages reveal how Franklin Roosevelt—a decades-long smoker of sixty-plus years in a precarious state of health—coped with the day-to-day demands of office during this critical period. It also provides an opportunity to reexamine some of the most contentious questions asked about FDR since the day he died: Was he too ill during these last months to properly carry the burdens of office? Did Stalin dupe him at Yalta because FDR was too weak to resist? Should he have run for a fourth term? Did he ever admit to himself how unwell he was? What role did the members of his family or his closest confidants play—if any—in his ability to lead despite his reduced capacity for work?

Fortunately, a number of new sources of information have come to light in the past few years that help round out this picture. Thanks to the work of a number of scholars and medical historians, and to the recent release of a confidential memo drafted by one of the physicians who examined the president in 1944, we now know a good deal more about the perilous state of FDR's health than we did in the past. In addition, the declassification and return to the FDR Presidential Library of a number of records of the Office of Strategic Services and other government agencies, as well as the accession of such important collections as the Grace Tully Papers, provide new information about the president's activities and the state of the war, including the secret negotiations over a possible German surrender in Italy that took place in Switzerland in March 1945. The release of the papers of Sarah Churchill, who was present at the Yalta conference, along with the opening of a number of other records held at the Churchill Archives Center in Cambridge, offers us a more complete view of the interplay between Churchill and Roosevelt, while the opening of a significant portion of the wartime Soviet archives provides us with a more detailed picture of how Stalin and the Russians approached their Western counterparts during this critical period.[8]

An intimate view of FDR's last months would not be possible, however, without the recently constructed day-to-day calendar of his activities and contacts. Previously, the full scope of FDR's day-to-day activities—including appointments he wished to keep confidential— was not readily available to researchers. To remedy this, the FDR Presidential Library has spent years meticulously recording and reconstructing FDR's schedule from a host of sources, making it possible, for the first time, to get a much better sense of what the president was doing at any given hour on any given day.

The portrait that emerges from these final months stands in sharp contrast to the vigorous and relatively youthful figure who inspired the nation and the world when he proclaimed in his first inaugural address that "the only thing we have to fear is fear itself." The FDR of the last 100 days is a much-diminished man, often near the point of physical exhaustion, yet determined to press on and achieve the goals he set for himself and the world as he led his nation into war. That he was able to accomplish as much as he did, in spite of his physical decline, is in itself a remarkable story. It is also a poignant one as it shows him seeking, time and time again, relief from the ceaseless burdens of office while simultaneously preparing himself and those closest to him for the end of his life, even as he refused to fully consider what the inevitable "drawing out of days" brings to us all.

The Last Christmas

LIGHT SNOW WAS FALLING AS THE PRESIDENTIAL TRAIN MADE ITS WAY up the Hudson River Valley on Christmas Eve morning. This was only the second time in over a decade that Franklin Delano Roosevelt spent Christmas at his home in Hyde Park, and like many individuals and families across the world, the president clung to the hope that this holiday season might be the last celebrated under the cloud of war.

Few presidents, with perhaps the exception of Thomas Jefferson, were more rooted in a particular place than Roosevelt. And with the 1944 election behind him, he was looking forward to spending a few restful days along the banks of this majestic river that had been such an integral part of his life. It was here, to this setting where he spent his youth wandering the woods and fields that surrounded the house in which he was born, that he returned again and again—seeking solace in the timeless quality of rural life, and a sense of community among the many friends and neighbors who made up the small village he called home.

The tranquility of the winter landscape that greeted FDR that morning stood in sharp contrast to the scene in the Ardennes forest in the border region between Germany, Belgium, Luxembourg, and France. There, a surprise German offensive had caught the Allies completely off guard. The Germans—aided by inclement weather that grounded the Allied Air Force—pushed the American First Army back more than sixty miles in some of the fiercest fighting of the Second World War. Hitler's aim was to sow dissension in the Allied ranks by driving a wedge between the British and American forces. He also hoped to disrupt the ability of the Anglo-American armies in northern

France and Belgium to resupply, by severing key road and rail lines and, ideally, capturing Antwerp. After the attack's initial success, Hitler even entertained the idea that he might be able to force a negotiated settlement in the West, leaving his military free to concentrate on the defense of the Third Reich's eastern frontier against Stalin's Red Army.[1]

The German attack provoked immense anxiety among the Western Allies. US casualties along the Western Front for the month of December alone totaled more than 74,000—nearly double the monthly losses sustained since the Normandy invasion. These were losses that the US army, plagued by an increasingly dire manpower shortage, could ill afford. How different things seemed from the heady days of July and August when the Allies swept across northern France, raising hopes that the war in Europe might be over by Christmas. Hitler's belief that he might be able to fracture the Allies with a spectacular victory on the battlefield was not entirely unfounded. There were deep tensions within the Alliance over, among other things, the futures of Greece, Italy, Romania, Poland, and even France.[2]

All of this weighed heavily on FDR's mind as he prepared to join his family for Christmas on the Hudson. But the most serious issue confronting the president concerned the impact that internal Allied tensions might have on the main reason FDR had decided to run for a fourth term: the fate of the United Nations. Indeed, it was less than twenty-four hours since he had met Democratic Senator Carl A. Hatch of New Mexico and Republican Senator Joseph A. Ball of Minnesota, two strong supporters of the proposed world organization, who had come to see the president to express their anxiety about "the gravity of the international situation" and the need for "a supreme effort . . . to overcome Allied disunity."[3]

What most alarmed the two men was the growing tendency toward unilateral action on the part of the major powers, which the senators argued might "hamper future cooperation to maintain the peace" and prevent the outbreak of another war. Compounding the matter was the recent revelation that the Atlantic Charter had never existed as a formal state document signed by Roosevelt and Churchill but, rather, was merely a press statement the two leaders had crafted.[4]

This news led to a great deal of initial confusion in Washington and elsewhere about the relevance of the proclamation. The *Chicago Daily Tribune* reported that the American people had been "fooled" by the president, while a *Washington Post* reporter lamented that getting all three major powers to adhere to the Charter's principles—which the American people had embraced "with the utmost seriousness"—was becoming increasingly unlikely in light of events in Europe. It was more and more apparent, for example, that the Soviet Union was intent on exerting direct control over Poland, and equally obvious that Churchill's government was intent on establishing a conservative pro-British regime in Greece—even at the cost of armed conflict with Britain's former allies, the anti-monarchist and largely communist Greek resistance. The British government had also recently intervened in liberated Italy, refusing to recognize any government in which Count Carlo Sforza, a prominent and highly respected leader of the parties of the left, might take part. These moves prompted newly appointed Secretary of State Edward Stettinius to issue a blunt statement condemning the British position on Sforza, in which he declared that the United States expected the Italians—and by implication the Greeks—"to work out their problems of government along democratic lines without interference from the outside."[5]

Not satisfied with this expression of disapproval, some members of Congress said that the Charter's principles were being "crucified in the current Polish and Greek crises," and they and others began to call for the administration to clarify US policy in Europe. In a press conference held on December 19, 1944, Roosevelt insisted that there was no need to do so, since his administration's foreign policy was already on record. As for the Atlantic Charter, FDR downplayed the importance of the disclosure. When asked about it again a few days later, he said that the Charter represented an important objective—one not unlike President Wilson's fourteen points, which signified "a major contribution to something we would all like to see happen . . . a step towards a better life for the population of the world."[6]

Although FDR did his best to give the impression that all was in order and that American foreign and domestic policy was proceeding apace, the challenges he faced in late December 1944 were grave. Throughout the fall—and certainly since October—FDR understood that the growing divisions among the Allied powers meant that another summit meeting with Churchill and Stalin was necessary. The fate of postwar Germany, the timing and extent of Soviet participation in the war against Japan, the question of whether France should be given a zone of occupation and a seat on the Allied Control Commission for Germany, the acrimony that had crept into the Alliance over Poland and Greece and other parts of Central and Eastern Europe—all of these matters remained unresolved.[7]

Looming above these questions was the fate of the United Nations Organization, the establishment of which was threatened not only by the growing dissention among the major powers but also by a serious impasse among the "Big Three" regarding the voting procedure for the proposed Security Council and the number of seats allocated to the Soviet Union in the General Assembly. Given the Kremlin's strong stance over these questions, FDR understood that obtaining a firm Soviet commitment to the new institution was not going to be easy. Nor could he afford to overlook the difficulty of maintaining the American public's support for the new international body, particularly given the recent disillusionment over the Atlantic Charter reported in the press and the growing isolationist sentiment it seemed to herald as the end of the conflict approached.

At home, FDR faced still other problems. He had to reconstitute his cabinet, deal with the threatened resignation of Labor Secretary Frances Perkins, and find a place for his soon-to-be-former vice president, Henry A. Wallace, who was strongly supported by the liberal wing of the Democratic Party. He also had to act to maintain war production, solve the growing manpower crisis, and reverse the sudden consumer shortage of gasoline, meat, and canned fruits and vegetables. Most important, FDR needed to find a way to balance all of these urgent matters while adhering to the rest-regimen that his two primary physicians insisted was critical to his survival.[8]

In fact, by this time, FDR's health had become a major item of concern among those who were closest to him. Since his return from the Tehran conference at the end of 1943, FDR had struggled with a number of illnesses that he couldn't seem to shake, including a lengthy bout of both flu and bronchitis. It was during these months that his daughter Anna, who had recently moved back into the White House, began to express alarm about the state of her father's health. This led to two extensive medical workups by a team of physicians in March and May of 1944. These examinations revealed that FDR was suffering from severe hypertension and the early stages of congestive heart failure.[9]

That the president of the United States was suffering from heart disease unleashed a fierce debate between Vice Admiral Dr. Ross McIntire, FDR's surgeon general and long-serving White House physician, and the other specialists brought in to examine him: Dr. James A. Paullin, former head of the American Medical Association; Dr. Frank Lahey, director of the Lahey Clinic in Boston and widely regarded as one of the most prominent surgeons in the country; and Dr. Howard Bruenn, the young naval cardiologist tasked by Dr. McIntire to carry out the initial cardiac examination. It was Dr. Bruenn who determined that FDR had heart disease and who was the most disturbed by the state of the president's health. He insisted that FDR's condition was serious enough to warrant aggressive treatment, including extensive rest as well as the administration of digitalis and two other medications.[10]

But McIntire was initially incredulous—"You can't do that," he said to Bruenn. "This is the President of the United States." Nor were Paullin and Lahey convinced that such treatment was necessary—in part, because they disagreed with Bruenn about the extent of the president's cardiac disease, but also out of concern that the sudden administration of a number of medications might cause the president distress.[11] Thus they tended to concur with Dr. McIntire's more conservative assessment and, according to Bruenn, "grudgingly" agreed to support a compromise proposal put forward by the young cardiologist at the end of March: the president would take digitalis, go on a low-fat diet, cut the number of cigarettes he smoked to six per day, and try to avoid stress and significantly reduce the number of hours he worked—not an easy task for a man charged with the responsibility of running a global war.[12]

By the time FDR had made the decision to run for a fourth term, however, the fragile consensus the team of physicians had reached over the state of FDR's health and treatment had broken down. Indeed, just days before FDR made his historic July 11 announcement to seek reelection, Lahey telephoned Admiral McIntire to inform him that the second round of tests they had conducted on the president in late May had convinced him that the president's heart condition was worse than he initially suspected and that he thus did not believe that the president "had the physical capacity to complete [a fourth] term." Lahey acknowledged that it was not his place to determine whether or not the president should run; but, suspecting that the president was on the verge of making his announcement, he insisted that it was the admiral's duty—as surgeon general and FDR's primary physician—to inform the president about the likelihood that he would *not* survive the strain of another four years in office and, in a clear indication of the gravity of the situation, argued that if the president did accept another term, "he had a very serious responsibility concerning who is Vice President."[13]

According to a secret signed, sealed, and witnessed memo that Lahey drew up recording his conversation with McIntire, the latter "was in complete agreement" about the state of FDR's health and had in fact "informed the President" about the nature of his condition. There is no way to confirm definitively whether or not this is true (and the Lahey memo would remain locked away in a safe in Boston for more than seventy years), but the balance of the evidence suggests that neither McIntire nor Bruenn—who would go on to become FDR's attending physician under the supervision of McIntire—ever provided FDR or his family with a blunt warning about the risks involved in his decision to seek another term. Nor was the public fully informed. The standard line taken by Dr. McIntire—an ear, nose, and throat specialist—was that FDR was in fine health for a man his age. This was the mantra that was repeated to the press whenever the issue of the president's health came up—which was often during the course of the 1944 campaign—and despite all of the evidence to the contrary, it appears that the surgeon general clung to this view right up until FDR's death.[14]

Still, there is no question that FDR understood that he had "some trouble with [his] heart," as he once informed his cousin, Daisy Suckley, and was well aware of his physicians' insistence that he had to cut back on his workload. Moreover, the weight loss that accompanied FDR's treatment, along with the ever more frequent bouts of fatigue brought on by his coronary disease and the gray pallor brought on by the digitalis, made it increasingly difficult for McIntire and other senior aides to simply brush aside both the private and public expressions of concern over the state of FDR's health. As the 1944 campaign intensified, these expressions broke out into the open. On October 17, the *Chicago Daily Tribune* insisted that the president's health be regarded as "one of the principal issues of the campaign" and two weeks later editorialized that "A Vote for F.D.R. may be a Vote for Truman." On October 25, the *Detroit Free Press* and the *Los Angeles Times* published an editorial that took issue with the Democratic Party's insistence that "Roosevelt's health is a private matter." Taking note of recent photographs that "revealed a man so changed" as to be almost unrecognizable, and calling Dr. McIntire's subsequent claim that the president "is a few pounds underweight" but is "otherwise in perfect health . . . nonsense," the two papers insisted that the president's health "is not a private matter at all" but an issue "of vital concern to all the people."[15]

Furious, FDR responded to these and other charges—which he attributed to his Republican opponent, Thomas E. Dewey—by engaging in a whirlwind tour of no fewer than seven states during the final weeks of the campaign, highlighted by a much-publicized tour through the four most populous boroughs of New York in an open car and driving rain. As Eleanor later recorded, FDR seemed to draw strength from this contact with the people. But this exhilaration soon wore off. The truth is that FDR often expressed ambivalence about the prospect of another four years in the White House. As he said in his July 11 announcement, after "many years of public service" his personal thoughts had turned to the day when he could return to civil life. "All that is within me cries out to go back to my home on the Hudson River," he famously quipped.[16] The conservative press dismissed these comments as "the usual fraudulent talk" based on "the artful pretense that he is another Washington craving the peace of his Mount Vernon."[17] FDR's private comments to numerous friends and acquaintances, however, reveal that these sentiments were genuine. "I shall not weep bitter tears if Dewey wins," he wrote to one colleague in early September. Yet the prospect of leaving office while the war still raged and before he had realized his dream of establishing the United Nations seemed unthinkable. So he marshaled on.[18]

To restore his energy in the wake of what turned out to be "the meanest campaign of his political life," FDR had spent only seventeen of the forty-six days since his reelection in the White House and was now on his way to Hyde Park for another six-day sojourn away from the Oval Office. His plan was to make this "a very quiet time with complete rest." But as both Head of Government and Head of State, he had to attend not only to the practical aspects of being the nation's chief executive but also to the ceremonial ones. Hence, at 5:15 p.m. that

FDR, Eleanor, and Anna enjoying Election Night victory on the porch of Springwood, November 7, 1944. (Getty Images)

evening, after his arrival in Hyde Park, his first duty was to address the nation in what had become an annual Christmas message. His goal, as so many times before, was to offer hope, to reassure the millions of men and women who gathered around their radios to listen to him speak that in spite of recent setbacks and difficult days ahead, the war was indeed drawing to a victorious close. Thanks above all, he said, "to the determination of all right-thinking people and nations that Christmases such as those we have known in these years of world tragedy shall not come again to beset the souls of the children of God."[19]

Accompanying the president as his train pulled into Highland Station, just opposite the river from Hyde Park, were his daughter, Anna, and her husband, John Boettiger, as well as Anna's children, Sistie, Buzzie, and young Johnny. FDR's friend and Hudson Valley neighbor Treasury Secretary Henry Morgenthau Jr., his wife Elinor, and a small contingent of White House staff were also on the train. Eleanor Roosevelt was already at "the big house," as the family often referred to Springwood, the home and estate that had belonged to FDR's family since his father purchased it in 1866. And the party would soon be joined by FDR's son Elliott and his new wife, the actress Faye Emerson; Mrs. Franklin D. Roosevelt Jr.; the Morgenthaus' daughter Joan; and the feeble Mrs. J. R. (Rosy) Roosevelt, daughter of FDR's late half-brother, James Roosevelt Roosevelt.[20]

The six days FDR spent in Hyde Park were relatively tranquil. On Christmas Day, he plumbed stockings and opened gifts with his family. He also spent a good deal of time with his cousin Margaret "Daisy" Suckley, who lived ten miles or so up the river near Rhinebeck. Daisy, who was unmarried and lived alone, had known FDR since they were teenagers and was utterly devoted to "the Pres.," as she often referred to him in her diary. Always concerned about his health, she gave him "medicinal" garlic pills and arranged for him to receive massage "treatments" from Harry "Lenny" Setaro, a masseuse who reportedly had a gift for restoring people's health through intense manipulation of muscles and internal organs.[21]

Thanks to a direct line that linked Springwood to the White House, and to the mail pouch that arrived each morning, FDR kept apprised of events overseas. He learned that Churchill spent Christmas Day on a surprise visit to Athens, in an effort to quell the violence and political unrest that had erupted in Greece after the Nazi withdrawal. In the meantime, the now-clear skies of Northern Europe allowed the British and American air forces to send seven thousand warplanes on a fierce attack against the Wehrmacht. And in the Philippines, American forces had closed in on the last Japanese stronghold on the Island of Leyte, before moving on to the all-important Island of Luzon for the final bloody assault on Manila.[22]

The weather remained crisp and cold in the days after Christmas. Perhaps recalling his boyhood days sledding on his estate, FDR took delight in the six inches of snow that blanketed the region. He also worked on his stamp collection, took some quiet moments with his son Elliott, and did his best to regain his strength. There was talk of the coming inaugural, which FDR insisted had to be kept as simple and uncomplicated as possible, and a mounting sense of anticipation about FDR's plan to organize a family reunion at the White House in conjunction with the event, with all of his thirteen grandchildren in attendance.

As one day merged into the next, the world, as Elliott later recorded, seemed "for a brief moment to be shut out." It wasn't long, however, before their varied responsibilities would take each of them away from the quiet tranquility of the Hudson Valley. On December 27, Elliott departed for England, where he served as a reconnaissance pilot, and the next day, Eleanor, who, as Grace Tully once noted, was "on the move . . . ad infinitum," left for New York. Before she did, she asked Daisy "to be with the President" for his meals in her absence—a request that Daisy was more than happy to fulfill. As FDR himself prepared to leave on the evening of December 29, the happy consensus among Daisy, FDR's longest-serving Secret Service agent Charlie Fredericks, and FDR's physiotherapist, Lieutenant Commander George Fox, was that the president looked refreshed—a fact that seemed to be confirmed by a drop in his blood pressure.[23]

There would be much to do when he returned to Washington, and as FDR's overnight train began to make its slow journey southward, he took a few moments to reflect on the many challenges that would confront him in the New Year. First and foremost was the need to craft his State of the Union Address, a task that, as he noted to Daisy earlier, "he planned to plunge into the minute he reaches the White House tomorrow." In the meantime, as his train slipped quietly and unannounced through the city of New York toward its scheduled arrival at 8:45 a.m. at the secret siding he used at the Bureau of Engraving in Washington, the fighting in the Ardennes continued to rage. There would be no end to the war this holiday season, and given the major blow the Wehrmacht had delivered to the Anglo-American forces still struggling to reach the Rhine, all thought of a quick victory had long since vanished.[24]

Chapter 1

An Uncertain New Year

THE WASHINGTON THAT FDR RETURNED TO ON DECEMBER 30 WAS still covered in the thick layer of ice that one of the worst sleet storms in recent memory had deposited on the city. Fortunately, the last day of 1944 brought a slight thaw to the capital, although the return of cold temperatures on January 1 meant that this respite would be short-lived. In New York, intermittent rain was forecast as revelers gathered for the New Year's Eve celebration in Times Square. By midnight an estimated 750,000 people had crowded into the space in front of the Times Tower, "joyously but not uproariously" welcoming in the New Year. Most were happy to put 1944 behind them and hopeful that "the 'five' in 45 would spell 'V' for victory and an enduring peace." The *New York Times* reported that there would be plenty of alcohol on hand to help keep the merrymakers warm, but in a reminder of the ceaseless demands of war, an estimated 20 percent of all the major restaurants in the greater New York City area would be closed that night owing to a shortage of meat.[1]

Unable to resist the onrush of events or to rid himself of what Dr. McIntire described as "a terrible sense of urgency" in the first three weeks of the New Year, FDR dismissed all entreaties—even from his beloved daughter, Anna—"to live within his reserves" and pressed ahead with a frantic schedule upon his return to Washington. In keeping with the directive he had issued to the senior members of his administration to work through the New Year's holiday, FDR got right down to work on January 1, meeting with a number of foreign representatives, engaging in a review of government finances with his budget director, Harold D. Smith, and hosting a luncheon with his wife Eleanor and fourteen guests. He also put the final touches on a statement to be read at the State Department later that day marking the moment at which, after three acrimonious years of struggle with Charles de Gaulle, France would finally be invited to sign the Declaration of United Nations.[2]

FDR kept up this pace for much of the next seven days, holding his first cabinet meeting and press conference of the New Year; meeting British Ambassador Edward Halifax to speak about the current state of Anglo-American relations and the coming summit; discussing the work of the United Nations Relief and Rehabilitation Administration with its director, Herbert Lehman; corresponding with Gifford Pinchot about the organization of a world conservation conference in conjunction with the end of the war; reviewing the need to recruit additional Army psychiatrists to help cope with the psychological rehabilitation—what today we would call PTSD treatment—of returning servicemen; and hosting a series of other meetings with senior members of Congress and his administration.[3]

Amid all this activity, on the morning of January 3, 1945, members of the House and Senate gathered to open the seventy-ninth Congress. Well aware that war in Europe was far from over, and deeply troubled by the president's frank admission the day before that "important differences" existed among the Allies, they were in a somber mood. There was a general feeling that this Congress might be "one of the most fateful assemblies in the history of the nation," and universal recognition that the challenge of ending the war and securing the peace was going to be formidable. Yet, in sharp contrast to the opening of the special session of the seventy-third Congress that launched the famous 100 days twelve years before, there was little interest among the House and Senate leadership in initiating any new legislation. Much of this reluctance stemmed from a desire to avoid any appearance of excessive optimism about impending victory in the wake of the Ardennes crisis. But it also resulted from a profound sense of uncertainty about the future. Indeed, on the very day that Congress reconvened, official Washington learned that the Soviet government was about to extend formal recognition to the Polish Committee of National Liberation that the Kremlin had brought into being in July 1944. This committee, often referred to as the "Lublin Poles," represented a direct challenge to the London-based Polish government-in-exile that had the support of the Western Allies, and its existence was further confirmation—if any was needed—of the "important differences" to which the president had referred.[4]

Thus most members of the House and Senate concluded that it would be better to wait until they had received the president's State of the Union Message before they set themselves to the tasks at hand—not knowing, of course, that the man to whom most of them looked to provide leadership during this critical period would fall victim to a massive cerebral hemorrhage exactly 100 days after the Speaker's gavel brought the new session into being.

FDR INITIALLY HOPED THAT HE COULD KEEP HIS ANNUAL REPORT TO Congress relatively brief. But given the many controversies that had arisen since early December, it would turn out to be the longest of his entire career. As he told his principal speechwriter, Samuel Rosenman, on January 4, he wanted the address to cover a wide field of matters, including the status of the war, the international situation after the war, and the United Nations Organization.[5]

Not willing to expend the energy to make the trek over to Capitol Hill to deliver the speech in person, FDR opted instead to deliver his 1945 State of the Union Address over the radio on the evening of January 6. He began by calling for the immediate passage of a National Service Act. He also recommended that Congress pass "work or fight" legislation aimed at requiring all young men classified as 4-F who were not currently working in war production facilities to do so or face limited military service. Legislation was also needed to meet the alarming shortage of nurses in the armed forces. And in reference to his call for the adoption of an Economic Bill of Rights a year earlier, the president insisted that the nation be prepared to take measures to maintain full employment once the war was over.

This initial focus on the manpower requirements needed to maintain the strength of America's armed forces and industry came at the direct behest of FDR's Chiefs of Staff. It was their view that in spite of the significant gains that had been achieved since the D-Day landings, the US Army—still staggering from the losses it had sustained from the sudden German counteroffensive—had been rendered understrength at the very moment it was about to enter what General George C. Marshall referred to as "the most critical phase of the war."[6]

FDR opened his discussion of the all-important international situation by reminding the American people that "the nearer we come to vanquishing our enemies the more we inevitably become conscious of differences among the victors." Anticipating the difficult negotiations that lay ahead over the future of Central and Eastern Europe with London and Moscow, he argued that it was vitally important "not to let those differences divide us and blind us to our more important common and continuing interests in winning the war and building the peace." Indeed, "in our disillusionment after the last war," he said, "we preferred international anarchy to international cooperation with Nations which did not see and think exactly as we did. We gave up the hope of *gradually achieving* a better peace because we had not the courage to fulfill our responsibilities in an admittedly imperfect world. We must not let that happen again, or we shall follow the same tragic road again—the road to a third world war."[7]

He then referenced the Atlantic Charter, admitting (in light of the recent revelation that it was an unsigned document) that the principles in the Charter do "not provide rules of easy application to each and every one of this war-torn world's tangled situations. But it is a good and useful thing—it is an essential thing—to have principles toward which we can aim." As to the recent criticisms in the press about what was going on in Greece and Poland, FDR admitted that he shared the public's concern. "But we must not permit," he said, "the many specific and immediate problems of adjustment connected with the liberation of Europe to delay the establishment of permanent machinery for the maintenance of peace."[8]

In retrospect, the speech reflects, perhaps more than anything else, FDR's own anxiety about the need to secure the American people's support for the United Nations Organization and the postwar order he hoped to establish. The fact that the United States, the United Kingdom, and the Soviet Union inhabited "an imperfect world" and differed on how best to protect their national security interests was no reason to give up on the idea of further cooperation. On the contrary, it was this hard reality that rendered the establishment of the United Nations—with its all-important Security Council—so important. As he said in closing: "1945 can and must see the substantial beginning of the organization of world peace. This organization must be the fulfillment of the promise for which men have fought and died in this war.

It must be the justification of all the sacrifices that have been made—of all the dreadful misery that this world has endured."[9]

Yet, in another indication that the US public was weary of war, the headlines that followed the address focused on the immediate matters, rather than the long-term aims, that Roosevelt had mentioned. The *New York Times* led with "Roosevelt Demands a National Service Act, Draft of Nurses and 4Fs, Postwar Training." The headline in the *Los Angeles Times* read "President Calls for Total Draft," while the *Washington Post*'s headline was "President Asks Full Use of Manpower." The *Chicago Daily Tribune,* always in opposition to FDR, blared "Draft War Deserters," with a sub-headline that read "Work or Fight, Forced Labor, New Sacrifices Asked." Nor was the new Congress enamored of FDR's proposals as the war entered its final "critical phase"—again, in contrast with his first 100 days. There would be no National Service Legislation, no bill passed to secure the induction of nurses, and no legislation focused on 4Fs. Congress did, at least, wrestle with the speech's larger implications. But mostly this resulted in critiques. On January 10, Senator Arthur Vandenberg, the ranking Republican on the Senate Foreign Relations Committee, launched a widely anticipated rebuttal, raising FDR's "deprecation of the Atlantic Charter" and apparent unwillingness to address the specific challenges presented by Soviet and British behavior. Although sympathetic to the need to maintain Allied unity and supportive of the president's call for the establishment of the United Nations, Vandenberg nevertheless insisted that "trends towards disunity cannot be reversed by our silence upon the issues . . . involved."[10]

FDR invited Vandenberg and the other members of the Senate Foreign Relations Committee to the White House for an extended discussion the next day, January 11. In a frank admission of the limits of American power, FDR argued that as early as the Tehran conference it had become apparent to him, Churchill, and Stalin that "the occupying forces had the power in areas where their arms were present and each knew that the others could not force things to an issue." In Eastern Europe, Russia had "the power" and thus the only practical course "was to use what influence we had to ameliorate the situation." It may be true, as one senator suggested, that the present Russian goal was to eliminate all opposition and "to settle all questions by force of arms . . . before the Dumbarton Oaks institutions were set up," but

FDR still believed "that much could be done by readjustment if the machinery could be set up and if the Russians could be brought in and could acquire confidence in it." This task was paramount, and due to the delicacy of the situation, FDR had decided that the best approach was to press American concerns over Soviet behavior at the coming conference—in Yalta, in the Crimea, in early February—not, as Vandenberg had suggested, in his annual message to Congress.[11]

Despite Vandenberg's criticisms, FDR told his cabinet later that afternoon that he was pleased about the overarching theme of the senator's foreign policy address, which to him indicated that the once-doctrinaire isolationist now understood the importance of the proposed United Nations Organization as well as the need for the United States to remain engaged in the world. Still, the senator's admonition—that American silence when "Moscow wants to assert unilateral war and peace aims which collide with ours" or "when Mr. Churchill proceeds upon his unilateral way to make decisions often repugnant . . . to our ideals" would do nothing to reverse these unfortunate developments—rang true with many members of Roosevelt's own cabinet. Vandenberg's address thus added to the immense pressure FDR was under both at home and abroad in the days and weeks before he would depart for his much-anticipated summit meeting with Churchill and Stalin in Yalta.[12]

Always alert to FDR's health and state of mind, Frances Perkins and Henry Wallace seemed reassured that the president appeared to be doing well at the cabinet meeting on January 11. FDR had certainly aged, but the fatigue and lack of focus that Wallace had observed in their last encounter before the Christmas holidays seemed to have subsided—a development that Wallace, like Perkins and other members of the cabinet, attributed to FDR's famous ability to "bounce back" following a period of rest. Yet these remained "hectic" times. As Perkins observed, the entire cabinet recognized that the president was "studying and working hard, going over a great mass of material . . . trying to learn all that he would have to know so that he could have it at his fingertips at the conference." This preoccupation was not without its consequences. FDR struggled to address certain secondary matters such as Wallace's oft-stated desire to become secretary of commerce as his tenure as vice president came to an end and Secretary Perkins's wish to step down at the close of FDR's third term.[13]

The president's workload also affected his relationship with Eleanor. FDR seemed to have lost all patience with Eleanor's determination to challenge some of his decisions and to press him to act on certain issues, often via memos that were placed in a special basket by his bedside each evening. At the same time, he clearly wanted Eleanor "to be around more," though as a friend and companion, not an adviser. FDR reacted angrily, for example, when Eleanor—at dinner a mere two hours before the president was scheduled to deliver his State of the Union broadcast—once again raised the issue of his recent State Department appointments, which she strongly opposed. And a few weeks earlier there was the scene that occurred during FDR's much-celebrated "children's hour"—the daily ritual of taking the thirty minutes or so before dinner to serve cocktails and relax, an almost sacred moment in FDR's day when policy talk was prohibited. Eleanor rarely engaged in the gentle banter of these gatherings, and in any case she usually joined at the very end, just before dinner was served. On this occasion, however, she entered the Oval Study in the president's private quarters with a sheaf of papers, sat down opposite her husband, and reached across his desk to hand them to him, exclaiming, "Now Franklin, I want to talk to you about this." FDR flew into a rage, taking the entire pile of papers, throwing them across his desk, and saying in a fury to his daughter, Anna, "Sis, you handle these tomorrow morning." At which point Eleanor quietly said she was sorry, got up, took her glass, and walked calmly away to join the others.[14]

Paradoxically, however, Eleanor was the one person, even more than Anna, who could relieve him of the pressures of office. Given his lack of mobility and her political and moral stature, it was Eleanor who frequently stood in for her husband at the myriad public and private events required of the nation's chief executive. She was a highly respected political counselor herself, but one whose relationship to the president was complicated by the fact that they were also man and wife. At this point in his tenure, FDR seemed to long more for the latter than the former. As he admitted to Elliott in a quiet conversation over the holidays, he still hoped for a return to the closeness he and his son's mother had once shared. But Eleanor, deeply concerned about the fate of the liberal agenda in which she so passionately believed and critical of what she saw as her husband's backpedaling on a number of major issues, found it hard to find fulfillment in her husband's simple need for companionship. So she pressed on, while Franklin, as he had so often done in the past, looked to others for the solace he craved.

FDR certainly did so on the night of January 11, when he set off for another four days' rest in Hyde Park, this time in the company not of Eleanor but of Lucy Mercer Rutherfurd. It was FDR's relationship with the un-married Mercer during his tenure in the Wilson administration that had led to his estrangement from Eleanor, who discovered the affair in 1918. We do not know the extent to which they were physically intimate, but given the intellectual nature of the relationship between Eleanor and her husband, FDR's emotional betrayal was perhaps of greater significance to her than any physical bonds that may have existed between FDR and Lucy. Eleanor's torment led to talk of divorce, and this, coupled with a threat by FDR's mother to cut off all future financial support if the relationship continued, prompted FDR to promise he would never see Mercer again.[15]

Lucy subsequently married, and though we now know that she and FDR stayed in touch by letter, and may have met from time to time, not until the spring of 1941 did the two of them begin to see each other more frequently. They would take drives together in the Virginia countryside, and occasionally meet in the White House, when Eleanor was absent. On these early visits Lucy often used the name Mrs. Paul Johnson. But as FDR's desire to see Lucy increased with the intensification of the war and the decline of his health, their encounters became more frequent and open. In late 1944 and early 1945, Anna—concerned about the president's well-being and recognizing his need for relaxed company—became the principal liaison between FDR and Lucy.[16]

As unusual as Anna's role was, she was not the only person close to FDR who abetted the relationship. Both Daisy and FDR's cousin Laura "Polly" Delano were well aware that the president and Lucy were spending time together. So too was Grace Tully, another person among the president's immediate entourage who helped arrange meetings between the two.

On this occasion, FDR and Lucy were joined by Daisy, who by then had grown quite fond of Lucy, whom she referred to as her "new cousin" and with whom she shared an "unselfish devotion to F." FDR had invited Lucy to Hyde Park ostensibly to show her some of the new items he had brought to his Presidential Library, and on the morning of January 12, the three of them thoroughly enjoyed themselves as

Daisy wheeled FDR around the library museum in his chair while he described each piece. They then enjoyed lunch together before Daisy "took herself off" after coffee, allowing FDR and Lucy to enjoy some private conversation before Lucy left for home on the 3:27 train from Poughkeepsie.[17]

FDR spent the rest of the long weekend preparing for Yalta and working on his inaugural address. He also took time to meet with a representative of the National Park Service to discuss the history of "the home place." In addition to building the nation's first Presidential Library, FDR had made the decision to bequeath much of his beloved Springwood to the public after his death, on the condition that his family be granted lifetime usage of the estate. He wanted to be sure the Park Service understood the full history of the house and grounds, including the century-old hemlock hedge that bordered the Rose Garden. FDR was concerned that the hedge had grown ragged and seemed to be failing, so he ordered the Park Service to replant it that spring.[18]

FDR left Hyde Park on the evening of Monday, January 15, 1945, and would spend the next five days meeting with a host of officials in preparation for his departure for Yalta and working on his fourth inaugural with his two principal secretaries, Grace Tully and Dorothy Brady. In the middle of one of these sessions FDR suddenly stopped his dictation, looked around the study, and asked the two women, "What in this room reminds you most of me?" Grace pointed to a naval print, while Dorothy Brady picked out a little French portrait of John Paul Jones that FDR's confidant Louis Howe had given to the president years ago. FDR thereupon dictated two notes that were immediately placed in his White House safe. These indicated that "in the event of his death" the two women should have these items. He then resumed his dictation.[19]

FDR also took the time on January 16, 1945, to send a note to Gifford Pinchot, the well-known conservationist and current governor of the state of Pennsylvania. The two men had been corresponding since August 1944 about an idea very close to FDR's heart: convening a world conference on conservation at the end of the war under the auspices of the yet-to-be-established United Nations. Convinced that "conservation is the basis for a permanent peace," FDR had asked the State Department to draw up a memorandum on the subject in the fall of 1944. Although incredibly pressed for time, FDR took a moment to

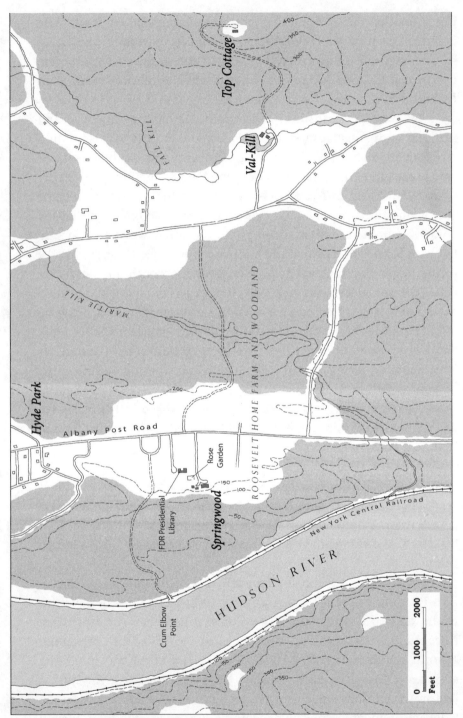

Hyde Park, New York

forward the memorandum to Governor Pinchot upon his return to the White House, and shortly thereafter invited the governor to join him for a luncheon meeting to discuss it. It was during the latter encounter, which took place on Friday, January 19, that FDR informed a delighted Pinchot that he was going to take up the idea of the proposed conservation conference during his forthcoming meeting with Churchill and Stalin. The two men also agreed, through Anna, that Pinchot should draw up a preliminary statement on the proposal that the president could take with him to the Crimea.[20]

As the week progressed, press speculation about Henry Wallace's status intensified. By this point, it had been widely reported that FDR offered Wallace the position of secretary of commerce. But at his press conference of January 19, the penultimate day of his third term, FDR refused to say anything about Wallace's future, other than to insist that "I don't think he'll starve."[21]

Just after this press conference FDR held what turned out to be his last private meeting with Wallace, telling his vice president what he would not confirm to the press: that he would indeed send Wallace's nomination as secretary of commerce to the Senate within the next couple of days. FDR also said that he would inform the current commerce secretary, Jesse Jones, of this decision over the weekend. The president indicated that he supported Wallace's request that the lending powers of the Department of Commerce, which fell under the authority of the Reconstruction Finance Corporation, not be stripped away as a consequence of his appointment—a move that Jones, and many conservative senators, had demanded as a condition for their support of Wallace's nomination.[22]

As their conversation drew to a close, the subject of FDR's health came up. Wallace told FDR about a talk he'd had with Senator Josiah Bailey, whose physical condition had deteriorated after he turned sixty-five. Following a long rest, Bailey was "taking things easy every day," which did wonders for him. FDR assured Wallace that "he was observing quite an easy daily schedule now . . . staying in bed each morning." He also added—untruthfully—that he rested for an hour after lunch each day. Moving on, FDR claimed to be "heartbroken" that Wallace had not been nominated for vice president at the 1944 Democratic Convention in Chicago. Unable to contain himself, the vice president countered that he would have won if FDR's postmaster general, Frank

Walker, had stayed out of it. When FDR said that Walker had acted "without his knowledge or consent," Wallace muttered to himself, in uncharacteristically blunt language, "bullshit." Yet when Wallace took his leave, and FDR reiterated how much happiness their relationship had brought him, "it was all so hearty," Wallace later wrote, "it seemed like he meant it."[23]

A few hours later, FDR hosted the last cabinet of his third term. He did not mention the location of his pending trip to meet with Churchill and Stalin, which remained a closely guarded secret, but indicated that he would be away for some time. He then surprised the members of his cabinet by raising the question of how they should carry on "while he was on his trip abroad—or in case he should become incapacitated like Wilson." Recalling Secretary of State Robert Lansing's decision to call a cabinet meeting while Woodrow Wilson was incapacitated, and Wilson's furious reaction—which included his firing of Lansing—Roosevelt said he did not subscribe to the same thinking. He made clear that he wanted the ranking cabinet officer of his administration to convene the cabinet if necessary. Since Secretary of State Edward Stettinius was going to accompany him at the summit, that responsibility would fall to Treasury Secretary Henry Morgenthau.[24]

To Wallace, listening intently, this was welcome news. As he recorded in the unpublished version of his diary, he did not entirely trust FDR's director of war mobilization, James Byrnes, who, in his unofficial role as "assistant president," might feel he was entitled to step in and run things in the event that FDR could no longer perform the duties of the office. Of course, if FDR were to die in office, this would be moot, as the vice president would take over. But if Roosevelt's failing health should render him unable to lead, the question of which cabinet officer had the authority to govern would be a somewhat open question, especially as the vice president has "no constitutional standing in the executive branch of the government." By making it clear that the highest-ranking cabinet officer present should step in to take charge, Roosevelt indicated that Morgenthau, not the ambitious Byrnes, would shoulder this responsibility.[25]

The rank of each individual cabinet officer, which is determined by the historical date on which his or her office was created, also determines the order in which cabinet members can speak with the president after a meeting. As the office of secretary of labor was the most recent creation, Frances Perkins was always the last to see FDR after a cabinet meeting—a fact that she frequently turned to her advantage. On this occasion, just a few hours before FDR's third term came to an end, Perkins was adamant about seeing the president. He had still not acted on his earlier promise to allow her to turn in her resignation at the time he took his fourth oath of office. Determined to do so, Perkins had already begun to empty her desk, and had sent FDR a note that morning to remind him of her wish that he announce her resignation to her colleagues during their last meeting. But FDR said nothing about it—much to the labor secretary's frustration.[26]

During the cabinet meeting, Perkins found the president alert and more or less himself. But afterward, sitting next to him in the Oval Office, she was shocked at the change in his appearance. "He had the pallor, the deep gray color, of a man who had been long ill. He looked like an invalid who had been allowed to see guests for the first time." Perkins hated to press him about her resignation but felt she had no choice.

"Don't you think," she asked, "I had better get [Stephen] Early to announce my resignation right now? I'll go in and write out the announcement."

"No," FDR pleaded. "Frances you can't go now. You mustn't put this on me now. I can't think of anybody else, and I can't get used to anybody else. . . . Do stay there and don't say anything." And with a hint of moisture welling up in his eyes he grabbed her hand and said, "You are all right."

Moved by FDR's appeal, Perkins decided, against her wishes, to stay on. She rang for Mr. Simmons, the White House Guard, who entered the cabinet room to push the president of the United States back to his Oval Study in the family quarters on the second floor of the White House. She implored Mr. Simmons in a whisper "to see that the President lies down. He is tired." She said the same thing to Grace Tully and, when she got back to her office, informed her long-standing administrative assistant in strictest confidence that the president looked terrible and that she was afraid he was ill.[27]

FDR did take a break that day, in the form of a drive with Daisy, who had accompanied him back to Washington for the inauguration. By this point, all of his grandchildren had arrived and the White House, according to his cousin, now resembled a kindergarten. Happily, the arrival of his brood seemed to revive FDR, who thoroughly enjoyed "the general excitement" and "orderly confusion" that evening. He even had the energy to read children's stories aloud after dinner, before getting back to work to put the final touches on the inaugural address he would deliver to the nation the next day.[28]

JUST AS FDR HAD WISHED, HIS FOURTH SWEARING IN WAS A BRIEF, straightforward affair. There was no Inauguration Day parade, and at the president's insistence the ceremony took place on the South Portico of the White House as opposed to the traditional site on the steps of the capitol. It was a cold day, with a fresh dusting of snow glistening on the leaves of the nearby magnolia trees. On the steps leading up to the portico, looking up in admiration and wonder as a brief patch of blue momentarily broke through the monotony of the gray sky, stood all thirteen of the president's grandchildren and, below them, the hundreds of official guests who filled a special section marked by a canvas spread on the ground to cover the snow. As FDR had intimated to Daisy earlier, the first thing he had done that morning was to test the steel leg braces that would make it possible for him to "walk" the short distance from the rear of the Blue Room to the edge of the South Portico. The president had also insisted—in a fitting reminder that the nation was still at war—that, amid the crowd of diplomats, governors, members of Congress, and other representatives of Washington officialdom, a space be reserved for fifty wounded servicemen, many of whom, like their commander-in-chief, were confined to wheelchairs.[29]

Beyond the canvas and the watchful eye of a phalanx of military police, a further crowd of lesser officials and everyday citizens—including Lucy Rutherfurd—stood in the snow, while a marine band played the national anthem. The first to take the oath of office was Vice President Truman. Then it was FDR's turn. Placing his right hand on the Bible that had been in his family's possession since 1686, and discreetly gripping the reading podium with his left hand with his braces locked in place, he turned to face Chief Justice Harlan Stone. He then swore to faithfully execute the office of president of the United States and to preserve, protect, and defend the nation's Constitution, "so help me God." As he repeated the oath for the fourth and final time, the crowd stood in utter silence, a stillness broken only by the soft whir of

FDR delivering his fourth inaugural address, moments after taking the oath of office, with his son James looking on. (Getty Images)

the newsreel cameras there to capture the moment. FDR then turned to address the crowd that had gathered.[30]

With the sight of the Jefferson Memorial glimmering in the distance, the president began by reminding his audience that the Constitution of 1787 "was not a perfect instrument." Indeed, "it is not perfect yet. But it provided a firm base upon which all manner of men, of all races and colors and creeds, could build our solid structure of democracy." Having learned through the experience of war that we "cannot live alone at peace," and that we must be "citizens of the world community," he urged his fellow countrymen to recognize that a lasting peace could not be founded on suspicion or mistrust or fear. Instead, what was needed was the confidence and the courage that flow from conviction, "the conviction that the only way to have a friend is to be one."[31]

By all accounts, FDR delivered the inaugural address, the shortest of the four he gave, in a clear and forceful voice. But Henry Wallace, standing near him, observed that FDR's whole body seemed to shake as he spoke, especially his right arm, which grasped the rail of the reading stand. The former vice president was also shocked at FDR's loss of weight, which was much more apparent in his standing position. "He was a gallant figure," Wallace recalled, "but also pitiable—as he summoned his precious strength." Seeing the president like this, Wallace doubted that FDR would ever again give a speech standing. He was right.[32]

Following the ceremony, FDR retired to the Gren Room, where he more or less excused himself from the normal postinaugural routine of greeting the hundreds of guests who were invited to attend a luncheon. This task fell to Eleanor, Anna, and other members of the family. After welcoming a few intimate friends and close associates—including the famous opera singer Marjorie Lawrence, who had contracted polio just as her career was reaching its peak but had somehow managed to return to the stage, singing from a sitting position—FDR asked that he and his eldest son James be left alone for a time.[33]

James had assisted his father in his first three inaugurals; though he was serving as a Marine combat officer in the Philippines in January 1945, FDR insisted that he be present at his fourth, and had issued a special order for his return to Washington. The president's ostensible reason was his desire to keep up this tradition. But in their private conversation that day, FDR intimated that there was a second, equally important reason he wanted to see James, and that was to discuss his will.

FDR informed James that he had selected him as one of three trustees and executors, and that he was the only family member among them. James said he would be honored to serve in such a capacity, but hoped it would "be a long time yet." FDR smiled at this, and went on to tell James about a letter addressed to him, in FDR's safe, that had instructions regarding his funeral. He also detailed the provisions in the will for FDR's longtime secretary, Missy LeHand, which no longer applied since Missy had died, but which FDR suspected would be misunderstood.[34]

FDR was right to suspect that later generations would misinterpret his act of generosity. Without a husband and children of her own, Missy had devoted much of her life to FDR and in essence became part of the family. She dined with them, acted as hostess in Eleanor's absence (a role Eleanor was often happy to relinquish), and even joined Anna and the family nurse in tucking Curtis and his sister into bed

Franklin and Eleanor and all thirteen of their grandchildren on the day of FDR's fourth inauguration, January 20, 1945. (Courtesy of the Franklin D. Roosevelt Presidential Library)

at night—a privilege that none of FDR's other secretaries, including Grace Tully, ever enjoyed.[35]

Missy had suffered a debilitating stroke in 1941. FDR subsequently changed his will to indicate that if he predeceased Missy, up to 50 percent of the income from his estate would go to cover her medical and living expenses. FDR acknowledged to James that some might try to make a story out of this, but as Missy had served him so well for so long and could no longer look after herself at the time, he felt it was the least he could do. Finally, they discussed various heirlooms that FDR had earmarked for members of the family. At the end of their conversation, FDR looked at his son and said, "I want you to have the family ring I wear. I hope you will wear it."[36]

At the time, James did not suspect, despite the content of their discussion, that his father was thinking about the possibility he might die soon. But looking back, he understood why FDR insisted that his mother go through the trouble of bringing all thirteen grandchildren to the inauguration, a reunion immortalized in the wonderful family

photo that FDR arranged to have taken in the Oval Study that morning. More and more, it seemed, FDR was thinking about posterity.[37]

FDR RETURNED TO WORK THAT AFTERNOON, ONCE AGAIN IN THE
company of Daisy, followed by a White House tea, given for roughly
250 members of the Electoral College and their spouses. Then he was
off to the "doctor's office," which on most days also meant a visit to the
top-secret Map Room, where a series of naval aides tracked the progress of the war, followed by dinner with Eleanor and sixteen guests.

Even though the day following the inauguration was a Sunday,
FDR met with his secretary of commerce, the curmudgeonly Jessie
Jones, who was about to be displaced by Henry Wallace. To soften the
blow, FDR offered Jones a number of other potential positions, including ambassador to France or membership on the Federal Reserve
Board. Jones rejected both. He also made clear his adamant opposition
to Wallace's insistence that the lending agencies Jones had supervised
under the aegis of the Reconstruction Finance Corporation (RFC) be
retained within the department.[38] FDR's initial rejection of Jones's view
prompted a public furor after Jones published both Roosevelt's letter
asking for his resignation and his own bitter reply; the latter included
his assertion that for the president to turn over all of the assets of the
RFC "to a man inexperienced in business and finance will, I believe,
be hard for the business and financial world to understand." This controversy would turn Wallace's nomination process into something of a
nightmare. Wallace would not see his position confirmed by the Senate
until March 1, one day after the president signed the George Act, sepa-
rating the Federal Loan Agency from the Department of Commerce in
yet another blow to his "old friend."[39]

FDR's next responsibility was to attend an official luncheon at
the White House. Unable to face the task, he asked Daisy, who had
returned to spend the morning in the president's study, "Do you want
to save my life?" She replied that she "would always be glad to save the
President's life."

"Well then, stay with me and have lunch on a tray. The so-in-sos
and so and sos are coming—they'll be a crowd, and I just don't want to
see them!"

As always, Daisy was happy to comply.[40]

The final event of the inaugural weekend involved a presidential birthday party and dinner, which the family decided to celebrate in advance as FDR would be at sea on his actual birthday, January 30. Attending were Eleanor, Anna, John Boettiger, FDR's son James and James's wife, the remaining grandchildren, the crown prince and princess of Norway, the Morgenthaus, Daisy, and the last vestiges of the old "cuff links gang," the group of close friends and confidants who had supported every one of his political campaigns since he first ran for vice president in 1920. The party delighted in FDR's enjoyment in opening the many gifts he received for the occasion, including a large print of a Hudson River scene presented by Princess Martha and her husband. Though fatigued, FDR invited a more intimate group to the Oval Study for a late-night game of cards, but not before the president and his son James took a moment to say their good-byes, as James was scheduled to depart from Washington's Union Station just after midnight—never to see his father again.

Chapter 2

Atlantic Sojourn

THE SPRAWLING AMERICAN NAVAL FACILITIES IN NEWPORT NEWS, Virginia, lie just to the southeast of the historic settlement of Jamestown. Possessed of an almost tactile sense of history and geography, FDR had long accorded Jamestown deep significance. He first visited on July 4, 1936, roughly a year after the passage of the act that made the preservation of historic sites, buildings, and objects a national priority, and approximately four years before Jamestown itself would receive federal protection under the new law. As with Plymouth Rock and Monticello, FDR saw Jamestown, the first permanent English settlement in the new world, as one of the cornerstones of American democracy, so it is perhaps not surprising that he referred to it in one of the most powerful addresses he made to the American people in the year prior to the nation's entry into the war.

The date was June 10, 1940. The occasion was a speech to the graduating class of the University of Virginia. Across the Atlantic the Italian dictator, Benito Mussolini, had just declared war on France, which was rapidly collapsing under the advance of the German army. Warning of the dangers that would ensue from abandoning "with deliberate contempt" the moral values to which the descendants of Jamestown and Plymouth Rock had been dedicated for more than three hundred years, FDR insisted that it was impossible for Americans to remain indifferent to "the destruction of freedom in their ancestral lands across the sea." To do so was to hold to "the now obvious delusion" that we can safely permit "the United States to become a lone island, a lone island in a world dominated by the philosophy of force . . . lodged in prison, handcuffed, hungry, and fed through the bars from day to day by the contemptuous, unpitying masters of other continents." Those "who still talk and vote as isolationists" were fatally misguided, he said. The intuitions of democracy could not survive in the United States if the wider world was dominated by "the gods of force and hate."[1]

In the months and years that followed his University of Virginia address, FDR labored hard to counter the forces of isolationism, which even after Pearl Harbor did not entirely disappear from the American political landscape. Certainly, Congress's passage in 1943 of the Fulbright and Connelly resolutions, which favored the creation of an "international authority with power to prevent aggression," indicated that the national legislature had come a long way from its forceful assertion of neutrality in the 1930s and its rejection of the League of Nations roughly a decade before that. But FDR still had his doubts. As he said to Robert Sherwood in October 1944, "Anyone who thinks isolationism is dead in this country is crazy. As soon as this war is over, it may well be stronger than ever."[2]

FDR's fear that the country might once again turn its back on the rest of the world grew more intense as the end of the war in Europe drew near. His fear stemmed in part from personal experience. Having served as assistant secretary of the Navy under Woodrow Wilson, FDR was an eyewitness to the rejection of US participation in the League. His anxiety was compounded by the reactions of the American people and press to actions by the British and Soviets in Greece and Poland— reactions strong enough to lead many officials in the British Foreign Office to speak of a "crisis" in Anglo-American relations.[3]

IT WAS WITH ALL THIS IN MIND THAT ON MONDAY, JANUARY 22, 1945, FDR boarded the special overnight train that would take him to Virginia. This would be the first leg of his final overseas journey, during which he would travel nearly fourteen thousand miles—more than half the circumference of the earth. He'd first take a ship across the Atlantic and through the still treacherous Mediterranean. Then he'd fly from Malta, his first port of call, to the Saki airfield on the western edge of the Crimean peninsula. His final destination, Yalta, summer home of the tsars, could be reached only by driving over the largely unpaved roads that snaked from the steppe-like terrain surrounding the airport at Saki, up past the craggy 5,000-foot summit of Mount

Roman-Kosh and down the steep, southern-facing slopes of the remote yet beautiful Crimean range that borders the Black Sea to the Livadia Palace, his home for the duration of the conference. It was there, in that distant corner of territory that lay astride the vast Eurasian continent Hitler had so desperately tried to conquer, that the critical mission of securing the future of the United Nations—and FDR's place in history—would be made or broken.[4]

The task of transporting a frail paraplegic halfway around the world fell to FDR's family and staff. Both Dr. Ross McIntire and Dr. Howard Bruenn expressed concern about the physical toll the trip would take. So, too, did Eleanor Roosevelt, who noted that her husband appeared "far from well" in the days following his inauguration. Yet there were those, including FDR himself, who professed that a long sea voyage might be just what the president needed to restore his characteristic vitality. In his quieter moments, however, including several conversations with Daisy, FDR admitted that the thought of the trip wearied him.[5]

Accompanying the president on his journey were Admiral William D. Leahy, James F. Byrnes, Edward J. Flynn, FDR's naval aide Vice Admiral Wilson Brown, General Edwin "Pa" Watson, Drs. McIntire and Bruenn, FDR's valet Arthur Prettyman, twenty members of the Secret Service, and the entire contingent of the much-loved "Potomac Stewards." These were the Filipino naval chefs and stewards of the Presidential Yacht, who had such a knack for anticipating FDR's needs that he insisted on bringing them with him whenever he traveled. General George Marshall, Admiral Ernest King, and the other members of the Joint Chiefs of Staff, along with Harry Hopkins, Secretary of State Edward Stettinius, Charles Bohlen, and other representatives from the State Department would rendezvous with the presidential party at Malta. Perhaps the most important passenger besides the president was Anna, whose charge was to protect FDR's privacy and to help him through the more stressful times.[6]

Like her mother, Anna was becoming something of a policy adviser—for instance, commenting on and helping to draft her father's public pronouncements. One result of her increased profile within the president's inner circle was a new tension between Anna and Eleanor—a tension that on this occasion was exacerbated by Eleanor's disappointment over not being the one invited to join Franklin on his

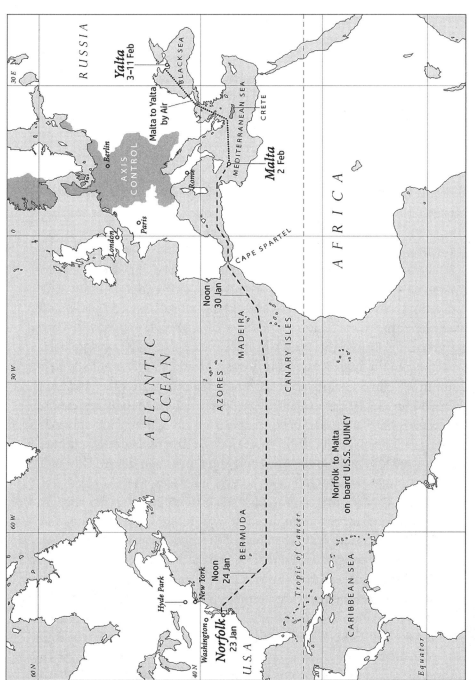

FDR outbound from Norfolk to Yalta

journey to Yalta, even after she had asked him directly if she could. FDR demurred, saying that her presence might create "difficulties," since everyone would feel they had to pay attention to her. As an alternative, FDR suggested Anna. She was quite anxious to go, and was clearly envious of her brothers, who had accompanied their father to a number of the major wartime summit meetings. Anna was also well aware that Churchill's daughters had often joined him on his wartime travels. Why should she be denied the same experience, especially once she learned that Sarah Churchill would be going to Yalta?[7]

On the morning the president and his party made their way up the gangplank to the deck of the USS *Quincy,* the weather was brisk. A strong wind from the northwest prevented the heavy cruiser from reaching full speed for about fifty minutes. As the ship made its way past Hampton Roads and out beyond the mouth of Chesapeake Bay to the open Atlantic, three escort destroyers formed an anti-submarine screen ahead of the *Quincy,* while the light cruiser USS *Springfield* sailed behind. Overhead, a squadron of P-38 fighters provided air cover.[8]

Despite the high seas and inclement weather, FDR spent the first hour of the voyage taking in the sights as the ship passed the busy harbor and the bay beyond. (To facilitate FDR's movement between decks, two special elevators had been installed on the *Quincy.*) At approximately 1:15 p.m., the task force increased the ship's speed to 22.5 knots and started to zigzag—a standard anti-submarine maneuver. Although it was possible for the *Quincy* to receive messages, the U-boat threat also made it necessary for the task force to maintain radio silence. Hence, any outbound communication with Washington, London, and Moscow was possible only when one of the escorting ships broke away from the group to send a message.[9]

Gloriously cut off from the world, FDR settled into a day-to-day routine that included informal conversations with Admiral Leahy about the agenda for the coming conference, midday and evening meals taken in the company of the rest of his immediate party, and an after-dinner movie in Anna's quarters. Aside from his talks with Admiral Leahy, which did not extend beyond an hour or so, and the occasional dinner conversation during which the conference was brought up, he mostly avoided lengthy discussions or formal meetings. Instead, he concentrated on getting as much rest as possible.[10]

Still, even in the middle of the Atlantic, it was not entirely possible to escape the exigencies of his job. On Wednesday, January 24, the president received word of a strike among the workers of the Bingham and Garfield Railroad, which served as a vital link between the massive open-pit copper mine at Bingham Canyon, Utah, and the mine's smelters roughly twenty miles distant. Given that copper was crucial to the manufacture of ammunition and other critical war materials, a strike was out of the question. Hence, amid a driving rain and rough seas, FDR ordered the destroyer *Satterlee* to break formation to transmit an urgent radio message to Washington, informing the War Department of his approval of an Executive Order authorizing the US Army to take over the railroad.[11]

Technically speaking, it was James Byrnes, in his capacity as director of war mobilization, who conveyed the message to Washington about the president's order—a somewhat ironic development given Byrnes's earlier insistence that instead of accompanying the president to Yalta it would be better for him to remain in Washington to handle just such an emergency. As a man of considerable ambition and pride, Byrnes assumed that FDR would take full advantage of his time at sea to consult with him on the host of political and economic issues facing the nation after the war. But much to Byrnes's chagrin, FDR did not avail himself of this opportunity.[12]

Initially, Byrnes believed the president's tendency "to stay in his cabin most of the time" was due to a worsening cold that FDR seemed to have contracted at the moment of their departure. But the more Byrnes observed the president, the more he feared that FDR's appearance reflected an underlying condition. Byrnes raised his concerns with Anna and Dr. McIntire, both of whom assured him that the president did have a sinus infection and a cold—but, as Anna put it, "He was not really ill."[13]

Byrnes was not the only person on board who was alarmed at FDR's poor appearance. FDR's longtime political associate Edward J. Flynn also expressed concern, deeming the president's physical condition "very bad." Indeed, Flynn was "shocked at the toll that had been taken [on FDR] by years of labor." At Yalta, his concern would be transformed into amazement when he noted FDR's ability, through "a supreme effort of will," to become "completely alive and alert to what was going on."[14]

That FDR was completely "alive and alert" to the larger issues at stake can be seen in the fact of Flynn's presence itself. FDR's decision to bring Flynn—a veteran of New York City machine politics and a former chairman of the Democratic National Committee—to a conference with Winston Churchill and Joseph Stalin was a puzzle to the others in the party. The mystery surrounding Flynn's mission was exacerbated by the secrecy FDR demanded, which included the requirement that Flynn not even fill out a passport application before their departure—a decision Flynn found more and more disconcerting as the days at sea went by. This soon became a source of great amusement for FDR; he brushed off Flynn's concerns and took great delight in drafting an unofficial passport in the form of Letter Signed by the President, to which Flynn attached a photo of himself taken by the ship's photographer.[15]

In fact, FDR's lighthearted demeanor masked the entirely serious reason he had invited Flynn to the conference: as a Catholic politician in a multi-ethnic and multi-religious city, Flynn knew a good deal about how to bring a diverse group of constituents together around a common set of values. Always thinking about the future, and well aware that the issue of religious freedom was one of the key points of domestic opposition to the Roosevelt administration's decision to recognize the "godless" Soviet Union in 1933, FDR had asked Flynn to attend the summit in the hope that he would be able to discuss this important question with both Stalin and Soviet Foreign Minister Vyacheslav Molotov. FDR was also convinced, he told Flynn, that there could never be a permanent peace unless the large Catholic populations in Poland, Lithuania, and the Balkans were permitted to practice their faith freely: hence he believed that the question of religious freedom would no doubt remain an important factor in whether the American public retained its positive wartime attitude toward the Soviets—an attitude that was already fraying as Moscow's intentions in Poland became clearer. All of this was especially disquieting to the Catholic hierarchy in America, whose bishops had sent a vigorously worded letter to FDR in December 1944 arguing that "a strong stand for justice in our relations with the Soviet Union is a postulate for our winning of the peace and for setting up an international organization which will command the support of our people."[16]

Mulling all this on board the *Quincy,* FDR decided that Flynn should not only meet with Stalin and his foreign secretary at Yalta but continue on to Moscow for further discussions, and that he should subsequently travel to Rome in an effort to encourage Pope Pius XII to seek an improvement in relations between the Holy See and the Soviet Union. The latter would not be an easy task given the pope's staunch anti-communism and unequivocal support of the London Polish Exile Government with whom the Soviets had broken off relations.[17]

As FDR TRIED HIS BEST TO RECOVER HIS STRENGTH IN HIS CABIN, Anna made the most of this highly unusual "cruise." Part of her delight in the voyage was the result of her being granted the admiral's quarters, which were located next to her father's and included a bedroom, bath, and sitting room. Given that Admiral Leahy was aboard, Anna's lodgings represented a breach of protocol, necessitated not only by her desire to remain close to her father but also by the fact that Captain Elliott Senn thought it inappropriate to lodge her on the lower decks where the men often ran around in their skivvies![18]

By the third day out, Thursday, January 25, the task force was approaching the island of Bermuda, which allowed for an exchange of escort destroyers, as the smaller vessels could not hold enough fuel to complete the crossing. The exchange of ships also afforded the *Quincy* the opportunity to transfer to one of its sister ships a "mail pouch" that, once it reached Bermuda, would then be flown by air to Washington. The arrival of the new escorts would also mean that for the first time since their departure from Virginia, FDR and Anna would be able to receive mail.

Curious about the means by which the mail pouch would be transferred in such high seas, Anna asked the officer in charge if she could observe the procedure. Not one to be outdone by his daughter, FDR insisted "that he would like to watch, too!" For a man in a wheelchair, though, such a request is easier said than done. The handover would take place at the stern of the nearly 700-foot-long *Quincy,* and knowing FDR's sensitivity to being seen in public in his wheelchair, his naval aide, Vice Admiral Brown, cautioned Anna that he did not think "the boss would like to be watched by all the gun crews and other members of the ship's party."

"This was no matter," Anna argued, "as long as we ignore this and tell him that he will not be under the gaze of the entire crew but just a few sailors manning the gun emplacements." Equipped with this fallacious argument, she and Brown wheeled FDR to the stern. Anna immediately began to wonder if she had made a huge mistake. Her father's wheelchair, which he himself had designed to be as unobtrusive as possible, amounted to little more than a narrow kitchen chair with wheels attached. It had no arms and no brakes to lock it into place. The *Quincy*, virtually dead in the water, pitched wildly while FDR clung to the wire railing "for dear life," watching in fascination as the mail was placed into an empty torpedo canister attached to a long rope and then dropped over the stern. Meanwhile, on board the destroyer, a small group of sailors perched on the bow flung a grappling hook forward to try to catch the canister, not securing it until the sixth attempt.[19]

The exchange of mail brought the first in a series of "disconcerting" messages that FDR received from Winston Churchill while crossing the Atlantic. These included a note from Harry Hopkins, who had been sent to London in advance of the Yalta conference to mollify Churchill, still fuming at Secretary Stettinius's earlier criticism of British policy in Greece and Italy. In the letter, Hopkins reported that Churchill had expressed the opinion that "ten years of research . . . could not have found a worse place in the world" to hold the conference than Yalta. The prime minister nevertheless felt they could "survive" the experience "by bringing an adequate supply of whiskey," which he understood is "good for typhus and deadly on lice which thrive in those parts."[20]

The second message, a more serious one, arrived by wire on January 26. In it Churchill conveyed his "great concern" regarding the "extreme difficulty" involved in reaching Yalta via mountain roads. Indeed, he was compelled to advise that two attempts made by a combined group of British and American officers "resulted in failure to pass mountainous track in blizzard," with one British officer describing the journey as "a most terrifying experience."[21]

Churchill's cables, coupled with the fact that the American delegation had not yet received word from the US advance team, sparked considerable discussion about what sorts of conditions they would confront once they reached the Crimea. Yet FDR remained confident that all would be well. He tended to brush off many of Churchill's concerns out of suspicion that the prime minister was still annoyed at Stalin's refusal to meet somewhere in the much more accessible—and warmer—Mediterranean.[22]

THE APPROACH OF THE GULF STREAM BROUGHT WARMER WEATHER and renewed air cover, provided by an escort carrier that had positioned itself ahead of the task force as the convoy entered the waters to the southwest of the Azores. These remote far-flung vestiges of the once-powerful Portuguese Empire held special meaning for FDR, for it was to these largely forgotten outposts that he took his first official trip overseas as a young assistant secretary of the Navy in the closing days of World War I. FDR was astonished by the abundance of flora and fauna that blanketed this rugged volcanic archipelago. It seemed to him that "anything" would grow in the Azores. "One sees bamboo next to English Oak and even White Pine," he noted in his diary— "a wonderful scene" of picturesque villages, volcanic craters, and "deep blue lakes and springs that threw off clouds of steam." Not wanting to forget the thrill he felt as "his ship," the USS *Dyer,* first made its way into the harbor of Ponta Delgada, the administrative capital of the Azores, FDR commissioned a painting of the scene that hung in his study for the rest of his life. In more recent times, he even entertained the thought that the Azores might serve as the headquarters for the Trusteeship Council of the United Nations.[23]

In keeping with his ardent desire to get away from the day-to-day pressures of the Oval Office, FDR had left his key aides and staff with strict instructions not to bother him during the voyage unless it was a matter of extreme importance. It would not be long, however, before the tranquility FDR enjoyed at sea was disturbed by news from Washington—now becoming more accessible as the slate of escort vessels changed with greater frequency. Once again, the matter at hand concerned a domestic issue: on Monday, January 29, FDR received a long telegram from Samuel Rosenman informing him that Henry Wallace's confirmation as secretary of commerce appeared "doomed." Rosenman urged FDR to tell Congress that he would transfer the federal lending agencies out of Commerce, as Wallace's critics had insisted. Otherwise, Rosenman insisted, there was no chance that

Wallace would be confirmed. And even such a transfer might not be enough to save him. A missive from Eleanor received two days later more or less made the same case.[24]

Keenly aware of the pressure that FDR was under due to the urgent demands of the war, Admiral Leahy was of the opinion that the president "is now faced with too many difficult and vital international problems to permit his getting into an acrimonious disagreement with the Congress, or even to warrant his being bothered by the personal troubles of any individual." Indeed, given the "equally impractical . . . idealistic attitudes" of both Eleanor Roosevelt and Wallace, Leahy regarded the president's decision to nominate Wallace as a mistake and had little sympathy for Wallace's plight. Leahy's view was that FDR should let matters take their course and "accept the decision of the Congress" whatever the outcome. But unwilling to abandon his former vice president, FDR sent word back to Samuel Rosenman indicating his support for the pending resolution.[25]

On Tuesday, January 30, FDR celebrated his sixty-third birthday. To mark the occasion, the crew presented him with a special gift: a brass ashtray fashioned out of a five-inch shell casing fired during the Normandy invasion. Anna organized a small convocation that evening. Five cakes were baked for the occasion; the first four represented FDR's four terms in office, and the fifth, procured at the last minute, was graced by a large question mark to represent the possibility of a fifth term, which brought hails of laughter from FDR. Unbeknownst to his assembled guests, FDR also enjoyed a more private celebration in his cabin that day, when Anna presented him with a series of little gifts and trinkets from Lucy Rutherfurd and his cousin Daisy.[26]

Now more than a week at sea, the task force was nearing the North African Coast and the Strait of Gibraltar. Passing through the strait, which is a mere nine miles wide at its narrowest point, would be the most dangerous moment of the entire voyage. Adding to the captain's concerns, on two occasions in the past forty-eight hours the escort destroyers believed they had detected a submarine in the vicinity, which raised the possibility of a security breach concerning the likely route of FDR's vessel and the location of the conference.

The responsibility of maintaining the safety and security of the Yalta party fell to Vice Admiral Brown. Fit, trim, and born the same year as the president, Brown first met Roosevelt in 1912, shortly after the latter had been appointed assistant secretary of the Navy. Brown went on to a distinguished naval career and for a brief time served in the White House as a naval aide to President Calvin Coolidge. In 1934 he returned to the White House to take up the same position for FDR; however, in accordance with the normal rotation between sea and shore duty, he was offered the command of the Atlantic Fleet in the summer of 1936—a move that FDR enthusiastically endorsed, telling Brown: "You are the luckiest man on earth. I would give anything in the world to change places with you."[27]

The bond that FDR and Brown shared became even stronger when the latter returned to the White House yet again to resume his duties as naval aide in February 1943. By this point, active duty experience had imprinted on Brown the value of secrecy for a vessel plying the Atlantic. Brown repeatedly stressed the importance of maintaining an absolute lockdown on any information regarding the president's voyage aboard the *Quincy*. Adding to his anxiety was the somewhat "lukewarm" attitude that FDR seemed to hold about the dangers involved. Brown was upset, for instance, when FDR sent the members of a Secret Service detail ahead as an advance team because they were always in pictures taken of the president and might be recognized abroad, providing a clue as to where and when the president might be meeting with the other members of the "Big Three."[28]

Brown was equally alarmed when he overheard Harry Hopkins explain that he would be traveling ahead of the party to London, Paris, and Rome for meetings with Churchill and de Gaulle before joining the president at Malta. This, too, might alert the enemy. More problematic still, Hopkins wanted to use the president's plane. Unable to contain his worry, Brown confronted Hopkins with the demand that he use the president's aircraft only as far as Gibraltar and then switch to a regular army transport to finish what Brown called a "most unfortunate venture."[29]

In the interests of security, Hopkins had received strict instructions to keep his mission to London secret and to say nothing to the press while he was in Paris or Rome. But as the task force steamed ever closer to the strait, report after report arrived about Hopkins's activities in Europe, including numerous press pieces and radio broadcasts describing his itinerary. These notices included rampant speculation that his presence in London, Paris, and Rome was part of the administration's effort to send key advisers aboard in advance of another meeting of the "Big Three." Hopkins also made himself freely available to reporters and even staged a press conference in Rome on the evening of January 29, during which he all but admitted that a meeting of Churchill, Roosevelt, and Stalin was imminent.[30]

On board the *Quincy*, news of Hopkins's parley with the press infuriated FDR's press secretary Stephen Early, upset the president, and seriously alarmed Brown, who felt that Hopkins's interviews seemed "to give warning that something was going on in the Mediterranean." To make matters worse, US naval intelligence had determined that German U-boats had indeed taken up positions in and around the strait. Whether this was a coincidence wasn't known, but there can be no doubt that tensions ran high on the bridge in the wee hours of Wednesday, January 31, when Captain Senn spotted the historic Cape Spartel Light on the north coast of Morocco that marked the entrance to the strait.[31]

To reduce the chances of even a "lucky hit" by a U-boat, the chief of US naval forces in the Mediterranean had increased the *Quincy*'s stable of escorts to six destroyers and a light cruiser. He also ordered a pair of the famous "Black Cat" Catalina Flying Boats to provide nighttime air cover. In addition, a K-Class Navy Blimp equipped with sonar flew above the strait ahead of the force. In the meantime, Captain Senn increased the speed of the task force, still zigzagging, to an extraordinary 30 knots.[32]

Just after 4:00 a.m., underneath a bright but waning moon, the task force finally entered the narrow waters that separate Europe and Africa. Having never sailed through the famous passage before, Anna decided that despite the hour she wanted to witness the occasion. From the flag bridge, as her father slept soundly below, she was able to make out the Rock of Gibraltar in the moonlight, the twinkling lights of the British naval base, and even the outline of a hospital ship. On the opposite shore was the stunning sight of Tangier, where it seemed that "every light in the town were lit." As dawn broke, the snow-covered mountains of the Spanish coast came into view, followed by the outline of the rugged North African shore near the Spanish enclave of Ceuta.[33]

Thursday, February 1—the last full day at sea before the landing at Malta—brought more warm weather. In an effort to conserve his strength before arriving at the ancient port of Valletta, FDR spent most of the afternoon on deck lounging in the Mediterranean sun. At home in Rhinebeck, meanwhile, his cousin Daisy waited anxiously for any word from "F" while she tended to his beloved Scottie, Fala. Due to the various communication restrictions placed on the presidential party, it would be some time before Daisy received a note from FDR. It came in the form of a brief diary that FDR had penned for her, sketching out his day-to-day routine and some of the high points of the voyage. Knowing that Daisy would be concerned about his health, FDR dutifully reported that he had made a point of getting plenty of rest. But the brevity of his descriptions and the overall lack of detail seemed uncharacteristic of him. His note showed none of his usual vitality, perhaps reflecting some of the dread he felt about the responsibilities he would soon confront as the relative quiet of his time at sea came to an end. "An awful day ahead," he wrote as the *Quincy* finally reached Malta on the morning of February 2, 1945, before "tonight at 10, we are off by air for the final destination."[34]

Chapter 3

Interlude at Malta

THE HISTORIC WALLED CITY OF VALLETTA, OR IL-BELT AS THE LOCALS call it, boasts one of the finest natural harbors in the Mediterranean. Protected on one side by the massive Fort St. Elmo and on the other by the ancient Castrum Maris, rebuilt and renamed Fort St. Angelo by the Knights of St. John in the first half of sixteenth century, the deep waters of the Grand Harbor that lies just to the east of the peninsula upon which Valletta rests have sheltered vessels for centuries. The city itself was established in the wake of the famous first siege of Malta that took place in the summer of 1565, when Turkish forces under the command of Suleiman the Magnificent invaded the island in an unsuccessful attempt to wrest control of the central Mediterranean from the sultan's archrival, King Philip II of Spain.

The gallantry of the knights, Maltese soldiers, and civilians who managed to hold out against far superior forces—an estimated forty thousand Turks against a force of fewer than ten thousand led by Grand Master Jean de la Valette and his six hundred knights—soon became the stuff of legend in Christian Europe. Although not apparent at the time, Malta's survival marked a turning point in the sixty-year struggle between the Ottoman Turks and the Hapsburgs of Spain for control of this vital sea and the shape of the Muslim and Christian worlds to follow.[1]

Malta's strategic location proved equally important two centuries later, when Napoleon Bonaparte conquered the island before attempting to seize control of Egypt in an effort to undermine British access to India. The British naval victory in the Battle of the Nile soon rendered Napoleon's position in Egypt untenable, and as a consequence of this defeat and the unpopularity of Napoleonic rule, Britain took possession of Malta in 1800, remaining in power there for the next 150 years.

Malta's value as a link between the British naval facilities at Gibraltar in the west and Alexandria, Egypt, in the east was immediately apparent, and became even more pronounced with the opening of the Suez Canal in 1869. This fact was not lost on Mussolini and Hitler in their efforts to drive the British out of the Mediterranean after the fall of France in June 1940. Located astride the main Axis supply route between Italy and North Africa, tiny Malta—with its airfields, submarine base, and surface ship facilities—proved an ideal launching pad for attacks against German and Italian shipping as the war in Libya and the Western Desert intensified. Churchill determined that Malta must be held at all costs, while Mussolini, and then Hitler, believed that the island must be either neutralized or brought under Axis control.

Given Malta's size—roughly seventeen miles long and nine miles wide—and its proximity to Sicily, a mere sixty miles distant, not to mention the more than one-thousand-mile sea expanse between the island and the nearest British supply base, it seemed inevitable that the Axis powers would bomb the island into submission. But like the Turkish forces arrayed against the protectors of Malta nearly four centuries before, the Italian and German air crews who blasted the island in what became known as the Second Siege of Malta learned a hard lesson about the tenacity of the Maltese people and the determination of the anti-aircraft gunners and RAF pilots defending the island. In January 1942 alone, for example, the Luftwaffe conducted 262 bombing raids on the island; in February, 236; and in March and April of that year the total tonnage of destruction that rained down from the sky measured twice the weight of the bombs dropped during the famous London Blitz. The ability of the Maltese to take such punishment served as an inspiration for people the world over, and on April 15, 1942, King George VI took the unprecedented step of granting to the entire population the George's Cross—the highest civilian honor for gallantry offered in the British Empire.[2]

FDR certainly understood the importance of Malta. In April 1942, at the very moment when the island was perhaps the most vulnerable, he responded to an urgent plea from Churchill for US help in ferrying British fighter aircraft to Malta by dispatching the US aircraft carrier

WASP into the Mediterranean laden with Spitfires. FDR's decision elicited a major protest from the chief of Naval Operations, Admiral Ernest King, who objected that this was all part of a British ploy to draw the United States into the Mediterranean Theater of Operations. But FDR persisted, and even authorized a second sailing of the *WASP* when the ever-present Luftwaffe destroyed the first delivery of aircraft on the ground within minutes of the planes' arrival.[3]

Equally moved by the uncommon valor of the population, FDR decided to present the citizens of Malta with a Presidential Citation as he made his way back from the Tehran conference in December 1943. During a brief stopover on the 8th of that month, FDR told the "good people of Malta" about the comments he had made to Churchill roughly a year earlier at the Casablanca conference, that "someday we would control once more the whole of the Mediterranean" and that when this day came, he "would go to Malta."[4] Now that the day in question had happily arrived, he was determined "to pay some little tribute to this island and to all of its people—civil and military—who during these years have contributed so much to democracy, not just here but all over the civilized world." In recognition of their courage, he had brought "a little token—a scroll—a citation—from the President of the United States, speaking in behalf of the people of the United States."[5]

In their name he continued:

> I salute the Island of Malta, its people and defenders, who, in the cause of freedom and justice and decency throughout the world, have rendered valorous service far above and beyond the call of duty.
>
> Under repeated fire from the skies, Malta stood alone, but un-afraid in the center of the sea, one tiny bright flame in the dark-ness—a beacon of hope for the clearer days which have come.[6]

The president dated the citation December 7, 1943, because he felt that the second anniversary of the American entry into the war better sym-bolized the American people's determination "to proceed until that war is won" and "to stand shoulder to shoulder with the British Empire and our other allies in making it a victory worthwhile."

Anti-aircraft emplacements at the entrance to the Grand Harbor in Valletta, Malta. (Imperial War Museum)

BY ALL ACCOUNTS, THE SCENE THAT GREETED THE MALTESE PEOPLE as FDR returned to the island on the morning of February 2, 1945, was magnificent. Moored along the quay in the Grand Harbor was the HMS *Orion*, the 550-foot light cruiser that had served as Prime Minister Churchill's headquarters and residence as he tried to recover from a fever in the two days he spent on Malta in advance of FDR's arrival. On the opposite side of the harbor stood the equally impressive HMS *Sirius*, another light cruiser, and next to it the *Eastern Prince*, a passenger liner–cum–troop ship brought in to help quarter the many hundreds of British and American officers and officials who made up the Yalta delegation.[7] Further down the quay stood the USS *Memphis*, the

cruiser that had served as FDR's flagship during the Casablanca conference and nearly two decades before that had earned fame as the ship
that transported Charles Lindbergh and his famous *Spirit of St. Louis*
back to Washington after his historic flight across the Atlantic.[8]

It was 9:30 a.m., beneath an absolutely cloudless blue sky, when the
massive *Quincy* first came into view at the narrow entrance to the harbor. High above the azure sea, a squadron of Spitfires, so critical to the
defense of the island, flew triumphantly overhead. On board the *Sirius*,
a company of Royal Marines stood at attention to greet the president
and his party, and as the *Quincy* carefully sailed by, aided by a pilot
tug, a Marine band on board struck up "The Star-Spangled Banner."[9]

Along the docks and from countless blown-out windows and shattered verandas, thousands of Maltese citizens waved flags and cheered
as the *Quincy* made its way further into the harbor. On board the
Orion, a second Marine band took up the American national anthem
as the *Quincy* slowly approached while Prime Minister Churchill,
dressed in a naval peacoat and cap, stood at attention and saluted President Roosevelt—the only seated figure among the hundreds of men,
and one woman, who lined the rail as the heavy cruiser finally reached
its berth, his wheelchair carefully hidden from view behind a canvas
screen.[10]

Churchill had hoped, as he did at Tehran, that he and the president would confer before the three-power summit to align British
and American strategy in advance of their discussions with Stalin.
On January 4, Churchill sent a cable to FDR, asking, somewhat dif-
fidently, if it might be possible for the president to spend two or three
nights at Malta to accomplish this task.[11] But Roosevelt—ever mindful of Soviet suspicions about possible Anglo-American conspiracies
against the Russians—refused. Concern over Soviet perceptions of
Anglo-American collusion was not the only factor that shaped FDR's
decision-making. He also wished to distance himself from the British out of his profound conviction that the United States must, as one
intelligence analyst put it, "start exercising the dominant influence
which power properly entitles us." To FDR the exercise of this "dominant influence" required above all else an independent relationship
with Stalin, the leader of the other emerging superpower.[12]

This attitude marked a dramatic shift, of course, from the early
years of the war, when Great Britain, with far more troops available

The USS *Quincy* arriving in Valletta Harbor, Malta, February 2, 1945.
(Courtesy of the Franklin D. Roosevelt Presidential Library)

for combat in the European Theater, remained the senior partner in the Anglo-American Alliance.[13] Thanks to this preponderance, Churchill and the British Chiefs of Staff largely determined the military strategy adopted for Europe in 1942. Much as Admiral King feared, and General Marshall opposed, this took the Allies to North Africa in November 1942 and on to Sicily and Italy in 1943 in pursuit of what eventually became known as the "Mediterranean strategy." Churchill, who preferred this indirect approach to the war (in part, out of his experience with the horrors of the trench warfare of World War I), and never stopped thinking about the impact that such a strategy might have on his desire to restore British influence in the region, was delighted at these developments, and would continue to press for the expansion of operations in the Mediterranean, even if this meant having to postpone the invasion of Northwest France.[14]

By the end of 1943, however, US mobilization had shifted the military tide rather dramatically in America's favor, with the result that Churchill increasingly found himself the junior partner in the Anglo-American Alliance. The most striking example of this shift came during the first two days of the Tehran conference of November–December 1943, where FDR all but ignored Churchill, held a number of one-on-one meetings with Stalin, and firmly supported Stalin's demand that the Anglo-Americans open a second front in northwest France in the spring of 1944—which was also the strategy vehemently favored by General Marshall.[15]

This pattern now repeated itself in the days leading up to the Yalta conference. Unable to convince FDR of the advantages of a pre-summit tête-à-tête and still distressed about Great Britain's diminishing influence over the course of the war, Churchill proposed at the very least a preliminary meeting of the Combined Chiefs of Staff as well as a conference involving the three Allied foreign ministers "of about a week's duration" prior to the summit. Churchill was also anxious to learn FDR's thoughts on the length of the Yalta meeting as he speculated that this "may well be a fateful conference, coming at a moment when the great allies are so divided and the shadow of the war lengthens out before us." Giving vent to the pessimism that seemed to plague him at the time, Churchill also expressed his fear that "the end of this war may well prove to be more disappointing than the last."[16]

After further entreaties from Churchill, FDR finally agreed to send both his military chiefs and Secretary of State Edward Stettinius to Malta in time for preliminary discussions. But he made certain that these talks would be of limited duration. General George Marshall, Admiral Ernest King, and General Laurence Kuter (who replaced the ill General Henry H. Arnold) would not arrive on the island until January 30, and Stettinius would fly in a day later, a mere forty-eight hours before the delegation was scheduled to depart on the evening of February 2.

Churchill and his foreign secretary, Anthony Eden, found Roosevelt's willingness to allow these brief discussions reassuring, although the prime minister confessed to being somewhat perplexed by FDR's response to his question about how long the president expected to remain at Yalta: five to six days. It was a good thing, Churchill mused in a mid-January cable he sent to FDR, that the president had agreed to the preliminary talks. Without them, he did not see how the Allies could realize their hopes for the creation of a world organization in just five or six days; after all, as he put it, "even the Almighty took seven."[17]

Left unsaid in these polite diplomatic exchanges was the fact that American skepticism over British policies and behavior was possibly greater than that over the Russians. The view in Washington, emanating from the president on down, was that the continuation of British imperialism was antithetical to the new world order the Americans wished to see emerge from war. Admiral King's opposition to the use of the *WASP* to deliver British aircraft to Malta in April 1942 was one example of this phenomenon. So, too, was the American insistence not to shore up what one US general called "Churchill's eternal and infernal Balkan enterprises," which persisted even after the successful Allied invasion of France in June 1944. The US Joint Chiefs of Staff remained vehemently opposed to this idea. Indeed, they regarded any British move to send additional forces to Italy or the Balkans as not only militarily counterproductive but a grave threat to Allied unity. Accordingly, when the idea reemerged in the fall of 1944, American military planners insisted that it was imperative to permit "no more diversions such as Winston Churchill is now asking," and by mid-October 1944 both FDR and Secretary of War Henry Stimson concurred that the United States should remain "absolutely inflexible" on this question.[18]

Unable to get Washington to support his calls for the strengthening of the Allied presence in the region—and lacking forces of his own to carry out such a mission—Churchill turned to diplomacy. Hence, at the very moment that FDR and his advisers had come to a firm decision not to support the dispatch of additional troops to Italy or the Balkans, Churchill flew to Moscow to meet with Stalin directly. On October 9, 1944, the two men negotiated Churchill's famous "percentages agreement." Under its terms, which came in the form of a note that Churchill passed across the table to Stalin, the prime minister proposed that the Soviets would retain 90 percent influence in Romania and that Great Britain would hold the same figure for Greece. The two powers would split Hungary and Yugoslavia 50/50, while the Russians would retain a 75 percent influence—and Great Britain a 25 percent interest—in Bulgaria.[19]

FDR was aware that Churchill had decided to fly to Moscow to meet Stalin, and he made no objection, so long as both leaders understood that "in this global war, there is literally no question, political or military, in which the United States is not interested." The president also insisted—as he put it in a private message to Ambassador W. Averell Harriman (whom he instructed to attend as an observer)—that the talks be regarded as "nothing more than a preliminary exploration" by the two powers leading up to "a full dress meeting between the three of us."[20]

Churchill had conveniently organized the "percentages agreement" talks shortly after his arrival and at a time when Harriman could not be present. But his motivations were clear: to protect the British sphere of influence in the Eastern Mediterranean—an objective confirmed by the forceful British intervention in Greece at the end of 1944. Both FDR and Harriman soon became aware of the percentages agreement, and even though FDR would subsequently inform Churchill in private that he understood "the anxious and difficult alternatives" that his government faced in Greece, Churchill's machinations did nothing to allay the overall apprehensions that many of FDR's senior advisers harbored about the political motives underlying British military strategy. These remained as strong as ever, with the result that the pre-summit meetings that took place on Malta shortly before FDR arrived turned out to be what General Marshall termed "the stormiest of the entire war."[21]

Secretary Stettinius, Ambassador Harriman, and Harry Hopkins were the first officials to come aboard the *Quincy* to welcome the president upon his arrival in Malta. After exchanging a few words about the voyage, FDR and Stettinius took a few moments to review two urgent matters, the first of which concerned Flynn's need for a passport, so that, as FDR put it, his friend would not have "to spend the rest of his days in Siberia." The second one was far more important: FDR's latest thoughts on how best to overcome the Soviet objections to the proposed voting procedure in the Security Council that would make up such an important part of the postwar United Nations Organization.[22]

The question of how to come to an agreement on the two outstanding issues that stood in the way of the creation of the world organization—on voting and the number of seats granted to the USSR in the General Assembly—was the first priority among the American delegation to the Yalta conference. All three of the major powers agreed that

FDR confers with Admiral Cunningham, commander-in-chief of the British Naval Forces in the Mediterranean, Valletta Harbor, February 2, 1945.
(Getty Images)

the five permanent members should have the right to exercise a veto, but a significant dispute arose over the question of when this power should be exercised, particularly in cases where one of the permanent members was a party to a dispute. By the time the Dumbarton Oaks conference wrapped up in the fall of 1944, the Soviets had made it clear that they favored an "unlimited veto." This would allow each of the five permanent members the power not only to veto any potential Security Council enforcement action but to block mere discussion of it. In light of the still-strong isolationist sentiment in America and the failure of the Senate to endorse US membership in the League of Nations over the fear that US involvement in the international body might threaten the sovereign exercise of US foreign policy, FDR recognized that the possession of a veto would significantly enhance his ability to gain Senate acceptance of the United Nations. But in his view, the permanent members should exercise this right regarding only questions, as former Secretary of State Cordell Hull put it, "of the gravest concern, . . . never on secondary matters, and never in a way to prevent thorough discussion of any issue."[23] Hence, in lieu of the unlimited veto favored by the Russians, what Hull, Leo Pasvolsky, and other officials within the State Department favored was a "limited veto" that would allow the free airing of grievances. Failure to allow such open discussion, they argued, might result in a backlash against the organization among the lesser states, whose spokespeople could justifiably argue that the five permanent members had been granted such sweeping powers as to place them on a higher plane than smaller nations in attempts to resolve potential conflicts.[24]

In an effort to sway Soviet opinion on this question once it became clear that the Anglo-Americans and the Russians had reached an impasse at the Dumbarton Oaks gathering, FDR agreed to meet with Soviet Ambassador Andrei Gromyko in September 1944 to discuss the matter. Using one of his homespun analogies, FDR noted that "traditionally in America, husbands and wives having trouble never have the opportunity to vote on their own case, although they are always afforded the opportunity to testify—to state their case. It should be the same," he thought, "within the family of nations."[25] FDR sent a note to Stalin in which he made the same argument. But Stalin remained unmoved, even in the face of the American argument that the impasse might destroy "the prospect of ever having a world organization."[26]

Determined to resolve the issue, the State Department put together a detailed proposal on the voting procedure that spelled out the exact nature of the powers that the permanent members would possess under the limited veto by offering a more complete definition of "enforcement actions." These included all sanctions or military operations, as well as membership questions and determinations of "threats to the peace." This more detailed proposal was sent to the Kremlin in early December in the hope that the Soviets would be prepared to accept it at the Yalta gathering.[27]

Unable to put aside his fears that the Soviets might continue to maintain their hard-line position on the matter at Yalta, the president, during the voyage, had worked up a short memorandum on the subject that he passed on to Stettinius on deck that morning. For his part, Stettinius reported that the conversations he'd had with Eden the day before over the voting question had gone very well, as Eden, who had read the State Department's proposal, indicated that he fully approved of it and was prepared to support it at the conference.[28]

Having finished his brief talks with Stettinius, FDR left the bridge for a deck chair on the port side of the ship, away from the shore, where for the next hour he would begin the task of receiving the many visitors who expected to see him that day. Just before noon, Prime Minister Churchill was "piped" on board (the shrill sounding of a bosun's pipe is a traditional honor accorded to flag officers and other dignitaries), followed a few minutes later by Eden and Churchill's daughter Sarah. While Eden spoke with Stettinius, the two leaders and their daughters spent about an hour on deck enjoying each other's company. At 1:00 p.m., they moved to the president's cabin for a lunch that included Eden, Stettinius, Director Byrnes, and Admiral Leahy.

Churchill was in fine form as he took his seat to the right of the president. The prime minister particularly appreciated the small candle that FDR had placed next to his plate so that Churchill could light his cigars. Still, any hope (specifically felt by Eden) that this first semi-official gathering would include a serious examination of the issues the two leaders were about to confront at Yalta was quickly put to rest, though FDR did raise the issue of the Atlantic Charter. Remarking on the unofficial nature of the document (which had created such a furor in the press in December), the president wondered if the prime minister might have a moment to countersign the only draft FDR had in his possession, which included his own signature but not Churchill's. Churchill was happy to do so, and then launched into a lengthy discourse about the Declaration of Independence, Roosevelt's Four Freedoms speech—both of which he greatly admired—and the nature of democracy. He also mentioned that he was quite confident he would be returned to office when the British people next went to the polls. The two also briefly discussed China, which, given recent difficulties, Churchill somewhat caustically referred to as "the Great American Illusion," and engaged in some speculation about when the war against Japan might come to an end. Beyond this, "no business whatsoever" was discussed, as Eden lamented in his diary.[29]

While Churchill returned to the *Orion* for his daily hour-long nap, FDR went on a motor tour of Malta accompanied by its governor, Lieutenant General Sir Edmond Schreiber, his wife and daughter, Sarah

Churchill, and Anna. As the party made their way from the harbor to the medieval walled city of Medina, the ancient hilltop town that once served as Malta's capital, Anna quickly fell in love with the soft hues and texture of the local limestone and the colorful luzzu fishing boats, whose sturdy construction and painted "eyes of horous" were said to date back to the Phoenicians. But as she also recorded in her diary, the contrast between these peaceful scenes and the massive destruction she witnessed in Valletta left her feeling somewhat overwhelmed by the brutality of modern war.[30]

After viewing the plaque of FDR's citation that had been mounted on the wall of the grand master's palace in Valletta, the party returned to the ship at 4:30 p.m. FDR then went straight into a meeting with his military advisers, where he was finally able to obtain a more complete picture of the acrimonious meetings that had taken place over the past two days among the Combined Chiefs of Staff. As Marshall reported—and in sharp contrast to the more harmonious encounter between Eden and Stettinius—the American Chiefs had gone into the meeting with every intention of maintaining Eisenhower's broad-front strategy. This meant that while the weight of the Allied thrust would proceed north of the Ruhr, a simultaneous attack would be mounted in the south. The Americans insisted that the southern thrust was essential. Without it, the Germans would be able to concentrate their forces against the Allied attempt to cross the northern reaches of the Rhine, slowing or perhaps even halting it.[31]

But Hitler's stunning offensive in the Ardennes in December had revived earlier British objections to this approach. It would be far better, Churchill and his military chiefs argued in the days leading to the conversations on Malta, to concentrate Allied forces in a single thrust north of the Ruhr and to "pass to the defensive all other parts of the line." Never a fan of Eisenhower, Churchill and his chiefs also used the Ardennes setback as an opportunity to reissue their call for the appointment of a British officer as commander-in-chief of all Allied ground forces on the Western Front—a responsibility that Eisenhower had assumed by design following the Normandy breakout. Convinced that Churchill's promotion of this idea would mean that "the British had won a major point in getting control of ground operations," General Marshall made it clear to both Eisenhower and Roosevelt that he was adamantly opposed to the idea. Moreover, both Marshall and the president suspected that, as with Churchill's proposed "infernal" adventures in the Balkans, the motives behind London's advocacy of the single-thrust strategy were political—an attempt to sweep across northern Germany to grab the ports and naval bases along the North Sea and Baltic coasts ahead of a possible Russian attempt to do the same.[32]

The American Chiefs were adamantly opposed to this idea. From the moment the United States joined the war, American strategists had repeatedly stressed the importance of the Soviet Union in the Allied effort to defeat the Nazis. With the Red Army facing roughly 90 percent of the German Divisions and having inflicted 93 percent of German battle casualties between 1941 and 1944, a Russian defeat or separate peace would—in the Joint Chiefs' view—make victory over the Germans impossible.[33]

A corresponding factor was the problem of manpower. Even though the US population might have appeared to offer an advantage over the Axis, the nature of America's role in the war—as the "great arsenal of democracy"—made it difficult for the United States to field an army as large as the forces arrayed against it. Out of some 25 million Americans fit for military service during the war, the absolute ceiling on the number who could be used for active duty was somewhere between 15 million and 16 million. Most of the rest were needed by the American war industries. Hence, the US Army had to compete for manpower, not only with the needs of the other services but also with the claims of industry. To make matters worse, prior US assumptions about the Chinese Army tying down large numbers of Japanese troops in Asia had all but collapsed in the wake of the successful Japanese *Ichi-Go* offensive in the summer and fall of 1944, which led to the virtual collapse of the Chinese front by December. Taken together, these considerations made cooperation, not confrontation, with the Russians a military imperative from the US point of view. Thus, FDR and his military advisers regarded the efforts of the British to beat the Russians to the punch in Europe as nothing less than a threat to American national security.[34]

All of these disputes resurfaced and came to a head during the Combined Chiefs of Staff meeting that took place on Malta on January 30, 1945. As the arguments intensified, the normally calm and soft-spoken Marshall demanded that he and General Alan Brooke and

their top advisers go into a closed session—that is, without any stenographers. There Marshall gave full vent to his frustration. He lashed
out at the British so severely that "he carried everything before him,"
clinching the argument with his insistence that if the Supreme Commander's plans were not acceptable to the British he would recom-
mend to Eisenhower "that he had no choice but to ask to be relieved
of his command." Impressed by Marshall's conviction, and with much
less leverage now that the American forces on the Western Front far
outnumbered their own, the British relented and the matter was settled in favor of Eisenhower, "without the need for reference to higher
authority."[35]

Having settled this critical strategic question, Marshall was happy
to inform the president, during the debriefing he gave FDR on board
the *Quincy* on February 2, that the Combined Chiefs had little trouble
coming to an understanding about various other matters—including
the withdrawal of five divisions from the Mediterranean to France—
during the remaining discussions that took place in the two days
before FDR arrived on Malta. But in the subsequent meeting with
Churchill and the Combined Chiefs of Staff that immediately followed
General Marshall's report to the president—where all concurred that
they were in "complete agreement" about how to proceed in northwest Europe—Churchill suddenly surprised both his own military
chiefs and the Americans by indicating that he continued to attach
the utmost importance to the possibility that the Allies would be able
to follow up any German surrender or withdrawal from Italy with a
rapid thrust from the Balkans into Austria. Perhaps taken aback by
this abrupt outburst, neither FDR nor any of the British or American
military chiefs present made any comment, and with that the discussion turned to the war against Japan.[36]

Not unlike the case over what strategy to pursue in Europe, it soon
became apparent that there was a divergence of opinion over how best
to prosecute the war in the Far East. Churchill wondered—after indicating how dissatisfied he was with the progress of the war in China
and Southeast Asia—if it might not be advantageous for the British
to move a number of divisions from Burma into China to take part in
operations there. But General Marshall rejected this idea as impractical, and although FDR did not say so during the meeting, his opposition to such a move was unequivocal and long-standing. Fully alive

to the idea that "the raising of the Union Jack over Singapore is more important to the British than any victory parade through Tokyo," FDR viewed any such suggestion as little more than a brazen attempt to reestablish the Empire in the region.[37]

As FDR explained to Stettinius and Hopkins in a conversation they had in early January, the British "were working to undermine our whole policy with regard to China." Indeed, it appeared to the president that London "still clung to the idea of White supremacy in Asia" and did not want to see a strong China. By contrast, his approach to the region was based on the recognition that despite "temporary weakness," and the possibility of revolutions and civil war, the 450 million Chinese "would someday become united and modernized." When this occurred, they "would be the most important factor in the whole Far East."[38]

Given that FDR was even less enamored with the idea of a return of the French to Indochina,[39] these differences point toward a fundamental split over the very purpose of the war in Asia. Whereas FDR looked at the conflict as an opportunity to rid the region of colonialism and create a new world order, Churchill and de Gaulle seemed mired in the past, unwilling or unable to embrace FDR's forward-thinking ideas about what he saw as the essential nature of the struggle. Indeed, in another indication of the increasingly disparate geopolitical strategies of the two powers, FDR and his military advisers had by this point shifted their emphasis away from support for a British drive into Malaya and other parts of Southeast Asia. Their focus was now centered on bringing Russia into the war against Japan.[40] This was undoubtedly a welcome development in Washington, where the acronym of the British-led Southeast Asian Command, SEAC, was frequently translated as "Save England's Asian Colonies."[41]

Leaving the issue of China unresolved, but satisfied that "such a great measure of agreement had been reached" on all other issues, FDR adjourned the meeting. At this point, Anna took it upon herself to explain to any lingering officials—including Secretaries Eden and Stettinius—that she wanted her father "to have a little rest time to himself." The prime minister had had his nap, and now planned to take his usual bath before dinner. FDR, in contrast, "had been going strong since 9:30 a.m. without a break." She therefore insisted that he return to his cabin for some quiet time before cocktails were brought in at

8:15 p.m. That would allow FDR forty-five minutes of peace. To her and Dr. McIntire's great annoyance, however, Eden and Stettinius snuck into FDR's cabin to engage in a further review of the previous day's discussion on the UN voting procedure, among other matters. Anna was right, however, about her father's need for a rest. Seeing the president in such close quarters for the first time since the Quebec conference in September, Eden thought FDR looked considerably older, writing in his diary that "he gives the impression of failing powers."[42]

Though the evening meal had been arranged for the express purpose of serious discussion, the lighthearted conversation that ensued made dinner, as Eden later recorded, "no more successful than the luncheon" in this regard. Churchill raised his oft-expressed desire to see General Harold Alexander replace Air Marshal Arthur Tedder as Eisenhower's deputy commander, and there was some general talk about the issues that Eden and Stettinius had discussed the day before, but overall, it turned out to be "impossible to even get near business." Frustrated, Eden spoke "pretty sharply" to Harry Hopkins about this circumstance later that evening, "pointing out that we were going into a decisive conference and had so far neither agreed what we would discuss nor how to handle matters with a Bear who would certainly know his own mind."[43]

Concerned about her father's well-being, Anna tried her best to get the dinner party to break up at 10:00 p.m., but it would be 10:30 before FDR finally found himself alone in his cabin. He spent the next half hour on his correspondence. Then he, Anna, and the rest of the delegation departed the *Quincy* for the Luqa Airfield and the 1,400-mile flight to the Crimea. At 11:15, FDR at last found himself able to retire to his bedroom in his new presidential plane, to attempt to get a good night's sleep before landing the next morning in Saki. In the mail pouch heading the other direction was the brief diary that FDR had penned that morning for Daisy. "The awful day" that began thirteen hours earlier had finally ended. It would soon be time to set off on the last leg of his 14,000-mile journey to try to secure the "worthwhile" peace he had promised to the "good people of Malta," and to the rest of the world.[44]

Chapter 4

On to the Crimea

THE BRITISH AND AMERICAN DELEGATIONS FOR THE YALTA CONFERence totaled more than seven hundred people, making Yalta the largest of any of the wartime summit gatherings to date. Needless to say, transporting the group by air from Malta to the Crimea was no small undertaking, particularly in the days before the advent of large-scale air transport. The flight was also not without risk. The route for the 1,400-mile journey took the delegation across the Mediterranean due east from Malta. Before reaching Crete, still under German control, the planes would make a sharp 90-degree northerly turn toward the southern coast of Greece, where they would then head northeast across the Aegean, past northwestern Turkey and the Dardanelles, and finally over the Black Sea for the final descent to the Crimea. Even though both governments had taken special measures to secretly inform the Turks, there was still the possibility that the planes might be fired on accidentally by Turkish anti-aircraft batteries. At the very end of the flight, each pilot had to execute another 90-degree turn to identify himself as friendly aircraft to the radio transmitter at Saki airfield.[1]

For security reasons the decision was made to fly at night, and in order to take full advantage of the darkness, the first of the twenty C-54 Skymasters and five RAF Avro Yorks began taking off at ten-minute intervals shortly after midnight, with strict instructions to maintain constant air speed and observe radio silence. Meanwhile, all along the flight path, US and Royal Navy rescue craft had been stationed, in the event that something went wrong, despite all the precautions.[2]

Not until 3:30 a.m. did FDR's aircraft, nicknamed "the Sacred Cow," take off. This was the first time the president had flown in the precursor to "Air Force One." The plane had been outfitted with a specially designed retractable lift to hoist FDR on board in his wheelchair, a mechanism that FDR, always trying to downplay his disability, had objected to as an unnecessary expense. The plane boasted a private compartment for the president, complete with a bathroom, a closet, an armchair, a table, communications equipment, and a wide bed adjoining the fuselage. Anna, who accompanied her father along with Admirals Leahy, Brown, and McIntire, Pa Watson, Michael Reilly, and Arthur Prettyman, found the plane "quite luxurious." Also on board was Dr. Bruenn, whose presence, as always, was a closely guarded secret.[3]

Churchill's plane took off ten minutes after FDR's. Because there were still rump German forces and potential enemy aircraft located on the Dodecanese, and owing to the proximity of the flight path to Nazi-occupied Crete, both the prime minister's and the president's planes had been assigned six P-38 long-range fighter aircraft as escorts. As they took off, they might have reflected on the sad news that less than forty-eight hours earlier one of the aircraft transporting senior Foreign Office personnel from London to Malta had mistakenly flown over the island of Pantelleria at night, and, unable to find the aerodrome, had crashed into the sea. Among the dead were Alexander Cadogan's private secretary, Peter Loxley; Albany (Barney) Charlesworth, the trusted confidant and aide-de-camp of Field Marshal Sir Alan Brooke; Anthony Eden's bodyguard; and twelve of the other nineteen people on board.[4]

Worried about the effects that a high-altitude flight might have on FDR's delicate heart, Dr. McIntire had instructed the pilots of his plane not to exceed 10,000 feet. Meanwhile, FDR refused to wear the specially designed belt that had been fitted to the bed in his cabin; to counter the possibility that FDR might suddenly be thrown out of bed, Dr. Bruenn slipped quietly into the slumbering president's cabin just before takeoff to sleep on the floor next to him.[5]

Shortly before noon, local time, the Crimean peninsula finally came into view, and at exactly 12:15 the president's plane bolted down the concrete block runway, which was just long enough to accommodate the C-54s. Eight inches of new snow had been swept off the runway by a host of sturdy Russian *babushkas*. Stationed along the perimeter of the airfield, at 20-foot intervals, were Russian guards armed with tommy guns, while a crack regiment of Red Army troops and a military band stood at attention as the Skymaster slowly taxied past.

Since Churchill's plane had not yet landed, FDR decided to remain in his cabin, where Soviet Foreign Minister Molotov and his interpreter, Mr. Pavlov, immediately came to greet him. Anna, in the meantime, slipped out of the aircraft with the other members of the president's delegation to sample some of the lavish refreshments the Russians had provided for their guests, including the ubiquitous vodka.[6]

As soon as Churchill had landed and disembarked, and greeted Molotov and Deputy Foreign Minister Andrei Vishinski, the three walked over to the president's plane. As Churchill later recalled, watching FDR coming down from the aircraft in his special elevator, and then being lifted by a Secret Service agent from his wheelchair into the waiting lend-lease jeep, made him seem something of a "tragic figure." Conscious of the president's desire to maintain his dignity, his hosts had draped a hand-woven Kazak carpet from the Caucasus over the back of the seat behind him. They had also outfitted the jeep with a special booster chair that would elevate FDR to a height roughly equal to that of the dignitaries who strolled beside him as the party inspected the guard of honor there to greet them.[7]

Observing the scene, Alexander Cadogan recorded that the prime minister "walked by the side of the President, as . . . an Indian attendant accompanied Queen Victoria's phaeton," preceded by a throng of cameramen, "walking backwards as they took snapshots." In the intense winter light that even at this hour cast lengthy shadows before them, "the President looked old and thin and drawn," a "shrunken" figure under the dark naval cape wrapped around his shoulder to keep out the damp air. Following a short speech by the commander of the Russian regiment and the playing of the three national anthems, the honor guard paraded in goosestep. "A fine, strong, and healthy looking bunch," Anna observed, made all the more interesting "because they represented so many different races."[8] Like Cadogan, she had noticed the weary look on FDR's face as he reviewed the Russian troops. Ever protective, she insisted that she and Secret Service Agent Michael Reilly would ride alone with her father in the car that was to take them to Yalta "so that he could sleep as much as he wanted and would not have to 'make conversation.'"[9]

FDR greeting Harry Hopkins a few minutes after the president's arrival at Saki Airfield in the Crimea. Note the special booster chair that would bring FDR to the same height as his guests. (Courtesy of the Franklin D. Roosevelt Presidential Library)

The distance from Saki to Yalta is only about ninety miles, but the journey on mountain roads took more than five hours. As in Malta, Anna was taken aback by the destruction in and around the airport, which had been heavily bombed by the Germans. As they crossed over the snow-covered steppes to the southeast of Saki, a desolate scene came into view, the result of the scorched-earth tactics the Nazis employed as they withdrew west. Anna noted a few rebuilt homes, but most of the farming villages they passed had largely been destroyed, with barely a barn left standing. Burnt-out tanks and vehicles littered the sides of the road. Here and there they saw small flocks of sheep but very few civilians, mostly grim-faced peasant women. The road, which was unpaved in places, left Admiral Leahy wondering if the trip would "break every bone in his body."[10]

As the president's car reached the foothills, the road rose rapidly. In keeping with his passionate interest in geography, FDR noted their

65

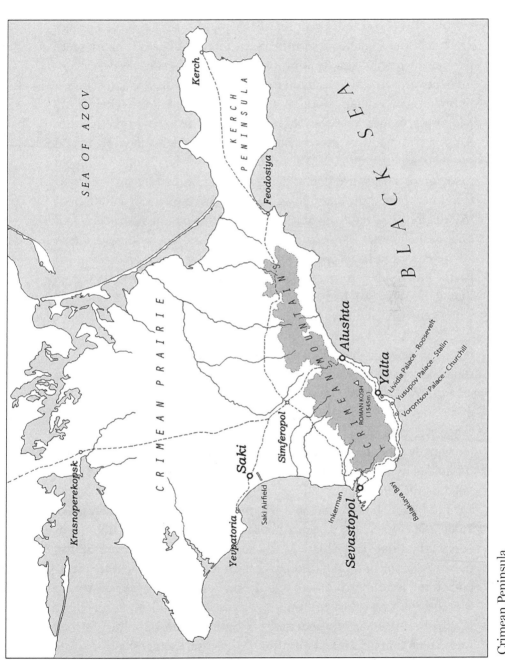

Crimean Peninsula

position: nine hundred miles south of Moscow and three hundred miles east of Romania. He also informed Anna that he was going to tell Marshal Stalin that this part of the country should be reforested. The turns and switchbacks in the ascending road became much more frequent, with the car seeming to go three miles sideways for every mile forward. At 1,000-yard intervals along the route, Russian sentries, most of them women, stood at attention as they passed. Their hosts had also arranged an elaborate luncheon for the party in the town of Alushta with vodka, wines, caviar, fish, bread, butter, stewed fruit, and sweet champagne. But Anna was fearful that the luncheon would hold them up for at least two hours; stepping out of the car, she pulled Molotov's interpreter aside and did her best to "pave the way . . . for a refusal from Father," without informing him of her intentions. She then told FDR that she was sure they could skip the luncheon without causing any offense, and so off they went, much to their mutual relief. For his part, Churchill felt no such reticence. He accepted the invitation, even though he and Sarah had already fortified themselves with "a very stale ham sandwich" and numerous swigs of "some very good brandy."[11]

Thanks to Anna's intervention, she and her father made the rest of the journey in the daylight. From Alushta the road turned to the southwest, past the summit of Mount Roman Kosh, and then wound its way up to dizzying heights. Since the road had no guardrails, the drive was a terrifying experience. Once over the crest of the Crimean range, however, they seemed to arrive "in a different country," one dotted with cypress trees, "almost like Italy." The snow was gone, and they immediately noticed that the air was much balmier than it had been north of the mountains.[12]

Just before dark, Anna and FDR finally passed through the town of Yalta. The city had once been a popular destination for wealthy members of the Russian aristocracy, whose palaces lined the shore. It also possessed a fine natural harbor, to accommodate the yachts that transported the wealthy from Sevastopol—the terminus of the train from Moscow—to this resort community on the "Russian Riviera." Following the Bolshevik Revolution, many of these palaces were transformed into either sanatoriums or vacation hostels for Russian workers. The Wehrmacht, which had occupied the city from 1941, had made sure to render the harbor nearly useless by strewing the bay and the sea beyond with hundreds of mines. Hence, the USS *Catoctin* and most of the other support vessels had to weigh anchor in the harbor at Sevastopol, which had been cleared of mines. FDR was appalled by the destruction of the city itself. "There was no military reason for it," he said to Anna. "Yalta had no military value and no defenses." The sight of it "now made him want to exact an eye for an eye from the Germans, even more than ever." Virtually all of the palaces within or close to the town had been destroyed or badly damaged by the Germans. The three intact ones were to be used by the British, American, and Russian delegations to the conference.[13]

THE AMERICAN CONTINGENT WOULD STAY IN THE LIVADIA PALACE, which was built by Russia's last tsar, Nicholas II. The Livadia sat atop a ridge, overlooking the sea nearly 200 feet below. It had magnificent views in three directions, while the slopes surrounding the palace were covered with Mediterranean pine, yews, tall cypress, and craggy cedars. Centered on a small Italianate courtyard, the palace itself was not huge by the standards of the tsars, but still boasted over fifty rooms on three floors. The Americans also occupied two adjacent buildings, one used to house the president's Secret Service detail and additional military personnel, the other refitted as a communications command center. To facilitate the ability of the president and his Chiefs of Staff to send secure messages to the USS *Catoctin* and then on to Washington and the Supreme Allied Headquarters in Europe (without the Soviets listening in), US naval engineers installed a landline between this building and Sevastopol, eighty miles to the northwest, over rugged terrain and deep snow at the higher elevations.[14]

FDR, who had been warned that he'd be put up in shoddy accommodations, was surprised as he was wheeled around the palace. There was a large ballroom, which would serve as the main conference room for the summit. To the left of the entrance hall were his quarters—rooms that had been Nicholas II's study and bedroom suite. The retreating Germans had stripped the building of almost everything of value, including most of the plumbing. Thus all of the furniture, bedding, kitchen utensils, tableware, bathroom fixtures, and wall décor placed in the palace for the conference had been shipped from Moscow, which left many of the city's hotels, including the historic Metropole, denuded.[15]

Since the building had been in a state of disrepair and was infested with vermin and insects, the Russian high command had sent, in the

The Livadia Palace, 1940. (Imperial War Museum, London)

weeks prior to the summit, a contingent of soldiers, painters, plumbers, plasterers, gardeners, hotel staff, and housemaids, all of whom contributed to making the accommodations livable. Perhaps the greatest challenge, however, was the lack of toilets and hot water—not to mention the chambermaids' custom of walking into toilet facilities without knocking. The Americans built latrines outside, and the naval medical team forewarned the delegates that cooperation and "a little good-naturedness on the part of all concerned" would be required. The medical advance team also sprayed every bed, bedspring, mattress, rug, and palace wall hanging with a 10 percent DDT solution to guard against lice and bedbugs.[16]

About twelve miles to the southwest of the Livadia was the Vorontzov Palace, to which the British delegation had been assigned. In contrast to the Livadia, its furnishings had largely been left in place by the Germans, so at first glance the Vorontzov appeared to be in better shape than the American accommodations. But as Churchill's doctor, Lord Moran, discovered the first morning, first appearances were deceiving. The delegation soon learned that Churchill's feet had been bitten overnight, that "a more thorough assault" had been carried out on Churchill's valet, the indefatigable Frank Sawyers, and that "Eden's right-hand man [Piers] Dixon had been eaten up." Desperate, Lord Moran immediately contacted Dr. McIntire with the request that he send over his medical team to spray every nook and cranny of the Vorontzov with the same DDT solution.[17] The toilet facilities at Vorontzov were not much better than those at the Livadia, although the British delegation did have the use of two bathhouses adjacent to their villa. These were attended by two sturdy Russian ladies who, according to one of Churchill's female stenographers, "always insist on scrubbing you all over." This made it much more difficult for the female staff to gain access to the facilities, as there was "always such a run on this . . . especially by the men!"[18]

Stalin and the Soviet delegation were housed in the Yusupov Palace, named for the prince who had reputedly assassinated Nicholas II's close adviser, Rasputin. At Yusupov, which was midway between the other two palaces, Stalin and his generals maintained contacts with generals on the Eastern Front, and refined their tactics to the approaching deliberations—their work supplemented, naturally, by daily intelligence summaries of the bugged conversations of the American and British delegations.[19]

ANNA'S FIRST ORDER OF BUSINESS AFTER THEIR ARRIVAL WAS TO SEND one of the Secret Service staff on a mission to procure gin for her father's pre-dinner martini ritual. She soon learned that there was not only no gin but no ice or lemon as well. Anna then drew up a dinner list in consultation with her father and immediately sent word out to his chosen invitees.

In lieu of martinis that evening, the maître d' brought FDR and the hastily assembled dinner party "some sweet concoction" that apparently was a mixture "of just about everything." Dinner, which included Secretary of State Stettinius, Admirals Leahy and Brown, General Watson, Anna, and Ambassador Harriman and his daughter, Kathleen, was a relaxed affair. An accomplished journalist who was fluent in Russian, Kathleen found FDR "absolutely charming." She also thought he looked "in fine form" and did not fail to note the irony that their first meeting took place so far from their native New York. Over the coming week, she and Anna, as the only two female guests among the American delegation, would become fast friends, joined by

Sarah Churchill, who, like Anna, was there in part to keep her "unruly father" in line.[20]

The eight-course meal included caviar, cured fish, game, skewered meat and potatoes, two kinds of dessert, white wine, red wine, champagne, and vodka—all of it topped off by a liqueur and coffee. Afterward, FDR was ready to head straight to bed but had to wait until Drs. McIntire and Bruenn checked his blood pressure and heart rate, which were much improved since the flight—a change that Anna attributed in part to her determination not to let any of FDR's advisers ride with him on the drive from Saki.

Over dinner, FDR instructed Ambassador Harriman to extend an invitation to Stalin to visit the president at the Livadia at 3:00 or 3:30 the next afternoon for a "purely personal talk." This would be followed by the first plenary session of the conference, which FDR wanted to devote to military matters. Then, if agreeable to the Soviet leader and his foreign secretary, FDR would host them for a small "unofficial dinner" at the Livadia.[21]

With FDR safely ensconced in his bedroom, Anna took the opportunity to drop in on Harry Hopkins, who had arrived at the palace from Malta earlier that day. Hopkins's relationship with FDR went all the way back to the latter's days as governor of the state of New York. As the two men became better acquainted, a mutual respect and affection developed between them that was unique among FDR's inner circle. This closeness was partly due to their shared conviction that "human welfare is the first and final task of government." But it also resulted from Hopkins's uncanny ability to sense when FDR wanted to discuss affairs of state and when he wanted "to escape from the awful consciousness of the Presidency." In this respect Hopkins was not unlike Daisy Suckley, in that FDR found he could relax in Hopkins's company when the two of them were not engaged in business. FDR also had a profound sense of trust in Hopkins's judgment and ability to act on his behalf as an overseas envoy to both Churchill and Stalin during the war.[22]

Yet by the time the two men had reached Yalta, Hopkins's stature as the president's most intimate and trusted adviser seemed a thing of the past. Anna found "Harry in a stew" over the fact that FDR had refused to confer with Churchill before the summit. As soon as Anna arrived, Hopkins launched into a tirade.

"FDR *must* see Churchill in the morning for a long meeting to dope out how those two are going to map out the conference," he told Anna. After all, "FDR had asked for this job, and whether he liked it or not, he had to do the work. It was imperative that FDR and Churchill make some prearrangements before the big conference started."

"Don't you think this might stir up some distrust among our Russian brethren?" Anna asked.

Brushing off Anna's comments with a dismissive wave of the hand, Hopkins made no comment. At which point Anna, in her role as her father's protector, asked: "Why don't you and Stettinius and Eden get together beforehand?" This would certainly be "ok," she went on, promising to raise the matter with the president in the morning.

Hopkins still did not reply. "It certainly did not appear," Anna later recorded, that "Harry's mind was clicking or his judgment good." Perhaps this was understandable, given Hopkins's chronic health issues, which included terrible bouts of dysentery exacerbated by his penchant for coffee, cigarettes, and late nights and his tendency to abandon the dietary restrictions placed on him by his doctors. "Or maybe," Anna mused, "it was just that I never realized how pro-British Harry is."[23]

Of course, Hopkins's anger may also have been a sign of his mounting frustration over his diminishing influence within the administration. This could be attributed not only to his health struggles, which necessitated a number of long absences from Washington, but also to Anna's ascendance. She now occupied a boundary area between her father and the man who once had been his most intimate adviser. No fool, Anna was convinced that Hopkins was resentful over this change of roles, and probably had taken some offense at her determination to act as FDR's protector—a determination that would be tested in the days ahead. For now, though, it was time to retreat to her room, with its tiny wrought-iron bed. It had been a very long day.

Chapter 5

Sunrise over Yalta

THE HISTORIC CONFERENCE THAT WOULD DO SO MUCH TO DETERMINE
the postwar legacy of Franklin D. Roosevelt began on a bright, clear
Sunday morning. Had FDR decided to rise at dawn that day, he would
have witnessed the magnificent sight of the sun breaking above the
bay and the rugged coastline that juts out into the Black Sea to the east
of the Livadia Palace. But FDR did his best to remain in bed well past
dawn that morning. The extra rest would do him good, and the journey to this moment had been long and arduous.

In many respects it was a journey that began in the days that followed America's dramatic entrance into the war in the wake of the
Pearl Harbor attack more than three years before. It was then, at that
all-too-perilous moment—when Hitler's Wehrmacht was but fifteen
miles from Moscow, the British army was locked in a desperate struggle with Rommel in North Africa, and the Japanese were furiously
advancing on Hong Kong, the Philippines, and Malaya—that FDR, in
his first wartime fireside chat, warned the American people that the
world and all its oceans and continents had become "one gigantic battlefield." It was not going to be easy to achieve the "absolute victory" he
called for in his famous Pearl Harbor address, he cautioned. This was
going to be "a long . . . hard war." But given that the American people
were now "all in" this struggle, he was confident that the United States
and its Allies would not only win the war but also "win the peace that
follows." After all, he observed, we Americans "are not destroyers—we
are builders." We fight "not for conquest . . . or vengeance, but for a
world in which this nation, and all that this nation represents, will be
safe for our children."[1]

As FDR prepared to greet this thirty-third of his last 100 days, it was clear that the moment at which America and its Allies must begin to win the peace and construct that better world had now arrived. But the circumstances in which the president found himself at Yalta differed from those he envisioned in the dark days following Pearl Harbor. Pressed, even at that early date, to support a list of territorial demands delineated by Joseph Stalin—a list that included the Baltic States and much of the ground gained by the USSR through the 1939 pact with Hitler—FDR insisted that it was far too early in the conflict to begin any discussion of a postwar settlement. This resistance stemmed in part from his belief that the Allies should concentrate on the war—the actual outcome of which was still very much in doubt. But it also resulted from his conviction that these matters would be best left until victory had been achieved, at which point FDR fully expected there would be a major peace conference. Equally important, however, was his conviction that the United States—under-armed and still reeling from the devastating Japanese attack on Hawaii and the Philippines—was in far too weak a position to enter into any serious discussion about the nature of the world after the conflict. Far better to wait until US armed forces had been brought up to strength and were fully deployed in the struggle against Germany and Japan, before he or members of his administration entered into any negotiations about the future of Poland or other parts of the world. For all these reasons, then, FDR tended to follow what one of his advisers called "a policy of procrastination." This entailed putting off difficult discussions about future issues in the full expectation that the United States would be in a far better position to come to a settlement over various territorial questions and other political matters later in the war.[2]

But there was an important flaw in FDR's early thinking that had now returned to haunt him, for it was not only the United States that was stronger: Russia, too, had gained strength—tremendous strength. Indeed, the Soviets not only had survived Hitler's initial onslaught but had driven the Wehrmacht from Russian soil, had overrun Poland, and were now poised to begin the final assault on Berlin. Stalin, in short, had achieved his territorial ambitions on his own, without the need for negotiations, although at a staggering cost in blood and treasure.

FDR, in the meantime, had not only overseen an astounding buildup in US military and industrial power but had also come a long way toward establishing the institutional structure he needed to bring his postwar vision for the world into reality. He, too, had marched forward—through the Four Freedoms, the Atlantic Charter, the Declaration of United Nations, and the Dumbarton Oaks conference—to bring the world but a few short steps away from the creation of the United Nations Organization that would serve as the basis for the future peace and Great Power cooperation. And while FDR had always intended to use the crisis of the war and the cooperation it entailed to move his vision forward, he still clung to the hope that such important questions as the future frontiers of Poland and the final disposition of Germany might be held in abeyance until the war was truly over and a proper peace conference—held in collaboration with the new world organization—could be organized. Unfortunately, however, Stalin's victories on the battlefield, and his insistence that his government had every right to establish a buffer of friendly states on his Western border, had rendered it impossible for FDR to avoid coming to terms with such issues as the final disposition of Poland. The unintended consequence of such developments was to turn Yalta into something it was never intended to be: a kind of "premature peace conference," pitting the security demands of the Soviet Union against the principles that were supposed to stand behind the yet-to-be-constructed United Nations Organization. This placed FDR in one of the most profound dilemmas of his political career.[3]

WELL AWARE OF HER FATHER'S DESIRE TO HAVE A LIE-IN ON THAT first morning in Yalta, Anna managed to slip quietly into the private bathroom that adjoined FDR's suite before returning to take breakfast in her small room. She then made a quick visit to check in on Harry Hopkins, who, to her relief, was in a much calmer mood than on the previous evening, and seemed to have given up on his insistence that FDR and Churchill hold a long tête-à-tête before seeing Stalin. By the time she looked in on FDR it was shortly before 10:00 a.m. Pleased that her father seemed fine and that Hopkins was no longer on the warpath, Anna made no mention of their discussion the prior evening. Afterward, she felt free to take a walk with "Kathy" Harriman and Dr. Bruenn, who had finished his morning checkup of the president.[4]

As agreed the prior evening, FDR began his day meeting his Chiefs of Staff and senior foreign policy advisers. The discussion with the Chiefs focused mainly on how best to establish communication between the Western Allies and the Russian High Command during the final push into Germany. Secretary Stettinius then presented the attendees with a seven-point document, outlining the main political questions that the State Department believed the conference needed to address. These included not only the future of Germany and Poland and the outstanding issues concerning the United Nations Organization but also whether France should be granted a zone of occupation and a role in governing occupied Germany after the war. Then there was the question of a proposal for the establishment of a European High Commission to oversee the transition from war to peace in liberated areas as well as a set of guidelines to govern their conduct in these areas, titled the Declaration of Liberated Europe.[5]

After the meeting, Anna found her father alone, "wheeling around the [sun] porch" outside her room, taking in the view. As was now her routine, she asked him whom he would like to dine with at noon. The names in hand, she dashed off to extend the invitations and to arrange the seating in the president's private dining room. Following this "very quiet lunch," Anna put "the clamps on" and insisted that the luncheon party leave, so that her father, who was clearly fatigued after the long journey from Malta, could take an hour or more's nap before his scheduled meeting with Stalin.[6]

RESOLUTE, ENIGMATIC, AND AT TIMES UTTERLY CHARMING, THE MAN who was born Joseph Vissarionovich Dzhugashvili but was known to the world by his revolutionary moniker, Stalin, or "the Man of Steel," had also endured a journey to Yalta that was long and arduous. Not unlike FDR's, his had begun with a devastating surprise, rendered not so much by the German attack on Russia launched on June 22, 1941, as by the catastrophic failure of the Soviet Union's defenses and the rapid advance of the Wehrmacht in the months that followed.[7]

Given America's nonbelligerent status and Great Britain's inability to field an army large enough to defeat the Wehrmacht on the continent in 1941, Hitler's assault on Russia in June of that year was viewed as a godsend in both London and Washington. Within hours of the attack, both Churchill and Roosevelt announced that the British and

American governments would give whatever help they could to the Soviets, and by the end of September 1941 the three governments had negotiated a detailed agreement on the shipment of Anglo-American supplies to the Soviet Union.[8]

What is most interesting about these early tripartite conversations is that even in the midst of the initial collapse of the Red Army, Stalin had the audacity—or the guts or courage, depending on your point of view—to bring up the issue of the postwar settlement. By early November he had put this in writing in a cable to Churchill—a move that ultimately led to the negotiation of the Anglo-Soviet Treaty of Alliance of May 26, 1942. Viewed from the perspective of what we now know about Soviet wartime policy, these early conversations are especially illuminating. That Stalin initiated talks on wartime cooperation and "the postwar organization of the peace" tells us something about his persistent fear of a Western-negotiated separate peace with Hitler and/or a repetition of the Allied intervention in Russia that took place in the wake of World War I. These talks also serve as an early example of the willingness of both the Soviet and British governments to reach a concordance over the future of Europe negotiated outside the formal control of the United States—as further evidenced by the October 1944 percentages agreement. But most important is what these early negotiations tell us about Stalin's remarkably consistent territorial ambitions in Eastern Europe, all of which renders Eden's comment to Hopkins on the eve of the Yalta conference—that the Allies were dealing with "a Bear who would certainly know his mind"—eminently correct.[9]

It is also true that Stalin—much like FDR—hoped to make use of the Yalta conference as a means to bolster the sense of trust and cooperation between the United States and the Soviet Union. As Andrei Gromyko, the Soviet ambassador to Washington, put it in a document he issued in July 1944, he could see no reason why the Soviet-American détente should not continue after the war, as the United States and the Soviet Union shared "a common interest . . . in dealing with the German threat and in securing conditions for a prolonged peace." Stalin shared this assessment. Moreover, his views on the spread of communism to Western Europe also appeared to have moderated. As he said to a group of Bulgarian visitors to Moscow just days before the start of the Yalta conference, "We have to forget the idea that the victory of socialism could be realized only through Soviet rule.

It could be presented by some other political systems—for example by democracy, a parliamentary republic and even by a constitutional monarchy." Stalin's recognition of the persistence of the German threat, coupled with this more moderate view of the means by which socialism might advance in the West, pointed toward the possibility that the cooperation the Allies had achieved in their mutual struggle against Hitler could continue—provided that the Anglo-Americans recognized Stalin's unequivocal demand for a sphere of influence in Eastern Europe.[10]

At 4:00 p.m. on Sunday, February 4, 1945, amid much anticipation of the arrival of the man Churchill and Roosevelt referred to privately as "Uncle Joe," Stalin appeared at the Livadia Palace for the "personal private chat" FDR had requested. Preceded by a host of NKVD secret police and American Secret Service agents, the Soviet dictator made his way to FDR's private study. As FDR's interpreter, Charles Bohlen, noted, "the two leaders greeted each other as old friends." Smiling broadly, the seated FDR "grasped Stalin by the hand and shook it warmly," while the Soviet leader, "his face cracked in one of his rare, if slight, smiles, expressed pleasure at seeing the president again."[11]

FDR thanked his host for making him feel welcome, and commented on the improvement of the military situation since their last meeting in Tehran. Ever the geographer, FDR also conveyed the pleasure he derived from the climate and topography of the Crimea, adding that he was shocked by the extent of the destruction wrought by the Germans on the peninsula. He told Stalin that the sight had left him "more bloodthirsty in regard to the Germans than he had been a year ago." He hoped Stalin would once again propose a toast—as he had done at Tehran—"to the execution of 50,000 officers of the German army."

"Everyone was more bloodthirsty than they had been a year ago," Stalin responded through his interpreter. "[But] the destruction in the Crimea is nothing compared to that which occurred in the Ukraine. In the Crimea, the Germans had been outflanked, and had little time to carry out planned destruction, whereas in the Ukraine they had done it with method and calculation. The Germans were savages," he said, "and seemed to hate with a sadistic hatred the creative work of human beings."[12]

FDR and Stalin meeting in FDR's study at the Livadia Palace, February 4, 1945.
(Courtesy of the Franklin D. Roosevelt Presidential Library)

The two men turned to the military situation. FDR gave Stalin a brief overview of the Western Front and indicated that the Anglo-American armies planned to launch a new push toward the Rhine with two immediate small-scale offensives, followed by a major drive to begin in March. As a means of reminding Stalin that the Americans, not the British, were now leading the way on the Western Front, FDR added that Churchill's commanders had argued for a single thrust in the northern sector, but given that the United States "had four times the number of men in France than the British, we felt we were entitled to have an alternative, which would be either in [southern] Holland or in the region of Mainz." Stalin expressed his satisfaction at this summary and, in response to a question from FDR about the Red Army's status on the Oder, indicated that although the Soviets had established five or six bridgeheads on the river, much fierce fighting would be required before they could expect to break out.

Anticipating that the matter of France might come up during the tripartite talks, FDR raised it with Stalin, no doubt to gain Stalin's trust and make clear that he and Churchill did not always see eye to eye. Well aware of the chilling effect that Charles de Gaulle's haughty demeanor had on even the most hardened personalities, FDR took advantage of Great Britain's support for the Free French leader as a relatively harmless means of indicating his differences with the British. The president, recalling de Gaulle's portentous assertion at the Casablanca conference that he could be compared to Joan of Arc in his role as "spiritual leader of France," wondered how Stalin and de Gaulle had gotten along during the latter's visit to Moscow. When Stalin replied that he found de Gaulle unrealistic in his demand that France should enjoy "full rights with the Americans, British and Russians," FDR saw his opening.

Roosevelt confided that he wanted "to tell the Marshal something indiscreet" that he "did not wish to say in front of Prime Minister Churchill"—namely, that for the past two years the British had been plotting to build France into a major power, with an army of 200,000 men that could hold the line against Germany for the period of time the British would need to assemble a strong army of their own.

"The British," the president said, "are a peculiar people" who "wished to have their cake and eat it too."

FDR also claimed that "he had had a good deal of trouble with the British in regard to [the] zones of occupation," particularly as he "would . . . have preferred to have the northwest zone, which would be independent of communication through France." He then remarked, caustically: "But the British seemed to think that the Americans should restore order in France and then return political control to [them]."

As to the question of whether France should receive a zone of occupation, FDR admitted that it was "not a bad idea," but one that he felt could be justified only "out of kindness." Stalin and Molotov emphatically agreed, since the French contribution to the war had been quite small in comparison to that of the other Great Powers.[13]

On this convivial note, the first meeting between the president and Marshal Stalin at Yalta drew to a close, but not before Stalin, who had learned about FDR's disappointment at not having any lemons for his martinis, promised to rectify the situation. The next morning, a potted lemon tree bearing an enormous amount of fruit arrived, along with a small Frigidaire for making ice. In the meantime, a reassured FDR took a few minutes to review matters with Hopkins and Bohlen before making his way to the ballroom in advance of the other delegates, so as to be transferred from his wheelchair to his seat at the head of the conference table with no other officials looking on.

THE LAST TIME THE BALLROOM AT THE LIVADIA HAD HOSTED SUCH AN elaborate affair was in 1911, when Nicholas and Alexandra had organized a full dress ball in honor of their eldest daughter Olga's sixteenth birthday. For the purposes of the Yalta gathering, the Soviets had placed a large round table at the end of the rectangular ballroom, close to the fireplace, but left enough room for a concentric ring or two of chairs to surround the principal negotiators and their interpreters. The timing of this first meeting also established the schedule for the remainder of the conference, with the plenary sessions being held in the late afternoons, starting on all but this occasion at 4:00 p.m., while the three foreign ministers held daily "advance" meetings at noon.[14]

As FDR was the only head of state among the three leaders at the Yalta conference, Marshal Stalin asked the president if he would preside over the discussion—a role that FDR was more than happy to assume and a reprise of the protocol at Tehran the year before. In keeping with his desire to set the tone for the entire conference, FDR began the session not only with the customary note of thanks to Marshal Stalin and his staff for all of "the splendid arrangements" they had made for their guests but also with a reference to his hopes for the talks. "We all understand each other much better now than in the past," he said, and because of this, he felt safe in proposing that the sessions be conducted "in an informal manner in which each would speak his mind frankly and freely, since he had discovered through experience that this was the best way to conduct business expeditiously."[15]

In sharp contrast to the rigid protocols often observed at later summit meetings, there were no formal introductions, no place cards, no official secretarial staff (although the three interpreters and some other aides took notes), and no advanced agenda. This informality carried great risks, as negotiations among heads of state or heads of government placed tremendous pressure on the participants not to leave the summit without some sort of agreement. But this was the way FDR insisted on conducting summit diplomacy, and in this he was not alone. Churchill's penchant for face-to-face meetings became something of an obsession during the war. It is estimated that the British prime minister flew more than 100,000 miles to attend the fifteen major summit meetings he carried out between 1941 and 1945.[16]

Even Stalin, the most reluctant traveler of the three, seemed to appreciate the value of a face-to-face encounter. In a conversation that Molotov had with Harry Truman shortly after Roosevelt's death, the foreign secretary urged the new president to take up the idea of a meeting with Stalin, as the Soviet leader had found that his direct talks with Roosevelt "always had great positive significance." Indeed, the "establishment of personal relations between government leaders was always highly important." A key difference between Roosevelt and his two counterparts, however, lay in FDR's faith in his intuitive ability to read the tenor of every conversation, and to influence the outcome through his powers of persuasion. It was largely for this reason that FDR preferred not to be boxed in by a set agenda, and why he often shunned Churchill's persistent entreaties to work out a formal position on every issue in advance.[17] FDR's breezy and somewhat casual manner would lead to the charge that he "lived on charm," and that he even thought, as Harold Macmillan once put it, that "he could charm Stalin." But FDR's skilfully cultivated outward manner—which was developed in part to make those around him not notice or feel comfortable with his disability—also masked the much more Machiavellian side of his personality. As Walter Lippmann, another astute observer of the president, once wrote: "What [FDR] thought he could do was outwit Stalin. Which is quite a different thing." Given FDR's refusal to engage in serious conversations with Churchill at both Tehran and Yalta, the same might be said about his treatment of the man he referred to as "Winston."[18]

THE FIRST DAY'S DISCUSSION OF THE MILITARY SITUATION OPENED with a frank exchange of information and plans. There followed a discussion of how best to facilitate communication between the Eastern and Western Fronts. There was nothing overtly contentious in any of this. But from the Russian perspective, both the military and the political discussions that took place over Germany during the first two days of the conference were unsettling.

The fact that the Anglo-Americans did not expect to cross the Rhine until March, for example, and thus were lagging behind the Soviets in their drive into Germany, was not welcome news to Stalin. Indeed, his primary goal the first day was to induce the Allies to launch a major attack on the Western Front as soon as possible. That this would not happen until March had a significant impact on his strategic calculations. On the one hand, the military situation along the Oder, while encouraging, was also precarious. The rapid advance of General Georgy Zhukov's forces in the center front had exposed his flanks to a possible German counterattack, particularly from the north where the Soviets' Second and Third Armies were bogged down by fierce German resistance in East Prussia. To continue the Red Army's drive toward the prize of Berlin could be to court unnecessary risks. Moreover, even though the USSR clearly held the upper hand in the eastern stretches of the Reich, and even though some of Stalin's commanders urged him to press on despite the risks, a precipitous lunge into Berlin might—in the paranoid workings of his mind—tempt the Western powers into a last-minute deal with Hitler or some post-Hitler group, as Stalin had feared since the start of the war.[19]

For this reason and others, Stalin was quick to point out, at this first plenary meeting, that his government considered it "a moral duty" to help its ally in the midst of the Ardennes crisis. It explained why he couched his decision to advance the start date of the Red Army's January offensive—though largely planned without consultation with the Allies—as the responsibility of a faithful partner prepared to sacrifice its own troops and strategic interests in support of the others. Stalin also concurred with an assertion FDR made that it was time for the two sides to synchronize their military efforts. The meeting concluded with all three leaders agreeing that the British, American, and Soviet Chiefs of Staff should reconvene at noon the next day to coordinate their plans for the final destruction of the Wehrmacht.[20]

As Stettinius notes in his memoirs, the proposal that the three Chiefs of Staff meet to coordinate their military plans was the first time such a step had been taken in the entire war. To him, this was representative of the "cooperative" spirit of the first day of Yalta. For the most part his assessment was accurate, although securing Soviet agreement to direct communication among the three operational staffs would prove impossible in the end. But the overall strategic picture that Stalin was confronted with over the first two days of the conference convinced him that it would be some time before his Western Allies would be in a position to ease the pressure on the Red Army. Hence, on the third day of the conference Stalin informed General Zhukov that he should halt his drive to the west and turn his attention to his northern flanks. The capture of Berlin would have to wait.[21]

Not every senior member of the American delegation was in such a sanguine mood as the first plenary drew to a close. As Anna Roosevelt would soon discover, while scrambling about to make preparations for the dinner that FDR had scheduled that evening, one member of the US delegation, James Byrnes, was in such a rage he had "fire shooting from his eyes."[22]

ANNA WELL UNDERSTOOD THAT BEING THE DAUGHTER OF THE PRESIdent of the United States came with certain advantages. Given her father's love of gossip, Anna frequently found herself privy to some of the more important goings-on during the conference, especially anything that inspired FDR to spin one of his humorous anecdotes. But her privileged family position did not entitle her to sit in on the conference sessions, nor did it mean that she was able to escape certain responsibilities—helping him make his dinner arrangements, delivering messages to various members of the American delegation, and, most important, trying to protect her father from any undue stress. These tasks might seem straightforward enough, but thanks to the ad hoc manner in which FDR ran his affairs, Anna frequently found herself "sitting on tacks" due to the last-minute nature of his decisions. Such was the case as this first all-important day of the conference drew to a close.[23]

As Ambassador Harriman had indicated to Molotov the night before, FDR intended to host a dinner for Churchill and Stalin that first evening. Yet, even though FDR had let Anna know of his plans in advance of the first formal meeting of the conference, no definite list of invitees had been drawn up as the delegates entered the first plenary at 5:00 p.m. All Anna could manage was to tell the Russian staff to set FDR's private table for the maximum number of guests—fourteen— while nervously awaiting word from Harriman, her collaborator on this occasion, who promised that he would do the inviting during a lull in the session.

Not until 8:00 p.m. did Harriman emerge from the conference room to tell Anna whom the president, in consultation with the British and Soviet delegations, had decided to invite. With the dinner scheduled to begin in thirty minutes, Anna and the ambassador immediately set to work on the seating arrangements, while Commander William Rigdon, assistant naval aide to the president, hastily drew up the place cards, taking care not to misspell the various names of the Russian and British guests.

Amid this frenzy, Dr. Bruenn—Anna's partner in trying to keep any unnecessary "crises" away from FDR—burst into the dining room to inform Anna that she needed to drop everything at once and go see Justice James Byrnes, who was so upset at the way he had been treated that first day that he had not only decided to refuse the president's invitation to dinner but was also threatening to "order a plane to take him home." The "Assistant President" was furious because he had not been invited to the first plenary session. As the meeting was devoted to military matters, and as FDR was convinced that Stalin would speak more freely about these questions if the number of civilians in the room was kept to a minimum, FDR had asked Byrnes not to attend, but to come along at 6:00 p.m., by which point FDR assumed they would have moved on to nonmilitary matters and Byrnes would be summoned into the conference room.[24]

Byrnes arrived on schedule, only to "cool his heels" outside the closed doors for the next forty-five minutes without anyone saying "boo to him" as the military discussions went on much longer than FDR expected. Now even more enraged, Byrnes retired to his room to vent his anger on anyone within reach, including Drs. Bruenn and McIntire. Now it was Anna's turn. "I have never been so insulted in my life," he fumed. "I should have been included in these first discussions, even though they were military in character." "At home," he stormed, "I could and did consult with the military, but here I am not considered important enough. I told the President," he went on, "that I had come along [to this conference] to work and not for the ride. Harry Hopkins had been at the conference," he erroneously insisted. "Why not me?"

Anna argued with and cajoled Byrnes for the next fifteen minutes, insisting that she did not want to go to FDR and Uncle Joe with "this little problem." But Byrnes refused to be consoled, even after

Sarah Churchill, Anna Roosevelt, and Kathleen Harriman at the Livadia Palace, February 8, 1945. (Courtesy of the Franklin D. Roosevelt Presidential Library)

Ambassador Harriman arrived "to join the fray." It was only after Anna had told him that having thirteen at dinner "would give the superstitious FDR ten fits" that the sulking Byrnes finally agreed to attend, with the promise—broken almost immediately—that he was not going to say "one word." Having won her argument "on this stupid basis," Anna went off to dine with Sarah Churchill, Kathy Harriman, and some generals Kathy "had corralled."[25]

While Anna coped with Byrnes and Churchill headed to Stettinius's room to take a few minutes to freshen up, FDR and Stalin retired to the president's study for a few moments of private conversation. There is no record of what the two leaders discussed, but given that Stalin raised the issue of the "rights of small powers" in the proposed world organization a number of times that evening, it seems likely that the two men may have broached this question. Indeed, in numerous "toasts"—which in Russian tradition often involve a fairly lengthy oration—Stalin returned again and again to this theme during the meal, insisting that the three Great Powers who had borne the brunt of the war had earned "the unanimous right to maintain the peace of the world" and thus should not be expected to stand by while the many smaller states they had liberated during the war sat in judgment.[26]

Not wanting to open a breach on this critical question before the three leaders had had the chance to address it formally, FDR responded somewhat diplomatically by concurring with the view that the Great Powers bore a greater degree of responsibility for what happened both during and after the war and that the peace should be written by them. Churchill, though more poetic, was less diplomatic when he challenged Stalin's assertion with a paraphrase of Shakespeare's line from *Titus Andronicus:* "The eagle should permit the small birds to sing and care not wherefore they sang."

Overall, the dinner that FDR hosted that evening was largely a social affair marked by good humor and the consumption of much champagne and vodka. By the end of the evening, FDR felt relaxed enough to confide to Stalin that he and Churchill affectionately referred to him as "Uncle Joe" in their correspondence—a remark that required some hasty further translation as the word for *uncle* does not connote the same affectionate meaning in Russian. Meanwhile, the staunchly anti-communist Churchill went so far as to raise a glass "to the proletarian masses of the world!"[27]

As usual, before retiring for the night Anna dropped in to check on FDR, who seemed quite happy at the way both the dinner and the first day's sessions had gone. Anna, too, was pleased, though in her case it was because the dinner had broken up early and all seemed well. "Jimmy made a fine toast," her father enthused. But Anna, as amused and tempted as she was, decided to say nothing about the Byrnes incident. Better to wait and recast the episode as a "light story" for FDR to enjoy in the morning. He had had enough excitement for one day.[28]

Chapter 6

Coming to Grips with "The German Problem"

As in Washington, FDR began the second full day of the Yalta conference with a visit from Dr. Bruenn, who checked his heart—by administering the first of the electrocardiograms he performed twice daily—as well as his lungs, blood pressure, and overall condition. The president's lungs were clear and there had been no change in the function of his heart or in his blood pressure since the evening before, but his usual sinus troubles had returned and he had developed a nocturnal paroxysmal cough that would awaken him at night. This was not a welcome development in view of the long days and late evenings that the conference required, although the president said he had been able to get back to sleep after being roused by the coughing spells.

Dr. Bruenn treated the cough, which continued for the next three nights, with terpin hydrate and codeine, and the sinus troubles with nose drops that were administered each evening before FDR retired. He also urged the president to limit his activities in the mornings and reiterated his request that he take a rest in the afternoons. But these pleas were no more successful than they had been over the course of the past few months in Washington. On most days, FDR entertained a steady stream of advisers and officials. He found it difficult to catch any sort of rest in the afternoon, although on a few occasions, when time permitted, he set aside a few minutes to receive a rubdown from Lieutenant Commander George Fox just before dinner.[1]

FDR's first meeting that day was Secretary of State Stettinius, who made it a point during the Yalta conference to drop by for a talk in the mornings, when the president's "mind was fresh and he was unhurried by outside pressure." Over forty-five minutes or so, the two men discussed a host of topics, including FDR's continued opposition to the Soviet request for sixteen seats in the General Assembly, the list of possible locations for "the world organization conference," and the president's and Ambassador Harriman's plan to discuss with Stalin the Soviets' entrance into the Japanese War—a topic the president insisted there was no need for Stettinius to take part in given the "heavy burden" he was carrying.[2]

Satisfied that he had obtained his chief's "innermost feelings" about some of the critical issues in front of them, Stettinius left the president to take a short stroll on the palace grounds, before he would attend the first of the daily lunchtime meetings with his two counterparts, Foreign Ministers Anthony Eden and Vyacheslav Molotov. In the meantime, FDR had lunch in his private dining room with Anna followed by a 2:30 discussion with Harry Hopkins, H. Freeman Matthews, and Charles Bohlen. Each man in turn did his best to convince FDR to support granting France both a zone of occupation and a seat on the Allied Control Commission that would govern Germany in the immediate aftermath of the war. FDR agreed with their position on the zone, but still refused to commit to the idea of France being granted a role in the governance of Germany—the subject slated to be discussed in that day's plenary session.[3]

BECAUSE YALTA LATER BECAME KNOWN AS THE PLACE WHERE THE BIG Three decided the future of Eastern Europe, it is easy to forget one of the primary reasons they reassembled in 1945 was to discuss not Poland but Germany. Perhaps the most striking indication that this was the case can be derived from the original name the Allies used in referring to the proposed second summit—namely, Eureka II. This term points to the unequivocal link between the first Big Three conference at Tehran, code-named Eureka, and the second one at Yalta.[4]

It was at this first all-important—and often overlooked—meeting between Churchill, Roosevelt, and Stalin in late 1943 where the three leaders sketched out much of the framework of the Yalta conference. Indeed, virtually all of the major military and political issues that were discussed in the Crimea in the spring of 1945 were first broached at Tehran, including Soviet participation in the war against Japan and recognition in principle that the eastern border of Poland would follow the so-called Curzon Line first proposed by the British foreign minister in 1920 as part of the reconstitution of the Polish state called for by the Treaty of Versailles.[5] It was also during the Tehran gathering that the Allies engaged in their first serious discussions of what their generation referred to as the "German problem," the idea that the existence of a powerful and united Germany was incompatible with world peace. One solution to the German problem that received a good deal of attention at Tehran was the possible breakup of Germany into several smaller states after the war. Another solution, first articulated by Henry Morgenthau at the Second Quebec Conference in September 1944, was to "pastoralize" Germany—that is, to demolish the German state's war-making capacity, which Morgenthau insisted was the only way to root out and destroy the twin evils of German Nazism and Prussian militarism. Like many of his generation, Morgenthau viewed a resurgent Germany—not the Soviet Union—as the greatest threat to international security. He titled his plan "Program to Prevent Germany from Starting World War III" and remained vehemently opposed to any suggestion—such as that first put forward by the State and War Departments in the summer of 1944—that the Allies would have no choice but to rehabilitate the German economy after the war.[6]

To a certain extent, FDR shared these sentiments. Having spent his summer holidays in Germany during his boyhood, and as assistant secretary of the Navy during World War I, when the Germans introduced the world to unrestricted submarine warfare, FDR had already developed an antipathy for the German people. His youthful exposure to Germany—which included attending school there and studying the German language—led him to believe that the cult of militarism had poisoned the German mind.[7] FDR dismissed any notion that the Germans were not responsible for what had taken place during the war—that "only a few Nazi leaders are responsible." As he once wrote to Secretary of War Henry Stimson, this idea "is not based on fact. The German people as a whole must have it driven home to them that the whole nation has been involved in a lawless conspiracy against the decencies of modern civilization."[8]

FDR initially concurred with Morgenthau's view that any plan that called for the immediate rehabilitation of the German economy after the war, including the summer 1944 plans of the War and State

Departments, must be rejected. It was of "the utmost importance," he wrote, "that every person in Germany should realize that this time Germany is a defeated nation. I do not want them to starve to death but . . . if they need food to keep body and soul together beyond what they have, they should be fed three times a day from [US] Army soup kitchens. That will keep them perfectly healthy and they will remember the experience all their lives."[9]

With the Red Army now on the Oder and the Anglo-American armies within reach of the Rhine, that final defeat, so necessary to the reform of the German character, seemed tantalizingly close. But aside from an agreement reached at Tehran to grant each of the three powers a zone of occupation once the Reich had been defeated, the Allies had still not come to a final decision about the status of the German state after the war. One reason FDR found it so difficult to arrive at a settled policy for postwar Germany stemmed from the intense debate that the president's initial approval of the Morgenthau plan had unleashed in Washington following the Quebec conference. Both Cordell Hull and Secretary Stimson were adamantly opposed to the plan. A second reason came as a consequence of the growing opposition to the notion of a Carthaginian peace that emerged in the press in the fall of 1944, where "fanatical, bitter-end resistance among German front line troops" attributed to the announcement of the Morgenthau plan were being reported. By this point the Soviets had also made clear their desire for postwar German reparations—a notion that militated against the deindustrialization of Germany after the war. The difficulties FDR encountered over postwar German policy in the fall of 1944 pushed him to postpone the matter. But the imminence of Germany's final collapse meant that it would be impossible to avoid coming to a decision over three issues of immediate concern at Yalta: how to coordinate the final assault on the German state, what the exact borders of the proposed zones of occupation were, and whether France should participate in the occupation.[10]

In his capacity as chair of the proceedings, it had been FDR's intention to begin the political negotiations on Germany with a focus on the proposed zones of occupation and what role France should play in the Reich after the war. But Stalin was clearly not pleased with this agenda. He insisted that there were a number of other vital questions he wished to examine, including the resumption of discussion of the dismemberment of the German state that the three powers had begun at Tehran. Equally important was the question of the payment of reparations. Indeed, given the extent to which the three powers had discussed the possible breakup of Germany at their last summit, FDR's decision not to raise the dismemberment issue as the first order of business came as a surprise to the Soviet dictator.[11]

It may not have been Stalin's intention, but by bringing up these matters at the outset of the discussions on the future of Germany, the Soviet premier put FDR and Churchill on the defensive. Churchill faced a special quandary. His concern over Germany was linked to the larger question of the security of Western Europe. Like Roosevelt, Churchill had supported the idea of dismemberment earlier in the war, but by the time he had reached the Crimea, he and his government were of two minds. On the one hand, Churchill, and much of Whitehall, had always favored the separation of East Prussia from the rest of Germany—a region that, since the days of the 1907 Crowe Memorandum describing the potential threat that Germany posed to Great Britain, was widely viewed in British circles as "the cauldron of wars."[12]

On the other hand, the forced breakup of the German state might inflame the German public and rekindle the same nationalism that had proved so destructive in the past, necessitating a substantial and prolonged period of occupation—a responsibility that Great Britain could ill afford. The British also worried that a weak and dismembered series of small German states could easily fall prey to Soviet domination, particularly in the east.[13]

Churchill was thus unprepared to commit to a decision on dismemberment. In a frank and often tense exchange with Stalin, he insisted that the matter was "too complicated . . . to be settled in five or six days." At the very least a decision on dismemberment would require a "searching examination of the historic, ethnographic, [and] economic facts" involved. He also pointed out that under the terms of unconditional surrender, "we reserve all our rights over their lands, their liberties, and even their lives," which meant that there was no need to rush the matter as the question could be decided at any time in the wake of the defeat.[14]

FDR was certainly not opposed to dismemberment; in fact, he frankly acknowledged that his personal preference was to see the breakup of Germany into as many as five or even seven states. But he, too, had been strongly cautioned by both Stimson and Hull in the wake of the Morgenthau plan that a forced dismemberment might entail a prolonged occupation—necessitated, as the Foreign Office argued, by a resurgence of German nationalism.[15]

Given the war against Japan, and the latent domestic hostility toward US involvement in European affairs, the idea of stationing a large number of American troops in Europe after the war was widely viewed as unacceptable. This public opposition strengthened the argument among US military planners to maintain Soviet-American cooperation after the war. As with many of the issues that arose in the early days of the Yalta conference, FDR's preferred stance when a debate arose between Churchill and Stalin was not to take a position that might be regarded as hostile to one side or the other but, rather, to play the role of "honest broker"—a position that drove Churchill to distraction but that Stalin found reassuring. This moderation was no accident, but part of FDR's overall plan to use the Yalta meeting as a means to enhance the degree of trust between himself and the Soviet dictator. Hence, his initial and somewhat rambling response to the dispute that had emerged over this question—during which he reflected on the largely decentralized Germany he had visited in his youth—was actually an effort to diffuse the tension in the room. Bohlen found FDR's foray into the past somewhat alarming; in his memoirs he speculated that this was the one time during the Yalta conference when the president's ill health might have affected his thinking. But as Anthony Eden observed to the contrary, "Roosevelt was, above all else, a consummate politician. Few men could see more clearly their immediate objective, or show greater artistry in obtaining it."[16]

Thus, having tipped his hat to Stalin by registering his own preference for dismemberment—a position that placed FDR at odds with the official position of his own State and War Departments—while at the same time concurring with Churchill's observation that the question of dismemberment required "further study," FDR suggested the matter be turned over to the three foreign ministers, who were tasked with reporting back to the three leaders later in the week. The practice of turning over major disagreements to the three foreign ministers became a habit of the three leaders at the conference, with mixed results.[17]

Indeed, FDR took this approach to the contentious question of what role France should play in Germany after the war. Here, even though the three leaders quickly came to the agreement that France should be granted a zone of occupation, the question of a French seat on the Allied Control Commission that would govern postwar Germany was largely worked out during the Foreign Ministers meetings that followed in the days ahead.

In many respects the dissension over France among the Big Three was linked to each leader's perceptions of the French nation. Both FDR and Stalin still tended to view France as a lesser power, or even perhaps as the most significant of the "smaller powers." Thus the discussions over France were linked to the discussion of how the Allies should treat the other "small powers." This connection was particularly strong for Stalin, whose opposition to granting France a role equal to that of the other Great Powers was based on his fear of the impact that elevating France's status might have on the aspirations of other "small" states, particularly over the question of reparations.[18]

As Stalin noted at the outset of the political discussions over Germany, the Soviet Union regarded the question of reparations as absolutely vital. He acknowledged that the final dollar amount would be difficult to determine, but the Soviets proposed a formula based on the concept that the countries that had made the greatest contribution to the war effort and had suffered the highest material losses should receive the highest level of reparations. Moscow estimated the total value of the reparations due to the Allies for "direct material losses" to be roughly $20 billion (equivalent to about $265 billion in 2017) and, based on the Soviet Union's own internal assessments, determined that Russia should expect to receive no less than half this amount.[19]

As Ivan Maisky, the former Soviet ambassador to Great Britain, then explained, the Soviets envisioned the extraction of reparations payments from Germany for Russia by two principal means: first, through the removal of "Germany's national wealth" (the factories, machine tools, rolling stock, and other components of German heavy industry) and, second, through annual payments-in-kind that were to last for ten years. Overall, the Soviets envisioned removing all but 20 percent of Germany's heavy industry, including the country's electrical and pharmaceutical plants.[20]

Once again, Churchill objected to the Soviets' proposals. He admitted that no country had suffered more than Russia in this war, and that it therefore deserved reparations, but based on the experience of Versailles he was "quite sure" Russia would never be able to get "out of ruined Germany" the amounts that Maisky was suggesting. "We named astronomical figures in the last war," he noted, "and it turned out to be a disappointment." Churchill also asserted that, even though there was "no victorious country that will come out of the war so burdened financially and so stricken economically as Great Britain," he remained doubtful that the British economy would benefit from reparations.

"If our treatment of Germany's internal economy is such as to leave 80 million people virtually starving," he continued, "are we to sit still and say, 'It serves you right?' Or will we be required to keep them alive? If so, who is going to pay? I am sorry to ask these questions, but they occur to me. If you have a horse and you want him to pull a wagon, you at least have to give him fodder." Stalin remained unimpressed, retorting, "Care should be taken to see that the horse did not turn around and kick you."[21]

Again, FDR mediated. He, too, did not want to see a repeat of the mistakes of the last war, and of the 1920s more generally, when the United States had lent more than $10 billion to Germany for little in return. Roosevelt agreed that Germany should retain enough industry to keep the German people from starving, but he also insisted that they should not have a higher standard of living than the people of the USSR. The US objective, he went on, is to see Russia "get all it can in manpower and factories" and the United Kingdom "get all it can in exports to former German markets." But owing to the challenge of determining the best means of securing compensation—and in keeping with his practice of pushing troublesome issues into the future—FDR suggested that the time had come to set up a reparations commission, which, given the importance the Soviets attached to this issue, should be centered in Moscow.[22]

Churchill concurred with this idea, but he continued to argue that the expected level of reparations was too high—and he refused to endorse a specific dollar amount. With the three parties unable to agree on a total figure or on the precise charge to the proposed reparations commission, FDR once again argued that the matter should be turned over to the three foreign ministers for further consideration. With that, the second day's plenary session came to an end.

FDR MAY HAVE BEEN ABLE TO TAKE SATISFACTION IN THE FACT THAT there had been no open breach on any of the issues the three powers confronted as they wrestled with how best to bring the war against Germany to a close. But it was also the case that, after two days of wrangling, the three leaders had managed to settle only one of the remaining political questions facing them as they contemplated the future of Germany—namely, granting France a zone of occupation. Moreover, even though the military discussions of the day before had gone reasonably well and the question of granting France a seat on the Allied Control Commission would be settled in France's favor by the end of the week, the lack of agreement on repatriations—coupled with the somewhat discouraging disposition of the Anglo-American forces on the battlefield, along with the all-important revelation that there was still no agreement about the possible dismemberment of the German state after the war—meant that for all intents and purposes "the German problem" remained unresolved. Given that it was the threat of a resurgent Germany that, above all else, drove Soviet foreign policy—a threat that not only necessitated the need for a series of friendly states on Russia's western frontier but also informed the Kremlin's desire for cooperation with the West after the war— the inability of the three powers to come to a settled policy on postwar Germany had important consequences. It made the question of Poland all the more important in Soviet calculations, significantly decreasing the likelihood that Stalin and Molotov might show a measure of flexibility on the matter. This harsh reality became eminently clear as the three powers turned their attention to the two issues that the circumstances of the war seemed to have joined at the hip: the critical need to secure Soviet support for the United Nations and the coming to terms with the future of Poland.

Chapter 7

The Polish Quandary

To FDR AND HIS ADVISERS, THERE WERE THREE CRITICAL ISSUES that had to be settled at the Yalta conference: orchestrating the final defeat of Germany, obtaining Soviet participation in the war against Japan, and securing Soviet support for the United Nations Organization. This is not to say that the United States had no interest in the future dispensation of Poland or other parts of Central and Eastern Europe. But just as military expediency often took precedence over political considerations, diplomatic expediency necessitated the subordination of certain issues. That was certainly the case with Poland. On this matter—and on the question of the future of the Baltic States— FDR regarded himself as "a realist." He was quite willing to try to ameliorate the situation in which the Poles found themselves in the wake of the Soviet advance, but he pursued this aim within the context of larger objectives, and was unwilling to allow the "Polish question" to stand in the way of Great Power cooperation or Soviet participation in the new world body.[1]

Still, it was impossible for FDR to ignore the increasing interest that the American people had begun to show about the Soviet treatment of the Poles, which by January 1945 was widely viewed as a litmus test of the Kremlin's willingness to adhere to the values articulated in the Atlantic Charter. The issue of Poland was further complicated by the fact there were now two Polish governments in place: the London-based Polish government-in-exile, recognized by the Anglo-Americans, and the Lublin-based Provisional Government of the Republic of Poland, which had been granted recognition by the Kremlin a mere four weeks before the start of the Yalta conference.

Keenly aware of their public's perception that the Soviet-backed Lublin regime was little more than a puppet of Moscow, both FDR and Churchill had arrived in the Crimea determined to orchestrate the creation of a new, interim Polish government—one that at the very least, as one Foreign Office official put it, was "sufficiently respectable in the eyes of the world . . . to be recognized." Indeed, without some means to show that the two sides had agreed to replace the Lublin status quo with a more democratic or otherwise inclusive alternative, both men feared that the entire conference might be regarded as a failure—with untold consequences for the future. This rendered the settlement of the Polish question one of the most daunting and controversial issues at Yalta.[2]

That Poland should take up such a large part of the conference deliberations must have come as a surprise to many members of the US delegation. Indeed, American policy with respect to Poland in the years prior to Yalta might best be described as purposeful non-involvement. Far more important, after all, was the defeat of the Axis and the establishment of the world organization. Secretary Hull preferred not to even discuss Poland—"that Pandora's box of infinite trouble"—at the Moscow Conference of Foreign Ministers in October 1943, while FDR pretended to fall asleep when the discussion of Poland came up at the Tehran conference a month later. As the president said, "Wake me up when we talk about Germany."[3]

FDR recognized what a full-scale confrontation with the Soviets over the future of Poland might entail. When pressed by Arthur Bliss Lane, the newly appointed US ambassador to the Polish government-in-exile, to take a strong stand against the Soviets in November 1944, FDR responded by asking, "Do you want me to go to war with Russia?" And when the two men turned to the eastern-boundary dispute between the London Poles and the Soviets—at that time, a critical matter—FDR observed that perhaps the best way to settle the question was to organize a plebiscite in the disputed regions in ten or fifteen years' time. He urged Bliss Lane to greet the Czech leader, Dr. Eduard Benes—who had managed to establish amiable relations with Moscow—once the ambassador arrived in London. And as if to remind Bliss Lane that the interwar Polish government was not without sin, FDR closed the conversation by noting: "I have never forgiven the Poles for having taken Teschen after Munich in [19]38"—or, for that matter, for invading

Vilna, Lithuania, during the same year, a move that FDR described as "unfair . . . and very ill-advised."[4]

FDR's reference to a future plebiscite hints at his expectation that the Soviet Union was inching its way toward a more tolerable form of socialism. As FDR explained to Richard Law in a conversation held near the end of December 1944, "There were many varieties of Communism, and not all of them were necessarily harmful." Nor did the president harbor the same apprehension as others about the possibility of communist agitation in the shattered economies of Europe once the war was over. He himself had lived through such a troubled period. When he first became president at the height of the Great Depression, "there was a great deal of fear of communism and some danger of it," he told Law, "but he knew that as soon as the conditions of 1932 had been changed, the fear and the danger would pass."[5]

FDR's reference to Eduard Benes and his comments about a possible war with Russia, meanwhile, fly in the face of later accusations that FDR's dealings with Stalin were founded on naïveté. Soviet power was a reality, and war with Russia over Stalin's ambitions in Eastern Europe was unthinkable—particularly with Germany still at war and with FDR's own military chiefs insisting that it was vital to secure Russia's help in the defeat of Japan. The only alternative was to seek a compromise solution, such as the kind Dr. Benes had successfully achieved through the negotiation of the Czechoslovak-Russian Treaty of Friendship that was signed in Moscow on December 12, 1943.[6]

Well aware of the background of the negotiations that led to the signing of this treaty—which included language calling on each state to act "in accordance with the principles of mutual respect for the independence and sovereignty" of the other state—FDR saw the highly popular Czech leader's determination to pursue a settlement with Stalin as a potential model for the type of agreement that the Poles might achieve. This impression was further strengthened in the spring of 1944 when the Czechs signed a subsequent understanding with Moscow that placed territory liberated by the Russians under Soviet military command, but with a Czech administration governing the area once it no longer remained a combat zone.[7]

Under more pressure to take up the Polish cause as the end of the war approached, both FDR and Churchill had urged the London Polish government-in-exile to negotiate a similar understanding with

Moscow. For example, in a June 1944 meeting with Stanislaw Miko-lajczyk, the then–premier of the London Poles, FDR insisted—in a remark that presaged his comments to Ambassador Bliss Lane—that the Poles "must find an understanding with Russia," as, on their own, they'd have no chance to beat them, "and the British and the Americans have no intention of fighting Russia."[8]

Two months later—under further pressure from both London and Washington—Mikolajczyk agreed to travel to Moscow to meet with Stalin. The workmanlike nature of these conversations, which included a frank discussion of Stalin's insistence that the Curzon Line form the eastern border of Poland, seemed encouraging, particularly as both sides seemed willing to embrace some flexibility on the border question. But this relatively warm atmosphere was soon shattered by the decision of the London-sponsored Polish resistance in Warsaw to try to liberate the capital in advance of—or in conjunction with—its capture by the Red Army, which, after four weeks of intense fighting, suddenly found itself on the east bank of the Vistula River on the outskirts of the city. Both Churchill and Eden had strongly advised the Polish government-in-exile not to proceed with the uprising without first obtaining the full collaboration of the Soviet Union. The Polish underground leadership in Warsaw refused to heed this advice, however, and on August 1, 1944, the Home Army (as the resistance was called) launched a full-scale assault on the German forces in the city without informing the Kremlin.[9]

The Warsaw uprising was a disaster for all concerned. It resulted in the destruction of the Polish Home Army and the deaths of upwards of 200,000 civilians. It also led to serious tensions within the Grand Alliance over Stalin's indifference to the plight of the Home Army—whose leadership was intensely anti-Soviet—and initial refusal to airdrop supplies to the insurgents or offer any assistance to the British and American air forces that wished to do the same. The disaster also weakened the ability of the London-based Poles to influence events in Poland both during and after the war, and—thanks to the bitter recriminations that emerged on both sides of the Vistula about who was to blame for the catastrophe—all but destroyed any chance that the talks initiated among the London Poles and Moscow in early August would lead to a rapprochement and the restoration of diplomatic relations.[10]

In his October 1944 percentages meeting with Stalin, Churchill tried to revive this effort, going so far as to arrange a face-to-face meeting between Mikolajczyk and the Soviet leader. But these talks soon failed over the continued refusal of Mikolajczyk's colleagues in London to even discuss Stalin's demand that the Curzon Line form the eastern border of Poland. Frustrated at his inability to make progress, and by the lack of support he received from the Polish government-in-exile in London, Mikolajczyk resigned as premier at the end of November 1944. Both Churchill and Roosevelt regarded this as a serious setback.[11] Then came the news about the Soviet recognition of the Lublin regime in early January and the equally disturbing news from Greece, all of which led Secretary Stettinius to report that public "confidence that Britain and Russia can be trusted to cooperate with the United States after the war had reached its lowest point since the [1943] Moscow conference." Ever fearful of the reemergence of American isolationism, and the possibility that the American people might repeat the mistakes of the past and reject the United Nations, FDR could not afford to ignore these ominous signs, particularly over Poland. A solution to the Polish problem thus became the *sine qua non* upon which the success or failure of the entire effort to establish the world body now seemed to rest, rendering the discussions over Poland the most protracted and difficult of the Crimean conference.[12]

OF COURSE, THE ISSUE OF POLAND WOULD BE IMMATERIAL IF FDR failed to secure Soviet participation in the United Nations. To date, however, the prospects that the Soviets would embrace the US formula on voting in the Security Council were far from encouraging. As Andrei Gromyko had put it during the last discussion he had with Leo Pasvolsky on the matter, the Soviets' demand for an unlimited veto (as opposed to the limited veto proposed by Washington) was their final word, "and would not be changed regardless of whether the conversations [on the question] were prolonged a week or a year."[13] Fully aware of what was at stake, FDR spent the morning of Tuesday, February 6, in his room, going over the December 5 proposal that Pasvolsky had so assiduously drafted in an effort to break the deadlock. He also instructed Secretary Stettinius to be ready to present the plan at the plenary session that afternoon—a request that Stettinius regarded as perhaps the most important assignment he had ever received from the president.[14]

Harry Hopkins was also anxious about the future of the world organization, though from a slightly different perspective. He knew from past experience that Churchill's views on the structure of the United Nations were mercurial, and in an effort to harmonize the stance taken by FDR and Churchill on the voting procedure in advance of that day's plenary session, he insisted that Anna arrange a meeting between the two. Speaking from his sickbed, Hopkins expressed deep concern about "the Dumbarton Oaks part of the conference." He urged Anna to arrange for the two men to dine together at noon. Anna agreed, but only on the condition that W. Averill Harriman attend with instructions "to shoo the PM out at 2:45" so that her father could get an hour's rest before the plenary started and thus "would not have to work steadily from one o'clock to seven-thirty or eight pm when the conference usually comes to an end."[15]

The luncheon went ahead as arranged, with Hopkins, Byrnes, Harriman, and Cadogan also in attendance. Although the conversation continued until 3:00, it turned out to be mostly a social affair. "Quite agreeable and amusing," Cadogan recorded in his diary, "but not awfully useful." The most exciting aspect of the afternoon, in fact, was finding a room in which Churchill could take his daily afternoon nap, since there would not be time to transport the prime minister back to his residence before the start of the plenary at 4:00. Churchill's needs resulted in Vice Admiral Brown and General Watson being kicked out of their shared room, much to their displeasure.[16]

In keeping with his concerns about the need to reassure the America people about the larger purposes of the conference, FDR began the plenary negotiations on the world organization with a blunt warning about the precarious state of American public opinion, which the president characterized as "decisive." In later years, conservative critics would assail FDR for this tendency to stress domestic sentiments, but his actions represent far more than crass political calculation. Few presidents have understood the necessity of public support more than FDR, and with Stettinius's alarming report about the fall in the American people's confidence in future Great Power cooperation still ringing in his ears, his decision to begin with this reference made perfect sense. Moreover, by the time he had reached the Crimea, the advisability of stressing this aspect of US foreign policy had gained considerable currency in the State Department. As *Foreign Affairs* editor Hamilton Fish Armstrong put it in a letter to Secretary Stettinius near the end of January 1945, one of the chief barriers to understandings between representatives of a totalitarian state like Soviet Russia and those of a democracy like the United States "was not the difference in language or custom but the fact that they do not know what we mean by public opinion." The Russians hear us talk of "the necessity of satisfying public opinion," Armstrong observed, "but it always sounds to them a little like an alibi for not doing what they want." He urged that "no opportunity should be lost . . . to impress on them that public opinion in this country is an absolute imperative . . . and that no official policy can long survive if it runs counter to what the people think is right."[17]

In his initial remarks, FDR said that if it was possible "to get agreement on the Dumbarton Oaks proposals," it would be much more probable "that the United States would be prepared to take a full part in organizing the peace throughout the world." But to support this plan, the American people would want to see "concrete proposals to prevent war for as long a period as anybody could foresee." He was not so optimistic "as to believe in eternal peace," but he did think fifty years without war was possible and with this in mind expressed the hope that his counterparts would now give careful consideration to the American proposal for the voting procedure in the Security Council of the world organization.[18]

Despite the fact that Stalin had received the American proposal more than a month before, Stalin insisted—somewhat apologetically in the wake of Secretary Stettinius's review of this matter at the plenary—that he had not had the time to read the document carefully. He also professed a lack of understanding regarding certain aspects of the proposal.

Stettinius tried to counter Stalin's apparent, or feigned, ignorance with a number of examples of how the voting procedure would work in practice. But none of these seemed to satisfy Stalin, who expressed grave concern about the ability of the smaller powers to air their grievances and make recommendations, which in his view constituted a form of action. He then reminded his colleagues that in December

1939, during the Russo-Finnish War, "the British and the French had used the League of Nations against them and succeeded in isolating and expelling the Soviet Union."[19]

Both Churchill and Eden insisted that this misuse of the international community's power within the world body could not happen under the American formula, and they offered further examples of how the prerogatives of the five permanent members would be protected. But Stalin remained unconvinced. To him, Allied unity, especially among the Big Three, was far more important than the rights of the lesser states. If Russia is accused "of attaching too great importance to the procedure on how to vote," he said, "[w]e are guilty."[20]

Alarmed, FDR noted that of course there would be differences among the Big Three in the future, but permitting discussion of these differences in the Security Council would highlight their ability to solve problems and would "demonstrate the confidence the Great Powers had in each other and in the justice of their own policies." Stalin countered that this might be true, but continued to insist that he needed more time to study the proposal and suggested they table the discussion on the United Nations for the following day—a suggestion to which FDR reluctantly agreed.[21]

Observing the proceedings, James Byrnes could not help feeling "deeply disturbed by the clear evidence that Stalin had not considered or even read our proposal on voting in the Security Council even though it had been sent to him . . . on December 5." He'd had "sixty-three days" to "familiarize himself with the subject," and thus it seemed clear to Byrnes that Stalin "was not greatly interested in the United Nations organization."[22]

Another observer, Lord Moran, agreed. The discussion on the United Nations Organization brought the differences between Stalin and Roosevelt into sharp relief, he noted in his diary: "In American eyes, the first purpose of this conference is to lay the foundation of an international peace organization. . . . But Stalin can see no point in vague sentiments and misty aspirations for the freedom of certain small nations. He is only concerned with the borders of Poland, with reparations and with what he can pick up in the Far East. These are tangible things that he can get his teeth into. . . . Roosevelt would like to proscribe for the world, Stalin is content to make clear what the Soviet Union will swallow."[23]

IT WAS ON THIS LESS THAN AUSPICIOUS NOTE THAT THE THREE POW-
ers began the difficult and seemingly endless effort to reach a settlement to the Polish question at Yalta. There were two main issues that
stood in the way of a final agreement: the frontiers of the future state
and the creation of a new interim government that all three powers
could recognize. Thanks to the discussions over Poland that had taken
place at Tehran, the question of Poland's eastern frontier had been
largely decided, as both Churchill and Roosevelt had agreed in principle to support Stalin's demand that it follow the Curzon Line. The one
significant modification to this proposal—suggested by FDR at Tehran
and reiterated in his opening comments on Poland at Yalta—was the
inclusion of Lvov and the oil fields of Galicia to the southwest of the
city on the Polish side of the border. This stance was also in keeping
with the conversations FDR had with Mikolajczyk at the White House
in June 1944, and with the briefing papers FDR had received from the
State Department before his departure. Furthermore, all three powers had come to a general understanding that in return for the territory lost in the east, Poland would receive compensation through the
acquisition of territory in East Prussia and additional German lands
in the west. Having recapitulated all of these points as he opened the
negotiations on Poland, FDR reverted to his earlier argument about
the importance of public opinion with the observation that there were
6–7 million Poles in the United States, most of whom were willing to
accept the Curzon Line as the eastern border of postwar Poland. The
president said he would have an easier time convincing his nation to
support the new Polish border if the Soviet government would yield
Poland the city of Lvov and perhaps the oil lands to its southwest.[24]

The most important question, however, was the one concerning the
permanent government of Poland. The general opinion in the United
States, FDR said, "is against our recognizing the Lublin Government
on the grounds that it represents only a small section of the Polish
population. We favor the creation of a Polish government that would
resolve the political differences by creating a government of national
unity, a government which would represent all of the major Polish
political parties," which he identified by name. He then recommended
that the Allies establish a Presidential Council, composed of a small
number of Poles from both within and outside Poland—including,
perhaps, Stanislaw Mikolajczyk—who would be charged with the duty

of creating a more permanent government, which, of course, would maintain friendly relations with Russia in the years ahead.[25]

Roosevelt's plea on behalf of Poland inspired Churchill to mount a much more spirited defense of Polish independence than the one he had made to Stalin in October 1944. Consistent with his previous stance, Churchill endorsed the Curzon Line and like FDR, said he was more interested in Poland's sovereign independence and freedom than in its borders. For the British, this was a matter of honor, since they had gone to war in the first place in defense of Poland. Yet freedom for Poland, he went on, should "not be made to cover any hostile design by Poland or any Polish group, possibly in intrigue with Germany, against Russia."[26]

Stalin was not impressed by these arguments, however, and after a ten-minute recess he returned to the table to counter Roosevelt's and Churchill's calls for concessions with stern conviction. He understood that for Great Britain, honor dictated a secure and independent future for Poland, but he reminded the prime minister that for Russia the future of Poland was not merely a matter of honor but also one of survival. Throughout history, Poland had been the corridor through which Russia's enemies had attacked it. Over the previous thirty years, the Germans had done so twice. This had been possible because Poland had been weak. Russia thus wanted to see a strong, powerful, and independent Poland.[27]

As for Poland's eastern frontier, Stalin maintained that it had been determined not by Russia but by Lord Curzon and Georges Clémenceau after World War I, and that FDR and Churchill could hardly expect him to be "less Russian" than these two statesmen by ceding this territory to the Poles. Stalin also refused to grant Lvov and the oil fields near it to Poland. This area was populated largely by Ukrainians, he insisted, who had suffered greatly in the war. Maintaining the region as part of the Soviet Republic of Ukraine was therefore just.

Stalin also brought up a claim he had made earlier about agents of the London Poles engaging in violent activities in the rear of the Red Army, killing Russian soldiers and attacking supply depots. He further maintained that the Lublin Poles, whom he said should now be referred to as the Warsaw Poles, had as great a "democratic base" as de Gaulle had in France, and that the composition of the Polish government was an internal Polish matter. Finally, in reference to the proposal that the three powers create an interim government for the country, he wryly observed that even though he was often accused of being a dictator, "he had enough democratic feeling to refuse to create a Polish government without the Poles being consulted."[28]

Stalin's impassioned oration on Poland, which included an offer to bring some members of the Lublin Poles to the Crimea for consultation, turned out to be the longest speech made by any of the three leaders at Yalta. He was clearly vexed by the Polish question and made the unusual decision to stand while he spoke. It was clear, Bohlen recorded, that "the Americans and the British faced a formidable task in trying to salvage anything on Poland." When Stalin finished talking, Hopkins passed a note to a grim-faced FDR suggesting that they return to the matter tomorrow. Roosevelt did not take much convincing and, noting the lateness of the hour, brought the meeting to a close at 7:45 p.m.[29]

Unsettled by the vehemence with which Stalin defended the Soviet position on Poland, FDR decided to issue a direct written appeal to the marshal, instructing Bohlen and Hopkins that evening to prepare a letter that could be delivered to Stalin that very night. After conferring with Bohlen on the draft, and making arrangements for both Eden and Churchill to see it, he sent the missive by courier to the Yusupov Palace. In it, FDR indicated he was "greatly disturbed" that the three leaders had not been able to come to "a meeting of minds about the political setup in Poland." The president stressed that it was vitally important to put this issue behind them in large part because the American people "will look with a critical eye on what they consider a disagreement between us at this vital stage in the war." Indeed, they might conclude that "if we cannot get a meeting of the minds now, when our armies are converging on a common enemy, how can we get an understanding on even more vital things in the future?" FDR understood Stalin's determination to safeguard the Red Army from attacks from the rear as it moved into Germany, but he stated categorically that the United States "cannot recognize the Lublin government as now composed." Noting that Stalin had suggested at the end of his lengthy oration that the Big Three could bring representatives from Lublin to Yalta for consultation, FDR suggested that he do so at once, including, at the suggestion of Churchill and Eden, at least three non-Lublin Poles.[30]

THE NEXT MORNING, WEDNESDAY, FEBRUARY 7, FDR TOOK A LATE breakfast and tried to get a little extra rest in preparation for the day ahead. The lack of progress on Poland the day before was troubling, but like others in the American delegation, his foremost concern that morning was the fate of the United Nations, which now seemed to be inextricably linked to the fate of the Polish state. Secretary of State Stettinius was also worried and, at FDR's instruction, went off to see Hopkins, Byrnes, and other members of the State Department staff to discuss the UN impasse in advance of the noon meeting of the foreign ministers. The US delegation's hope was that Stettinius might be able to shift the original agenda for the luncheon meeting and instead convince Foreign Ministers Molotov and Eden to concentrate on the United Nations. But Molotov, the host of the gathering on this occasion, refused Stettinius's request to take up the voting procedure. Thus, by the time Stettinius returned to the Livadia Palace that afternoon to report back to the president and his colleagues, his anxiety over the future of the United Nations was even more pronounced than it had been that morning.[31]

Unbeknownst to the Americans, however, Stalin had been thrown somewhat on the defensive by the strong stand FDR had taken in his letter on Poland. Coupled with Churchill's firm stance the previous afternoon, the letter led Stalin to conclude that he faced a united Anglo-American front on a question that he believed vital to Soviet security. The plenary session that afternoon thus became a critical moment for all three powers: the start of an intense period of negotiations that would determine the fate of millions of people. It also represented a test of each man's abilities as a negotiator, and here Stalin would prove himself, as Anthony Eden later commented, a man of considerable skill.[32]

FDR opened the fourth plenary session by asking the foreign ministers if they had anything to report, which led to a brief overview of a number of issues, none of which had been settled. He then requested that the group return to the discussion of Poland. Stalin immediately interjected—in a likely fabrication—that he had just received the president's letter an hour before. Then, taking note of the suggestion that he follow up on the idea of inviting members of the Lublin Poles to Yalta, he explained that he had tried to do so, but unfortunately they could not be reached. He felt there was little hope of finding the representatives that FDR had mentioned in his letter, but he would keep trying. In the meantime, he assured the president that his typists were busy preparing a document on Poland that he believed would please his counterparts. But since this was not yet ready, he suggested they return to their discussion of the voting question; then, turning toward Foreign Minister Molotov, he asked him to state the Soviet position.[33]

As FDR and Stettinius listened intently, Molotov announced that after due consideration of Stettinius's report, the Soviet government was ready to accept the American voting formula in its entirety "without further comment or amendments." After months of struggle over the issue, Molotov's unexpected proclamation was a major breakthrough; as former Ambassador Maisky recorded, an audible sigh of relief swept through the American delegation at this news. But Molotov was not finished. He added that the Soviets would no longer insist on UN membership for all sixteen of the Soviet Republics, as they had at Dumbarton Oaks, but would now be content with two or three, suggesting Ukraine and Byelorussia as the two most viable candidates.[34]

FDR was understandably delighted at the Soviets' sudden change of heart on the voting procedure in the Security Council, which he characterized as "a great step forward." On the other hand, even though the Soviet proposal to reduce the number of seats the USSR held in the General Assembly from sixteen to three was welcome news, the fact that the Soviets had made this offer more or less in conjunction with their sudden about-face on the voting procedure placed FDR in a difficult position. The president had consistently and quite publicly argued in favor of "one nation, one vote," and hence his initial response to Molotov's proposed reduction was to pass a note to Stettinius on which he had scribbled "Not so good." Still, he did not want to endanger this chance to move the United Nations effort forward, and after acknowledging how close they were to a final agreement on the matter, he suggested that the three foreign ministers study the question of granting Ukraine and Belarus seats in the General Assembly while preparations were made to convene a conference to set up the world organization as soon as possible, preferably before the end of March.

No doubt excited by the prospect that the world organization he had worked for might in fact be up and running in the relatively near future, FDR took a moment in the wake of Molotov's announcement to engage in a brief exposition on the need for the forthcoming United Nations to turn its attention to economic development among the less well-off areas of the world. In an oblique reference to the proposed international conservation conference FDR had been exploring with Gifford Pinchot, FDR spoke of the tremendous impact that the reforestation of Persia might have on the social and economic well-being of the local inhabitants as one example. Persia had once been "well-wooded" and prosperous, he noted, with plenty of "surface water . . . and no soil erosion." Now, however, thanks in large part to the loss of its timber, Persia had become "one of the poorest countries he had ever seen." Having thus made the link between environmental degradation and poverty, FDR argued that one reason the United Nations should come into existence as soon as possible is so that a worldwide study could be made of how impoverished nations with no purchasing power could be enabled to get it.[35]

Much to FDR's annoyance, however, Molotov's proposals on the General Assembly led Churchill to embark on a long discourse about the importance he attached to seeing not only the Dominions but also India possessing a seat in the body. Churchill enthusiastically welcomed the Soviet proposal, specifically endorsing membership for Byelorussia, "bleeding from her wounds and conquering and beating down the tyrants." Growing more emotional, the prime minister dismissed FDR's suggestion that the foreign ministers take up the question, claiming they already had too much to do. He also criticized Roosevelt's call for a United Nations planning conference in March, arguing that the "battle" for Europe would be at its height and that domestic issues in Britain would make it difficult for his nation's ministers to concentrate on the proposed conference.[36]

Irritated over Churchill's precipitous support for the Soviet position, FDR scribbled a note to Hopkins during Churchill's harangue that said "All this is rot," which he quickly crossed out and amended to say "local politics"—evidence of his suspicion that Churchill was worried about a possible election in Britain. FDR tried to calm Churchill by explaining that all he was suggesting was that the foreign ministers turn their attention to three simple questions: the Soviet proposal regarding membership, the date and location of the conference, and who should be invited. Churchill responded that he had no objection to the three foreign ministers discussing these points, so long as it was understood that these were not mere technical questions but matters of great moment.

Churchill's sudden and quite unexpected rant about the world organization—which, as Alexander Cadogan noted, was "completely contrary to the line already agreed with the Americans" at Malta—did not go down well with the members of the US delegation. Nor was Anthony Eden pleased, seeing it as a consequence of Churchill's reluctance to devote his attention to peacetime matters. This incident also represented the first public display of tension between Churchill and Roosevelt at the conference—a potential confrontation that, ironically, Stalin brought to a close by reminding his colleagues that the foreign ministers would not make decisions, but merely report back to the three leaders.[37]

Eden's observations about the skill with which Stalin orchestrated the Yalta negotiations now came into full view as Molotov, after having proffered the Soviet concessions in the United Nations, now presented the proposal on Poland that Stalin had alluded to at the start of the plenary. This consisted of a six-point plan that included a reiteration of the Soviet call for the Curzon Line—with some minor adjustments—to serve as the eastern boundary of Poland; a recommendation that the Oder River and the Western Neisse River constitute the western frontier; and, most significantly, a series of provisions that called for the enlargement of the current Lublin regime to include "some democratic leaders from Polish émigré circles" as well as elections for a new permanent government as soon as possible. The fact that Moscow had finally placed the composition of the Lublin government on the table—with a specific reference to the inclusion of "democratic leaders"—was widely regarded by the Anglo-Americans as an important "step," as FDR put it, "along the general plan we have been talking about." But after noting his own dislike of the term émigré—which seemed to imply that there were no democratic representatives within Poland—FDR asked for further time to study the proposal and, at Hopkins's recommendation, suggested they adjourn for the day.[38]

Stalin was quite happy to defer further discussion, but Churchill, who took even greater offense at the use of the word émigré, launched into a ringing defense of the Polish government-in-exile. This prompted an exasperated FDR to pencil a note to Stettinius saying "Now we are in for a ½ of it." Churchill also raised objections to Molotov's suggestion that Poland's border with Germany be moved to the Western Neisse River, as "it would be a great pity to stuff the Polish Goose so full of Germans that it died of indigestion." Furthermore, if the solution to this dilemma was to force the German population of East Prussia and Silesia to emigrate, it was the prime minister's understanding that this would mean moving about 6 million people. This remark prompted a rather remarkable exchange about the consequences of the Allied decision to move Poland to the west. Stettinius speculated that the total number of people forced to move would be "four million," while Eden interjected to say that, in fact, "including East Prussia," it would be "six million four hundred thousand." Stalin countered that "there will not be that many people . . . because where our troops come in they run away."

Churchill, in response, said that Stalin's observation "simplifies the problem. But one has to consider also where are those Germans who run away? Will there be room for them in what is left of Germany?"

Stalin said that the Red Army had already "killed six or seven million Germans and probably there will be another million or so killed before the end of the war."

"I am not proposing we take any steps to stop it," Churchill replied, "but I think there ought to be room . . . for the people transferred to Germany up to a certain point. So I am not afraid of this problem of transferring populations so long as it is proportioned to what can be properly managed. It requires study. Not as to a matter of principle, but as to the actual numbers to be transferred."[39]

After Stalin nodded in agreement, Churchill closed the grim conversation by saying he agreed with the president that "we should sleep on" the question of Poland and speak about it tomorrow. "We are making progress in a difficult field."[40]

Churchill may have been correct on this count, but so was Stalin in his assessment of the heavy German casualties to come. At the much-heralded first meeting of the three nations' Chiefs of Staff earlier that week, the Soviets pressed the Anglo-Americans to do all they could to disrupt the potential movement of German reinforcements from the west to the east. The Anglo-Americans decided to strike at German lines of communication by bombing the cities of Berlin, Leipzig, and Dresden. Just two days after the Yalta conference ended, over 1,300 British and American heavy bombers dropped nearly 4,000 tons of high-explosive and incendiary bombs on Dresden, creating a firestorm of unprecedented proportions that all but destroyed 13 square miles of the once-magnificent medieval city and incinerated more than 25,000 men, women, and children.[41]

AT DINNER THAT NIGHT, THE FOURTH EVENING MEAL OF THE CONFER-ence, FDR and Stettinius agreed that it had been "a most fruitful day," during which they had come one "step further along the difficult path to a world organization." As their conversation turned to the composition of the United Nations, FDR conjectured that "there would be approximately fifty seats in the assembly." He wondered "what practical difference it would make to the success or failure of the Assembly for the Soviet Union to have two additional seats to represent its vast population and territory"—particularly when "the actual power would rest in the Security Council" and "each country in this body, large or small, would have only one vote." Although he did not say it out loud, it was clear that FDR's formerly strong opposition to the inclusion of some of the Soviet Republics in the United Nations was softening, especially now that the realization of the proposed world organization was so close at hand.[42]

It was also clear, as FDR's conversation with Stettinius stretched into the night, that the pace of the conference—including "the grueling five-hour [plenary] session" held earlier that day—was taking a toll on him. No one was more aware of this than Anna, who, despite the progress the American delegation seemed to be making on the issues she knew were closest to her father's heart, could not help but dwell on her concerns in a letter she wrote to her husband that evening.

After inquiring about their children and offering some impressions of the largely destroyed city of Sevastopol, which she had visited that afternoon, she wrote about the "OM," or "old man," or "Oscar Meyer," as she frequently referred to her father in her correspondence:

Just between you and me, we are having to watch [the] OM very carefully from the physical standpoints. He gets all wound up, seems to thoroughly enjoy it all, but wants too many people around, and then won't go to bed early enough. The result is that he doesn't sleep well. Ross and Bruenn are both worried because of the old "ticker" trouble—which of course no one knows about but those two and me. I am working closely with Ross and Bruenn, and am using all the ingenuity and tact that I can muster to try and separate the wheat from the chaff—to keep unnecessary people out of OM's room and to steer the necessary ones in at the best times. This is actually taking place at the conference, so that I will know who should and who should not see OM. I have found out through Bruenn (who won't let me tell Ross that I know) that his "ticker" situation is far more serious than I ever knew. And the biggest difficulty in handling the situation here is that we can, of course, tell no one of the "ticker" trouble. It's truly worrisome—and there's not a helluva lot anyone can do about it.

Anna then wrote, in words that thankfully were not heeded by her husband, "Better tear off and destroy this paragraph."[43]

Chapter 8

The Birth of the United Nations

FEBRUARY 8, 1945, WAS A DAY OF GREAT ACCOMPLISHMENT AND GREAT frustration for FDR. In many respects the United Nations was born that Thursday, as by the time the plenary session opened at 4:15 p.m., the president had made up his mind to support the Kremlin's request for the Soviet Republics of Byelorussia and Ukraine to join the General Assembly. Though the process by which the two republics would be admitted had yet to be determined, this agreement removed the last major obstacle to the establishment of the United Nations.

Just what led FDR to back down on an issue he felt so strongly about before he left for Yalta is not entirely clear. That the Soviets decided to embrace the US voting formula, and to lower the number of client states they hoped to have admitted to the General Assembly from sixteen to two, certainly played a role. Moreover, Churchill strongly supported the Soviet position, due in part to his desire to see the Dominions and India represented in the Assembly. FDR was reluctant to go against the prime minister in this case, even if his vision for the postwar world did not include the perpetuation of imperialism, British or otherwise.[1]

February 8 was also the day that FDR secured Stalin's agreement to enter the war against Japan, although the formal terms of that understanding would not be signed until the last day of the conference. The day's frustration came from the intractable problem of Poland, which FDR found more and more troubling.

For the US delegation, the first order of business that morning was to circulate an American counterproposal to the six-point plan on the Polish question that Foreign Minister Molotov offered the day before. Drafted largely by Charles Bohlen and approved by FDR, this document reiterated the American demand for the creation of a new government in Poland through a Presidential Council of three individuals drawn both from the Lublin regime and from democratic elements within Poland and abroad. The Presidential Council would hold elections for a constituent assembly, which, in turn, would draft a constitution. Following this would be a general election and the establishment of a permanent government. The US counterproposal also called upon the three powers to recognize the proposed provisional government and indicated American acceptance of the Curzon Line as the eastern boundary of Poland. It rejected, however, the western frontier that Molotov's document had put forward. The British also drew up and circulated a counterproposal that morning. Although the two plans were similar in that the British proposal likewise called for replacement of the Lublin regime, in this case by a Regency, FDR's preference for a unilateral American approach to the Soviets weakened the overall Anglo-American effort.[2]

In the meantime, Stettinius asked Dr. McIntire for his opinion on whether former Secretary of State Cordell Hull, who was recovering from exhaustion and remained hospitalized in Bethesda, Maryland, would be well enough to chair the founding UN conference. Given Hull's age and frail health, McIntire advised against it and suggested instead that the president appoint Hull as senior adviser to the American delegation—an ironic response, coming from a man who had done nothing to discourage an unwell FDR from running for a fourth term or from traveling halfway around the world to meet with Churchill and Stalin.[3]

Stettinius then went to see Hopkins, another desperately ill figure who, aside from his attendance at the plenary sessions, and an occasional luncheon, was more or less confined to his bed. Harriman, Bohlen, and Byrnes joined them for this discussion. Here, the five men, reflecting the cautiously optimistic mood that prevailed within the American delegation that morning, discussed the preparation of a draft communiqué about the proposed UN conference in anticipation of a final settlement.

FDR remained in his quarters that morning, to take some quiet time to rest and prepare for his midafternoon meeting with Stalin, where the two men, accompanied by Foreign Minister Molotov and Ambassador Harriman, planned to discuss the proposed Soviet entry into the war against Japan. Not far away, while the president worked and sun broke through a bank of misty clouds over the sea, a small group of Russian peasant women gathered in the little stone market square that stood at the center of the village of Yalta to ply their wares. Aside from a few crumpled and old paperbound books, however, and some "dried half-pumpkins" and a few strange-looking half-bottles of yellow oil, there was little to buy, as Valentine Lawson, Anthony Eden's private secretary observed while out for an early morning walk. "God only knows," he mused, "what these wretched people live on." Still, the morning was fresh and invigorating, and Lawson could not help but notice their friendly stares as he took a few precious moments to get away from the conference and feel what it was like "to be alone in Russia" before he hastily headed back to join his colleagues in their efforts to shape the world to follow.[4]

SECURING SOVIET PARTICIPATION IN THE STRUGGLE AGAINST THE JAPanese was one of FDR's main objectives at Yalta. FDR's top military advisers believed that the final defeat of Japan was going to be an enormously difficult undertaking, requiring an invasion of the Japanese Home Islands (which would take a minimum of eighteen months) and potentially costing the United States hundreds of thousands of casualties. Moreover, the United States had little faith in China's military capabilities; better, FDR's advisers thought, to encourage the Soviets to attack Japanese forces in Manchuria, which would have the effect of tying down large numbers of Japanese troops on the mainland when the final American assault on Japan began.

The first formal indication that the Soviet Union might join the war against Japan came at the Moscow Conference of Foreign Ministers in 1943. Shortly thereafter, at Tehran, Stalin assured FDR that he would open up a new front in Asia. But it was not until mid-December 1944 that Stalin, in response to a direct request from Roosevelt, finally put his terms on the table. In conversation with Harriman, he "brought out a map" and, pointing to the territory Russia lost in its 1905 war with Japan, said that Lower Sakhalin Island would have to be returned to Russian control. He wanted to annex the Kurile Islands, he argued, as "at present the Japanese controlled all of the approaches to the important port of Vladivostok." Stalin then brought up three additional issues—the lease of ports on the Liaotung Peninsula, the lease of the Chinese Eastern Railway, and the maintenance of the status quo in Outer Mongolia. All of these demands foreshadowed the agreement that was ultimately signed on the last day of the Yalta conference.[5]

Because these earlier talks had gone into such detail, the discussions between FDR and Stalin on February 8 amounted to little more than a chance for the two of them to put their seal of approval on a prior understanding. The one new item involved FDR's desire to secure Soviet support for the Nationalist regime in China. Here, taking note of his expectations about the final defeat of Japan and the establishment of international trusteeships after the war, FDR observed that the arrival of US forces in Manila meant that the war in the Pacific had entered a new phase. Thus "the time had come to make new plans for [the] additional bombing of Japan." Indeed, he "hoped that it might not actually be necessary to invade the Japanese Islands," as it may well be possible to "destroy Japan" and the "4,000,000 men in their army . . . by intensive bombing," which would "save American lives." The United States, he insisted, would invade Japan only if it were "absolutely necessary."[6]

Although FDR made no reference to the development of the atomic bomb, this argument in favor of bombing suggests that he may have had the new weapon in mind. He knew from his conversations with Secretary Henry Stimson and Lieutenant General Leslie Groves at the end of December 1944 that the weapon was projected to be ready by early August. Yet he may have simply been referring to the US Army Air Force's strategic bombing campaign against the Japanese Home Islands, which started in late November 1944. These raids—carried out by B-29 Super Fortresses dropping the Air Force's first incendiary cluster bombs—would intensify in the coming months.

In contemplating the use of air power as an alternative means to defeat the Japanese, FDR may already have moved ahead of the American Joint Chiefs of Staff in his thinking about this final stage of the conflict. This approach could render unnecessary Soviet participation in the Pacific War and give FDR more leverage when it came to Stalin's requested concessions in the Far East. But if an invasion of Japan was not going to be necessary, why did FDR press ahead with the request for the Soviets to enter the war?

The answer has to do with FDR's vision for the postwar world as well as with the part played by the United States and the Soviet Union as the two countries transitioned into the new era he hoped to launch in the wake of the final defeat of the Axis powers. Convinced that it was time for the United States to start "exercising the influence that power demands," FDR was thinking in geopolitical terms. Hence, in what could be described as a reversal of President Nixon's much-heralded overture to Beijing in the 1970s, he hoped to enlist Stalin's support in achieving the twin goals of building up a strong, unified, and reasonably democratic China, on the one hand, and eventually removing the European colonial regimes he found so antithetical to his democratic principles, on the other. Thus he pressed ahead with the effort to secure Soviet participation in the Pacific War, even though the defeat of Japan through the use of air power alone now presented itself as a possibility.[7]

It was for reasons of maintaining Soviet-American cooperation in the postwar world that FDR also invited Edward Flynn to Yalta. The president was keenly aware that the greatest opposition among the American public to Soviet-American cooperation after the war came from the Roman Catholic Church. After all, the Catholic Church put up the strongest objections to his decision to recognize the Soviet Union in 1933—objections that FDR was able to counter by including a clause in the recognition agreement between Moscow and Washington regarding the extension of religious freedom to foreigners in Russia (that is, Roman Catholics). FDR hoped that Flynn's current mission to secure the Freedom of Worship in Poland and the other parts of Eastern Europe that were bound to come under Soviet control after the war would help to placate American Catholic opinion. Instructing Flynn to continue on to Moscow and Rome after the conference, FDR even entertained the hope that he might be able to effect a rapprochement between the Kremlin and the staunchly anti-communist Holy See. Flynn would soon discover that this effort was in vain. The Soviets largely ignored his attempts to sign an agreement guaranteeing religious freedom in areas under their control. Nor was he any more successful in his conversations with Pope Pius XII. His Holiness, in fact, proved staunchly uncompromising in his attitude toward the Soviet regime and was nearly as hostile toward the Charter of the United Nations, which by April 1945 had been characterized by the Holy See as essentially nothing more than "an alliance among the Great Powers."[8]

FDR was well aware of the many challenges associated with attempting to cooperate with the Soviet Union, but this did not dissuade him from trying. Indeed, his approach to Stalin in 1945 was entirely consistent with his thinking on this question in 1933. At that time, his decision to recognize Soviet Russia was based largely on the notion that Soviet-American cooperation would serve as a counterweight to Japanese power in Asia. And while it is true that this first attempt to establish a Soviet-American power-bloc in opposition to Japan failed, the final defeat of Japan presented a second opportunity for the president to pursue this goal, which had taken on new importance given the relative weakness of China. More critically, the Cold War had not yet started, and even though both sides in the Soviet-American divide harbored certain strong suspicions about the other, FDR's forward-thinking geopolitical considerations in pursuit of Soviet-American cooperation had as much to do with his desire to counter British imperialism as with the need to maintain a strong front against Japan. FDR understood that there were certain "elements among the British, who, out of imperial considerations, desire a weak and disunited China in the post-war period." Viewed from this perspective, his conversations with Stalin on the Far East at Yalta represented an effort to enlist Soviet support for what were essentially American interests in the Pacific region after the war.[9]

Having sketched out his thinking about postwar Asia, FDR suggested that the United States, the Soviet Union, and China should manage the trusteeship of Korea. The president estimated that this would lead to full independence within a period of twenty-five to thirty years—a time frame significantly shorter that the fifty years first articulated in the Cairo Declaration of 1943. He also insisted that there should be no British participation in this effort, to which Stalin wryly responded by saying "Churchill will kill us." And FDR made it clear that he fully expected to establish a trusteeship in Indochina and had no interest "in giving it back to the French" as preferred by the

British, undoubtedly out of the latter's concern for the "implications" this might have for their control over Burma.[10]

Much like FDR's conversation with Arthur Bliss Lane at the end of November over the future of Poland, his conversation with Stalin over the future role of the Soviet Union and the United States in Asia had major import. His observation that France "had done nothing" to improve the lot of the native population indicates that FDR continued to view colonialism as a form of shameless exploitation. Moreover, even though FDR still insisted, though less strenuously, that he favored "international" as opposed to "national" trusteeships, his determination that "we must find a formula to resolve the relations between the White and Yellow races"—one that would ultimately lead to independence for peoples in the Far East—remained steadfast.[11]

Hence, there was a parallel between, on the one hand, Stalin's use of the German threat as a means to secure Anglo-American acquiescence over Poland and, on the other, FDR's hope to use the threat of a resurgent Japan as a means of fostering Soviet support for his efforts to establish a unified China, maintain postwar security in Asia, and bring an end to the bankrupt system of imperialism in the Far East. As FDR observed while bringing the conversation to a close, he had been trying to keep "China alive" for some time, not an easy task given the dissension between the Nationalist government "and the so-called communists." FDR allowed that the greater fault lay with the Nationalists. Still, the president was optimistic that he would be able to bring the two sides together now that he had established new American leadership in China under Ambassador Patrick Hurley and General Albert Wedemeyer.

Stalin concurred, noting that "there were some good people in the Kuomintang [and] he did not understand why they were not brought forward." Echoing FDR, he said that "he did not understand why they did not get together" to form a "united front" against Japan under Chiang's leadership. Stalin's reference to a "united front" was exactly the sort of comment FDR was looking for—an indication not only that the American and Soviet leaders understood each other but also that Soviet support for the American agenda in China and the Far East was possible. FDR must have felt a great deal of satisfaction as the two men finished this amicable tête-à-tête before entering what turned out to be the most difficult meeting of the entire conference.[12]

THE PLENARY SESSION THAT TOOK PLACE AT THE YALTA CONFERENCE on Thursday, February 8, 1945, was marked by a sharp contrast between the relatively agreeable opening discussions on the world organization and the angry stalemate that emerged over Poland. Owing to FDR's decision to accept the Soviet request for the addition of the two Soviet Republics in the General Assembly, Anthony Eden, who was tasked with giving the Foreign Ministers report that day, confirmed that a mutual understanding on the world organization had been reached. He also announced that he and his two Russian and American counterparts, Foreign Ministers Molotov and Stettinius, had agreed that the historic conference to draft the UN Charter would open in San Francisco on April 25, 1945.

FDR—mindful of the risk of waiting until war's end to convert the wartime cooperation of the "United Nations Alliance" into a long-term commitment to cooperation in the form of the new "United Nations Organization"—was delighted by this outcome, even though the conference would not open in March, as he had originally desired. Organizing a major international gathering in a mere two and a half months would be no small task. The first matter to be dealt with concerned which nations would be invited. As Eden explained, and as was widely understood by the three parties, the initial delegation to the San Francisco conference would include representatives from each of the states that had signed the "Declaration of United Nations"—in essence, a declaration of war—that FDR had crafted on January 1, 1942. As of February 8, 1945, the list of signatories included a total of thirty-seven states.[13]

A point of contention quickly arose, however, when Stalin remarked that ten of the countries represented in the Declaration of United Nations had no diplomatic relations with the USSR. FDR, who was perhaps overly optimistic about the prospects of the Flynn mission, brushed aside this concern, maintaining that he was quite sure most of these states wanted to establish relations with the USSR but had simply not got around to doing so. It was only in those countries "where the influence of the Roman Catholic Church was very strong," the president said, that there was any real reluctance to move ahead with recognition.[14]

The three leaders then turned to the question of whether an invitation should be extended to a number of other states, including many of the Latin American Republics, that had assisted in the war effort but had not yet signed the declaration. After a good deal of discussion, led largely by FDR, it was agreed that only those countries that had declared war against the Axis by March 1, 1945, would be invited; that former enemy states, such as Italy, would not be; and that the addition of Byelorussia and Ukraine to the General Assembly would not occur immediately, as Stalin proposed, but would be put before the conference for a vote; the full support of both Great Britain and the United States would virtually guarantee their admittance to the body.[15]

By proposing this process for the two Soviet Republics, FDR was seeking political cover, a means by which he might counter domestic criticism that he had abandoned the one-nation-one-vote principle. It would not be long, however, before he began to have second thoughts. A number of his senior advisers, including Leahy, Byrnes, and Hopkins, had not yet heard that FDR planned to support the Soviets on this matter. After the plenary, all of them voiced their objections, highlighting the possibility that FDR's decision might be used by isolationists in the US Congress to argue against American participation in the United Nations. Accordingly, FDR wrote a letter to Stalin asking the Soviet leader if the latter would object to the possibility of the Americans being granted an additional two seats in the Assembly (represented by two American states). Neither Stalin nor Churchill (who was also consulted) voiced an objection, and so FDR would return to the United States with this understanding—one that he kept secret for the time being.

That decided, the delegations returned to the thorny issue of Poland, which quickly devolved into an acrimonious standoff. In response to the counterproposals circulated by the British and the Americans earlier, Stalin and Molotov made quite clear that they would not accept any proposal involving the creation of a new provisional government, in any guise. They explained that the most they would accept was an expansion of the current Lublin/Warsaw regime, as put forward by Molotov in his six-point proposal. This led to a heated exchange between Churchill and Stalin, with the former declaring that, according to British sources, the Lublin government did not command the support of the vast majority of the Polish people. If the British were to "brush away" their support for the London Polish government under such circumstances, Churchill said, he would be denounced at home and "there would be a world outcry."[16]

In response, Stalin demanded to know why the Allies were willing to extend recognition to de Gaulle's provisional government, which was not elected, and yet were not able to do the same for the Lublin Poles, whom, he insisted—in a direct challenge to Churchill—had the enthusiastic support of the Polish people. Churchill all but scoffed at this notion, although he did admit that it was hard to gain a complete picture of what was happening in Poland—a comment that Stalin shrewdly rebuffed by noting how little the Soviets knew about events in Greece.

The vehemence with which the Soviets insisted that they would not agree to the formation of an entirely new government effectively meant that the two sides had reached an impasse.

In the moment, FDR decided there was no point in allowing this contentious debate to continue. Exercising his prerogative as chair, he shifted the discussion away from the makeup of the Polish provisional government and toward the question of elections. This proved to be a fateful move. Given that the Soviets, when pressed, said that a general election might take place in as little as thirty days, it appeared that the only remaining problem, the president remarked, was how Poland would be governed between now and the time of the election. Although FDR stopped short of saying it, implicit in this observation was the fact that the makeup of the interim Polish Provisional government was perhaps not as important as the democratic nature of the elections to follow, particularly if it was to be in power for such a short time. This opened up a whole new avenue of discussion about how the Allies might arrive at a solution to the Polish problem. FDR's comments and questions at this critical juncture also indicate that his worn appearance belied the sharp workings of his mind. He clearly desired a solution that would allow all three powers to move beyond the interminable discussions over Poland toward what he viewed as the far more important task of setting up the world organization. But in light of the tensions in the room, he thought it best to bring the plenary to a close and ended the meeting with the familiar suggestion that the matter of the Polish elections be turned over to the three foreign ministers.[17]

THE SESSION OVER, FDR PREPARED FOR A FORMAL DINNER HOSTED BY Stalin and the Soviet delegation. The president could take satisfaction in the fact that after five arduous days, he had achieved two of his three critical objectives—settling the outstanding issues blocking the establishment of the United Nations Organization and securing Soviet participation in the war against Japan. These were no small accomplishments. The breakthrough on the UNO was universally embraced, while Admiral Leahy remarked that the Russian agreement to declare war on Japan "was worth the whole trip."[18] But the difficulties over Poland continued to worry FDR as he was wheeled to the waiting car that would take him and Anna to the banquet that Marshal Stalin would host at the Yusupov Palace.

Like many previous dinners at Yalta, this one was largely a social affair, highlighted, on this occasion, by the presence of "the three ladies," Anna, Sarah Churchill, and Kathleen Harriman. After the afternoon's tensions, perhaps the most significant aspect of the soiree was the unexpected warmth with which Marshal Stalin toasted Winston Churchill, whom he saluted as the "bravest figure in the world," given the "courage and stanchness" he showed as England stood alone against Hitler.[19]

Clearly moved, and not to be outdone, Churchill reciprocated by raising a glass to Marshal Stalin, "the mighty leader of a mighty country that absorbed the full shock of the German war machine, had broken its back, and had driven the tyrants from her soil."[20] The two men then "rose to such heights of oratory" that their interpreters struggled to find adequate expressions in their respective languages. This fact apparently did not go unnoticed by Stalin, who, at one point in the evening, stood up with glass in hand to say: "Tonight, and on other occasions, we three leaders have got together. We talk, we eat and drink, and we enjoy ourselves. But meanwhile our three interpreters have to work, and their work is not easy. They have no time to eat or drink. We rely on them to transmit our ideas to each other. I propose a toast to our interpreters!" He then left the table to clink glasses with each of the three men in turn, while Churchill exclaimed to uproarious laugher: "Interpreters of the world unite! You have nothing to lose but your audience!"[21]

At this point Stalin proposed a toast to the president of the United States, whose nation "had been the chief forger of the instruments which had led to the mobilization of the world against Hitler." FDR responded by offering a toast to the family-like atmosphere that existed among the three of them, and to the hope that through the cooperation of the three powers gathered around the table they could "meet their objectives . . . to give every man, woman and child on this earth the possibility of security and well-being."[22] Stalin concurred, observing that "it was not so difficult to keep unity in time of war," when there was a "joint aim to defeat a common enemy." The more difficult task, he said, "came after the war when diverse interests tended to divide the allies." But he was "confident that the allies would meet this test," and that "their relations in peacetime would be as strong as they had been in war."[23]

All in all it was, as Stettinius later recalled, the most cordial of evenings, and perhaps the most important dinner of the entire conference. Kathleen Harriman was certainly in agreement, noting "that she had never seen Stalin in such great form."

FDR, however, had remained unusually quiet for most of the occasion. It was true, as he had said in his toast, that the three powers had come a long way and could accomplish a great deal if they continued to cooperate. But they had been arguing over Poland for three full days and, only hours before, had very nearly come to an open breach over the issue. The protracted discussions over Poland were clearly taking a toll on FDR's health. When he returned to the Livadia Palace at 1:00 a.m., Dr. Bruenn found him in a miserable state, gray in color and "greatly fatigued," after what FDR described as an "emotionally disturbing" session that had left him "worried and upset about the trend of the discussions . . . [over] Poland." Bruenn determined that the president was suffering from *pulsus alternans,* a condition that can indicate severe ventricular failure. He insisted that FDR's "hours of activity" be "rigidly controlled." This meant at least an hour of rest every afternoon before the start of the plenary sessions and no visitors allowed before noon—an order that FDR agreed to but that he would violate first thing the next morning.[24]

Chapter 9

The Final Turn

BECAUSE THERE WERE NO ELEVATORS IN THE LIVADIA PALACE, FDR spent the entire week of the Yalta summit on the ground floor of the building. Isolated in his suite of rooms, and focused on his own efforts to prepare for the daily plenary sessions, or to meet with his aides, the president was largely unaware of the comings and goings of the dozens of military aides and State Department personnel who inhabited the upper floors of the palace and whose job it was to ensure that the conference ran smoothly. Over the first few days of the summit, the consensus among much of the staff, including Ambassador Harriman's personal assistant, Robert Meiklejohn, was that the administrative side of the conference was functioning extremely well—much better, in fact, than it had at Tehran. It was Meiklejohn's responsibility to oversee the transcription of the various "unofficial" notes taken by FDR's interpreter, Charles Bohlen, and two other members of the State Department staff, into an official record for the president and secretary of state. Although Meiklejohn and his assistants had to put in long hours, they were pleased that they found themselves able to keep up with the work—that is, until the morning of Friday, February 9, when "all hell started popping," as the meetings got longer and more frequent, and the notes began to fall farther and farther behind.[1]

Much of this frenzied activity could be attributed to the intense negotiations over Poland, which by this point had already absorbed more attention than any of the other issues discussed at Yalta. This lack of progress—what Anna termed "one of the many worrisome things attached to this trip" in a letter she wrote to her husband that day—was clearly troubling FDR, who by this point had decided that it was time to take a different tack and make explicit what he had alluded to the day before: that the discussions over Poland should shift away from the exact makeup of the interim regime and toward the proposed elections that would follow.

This move had two important consequences. First, it expanded the time frame in which the three powers might achieve a final settlement of the "Polish question." Both Churchill and Roosevelt had in fact traveled to Yalta under the expectation that they might be able to establish a new provisional government for Poland while the conference was still in session. Hence, each delegation arrived in the Crimean peninsula with a list of possible candidates to be included in the new regime. After achieving this goal, both governments assumed that they would then be able to recognize the new authority and send ambassadors and/or observers to Warsaw to oversee the transition via the electoral process from a provisional to a permanent government. Neither man was so naïve as to think that the Poland born out of this process would stand as a shining example of democracy, or that the nation would not fall under the sway of a degree of Soviet influence. But each hoped that the government that would emerge would be stable, reasonably democratic, and willing to accept—as Eduard Benes had been—the reality of Soviet power. Most important, such an arrangement would provide an example of Soviet good faith that Churchill and Roosevelt could then point to upon their departure from Yalta.

The second consequence of FDR's decision to stress the importance of the coming elections—and in essence abandon all hope of establishing a provisional government while the Yalta conference was in session—is that it rendered the composition of whatever authority would be in power in the intervening period less important. This made the earlier Soviet proposal for the "expansion" of the existing Lublin regime, which up to this point FDR had rejected, much more palatable—so long as language could be found to ensure that the end result would meet the expectations of American public opinion. It was with this in mind that FDR instructed Stettinius in their session that morning to draft a new proposal that the secretary could then present to his counterparts at the noon meeting of the foreign ministers. Using the six-point plan that Molotov had presented earlier as the basis for an agreement, the new formula called for the existing Lublin government not to be "expanded" but "reorganized into a fully representative government based on all democratic forces in Poland and including democratic leaders from Poland abroad." It also stipulated that the existing regime, which the Soviets referred to as the "Provisional Government of the Republic of Poland," should change its name to the "Provisional Government of National Unity." The primary task of the provisional government would be to hold free elections as soon as possible. FDR also agreed that since it would take a minimum of thirty days to organize the elections, the required reorganization would not take place immediately, at Yalta, but instead, as suggested by Molotov the day before, would be handled by a committee in Moscow composed of Soviet Foreign Minister Molotov, British Ambassador Archibald Clark-Kerr, and American Ambassador W. Averill Harriman.[2]

FDR's decision to postpone a full and final settlement of the Polish question during the conference—or even to come to an agreement about which Poles should be called upon to orchestrate the reorganization—would turn out to be the most important decision he made on Poland at Yalta. The creation of the Moscow committee provided the Soviets with an excellent mechanism to delay, stall, and obfuscate the exact makeup of the "reorganized regime." This in turn made it impossible for either the British or the American government to extend recognition and, hence, send their respective ambassadors to Warsaw to oversee the proposed elections—in essence leaving the Polish question unresolved during the critical months to follow.

Nor did Roosevelt's new approach come as welcome news to Churchill and Eden. Indeed, as Eden explained at the Foreign Ministers meeting at noon that day when Stettinius presented the plan, the British had not given up their preference for a new interim regime. After all, at some point the British government would have to transfer recognition from the London Poles (whom they had had relations with since the very start of the war) to a new Polish government. It would be much easier for the British government to do so if they were transferring recognition to an entirely new authority, not to an expansion of the present one. Furthermore, even though Eden supported the American call for free and fair elections, he remained convinced that if the proposed elections were controlled by the Lublin government, which, he implied, was an obvious risk under FDR's new proposal, "they would not be free . . . or represent the will of the Polish people."[3]

Molotov was certainly pleased at the direction in which the talks were heading. But other than pointing out to Eden the advantages that would accrue from the expansion of the Lublin regime—which he characterized as a much more efficient means to get to the elections as soon as possible—he made no comment on the new proposal. Instead, he asked to have it translated so that he could study Stettinius's new formula before the start of the plenary session later that afternoon.

In the meantime, FDR and Churchill held a last meeting with the Combined Chiefs of Staff, followed by a luncheon where the main focus of conversation between the two leaders was on the voting procedure for the United Nations General Assembly. FDR also made reference to his anticipated departure in two days' time—a fact that Churchill would find more and more disconcerting as the day wore on.[4]

It was in the midst of all this frenetic activity that Churchill, Roosevelt, and Stalin gathered at just before 4:00 p.m. in the Italianate courtyard of the Livadia Palace for the renowned photo session that would immortalize this most famous of all the wartime conferences. In preparation for the shoot, three chairs were carefully placed on a series of oriental carpets laid at one end of the courtyard, while a throng of Soviet cameramen jostled for position at the other—accompanied by Robert Hopkins, the sole American photographer, whose father, Harry Hopkins, remained in bed. As at Tehran, FDR took the middle seat, Stalin sat on the left, and Churchill, who arrived after his two counterparts wearing a Russian fur cap and smoking one of his ever-present cigars, took the seat to the president's right. FDR was unable to rise to greet the prime minister but seemed to take great delight in Churchill's headgear, as the latter, perhaps in deference to FDR's senior position within the Alliance, or perhaps as a means of drawing attention away from FDR's disability, stood at attention and saluted the president, while Stalin jumped to his feet to extend his hand.

As Robert Hopkins later reported, the mood among the three leaders and their advisers in the courtyard that overcast afternoon seemed upbeat. Perhaps this stemmed from the historic nature of the occasion, or from the relief all three delegations felt at having a moment to put aside the remaining issues, while they milled about the courtyard, just moments before they would resume their efforts to finally come to an agreement over the Polish problem.[5]

The "Big Three" with Foreign Ministers Eden, Stettinius, and Molotov in the background, Livadia Palace, February 9, 1945. (Courtesy of the Franklin D. Roosevelt Presidential Library)

As the sixth plenary session got under way, it was clear that the American position on the Polish question was now closer to that of the Russians than that of the British. Not surprisingly, Churchill, who, like FDR, remained deeply concerned about British public opinion, found this tremendously frustrating. In a veiled reference to FDR's stated intention to leave the conference in two days' time—and perhaps thinking of his admonition to Roosevelt in January that the five to six days he had allotted for the conference were inadequate— Churchill noted that despite their desire "to put a foot in the stirrup and be off . . . [w]e could not allow the settlement of these matters to be hurried, and the fruits of the conference lost, for the lack of another twenty-four hours." He added that "[a] great prize was in view" and "these might well be among the most important days of the lives of those present." FDR concurred on the importance of the moment, but, in his view, because Poland remained an "urgent, immediate, and painful problem" driving the three parties apart, the sooner they could put the Polish problem behind them, the better.[6]

Delighted at FDR's change of heart, Stalin and Molotov presented only three small but still significant amendments to FDR's counterproposal. These were in keeping with their aim to ensure that the reorganized Lublin regime—not to mention the final government that would be put in place following the elections—would include Polish politicians prepared to accept the Curzon Line and willing to work with the Soviets and their communist allies. Unwilling to admit that the Lublin Poles did not enjoy the support of the Polish people, the Soviets requested that the phrase setting forth that the existing regime would be reorganized "into a fully representative government based on all democratic forces in Poland" be changed to "reorganized on a broader democratic basis." Molotov also requested the addition of the phrase "non-fascist and anti-fascist" to the reference to democratic parties as well as the elimination of the requirement that the three powers' ambassadors be "charged with the responsibility of observing and reporting . . . on the free and unfettered elections." The reference to the ambassadors, Molotov argued, would insult the Poles, and was unnecessary in any case, since reporting to their superiors at home was one of their normal functions.[7]

Arriving at an agreement on the final language proved no easy task. By this point, Churchill and Eden recognized that they had no choice but to fall in behind FDR's new plan. But they stood fast on the final wording regarding the composition of the "reorganized" Polish government and the requirement that the ambassadors be specifically tasked with observing the elections. As a result, there would be no settlement of the question on February 9, even though the three foreign ministers, at the request of FDR, met for a special late-night session at 10:30 p.m. in search of one.[8]

The inability of the three foreign ministers to reach a late-night accord (Eden would not arrive back at the Vorontzov Palace until 2:00 a.m.) meant that on the second-to-last day of the conference, Saturday, February 10, FDR would once again find himself engaged in an intense mid-morning meeting with Secretary Stettinius on the subject of Poland. At issue was the last sentence of FDR's protocol, with its specific reference to the requirement that the three ambassadors observe and report on the elections. No longer willing to risk the possibility of an

impasse, particularly in light of his impending departure, FDR decided
to withdraw this reference, but only on the condition that Stettinius
make it eminently clear that even though he had granted this concession, "the Russians . . . must understand our firm determination that
the Ambassadors will observe and report on the election in any case."[9]
Unhappy with FDR's decision, Eden and Churchill insisted in the subsequent plenary session that rather than remove any mention of reporting altogether, the sentence should at least indicate that the recognition
of the newly reorganized government would be accompanied by an
exchange of ambassadors "by whose reports the respective governments
will be kept informed about the situation in Poland." This would signify
that the British and American governments fully expected to be able
to report on the degree to which the agreements on Poland achieved
at Yalta were being followed. After further debate, the Soviets finally
agreed to these last emendations, which cleared the way for the three
parties to arrive at an agreement over how to settle the Polish problem.

In a concession to Churchill, the final declaration stated at the
outset that because the Red Army had liberated the country, "a new
situation existed in Poland"—an acknowledgment that in spite of
Whitehall's long-standing relationship with the London Poles, there
was very little the British could do to shape developments in Poland.
The declaration also called for the reorganization of the existing
Lublin/Warsaw regime "on a broader democratic basis" and for the
holding of "free and unfettered elections as soon as possible on the
basis of universal suffrage and secret ballot." But there were no strict
enforcement mechanisms, and because the selection of the proposed
candidates to make up the new regime depended on the subsequent
deliberations in Moscow, the Anglo-Americans had little power to
enforce these provisions.[10]

As Charles Bohlen observed, the overall intent of the plan—which
was designed to promote free elections and ensure that the government that emerged from this process was reasonably democratic—
is clear. But as he later admitted, its terms were not specific enough
and it bore the hallmarks of "hasty drafting." The Soviets approached
the wording of the final agreement with intense scrutiny; to them,
"even the last comma had meaning." But the Western Allies left
much of the language intentionally vague, and, as a consequence, the
Anglo-Americans would find their ambitions in Poland frustrated.

The agreement makes no mention, for example, of the exact number of non-Lublin Poles to be included in the provisional government, and unlike the proposals circulated earlier in the week, there is no reference to potential candidates or to the inclusion of representatives from specific Polish political parties.[11]

In the months and years following Yalta, FDR would come under heavy criticism for the decisions he made over the critical twenty-four-hour period from February 9 to February 10, 1945. The limited agreement he achieved on the Polish question—particularly in light of Soviet behavior in subsequent weeks and months—would increasingly be seen as tantamount to a sellout, and his call for free and unfettered elections as little more than a desperate attempt to paper over the harsh reality of the Soviet domination of the Polish people. In seeking an explanation for this turn of events, some of his contemporaries and later historians would speculate that FDR's health was to blame, or that his Russian adversaries had duped him.

But as FDR's forceful directions and instructions to Stettinius over these two days make clear, FDR was not only engaged but in charge. He made the decision to relent to the Soviet call for the expansion of the existing Lublin regime, and thus shifted the focus of the attention toward the proposed elections. FDR also agreed to the Soviet proposal to abandon any attempt to establish or at the very least select the Polish candidates involved in the proposed provisional government while the conference was still in session. These facts belie the notion that FDR was not in control of his faculties at Yalta. They also render him responsible for much of what took place.

Yet FDR's apparent acquiescence on the Polish question cannot be understood outside the context of his overall foreign policy agenda. This may have been small comfort to the Poles and the other peoples of Eastern Europe, but FDR never took his eye off the larger prize: the creation of the United Nations and maintenance of Great Power cooperation. While he hoped to be able to achieve an agreement with the Russians that would allow the Poles, like the Czechs, a measure of independence from Moscow, he had no intention either before, during, or after Yalta of allowing the Polish question to undermine his broader ambitions.

Nor should his decision to follow this approach at Yalta be viewed as an abrupt departure from his earlier stance on the Polish question.

On the contrary, it was entirely consistent with his earlier efforts to orchestrate some sort of rapprochement among the communist and noncommunist Poles and Moscow. As he said to British Ambassador Halifax in a conversation the two of them held in early January, just after the news broke that the Soviet government had recognized the Lublin Poles, the only sensible thing to do now was to convince Mikolajczyk (who remained FDR's preferred representative of the non-Lublin Poles) "to join up with the Lublin party and form a single government." Indeed, "all Poles must be brought to see that they could only exist by the good favor of Stalin. Benes had been wise enough to see this and had therefore managed to get along very well."[12]

It is also important to note the underlying assumptions upon which the Yalta accords were based. The first is that maintaining cooperation with the Soviet Union was regarded as a military imperative among FDR's senior military advisers. In the wake of the Ardennes crisis, no one in Washington believed that the final defeat of Germany was going to be easy—and based on American experiences in the Pacific, victory over Japan was going to be an equally daunting task. Second, both Churchill and Roosevelt felt that Stalin was a man with whom they could do business. The point here is not that negotiating with the Soviets was easy but, rather, that once an agreement had been reached, both Churchill and Roosevelt anticipated that the Soviets would work toward its reasonable fulfillment. As Churchill remarked to one of his aides less than two weeks after the Yalta conference: "Poor Neville Chamberlain believed he could trust Hitler. He was wrong. But I don't think I am wrong about Stalin."[13] A second important assumption was that Stalin had more or less abandoned the Bolshevik ideology of world revolution in favor of a more pragmatic form of socialism that was focused on internal development. Stalin's "Socialism in One Country" was one manifestation of this trend; another was his much-noticed decision to close the Comintern in May 1943, a move that was interpreted in the West as a clear sign that international cooperation rather than class war had become the Soviet method for securing the peace. Overall, these moves, especially when coupled with Stalin's promotion of the "Great Patriotic War" in the fall of 1943, made him seem more the heir of Peter the Great than of Vladimir Lenin, and the Soviet state as something akin to traditional continental power.[14]

Left unsaid, but clearly evident at Yalta and in the October 1944 percentages agreement that Churchill negotiated with Stalin, was a fourth assumption: that both FDR and Churchill were quite willing to grant the Soviet Union what is traditionally called "a sphere of influence" in Eastern Europe. FDR was of course loath to use this phrase, as it was often derided in the American press and in official Washington circles as another term for imperialism. Where the three leaders fell out is over the definition of the phrase. Roosevelt's interpretation of this concept was more akin to the so-called Open Door policy that the United States pursued in China. As such, Poland and Eastern Europe might fall under a Soviet sphere of influence, particularly in matters of security, but Soviet control would not be exclusive; it would be an open sphere, reasonably accessible to a degree of American trade and ideas. Churchill more or less concurred with this view, so long as these concepts did not interfere with his own government's ascendency in areas he regarded as falling under British influence. Stalin's paranoia and obsession with security militated against these notions, however. He was never able to rid himself of the fear that the Anglo-Americans might sign a separate peace with Hitler— best exemplified in his mind by what he saw as the Anglo-American delay in opening a second front. Having survived three and a half brutal years of war and turned the Nazi tide on its own, he firmly believed that the Soviet Union must provide for its own postwar security—and the biggest threat to that security remained Germany.[15] His failure to obtain a firm allied commitment to the breakup of the German state after the war, particularly when coupled with the knowledge that the United States was determined *not* to maintain a long-term military presence in Europe, rendered a compliant Poland, as he said to Churchill, a matter of national preservation.

The final assumption that must be taken into account if we are to understand the full dimensions of FDR's decision-making is perhaps best captured in his response to Admiral Leahy's famous remark that the agreement over Poland was so elastic "that the Russians could stretch it all the way from Moscow to Washington without ever breaking it." "I know Bill," FDR replied, "but it is the best I could do for Poland *at this time*."[16] As this remark indicates, FDR saw Yalta as but one step in a much longer process that he expected to continue in the months and years ahead. That FDR remained focused on his long-term objectives becomes even clearer when we consider that it was just when the discussions over Poland were reaching their climax that he introduced the Declaration of Liberated Europe. This proclamation, much like the statement on Poland, has been dismissed as a laudable but largely ineffectual edict that, owing to Soviet modifications at Yalta, could not enforce its major claim to guarantee "the right of all people to choose the form of government under which they will live." But much like the Atlantic Charter (which is mentioned not once but twice in the document), the Declaration of Liberated Europe was viewed by FDR as an inspirational promulgation—as an attempt to "frame the issues." As he put it to the Soviet premier during the plenary session that took place on the afternoon of Friday, February 9, 1945, he regarded the elections in Poland as the "first example" of how the Declaration of Liberated Europe would operate. "I want this election in Poland . . . to be beyond question," he said. "I don't want the Poles to be able to question [it]. The matter is not only one of principle, but also of practical politics."[17] He also cautioned his Russian colleagues that when it came to subsequent events in Poland, Stettinius would "feel free to make any statement he felt necessary relative to the fact that the American Ambassador would investigate and report to him about the conduct of the elections."[18]

FDR and Stettinius next brought up the highly sensitive issue of trusteeships, a firm indication that the president was concerned with more than just keeping future Soviet conduct within the frame of the Declaration. Churchill exploded in a "white heat" at this, insisting that the provisions in the Declaration of Liberated Europe referring to the Atlantic Charter did not apply to the British Empire. This had been the understanding that he and FDR had agreed to in August 1941, when the Charter was first drafted, and that he had articulated later in the House of Commons. Churchill added that he had reiterated all of this to Wendell Willkie during the latter's last visit to London, before Willkie suddenly died of a heart attack—to which FDR sardonically replied, to much laughter, "Was that what killed him?"[19]

Stettinius elaborated, in response, that neither the Declaration nor the proposal to open a discussion of trusteeships among the five permanent members of the Security Council in advance of the San Francisco meeting was meant to infringe upon the prerogatives of the British Empire. This was not exactly true. To FDR, Yalta was not fundamentally about the divisions of East and West—as it is so often interpreted today—but rather about the emergence of the "new world" in place of the "old." Indeed, FDR's hostility toward colonialism was at least as strong as his antipathy toward Soviet totalitarianism. And based on the assumptions that he and many of his colleagues held about the nature of the Soviet state, he viewed the USSR as essentially a continental power that, unlike its European neighbors, did not have colonial ambitions. Thus FDR saw Russia as a potential partner in his drive to build a "new world," a belief that inspired not only his negotiations with Stalin over Russia's role in the final stages of the war against Japan but also his approach to questions about postwar Europe.[20]

FDR's ultimate goal was to rally world opinion around a universal set of values supported by a universalist organization that would spell the end of colonialism and the eventual rise of democratic states in Eastern Europe, Asia, and other parts of the world. FDR was no fool. He understood that much would depend on the degree to which the Soviets and the British adhered to the understandings achieved at Yalta. But he also saw that if he did not affix a reiteration of the values articulated in the Four Freedoms and the Atlantic Charter to the overall purposes of the Yalta conference, the people of the United States—and much of the rest of the world—might lose faith in the grand purposes for which they had sacrificed so much over six long years of war.

THANKS TO FDR'S IMPENDING DEPARTURE, AND TO THE PROTRACTED discussions over Poland that had consumed so much of the delegations' time and energy, both Churchill and Stalin felt a certain sense of urgency as attention was finally directed to other matters at the plenary session that continued on the afternoon of Saturday, February 10. As was obvious to all concerned, it would be impossible to both deal with the number of issues still left on the table and draft the final conference communiqué in the hours that remained. Yet FDR remained adamant that he must leave by 3:00 p.m. the next day. One solution, suggested by Stalin, was to cancel the dinner that Churchill had planned for that evening so that the three leaders could continue working. Another, far more agreeable, was to set up an immediate committee of senior aides who would draw up a draft communiqué that would then be presented to the three leaders at 10:00 that evening. After some discussion, the latter solution was adopted. In addition, FDR agreed to hold an extra plenary session at noon the next day, followed by a luncheon that he would host.[21]

Having determined the schedule for the next twenty-four hours, the three leaders then pressed ahead with their discussions on the remaining issues that required either agreement or, at the very least, further deliberation. These included the final draft of the protocol that FDR and Stalin had negotiated over the Soviet entry into the war against Japan, an inconclusive discussion on oil concessions and the withdrawal of Allied troops from Iran, an attempt by Churchill to secure a more concrete understanding with Stalin on Yugoslavia, and the question of reparations.[22]

In the end, only the first issue would reach the status of a full agreement. As expected, the United States agreed to support Stalin's territorial claims in the Far East, while Stalin expressed his willingness to sign "a pact of friendship and alliance" with the Nationalist government of China. Stalin also agreed to render assistance in its efforts to liberate the country from Japan. FDR was tasked with the responsibility of securing the concurrence of Chiang Kai-shek, who, for the time being, would have to be kept in the dark given the military necessity of keeping the Russian decision to declare war on Japan secret.

Ironically, given all of the attention the issue had received during the Foreign Ministers meetings, the reparations question dragged on until virtually the last minute of the conference. At issue was the exact figure. Over the course of the week, the Soviets provided evidence to support their claim for $10 billion out of a total of $20 billion to be extracted from Germany. But the British continued to refuse to endorse a specific number. When Churchill said as much in the plenary meeting that day, an enraged Stalin rose from his chair and said with great emphasis, "If the British felt that the Russians should receive no reparations at all they should say so." Churchill empathically denied that this was the case.[23]

This deadlock was broken at the formal dinner hosted by Churchill that night, when the prime minister suddenly agreed to accept a proposal that Stalin had put forward that afternoon. It entailed, first, that the parties should agree in principle that Germany should pay reparations and, second, that the Reparations Commission that was to be established in Moscow should determine the final amount, using $20 billion as the basis for discussion, with 50 percent of the final determination going to the Soviet Union.[24] Having achieved a compromise, the three leaders enjoyed a more harmonious final dinner at the Yalta conference. As usual, there were many toasts and much good cheer. FDR seemed to take special delight in ribbing Churchill about the president's impending trip to the Middle East to see the kings of Egypt, Ethiopia, and Saudi Arabia. But as the evening wore on, Churchill could not help but notice that FDR looked quite tired.

THE FINAL MORNING OF FDR'S FINAL SUMMIT SAW THE RETURN OF the sun over the Crimea, or what the Russians by this point were calling "Roosevelt weather." Following breakfast, FDR and Anna managed to get in some last-minute sightseeing, taking a thirty-minute tour of the palace grounds in an open jeep so that FDR could observe the remarkable gardens, always a matter of deep interest to him. They then returned to the Livadia for the final plenary meeting and luncheon of the Yalta conference.

Both the meeting and the meal were held in the president's dining room, and the two more or less merged into one long session. The focus was on the wording of the final communiqué that would be released after the conference. Most of the changes made during this session were stylistic, including Churchill's insistence that the word *joint* be struck from the text at every turn—as in England it would invariably raise the specter of "the Sunday family roast of mutton."[25]

Finally, at 3:45 that afternoon, the communiqué was done. FDR, Churchill, and Stalin turned over the edited draft to the three foreign ministers and their staffs for polishing and release. The three leaders also provided their signatures on three blank sheets of paper, so that these could be affixed to the final document.[26]

After the formal adjournment, FDR bade farewell to Churchill, who left the Livadia immediately. He then took a few moments to thank Stalin again for his hospitality, and to present the Soviet leader with Legion of Merit medals awarded by the government of the United States to senior members of the Russian military. Stalin reciprocated with a series of gifts and packages for the president and his party, including several types of wine and champagne, caviar, butter, oranges, tangerines, and, of course, much vodka.

With that, the two men shook hands one last time, and less than ten minutes after Stalin had taken his leave, FDR was wheeled out to a waiting car, to be driven along the coast of the Black Sea for the last time. The Yalta conference was over. It was time now for FDR to journey to Egypt and his much-anticipated rendezvous with the "three kings."

Chapter 10

The Last Mission

THE CITY OF SEVASTOPOL, WHICH LIES SOME EIGHTY MILES TO THE west of Yalta, earned much of its fame during a siege that took place at the height of the Crimean War in the mid-nineteenth century. As was the case with Valletta, on Malta, World War II brought a second great siege to Sevastopol, as German forces in their initial drive to conquer Russia swept across the Ukraine and into the Crimea in the fall of 1941. By mid-November the entire peninsula, with the exception of the city, was in German hands.

Owing to Sevastopol's strategic significance as an important naval base and as the headquarters of Russia's Black Sea Fleet, leaving it under the control of the Soviets was deemed impossible by the German High Command. Thus, over the next eight months the Germans, in a strenuous effort to take the city, subjected Sevastopol to almost continuous bombardment—assisted by the heaviest artillery piece ever built, the Scherer Gustav railway gun, which could fire a seven-ton projectile a distance of twenty-nine miles. It would not be until late June 1942, however, that the 250-day siege finally came to an end.

For the next two years Sevastopol and the rest of the Crimean peninsula would remain under German control. Drunk with victory, General Gerd von Rundstedt and other leading figures in Hitler's regime soon entertained thoughts of turning the Crimea—and especially Yalta—into a kind of German, as opposed to Russian, "Riviera." But the rapid advance of the Red Army in the fall of 1943 and spring of 1944 saw Sevastopol once again besieged—this time by the Russians. Having encircled Sevastopol on May 6, 1944, the Red Army retook the municipality in three days of fighting that was so fierce that the *Chicago Daily Tribune* took to calling Sevastopol the "city of death."[1]

Often thought of as the most beautiful port city in Europe, Sevastopol had almost ceased to exist when FDR arrived in the fading evening light of February 11, 1945. All but a few thousand of the city's prewar population of 150,000 had long since fled, and according to the Russian authorities who greeted the president and his party, only six of the city's buildings were still standing. As Anna put it, she had never seen such "wanton destruction."[2]

Even though it was late, and it had taken them three hours to make the journey from Yalta, FDR insisted on taking a few minutes to be driven through the ruins. The scenes of "stark destruction" greatly disturbed him, even more than he had been at Yalta. After posing a few questions about the rebuilding of the port, FDR boarded the USS *Catoctin* for a night's rest in the captain's quarters. But as Ambassador Harriman later recalled, the president "had a ghastly night" and awoke the next day fatigued. When he was approached by Russian naval officers as he was about to leave for the Saki Airfield, he turned to his interpreter, Lieutenant Commander George Stroganoff, and said: "George, please tell them that I appreciate everything that they've done, but I am very, very tired and I am too exhausted to talk anymore and to answer any questions."[3]

The eighty-mile drive to Saki took roughly three and a half hours. Waiting for the president at the airfield were Harry Hopkins, Secretary Stettinius, Charles Bohlen, and other members of the American delegation, along with Foreign Minister Molotov. As protocol demanded, a Soviet band and Guard of Honor once again rendered full honors for the president before he got into his wheelchair and was lifted aboard his aircraft—the Sacred Cow—at 10:40 a.m. So exhausted were the members of the delegation that little if any conversation occurred during the tortuous five-hour flight that took them the one thousand miles from the Crimea to Egypt. If not for FDR's heart condition, they might have made the journey in less time, but since they were limited to a maximum altitude of 10,000 feet they had to follow a flight path that took the planes considerably westward, to avoid the high peaks of east-central Turkey.[4]

At 3:15 p.m. the president's plane put down at Deversoir Field on the shores of the Great Bitter Lake, which makes up part of the Suez Canal complex. Following the American minister to Egypt's customary greetings, the party motored to the nearby Suez Company boat landing, where they were ferried by small craft to the waiting USS *Quincy*. Relieved to be back on board that ship, FDR retired to his quarters, where he immediately dictated a note of thanks to Marshal Stalin for his hospitality. He also expressed how heartened he was as a result of the meeting between the three leaders at Yalta. "I am sure," FDR said, "that the people of the world will regard the achievements of this meeting not only with approval, but as a genuine assurance that our three great nations can work as well in peace as they have in war." Taking down this dictation, as he had dozens of times before, Assistant Naval Aide William Rigdon could not help but notice the president's upbeat mood. But this of course was no guarantee that what some were already calling "the spirit of Yalta" would endure.[5]

OF ALL FDR'S WARTIME EXPLOITS, HIS JOURNEY TO EGYPT IN FEBRUary 1945 is perhaps the least known and understood. That the president would insist on taking his leave—over the objections of Churchill and Stalin—from arguably the most important summit meeting of the war to undertake a costly and time-consuming detour must have puzzled his counterparts at Yalta. In fact, FDR undertook this journey—his last overseas mission—as part of a personal quest to solve one of the most intractable political problems of his era, and ours: how to reconcile the Arabs and the Jews in Palestine.[6]

There were other motivations, too, including US interest in the oil resources of the Middle East, FDR's desire to build air bases in the region, and his hope of extending the terms of the Atlantic Charter to the Arab world. But it was the "Palestinian problem" above all else that drove him to make this exhausting trek to a place few Americans had ever heard of, in a part of the world about which they knew little or nothing.[7]

FDR's interest in Palestine constitutes one aspect of his long-standing and controversial relationship with the Jews. His harshest critics have assailed him for not doing more to help German Jewish refugees escape persecution in the 1930s; some even

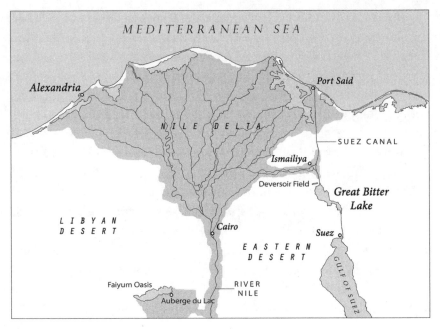

Great Bitter Lake

accuse him and his administration of complicity in the Holocaust in the years that followed. Meanwhile, his defenders insist that FDR simply could not open America to massive numbers of Jewish refugees in the 1930s because of the nativist—and in many cases anti-Semitic—attitudes of the US Congress and public. These tendencies were exacerbated by the economic conditions of the Great Depression, which made altering or overturning the highly restrictive immigration quotas established by the 1924 National Origins Act extremely unlikely. FDR's advisers urged him not to raise the notion in Congress, as doing so might have resulted in the passage of an even more restrictive piece of legislation. Still, in spite of these obstacles, between 1936 and 1940 the United States, thanks in part to FDR's leadership, admitted more German and Austrian Jewish refugees than any other country in the world. And the United States was the only Allied nation to set up an independent agency dedicated to rescuing Jews during the Holocaust—the War Refugee Board, which was established by FDR in January 1944 and saved the lives of an estimated 200,000 Jews.[8]

Whatever his failures on the question of Jewish immigration to America, FDR actively worked for the establishment of a Jewish homeland in Palestine. Having served in the Wilson administration during World War I, he was well aware of the 1917 Balfour Declaration, in which the British government expressed its support for "the establishment of a national home for the Jewish people" in Palestine. He was also familiar with the 1922 League of Nations Mandate that turned over control of the region to Great Britain after the dissolution of the Ottoman Empire, as well as the Resolution that was passed by the US Congress in September 1922 that endorsed the creation of a Jewish homeland in Palestine. In the two decades that followed, the British government adopted a fairly liberal policy with respect to Jewish emigration. As a result, the population of Jews in the region grew from roughly 80,000 in the early 1920s to more than 500,000 by the mid-1940s.

But there were also approximately 1.2 million Arabs living in the region, most of whom were vehemently opposed to Jewish immigration. This led to ever more frequent outbursts of sectarian violence. Then in 1936, soon after the Nazis passed the repressive Nuremberg Laws, Jewish immigration to Palestine came under a renewed threat with the outbreak of a major Arab revolt against British rule and Jewish settlement. As Jewish and Arab extremists exacted reprisals that cost dozens of British and hundreds of Jewish and Arab lives, pressure built once again within the British government to restrict or entirely cut off Jewish immigration to the Mandate.[9]

In late 1938, FDR sent a private message to British Prime Minister Neville Chamberlain via his friend, the Scottish Liberal, Arthur Murray, urging Chamberlain to continue to allow Jewish immigration to Palestine. Aware that the British government planned to host a conference of Arabs and Jews early in the New Year in search of a solution to the ongoing unrest in Palestine, FDR also asked Murray to convey the outlines of a "Palestine plan" for a "Transjordan Arab Settlement" that FDR had developed and discussed with Murray during the latter's visit to Hyde Park in October 1938. Chamberlain certainly appreciated receiving the president's views, and asked Murray to inform FDR that "knowledge [of it]" may be of assistance during [the] conference days." But as war with Germany became more likely, the deliberations that the British government engaged in over the next few months to try to find a solution to the Palestinian problem would ultimately prove antithetical to the Jews. By the spring of 1939, in fact, it was clear that the Chamberlain government intended to pacify Palestine through a rapprochement with the majority Arab population via the promulgation of a new White Paper that repudiated the Balfour Declaration.[10]

Issued in May, and approved by the British Parliament as the *de facto* policy of the British government during the war, the White Paper limited Jewish immigration to Palestine to 10,000 persons per year for five years, after which no further Jewish immigration would be permitted without Arab consent—which for practical purposes meant an end to further Jewish settlement. The paper also called for the establishment of a future Palestinian state to be governed by Arabs and Jews "in such a way as to ensure that the essential interests of each community are safeguarded." Based on population-growth projections, illegal Jewish immigration—which the British government was "determined to stop"—and the admission of an additional 25,000 Jews in response to the current refugee crisis, the British intended to limit the total increase in the Jewish population to 75,000. According to these projections, Jews would make up roughly a third of the population of the proposed new state. In Ambassador Joseph Kennedy's view, which he reported to FDR, this was in keeping with the ultimate objective of the proposal—namely, to ensure that any future Palestinian state would see the Jews in the minority.[11]

As FDR said at the time to Secretary of State Cordell Hull, he read the proposed White Paper "with a good deal of dismay." He also asked Hull to send him a copy of the original 1922 mandate, as he disputed the White Paper's claim that "the Framers" of the 1922 directive "could not have intended that Palestine should be converted into a Jewish State against the will of the Arab population." As FDR put it, "My recollection is . . . that while the Palestinian Mandate undoubtedly did not intend to take away the right of citizenship and of taking part in the government on the part of the Arab population, it nevertheless did intend to convert Palestine into a Jewish home in a comparatively short time. Certainly, that was the impression given to the whole world at the time." FDR also told Hull that he failed to see how the British government could read into the original mandate "any policy that would limit Jewish immigration."[12]

Concerned about Anglo-American relations on the eve of the war, the ever-cautious Hull was inclined to endorse the new White Paper, and he prepared a State Department release that implied US concurrence. But FDR refused to allow Hull to release this statement. He maintained that British attitudes with respect to Palestine might change, and because he believed the United States would likely be in a stronger position to argue the question later on, he said to Hull that it was "better to cross the Palestinian bridge when we come to it, instead of now." FDR further indicated that he welcomed Zionist pressure on the US Congress and ventured that the Arabs in Palestine could be placated through the purchase of more farms and the drilling of more wells for them, "so that any Arab who really felt himself pushed out . . . could go somewhere else."[13]

The outbreak of war in September 1939, and the first news about the killing of European Jews two years later, brought more urgent calls for the establishment of a Jewish homeland in Palestine. Notably vocal was the American Jewish community. Even those Jews who had been opposed to Zionism began to reconsider as word of Nazi atrocities reached them. By December 1942, enough evidence had been compiled to determine that the Nazis were in fact engaged in genocide. FDR supported the issuance of a joint statement released by the British and American governments and signed by nine other Allied nations—and, indeed, reported on the front page of the *New York Times*—"condemning Germany's bestial policy of cold blooded *extermination* of the Jews."[14]

At roughly the same time, FDR told Secretary Morgenthau that 90 percent of Palestine should be Jewish, that the Arabs should be moved to land elsewhere in the Middle East, and that Palestine should become an independent state. Six months later, at the Third Washington Conference in June 1943, FDR informed Churchill that he favored balancing out all concessions to the Jews in Palestine by transforming the Middle East into a bloc of independent Arab states, with Palestine as the exception—an idea that the imperialist Churchill found concerning. FDR also told the British Zionist leader, Chaim Weizmann, that he had convinced Churchill to support the convening of a postwar conference of Arabs and Jews, which was to be held in conjunction with the United Nations. Inspired in part by the work of Walter Clay Loudermilk, who would go on to write the best-selling book

Palestine, Land of Promise, FDR even speculated that the Jews might help the Arabs develop the region; like many Americans of his generation, FDR deeply admired the manner in which the Jewish population in Palestine had transformed their desert landscape into productive farmland.[15]

But FDR's arguments for a Jewish homeland in Palestine became increasingly complicated by his duties as commander-in-chief. The ongoing manpower shortage, and the opening of a Middle Eastern supply route to the Soviet Union, meant that in spite of the increasingly vocal public support for the idea of a Jewish homeland in Palestine, FDR found his senior military advisers opposed to the idea as the end of the five-year term of the 1939 White Paper approached in the spring of 1944.

Pressed by their counterparts in London, General George Marshall and Secretary of War Henry Stimson maintained that any overt move by the US government or Congress that might lead to further outbreaks of unrest in the Middle East—such as the passage of the Wright-Compton Resolution calling for a Jewish Commonwealth that was introduced in the spring of 1944—could impair the Allies in the lead-up to the long-anticipated Normandy invasion. Stimson went so far as to say that even the mere public discussion of the resolution might "provoke dangerous repercussions," as "any conflict between Jews and Arabs [that] would require the retention of troops in the affected areas" would "reduce the total forces that could otherwise be placed in combat against Germany."[16] Secretary Morgenthau also opposed the resolution, worried that the potential controversy would divert attention from rescue efforts in Europe led by the recently established War Refugee Board.[17]

Military necessity was not the only brake on FDR's ambitions in Palestine. Oil, too, played a role. By 1943, the United States was consuming oil at a rate that exceeded supply. As a result, the Roosevelt administration established a special Committee on Petroleum composed of representatives from the State, War, and Navy Departments, as well as other specialists, to determine how best to secure American access to Middle East oil, especially from Saudi Arabia.[18]

American relations with the Saudi kingdom dated to the spring of 1931, when the Hoover administration recognized the newly formed

Arab nation. In 1933, FDR expanded the relationship between the two states to include diplomatic and consular representation, and at roughly the same time, Standard Oil of California acquired the oil rights to a huge swath of territory along the eastern coast of the kingdom for a period of sixty years.[19] Yet Saudi Arabia, like much of the Middle East, still fell within the British sphere of influence, and as the US demand for oil skyrocketed, so, too, did American fears that the British might use their influence as a means to supplant American interests.[20]

To ensure that America's commercial activities were protected, FDR's Interior Department entered into negotiations with the British over a possible Anglo-American oil agreement. In a frank conversation with British Ambassador Halifax about the matter, the president pulled out a rough map of the Middle East that he himself had drawn and said in no uncertain terms: "Persian oil is yours. We share the oil of Iraq and Kuwait. As for Saudi Arabian oil, it's ours."[21]

FDR also faced strong arguments against a Jewish homeland in Palestine from the State Department. By this point, the Near East Division of the Department had received numerous reports from the Middle East about the strength of Arab opposition to the idea, including a detailed account by Lieutenant Colonel Harold Hoskins, whom FDR had sent to the region in the summer of 1943 as his newly appointed diplomatic emissary to Palestine. FDR had hoped that Hoskins might find some basis for a settlement over Palestine through conversations with the Saudi king, Abdul Aziz Ibn Saud, with whom FDR had maintained a cordial correspondence since the mid-1930s. But after a week of intense discussions with Ibn Saud, the Arabic-speaking Hoskins reported that owing to the Saudi ruler's profound political and religious feelings on the matter, there was "no possibility of his being any assistance to the Zionists in their efforts to come to terms with the Arabs in Palestine." Hoskins also spent time conferring with British officials in London, and afterward told FDR that he concurred with the Foreign Office's view that renewed clashes between Arabs and Jews over the question of Jewish immigration into Palestine could turn the Arab world against the Allies. Upon his return to Washington, Hoskins went to the White House, where in a long conversation with FDR he insisted that "the establishment of a Jewish State in Palestine can only be imposed by force and maintained by force." Hoskins recommended that the State Department issue a simple statement indicating that "any postwar decision [on Palestine] will only be taken after full consultation with both the Arabs and Jews." This soon became the State Department's official mantra on the subject.[22]

Yet despite the repeated warnings from two of the most important agencies in the US government, FDR did not renounce his support for a Jewish state. He also maintained his support for continued Jewish immigration to Palestine and, in March 1944, issued the first official American comment on British wartime policy in Palestine when he indicated that "the American Government had never given its approval to the White Paper of 1939." Of course, part of FDR's motivation for adopting this position was political. Jewish voters in the northeast United States were important constituents, and in addition to endorsing the provisions of the 1944 Democratic Party platform calling for the establishment of a Jewish commonwealth, FDR issued a statement in October in which he declared: "I know how long and ardently the Jewish people have worked and prayed for the establishment of Palestine as a free and democratic Jewish commonwealth. I am convinced that the American people give their support to this aim, and if I am reelected, I shall help to bring about its realization."[23]

Later critics have argued that these statements were mere rhetoric, pointing to FDR's refusal to support the Wright-Compton resolution in the weeks after his election as proof. But another explanation is that given the many complex considerations involved, FDR decided to set aside a more public approach to the problem and instead forge a solution through his own personal powers of persuasion. As he told Stettinius in a conversation the two men had just three days after the election, he had come to the conclusion that he would be able to "iron out the whole Arab-Jewish issue on the ground where he can have a talk." Shortly thereafter, FDR expressed similar confidence in personal diplomacy in a conversation he had about Middle East affairs with the economist Herbert Feis and other officials. As Feis left the White House, he found himself amazed that FDR "cherished the illusion that presumably he, and he alone, as head of the United States, could bring about a settlement—if not reconciliation—between Arabs and Jews." Feis had read of men "who thought they might be King of the Jews and other men who thought they might be King of the Arabs, but this is the first time," he mused, that "I've listened to a man who dreamt of being King of both the Jews and Arabs."[24]

THE MOST CONVINCING EVIDENCE OF THE SINCERITY OF FDR's commitment to a Jewish state can be found in his decision to go to Egypt after Yalta. In preparation, FDR had numerous discussions with Secretary of State Edward Stettinius. On January 2, 1945, he reiterated the basic outline of his plans to Stettinius: he would meet with Ibn Saud to discuss the issue. "He would take with him a map showing the Near Eastern Area as a whole and the relationship of Palestine to the area . . . and point out to Ibn Saud what an infinitesimal part of the whole area was occupied by Palestine." And he would note that "he could not see why a portion of Palestine could not be given to the Jews without harming in any way the interests of the Arabs, with the understanding, of course, that the Jews would not move into adjacent parts of the Near East." The president then directed Stettinius to have the appropriate maps drawn up.[25]

Shortly thereafter, FDR held a similar conversation with James Landis, the director of the American Economic Mission to the Middle East, indicating that a "rapprochement" between the Arabs and the Jews in Palestine might result from a personal appeal to King Ibn Saud. FDR asked Landis to draw up a report on the subject. Echoing Hoskins, Landis's report warned that Ibn Saud "feels very intensely about this subject [and] . . . recently threatened in the presence of one of my people to see to the execution of any Jew that might enter his dominion." Landis was extremely skeptical that FDR would be able to bring about a compromise. "The political objective implicit in the Jewish State idea," he argued, "will never be accepted by the Arab nations and is not consistent with the principles of the Atlantic Charter." Landis recommended that the United States oppose the creation of an independent Jewish state, arguing that the best that could be hoped for was "a Jewish National Home under Arab hegemony." He also feared that the "economic absorptive capacity of Palestine had been greatly exaggerated" and that the injection of this "highly charged moral issue" would severely disrupt budding Arab-American relations."[26]

Yet FDR pressed on, driven by his faith in his persuasiveness and by the conviction, as he expressed to Chaim Weizmann in March

1944, that in the end "full justice will be done to those seeking a Jewish National Home, for which our Government and the American people have always had the deepest sympathy." Armed with the maps that Stettinius supplied him, FDR went to sleep on board the Quincy on the night of February 12, 1945, in a hopeful mood, not knowing that the next two days would be among the most fascinating and frustrating of his entire twelve years in office.[27]

Chapter 11

Failure at Bitter Lake

Because the *Quincy* was moored in Egyptian waters, diplomatic protocol dictated that FDR's first caller on the morning of Tuesday, February 13, 1945, was that nation's young King Farouk, a ruler whose lavish lifestyle and ambivalent relationship with the British had made him a somewhat controversial figure during the war. Though this visit was not supposed to amount to more than a courtesy call, the two men seemed to enjoy each other's company as they sat on the deck under a bright but cool sky. They talked about cotton and trade, and about American tourism, which FDR predicted would explode after the war, necessitating an increase in air travel to the Nile region. After a leisurely lunch of American-style fried chicken and a tour of the ship, the king departed at 3:30 p.m.[1]

In the two hours that followed King Farouk's departure, FDR worked on his correspondence and took a few moments to review the briefing materials the State Department had prepared in advance of his next visitor, Emperor Haile Selassie of Ethiopia. Selassie was catapulted to fame when he went before the League of Nations to plead for international support in the wake of Italy's unprovoked attack on Abyssinia in the fall of 1935; his petitions—though they largely fell on deaf ears—represented the first real test of the world body. FDR had been at sea on a four-week fishing cruise off the coast of California when word of the Italian assault reached him, and although the conflict was confined to the Horn of Africa, the tensions it aroused among the major powers led to fears that war might break out in Europe. As the crisis dragged on, it became clear that the League would not be able to act with the decisiveness needed to meet the emergency. FDR, Admiral Wilson

Brown later recalled, "had an uninterrupted month to study what was going on, and how aggressors might be opposed more effectively by world forces in the future"—a critical period in what Brown called "the education of Franklin Roosevelt."[2]

The first thing that struck FDR as he watched Selassie being piped on board the *Quincy* was his small stature. Yet even though the emperor stood no more than five feet three inches tall, he possessed a quiet, dignified manner that made quite an impression on all who witnessed his arrival. For the first half hour or so, the two leaders exchanged pleasantries, conversing entirely in French, without the aid of an interpreter. After tea—and with the emperor switching to his native Amharic—the two men touched on territorial and economic concerns that had long plagued Ethiopia, including the country's need for a port, in either Djibouti or Eritrea, and the possibility that an American company might build a railroad to the latter, which FDR assured the emperor would not cost too much.[3]

They also discussed Italian Somaliland, the territory whose disputed borders had been used as the pretext for Mussolini's brutal incursion in 1935. As the conversation drew to a close, FDR invited the emperor to send a delegate to the San Francisco conference so that Ethiopia might be represented as one of the founding members of the United Nations—a suggestion the emperor appreciated immensely. After an exchange of gifts, Selassie left. Like many leaders in what we today call the developing world, he never forgot the gesture accorded to him by the US president; on his first official trip to the United States years later, he traveled to Hyde Park to lay a wreath on the grave of Franklin D. Roosevelt.[4]

The vibrant political and cultural exchanges that FDR had engaged in during his first full day on the Great Bitter Lake had certainly been memorable. But as much as he enjoyed meeting King Farouk and Emperor Selassie, these encounters would pale in comparison to what the president and the men of "his ship" would experience the next morning when the destroyer, the USS *Murphy*, hove to alongside the *Quincy*.

At 1,620 tons, compared to the *Quincy*'s 13,600, the *Murphy* seemed almost tiny. Sprouting a green shamrock welded to its funnel, the latter had a well-deserved reputation as a "good" and lucky vessel. Few destroyers had in fact seen more action than the *Murphy*,

from convoy duty in the treacherous North Atlantic to active participation in four of the most important amphibious landings of the European and Mediterranean theaters during the war, including operations
Torch, Husky, Overlord, and *Anvil.* But of all the *Murphy*'s wartime
assignments, nothing compared with the unusual operational orders
the ship's captain received on the evening of February 9, 1945. Having
accompanied the *Quincy* on its historic voyage across the Atlantic, and
now moored with the latter in the eastern stretches of the Great Bitter
Lake, the *Murphy* was to proceed "with upmost secrecy and dispatch"
south through the remaining portion of the Suez Canal to the Arabian
port of Jidda on the Red Sea, where it would embark King Ibn Saud
and return him immediately to the *Quincy* for a conference with the
president of the United States.[5]

Ibn Saud had never before left his kingdom, and given the size of
his entourage, and the myriad supplies and other requirements, transporting him from Jidda to the Great Bitter Lake proved a most chal-
lenging experience for the captain and crew of the *Murphy.* When
the ship arrived in Jidda on February 12, the Saudi prime minister,
who supervised such matters, first indicated that the king could not
be expected to travel with fewer than two hundred followers! Then
there was the problem of the king's proposed accommodations, the
Murphy's commodore's stateroom, which, with its spartan bunk, desk,
and private bath, was deemed "wholly unacceptable." So, too, were the
Murphy's steel decks, as the king suffered from arthritis and could not
possibly walk on such a hard surface. After a period of intense negotiations skillfully handled by Colonel William Eddy, the American
minister to Saudi Arabia, the two parties agreed that the total number
of the king's entourage should be capped at forty-eight, including an
astrologer, a food taster, two ceremonial coffee-servers, the king's physician, ten guards, three valets, and nine "miscellaneous slaves, cooks,
porters, and scullions." To accommodate the king's infirmity the deck
of the *Murphy* would be covered with oriental rugs, and in lieu of the
commodore's stateroom it was agreed that a large tent would be constructed over the ship's forecastle just as if the king were making a pil-
grimage somewhere in the vast desert regions of his homeland.[6]

The *Murphy* was soon a bustle of activity as colorful dhows drew
up alongside to unload the king's supplies. All seemed to be going
well when the American sailors spied an unforgettable sight: a barge

approaching with what appeared to be upward of a hundred sheep. Because it was the king's custom "to eat freshly slaughtered lamb on a daily basis," and to share his bounty with his hosts—in this case, the entire crew of the ship—his aides had determined this was the minimum number required. In the end, the *Murphy*'s captain agreed to take seven ewes on board, to be corralled on the ship's fantail, with the flagstaff used as a kind of "gallows" where twice a day, to the amazement of the crew, one of the unfortunate ewes would be hoisted, slaughtered, and prepared for the king's repast.[7]

Thus the *Murphy*, the first American warship ever to visit the port of Jidda, received its important guest, weighed anchor, and set off for its rendezvous with FDR. As the men worked in and around their Arab guests, the king and his party frequently offered them coffee. Near the end of the voyage the king revealed that he had brought a gift of ten pounds sterling for each member of the crew—a gesture that was hastily reciprocated by the captain's impromptu presentation of two of the ship's Browning submachine guns to the king and his delighted "security detail."[8]

IN THE MEANTIME, BACK ON THE *QUINCY*, ANNA WAS BUSY MAKING arrangements for the visitor who, "suffice it to say," as she wrote to her husband, "cannot be in the company of women outside of his own!" In light of this, Anna spent the evening of February 13 typing out "all instructions as to who was to lunch at which mess and the menu for the visitors" (an important task given the king's dietary restrictions) and making arrangements to go into Cairo first thing the next morning, well before their illustrious visitor arrived, since, as her father joked, "those women he does see, he confiscates!" As planned, Anna departed at 8:30 a.m. It was another bright sunny morning, and so FDR was soon out on deck, sitting in his wheelchair and enjoying the fresh air and the company of his longtime Secret Service agent, Michael Reilly. Shortly after 10:00 a.m., Reilly spied the *Murphy* approaching from the south—presenting, as it came nearer, "the most fantastic pageant." From his seated position away from the rail, however, FDR could not see the destroyer, so Reilly turned to him, saying, "Mr. President, you must see this. It's sensational." FDR "wheeled himself across the deck, and hiding behind a stanchion . . . watched the *Murphy* and her gay crew approach." Reilly could not help but notice how unusual an occurrence this was. Here was the president of the United States, hiding behind a post, "peeking at something, like a small boy sneaking a look at a ball game through a knot-hole," murmuring all the while "This is fascinating. Absolutely fascinating."[9]

High on the *Murphy*'s superstructure deck sat a huge man, on a large gilded throne, surrounded by dozens of retainers and members of the royal family in their flowing Arabic robes. Even more fantastic was the sight of what Reilly soon made out as the king's "secret service detail," who, lining the rail in their elaborately brocaded robes, made no "secret" of their profession, armed as they were with long files, curved scimitars, and the two Browning submachine guns the *Murphy*'s captain had presented to them. Then there was the rolled-up tent, the rugs, and the small flock of sheep nibbling away in the small coral that enclosed the slaughtering scaffold. One *Quincy* sailor, standing at attention as part of the ship's welcome party, and apparently unable to help himself, broke the disciplined silence by yelping, "For God's sake, look at those sheep!"[10]

Ever so slowly, the *Murphy* pulled up alongside the *Quincy*. Thanks to the ingenuity of one of the *Murphy*'s crew, the king, who was unable to climb a ladder, had been hoisted up to the destroyer's superstructure deck in a bosun's chair, bringing him to a height roughly level with the forecastle deck of the much larger *Quincy* and thus making it possible for him to navigate the gangplank that had been carefully lowered between the two vessels. Cutting an enormous figure at six feet four inches tall and well over two hundred pounds, the king, having been accorded full honors by the crew, slowly made his way over the gangplank. Thereupon he immediately approached the seated FDR, who reached up a warm hand in an enthusiastic welcome.

Sitting in the bright sunshine, the two leaders spent the next hour or so getting acquainted with one another. They quickly developed a strong rapport, with the king observing that he felt as if he were the "twin brother" of the president, "in years, in responsibility as Chief of State, and in physical disability."

"But you are fortunate," said a clearly touched FDR, "to still have the use of your legs to take you wherever you choose to go."

"No, it is you, Mr. President, who are fortunate," replied the Saudi ruler. "My legs grow feebler every year, with your more reliable wheelchair you are assured that you will arrive."

FDR, Ibn Saud, and Colonel William Eddy in conversation on board the USS *Quincy*, February 14, 1945. (Courtesy of the Franklin D. Roosevelt Presidential Library)

"I have two of these chairs, which are also twins," FDR said. "Would you accept one as a personal gift from me?"

"Gratefully," said the king. "I shall use it daily and always recall affectionately the giver, my great and good friend."[11]

The two leaders then retired to the president's private quarters for a more serious discussion over lunch. In keeping with Arab custom, the king—as the guest—did not broach any topics himself, with the exception of one question. He wanted to know whether the president would "greet with displeasure" his accepting Prime Minister Churchill's invitation to meet him—a meeting that Churchill had no doubt arranged as a means to remind the king of British influence in the region. FDR made no objection, saying, "Why not? I always enjoy seeing Mr. Churchill and I'm sure you will like him too." But he then went on to discuss "the English," whom he emphasized had a particular way of doing business.

"You and I," FDR said to the king, "want freedom and prosperity for our people and their neighbors after the war. How and by whose hand freedom and prosperity arrive concerns us little." He noted that the English shared this goal, but only "on the condition that it be brought by them and marked 'Made in Britain.'" The king smiled at this and asked the president, "What am I to believe when the British tell me that my future is with them and not with America?" What was he to think of their insistence that America's concern for Saudi Arabia is "a transitory war-interest, her aid as short-lived as Lend-Lease," and that "the security and economic stability" of Saudi Arabia "are bound up with British foreign policy?"[12]

In response, FDR expressed his conviction that the postwar world would see "a decline of spheres of influence in favor of the Open Door." In this new world the United States hoped that the door to Saudi Arabia would be open "for her and for other nations, with no monopoly for anyone," as only by "the free exchange of goods, services and opportunities can prosperity circulate to the advantage of free peoples." After discussing the imminence of the German defeat and the two leaders' mutual "compassion for the multitudes rendered destitute through oppression or famine," FDR decided it was time to broach the matter that had brought him to this point in the first place.[13]

FDR began the delicate conversation over Palestine by indicating that "he had a serious problem in which he desired the King's advice and help; namely the rescue and rehabilitation of the remnant of Jews in Central Europe who had suffered indescribable horrors at the hands of the Nazis: eviction, destruction of their homes, torture and mass murder." FDR said that he felt "a personal responsibility and indeed had committed himself to help solve this problem. What could the King suggest?"[14] To this, the Saudi ruler replied immediately, "Give them and their descendants the choicest lands and homes of the Germans who had oppressed them." "But," FDR interjected, "the Jewish survivors have a sentimental desire to settle in Palestine, and quite understandably would dread remaining in Germany where they might suffer again."[15]

The king understood that the Jews "have good reason not to trust the Germans," but surely the Allies will destroy German power forever, "and in their victory will be strong enough to protect [the] Nazi victims." Indeed, "if the Allies do not expect to firmly control future

German policy, why fight this costly war? He, Ibn Saud, could not conceive of leaving an enemy in a position to strike back." Still pressing, FDR said he "counted on Arab hospitality and on the King's help in solving the problem of Zionism." To this the king replied with some force, "Make the enemy and the oppressor pay; that is how we Arabs wage war. Amends should be made by the criminal, not by the innocent bystander, what injury have Arabs done to the Jews of Europe? It is the 'Christian' Germans who stole their homes and lives. Let the Germans pay."

Frustrated, FDR complained that "the King had not helped him at all with his problem," at which point the Saudi leader, having lost all patience, stated that this "over-solicitude for the Germans was incomprehensible to an uneducated Bedouin with whom friends get more consideration than enemies." In the Allied camp, he noted, "there are fifty countries, among whom Palestine is small, land-poor and has already been assigned more than its quota of European refugees."

FDR tried a less direct tack. Calling himself "a farmer at heart," he suggested that the Arabs could profit from irrigation and other methods of development that would increase the amount of land under cultivation, which would in turn make possible a larger population. Not willing to take the bait, the king thanked the president for promoting agriculture so vigorously, but said he could not support any expansion of agriculture and public works "if this prosperity would be inherited by the Jews." What he desired for his people, the king said, was independence, for without independence he and his country "could not seek an honorable friendship, because friendship is possible only with mutual and equal respect." The king also professed his sincere desire for FDR's friendship, because the president was known as the champion of the Four Freedoms, and the king had found that the United States "never colonizes or enslaves."[16]

FDR assured the king that he personally, as president, would never do anything that might prove hostile to the Arabs and—in line with the traditional State Department formula for the region—said that the Allies would make no decision on Palestine without first consulting both the Jews and the Arabs.[17]

At this point FDR indicated that the captain of the *Quincy* felt it would soon be time for the ship to get under way. Clearly disappointed that he would not be able to return the gesture of offering the president a meal (of fresh lamb) on board the *Murphy,* the king asked if the president would at least offer him the chance to serve him coffee. FDR readily agreed, and with the help of the two ceremonial coffee-servers, the president received two cups of a thick black liquid, which he later described as "godawful."

The two leaders exchanged gifts. The king presented FDR with a fabulously bejeweled sword, and Anna and Mrs. Roosevelt with fine perfume, dazzling jewelry, and beautiful "harem attire." In addition to the spontaneous gift of his spare wheelchair, the president gave the king a ceremonial medallion from his fourth inauguration and, as perhaps a not-too-subtle hint about the American desire to open an airfield in Dhahran on the Arabian peninsula, promised that a DC-3 Dakota, the twin engine, propeller-driven aircraft that was the mainstay of US commercial aviation, would soon be delivered to him. The king had never flown, and had no pilots or aircraft in his kingdom, so FDR said that he would arrange for an American pilot and crew to serve as the king's aircrew. The much-loved DC-3—in use for years and flown by the same pilot who delivered it, Joseph Grant—became "a fitting symbol of the US-Saudi relationship." It also stimulated the king's interest in developing air travel within the kingdom with the aid of American companies, which is precisely what Roosevelt hoped it would do.[18]

In the days that followed the meeting, Colonel Eddy sent in a number of reports detailing how much the king had enjoyed the experience. Owing to his strong desire not to let the Palestinian question cast a shadow over what he saw as a burgeoning relationship between the Arab world and the United States, Eddy was pleased at FDR's stated commitment "to make no change in its basic policy in Palestine without full and prior consultation with both Jews and Arabs." Admiral Leahy was also satisfied at the way the talks had gone, noting in his diary that the frank exchange between the king and FDR over the Palestine-Jewish difficulty "should be of great value to the President in his approach to or recession from the problem." Indeed, in Leahy's view "the King's directness" was most gratifying as "it may prevent our starting a bloody war between the Jewish inhabitants of Palestine and the Arab World."[19]

Leahy's assessment of the king's unyielding stance on the question of further Jewish immigration into the region is certainly accurate.

But given Eddy's proclivity for the Arab point of view, his official account of FDR's meeting with Ibn Saud may have left out some key information. One person who strongly suspected that Eddy was deeply anti-Zionist, and perhaps even anti-Semitic, was James G. McDonald, the former League of Nations High Commissioner for Refugees and chairman of the President's Advisory Committee on Political Refugees that FDR established in 1938. McDonald would go on to serve on the Anglo-American Committee of Inquiry that was established by the British and American governments in December 1945 to make recommendations regarding the resettlement of Jews after the war. Part of this effort also involved looking into the impact that further Jewish settlement would have on the political, economic, and social conditions in Palestine. McDonald was part of a team that interviewed—and rejected—Eddy for the position of secretary to the committee, as "within a half an hour, he evinced such marked anti-Zionist feeling that no further argument was necessary to convince my colleagues he was unacceptable."[20]

In March 1946, three of the six members of the Anglo-American committee would travel to Riyadh to discuss the question of Jewish immigration into Palestine with Ibn Saud, much as FDR had done a year before. From the record of these conversations it appears that FDR went even further than the somewhat tentative record left by Eddy. According to the king, FDR recommended that he allow 3 million Jews to settle in Palestine—a suggestion that the king flatly rejected with the remark that he found "it was strange that America had agreed to accept 30,000 persons in her territory while she wished to impose on our country some millions."[21]

Despite the persistent obstinacy that Ibn Saud exhibited on both of these occasions, FDR certainly enjoyed the cultural aspects of the encounter. As he wrote to his cousin Daisy a few days later, seeing King Ibn Saud with his whole court, including "slaves, taster, astrologer and 8 live sheep . . . was a scream!" Still, as FDR's subsequent comments make clear, he was not pleased with the substance of their talks. The meeting had certainly been "sobering and instructive," and the king was far more sophisticated and worldly than FDR had expected—but also far more obdurate. As FDR told his son Elliott some time later, "Of all the men he had talked to in his life, he had got the least satisfaction from the iron-willed Arab monarch."[22] FDR hinted at the same sentiment two weeks later, when he revealed in his Yalta address to Congress that he felt he learned more about the problem of Arabia—"the Muslim problem, the Jewish problem—in talking with Ibn Saud for five minutes, than I could have learned in the exchange of two or three dozen letters."[23] This was a frank admission that solving the Palestinian problem was going to be far more difficult than FDR had imagined.

As FDR's Yalta address was carried live on national radio, these extemporaneous comments led some among American Zionists to speculate that he may have abandoned his previous support for a Jewish homeland in Palestine. But as he told Rabbi Stephen Wise in a meeting in the White House on March 16—and as he authorized Wise to say afterward—his position on Palestine remained unchanged; he stood by the statement he made in October that he would seek to find ways to realize a Jewish state in the region.[24]

Wise's private record of this meeting is even more revealing. As he wrote in a letter to Chaim Weizmann shortly thereafter, FDR did something he almost never did: admit defeat. "The one failure of his trip," FDR confessed, "had been his meeting with Ibn Saud." Indeed, the president had arranged this meeting "for the sake of your cause" and he deeply regretted his inability to make any impression on the Saudi ruler. "I have never so completely failed to make an impact upon a man's mind as in his case," FDR said. Worse still, he now feared that if Ibn Saud united the Arab states in "a holy war," they could defeat the small contingent of Jews in Palestine. Perhaps the only course now, "since we cannot move Ibn Saud," is to put "the case up to the first meeting of the Council of the United Nations, whenever it meets."[25]

FDR made a similar statement to Harold Hoskins at roughly the same time. Over lunch at the White House, Eleanor observed that it now appeared as if the Zionists might be willing to risk a fight with the Arabs over their demands. FDR replied by reminding her that "there were 15,000,000 to 20,000,000 Arabs in and around Palestine and that, in the long run, he thought these numbers would win out." In the same conversation, FDR indicated he now agreed with Hoskins's previously stated claim that a Zionist state could be installed and maintained only by force. The two men thought that perhaps the sole solution might be to turn Palestine into an international territory for all three religions under some sort of arrangement worked out in the United Nations Organization after the war.[26]

No strong supporter of Zionism himself, Hoskins was anxious to know whether the subject had come up at Yalta, and in particular, if Stalin had expressed a view. To which FDR responded that Palestine had not been discussed in any substantive manner, but thanks to a brief conversation with the marshal on the question, he had been able to determine that Stalin was "neither pro-Zionist nor anti-Zionist" but "at least he was not the Jew-hater" that he was often made out to be.[27]

In the meantime, back in Egypt, Ibn Saud was busy speaking with Churchill, who, as Admiral Leahy recorded, insisted on seeing the Saudi monarch and the other two potentates "undoubtedly with the purpose of neutralizing any accomplishment the President may have made during his talks with the three kings."[28] To a certain extent, that was true, as Churchill began his talks by "confidently wielding" what Ibn Saud privately described to Eddy as "the big stick" and asking the king point-blank "for information regarding his conversation with President Roosevelt."[29] Prior to the meeting, Churchill had indicated to the British minister to Saudi Arabia that he had no intention of mentioning Palestine during his conversation with the king.[30] But after reading the record of the conversation handed to him by the Saudi monarch—which included a reference to FDR's persistent attempts to bring Ibn Saud around to a more sympathetic point of view on the question—Churchill intimated that the president had also spoken to him about the subject. Churchill pressed the king on the issue of a Jewish homeland. After reminding him that Great Britain had fended off various potential enemies and "had supported and subsidized" him for twenty years, he insisted that since his government had seen the king through difficult days, "she [Great Britain] was entitled to request his assistance in the problem of Palestine." Surely such a strong Arab leader as the king could "effect a realistic compromise with Zionism."[31]

But the king still absolutely refused to consider the request. "The promotion of Zionism from any quarter must indubitably bring widespread bloodshed and widespread disorder to the Arab lands," he said. A far better move would be for the British to stop Jewish immigration to the region at once. In the face of these arguments, Churchill "laid the big stick down" and in an echo of FDR indicated that though he could make no promise on halting Jewish immigration to Palestine he was willing to assure the king that "he would oppose any plan of immigration which would drive the Arabs out of Palestine or deprive them of the means of livelihood there."[32]

And so neither FDR nor Churchill was able to make any headway with the Saudi king on Jewish immigration or the question of a homeland in Palestine. Caught between his support for the Zionist cause, on the one hand, and his desire to maintain good relations with the Arab world, on the other, FDR would struggle with this dilemma right up to the moment of his death.

FDR's foray into the Near East, even though he largely failed to achieve his goals, nevertheless marks a significant turning point in the evolution of American foreign policy—a clear statement that the United States now regarded itself as a truly global power with global responsibilities extending far beyond the traditional US focus on the Western Hemisphere, Europe, and parts of East Asia.[33]

It also marks the first formal intrusion by the American government into the struggle between the Arabs and the Jews in Palestine. Like most of the presidents who succeeded him, FDR tried to follow a dual-track policy in this newfound area of American interest: refusing to abandon his support for the creation of a Jewish homeland while simultaneously trying to maintain good relations with the Arab world. Fearful, as he said near the end of his life, that continued agitation for a Jewish state "might cause a third world war" or lead to such intense disturbances in the region that the result would prove "most harmful to Jewish settlement," FDR did his best to placate both sides in the hope that the end of the war, and the establishment of the United Nations, would provide the context and opportunity needed to finally arrive at a definitive solution.

We will never know, of course, what FDR may have accomplished in Palestine had he lived but a few more years. What we do know is that, as with so many other matters, FDR's inclination in the final weeks of his life was to revert to the argument that any possible action on the question of a Jewish homeland would have to wait until "some future time," as he intimated to the Saudi king and other Arab leaders in the final weeks before his death.[34] This tendency toward procrastination—what FDR's harsher critics would call equivocation—has resulted in a great deal of *ex post facto* criticism. But as FDR frequently lamented in private, the harsh military and political realities of the moment—which in his mind included the possibility of a major war in the region—often left him no choice but to put the best face he could on some very difficult problems, while trying to lay the groundwork for solving them in the future. One of the ironies and tragedies of the last period of FDR's life is that, despite his poor health and his increasing premonitions of his own immortality, he believed he would have time to work through a number of monumental questions.

FDR may have failed in his mission to the Great Bitter Lake, but there can be little doubt that his support for the creation of a Jewish homeland in Palestine and his determination to find "ways to bring about its earliest realization" were sincere. As he said in a message delivered to the members of the National Labor Committee for Palestine as they prepared to celebrate the ancient feast of Passover less than two weeks before his death, he still harbored "sympathy with the Jewish People in the unparalleled sufferings they have been called upon to endure during these war years."[35]

Chapter 12

Going Home

ANNA RETURNED TO REJOIN HER FATHER ONLY A FEW MINUTES AFTER the Saudi king had safely departed the *Quincy*. The warship soon set off—bound first for Alexandria, to take on fuel and other supplies—before embarking for Algiers, and then the long voyage home to Virginia. As the ship made its way toward northern stretches of the Suez Canal, Anna took a few moments to type out another letter to her husband. She was not sure when there would be another "pouch drop," and there was much exciting news to report, about her trip, incognito, to Cairo and the "pageant" she had missed that day.[1] She was also happy to convey that the "OM" was "standing up under it all extremely well" since "the last scare" she had written about. Still, she was worried about the long journey that awaited them. Anna had just learned that one of her father's principal speechwriters, Samuel Rosenman, who was in London on a special mission, would be flying down to join them in Algiers, to help FDR draft a message to Congress about the Yalta conference as they traversed the Atlantic. Anna would have preferred that her father "spend the entire crossing resting up." Her worst fear was that he might experience a terrific "letdown" once he got home, and "crack under it as he did last year," after Tehran. All they could do at this point, she lamented, was keep their fingers crossed that this would not happen again.[2]

A few days before, FDR, too, had found some time to send a couple of quick notes home, both written on February 12, 1945, while he was on board the *Catoctin*. First, he penned a few lines to Daisy, whom he informed that though the evening meetings of the summit conference were "long and tiring" he was "really all right" as he had confined

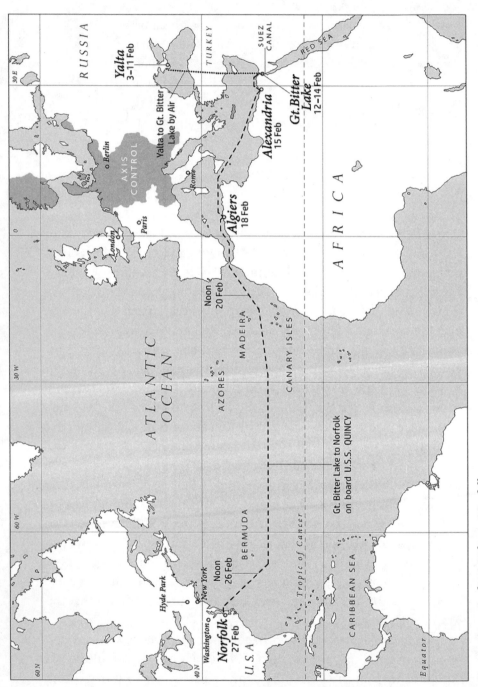

Return journey from Yalta to Norfolk

himself to "either work or sleep."[3] The second was a brief note to Eleanor—the first and only letter that he sent to her during the trip that conveyed a similar message, expressing his view that he thought the conference had wound up successfully and intimating that he was "a bit exhausted" but, using the same phrase, "really all right."[4]

Not mentioned in either of FDR's letters or in Anna's correspondence with her husband was that few of the travelers on board the *Quincy* were "really all right." Hopkins was still suffering from his many ailments, and on the very evening FDR wrote the brief assurances to Daisy and Eleanor, his longtime friend and personal secretary Edwin "Pa" Watson suffered a heart attack. This necessitated Watson's immediate transfer to the *Quincy's* sickbay upon the presidential party's arrival at the Great Bitter Lake, where he remained in an oxygen tent under the watchful eye of Dr. Bruenn.[5]

Now that they were finally under way again on this Valentine's Day, 1945, Anna found that she was too excited to sleep. So as the sun dipped below the horizon, she clambered up to the flag bridge in time to get a good view of Port Said, the historic city and gateway to Suez. At approximately 10:40 p.m., the ship passed through the port's submarine gate and out into the open Mediterranean for the overnight journey to their next port of call.[6]

As ANNA UNDERSTOOD IT, THE OSTENSIBLE REASON FOR THEIR LAYover in Alexandria, aside from the need to refuel, was to give Churchill the chance "to get a report" from FDR on his conferences with "the three kings" in advance of his own meetings with them. Like FDR, Churchill had left the Crimea shortly after the final luncheon meeting, in a hasty and unplanned departure that his daughter Sarah described as the very antithesis of the orderly and well-organized exit of the Americans.

Apparently seized by a sudden fit of loneliness, with the president gone and Stalin having vanished "like some genie," the impetuous Churchill, who originally had planned to leave Yalta the next morning, suddenly demanded that his party be ready to depart in fifty minutes. Much to Sarah's amazement, and to Churchill's valet's grief, this task was accomplished in just over an hour—inspired in part by the genial and sprightly behavior of the prime minister, "who like a boy out of school, his homework done, walked from room to room saying: 'Come on, come on!'"[7]

From Yalta, Sarah and her father spent two nights on the *Franconia,* which was anchored in Sevastopol. While waiting for his flight out, Churchill took the opportunity to visit the famous battlefield at Balaclava. On February 14 they flew on to Athens, where Churchill was relieved to see order restored and was deeply moved by the enormous crowd—estimated at forty thousand people—who had turned out to hear him speak in the city's Constitution Square. The mayor honored Churchill's presence in Athens by lighting up the Acropolis, the first time the ancient citadel had been illuminated since the arrival of the German forces in April 1941. As was often his wont, Churchill held court that evening at the British Embassy, where he regaled his guests deep into the night. At 7:35 a.m. the next morning, Churchill's Sky Master, escorted by three RAF long-range fighters, bolted down the runway bound for Egypt and the last face-to-face encounter he would ever have with Franklin D. Roosevelt.[8]

It was fitting that, as with their much-celebrated first wartime rendezvous in 1941, off the coast of Newfoundland—where they drafted the Atlantic Charter—the final meeting between these two iconic leaders took place on a warship. The historic port of Alexandria made for an apt setting in itself, and not only because it was named after one of history's great conquerors; the city is also a mere seventy miles east of El Alamein, another site of great significance. It was at El Alamein that the British achieved their first great land victory over the Axis in November 1942, a victory that would not have been possible without the sudden and decisive intervention of FDR six months earlier. In a scene that came to symbolize the bond forged between the two men during the war, Churchill was in the White House when FDR made this fateful move. The president had just handed the prime minister a telegram informing him that the besieged British garrison at Tobruk had fallen. Tobruk possessed the only major port in the Western desert, and holding it was viewed as vital to the British defense of Egypt. As such, the news of its capture by the Germans left Churchill stunned and speechless. FDR finally broke the silence by asking "What can we do to help?" and, in consultation with General George Marshall and Field Marshal Alan Brooke, who were also in the room, made the controversial decision to divert a squadron of A-20 light bombers destined for Russia to the retreating British forces in Egypt, along with three hundred Sherman tanks and one hundred self-propelled guns that proved decisive to the subsequent victory. Years later, Field Marshal Lord Alanbrooke wrote that "the Tobruk episode in the President's study" helped lay "the foundations of friendship and understanding that built up during the war between the President and Marshall on the one hand and Churchill and myself on the other."[9]

By the time Churchill's plane touched down in Egypt in February 1945, however, the relationship between the two leaders had entered a new phase. They still enjoyed each other's company, but the warmth that characterized the early stretches of the war—when Churchill referred to himself in their correspondence first as "naval person" and then as "former naval person"—had given way to more formal, and at times distant, interactions. Much of the shift can be attributed to FDR's objections to what he deemed Churchill's Victorian sensibilities—above all, his inability to imagine a world without the Empire. Then there was FDR's determination to maintain an independent relationship with Stalin and the Soviet Union. FDR never gave up the notion that he "could handle Stalin better" than Churchill or his British colleagues. "Stalin hates the guts of all your top people," he once remarked to Churchill, adding "he thinks he likes me better, and I hope he will continue to do so." Most distressing to Churchill, however, was the diminution of the British role in the war—and the loss of influence that it undoubtedly represented as the conflict drew to a close.[10]

One issue that drove a wedge between the two leaders, and that made manifest Great Britain's waning power, was the question of the joint development of the atomic bomb. The genesis of this all-important scientific endeavor dates to a letter President Roosevelt received in the fall of 1939 from Albert Einstein largely at the instigation of the physicist Leo Szilard. The letter noted the recent discovery of nuclear fission, and warned the president of the possibility that this breakthrough might lead to the creation of extremely powerful weapons. It also alluded to the likelihood that German scientists were already working to develop such weapons.[11]

FDR wasted no time in responding to these developments. He immediately established an Advisory Committee on Uranium under the leadership of Dr. Vannevar Bush, president of the Carnegie Institution in Washington. In the meantime, Great Britain launched a similar effort, which, over the next two years, made enormous scientific strides. In the fall of 1941, the British sent a copy of their findings—under the euphemism "the Maud Report," after the committee that carried out the work—to Washington. Its revelations spurred FDR to throw the entire weight of the American government into a massive effort to develop the atomic bomb. By January 1942 the program was fully under way; its code name—the Manhattan Project—was a reference to the Manhattan offices of the US Army Corps of Engineers, which had been assigned to oversee the construction of the initial facilities.[12]

At the time the Maud Report came out, FDR suggested to Churchill that the two powers might want to coordinate their scientific efforts.[13] But owing to a split of opinion in London over the degree to which Great Britain should collaborate with the Americans, it would take some time—and a good deal of rancor—before the two governments would be able to hammer out a formal understanding.[14] This document, known as the "Quebec Agreement," was signed in Quebec City in August 1943, and its terms called for "full and effective collaboration" between the two governments and their scientists. It further stipulated that any decision to use an atomic bomb or to share information about the project with a third party would require "mutual consent."[15]

The Quebec Agreement also addressed the non-military uses of atomic energy that might result from the Manhattan Project. In a clear expression of American suspicions of the British, and of the competitive nature of the transatlantic relationship, the agreement demanded that the latter "recognize that any post-war advantages of an industrial or commercial character shall be dealt with as between the United States and Great Britain on terms to be specified by the President of the United States." In addition, it stated that the prime minister "expressly disclaims any interest in these industrial and commercial aspects beyond what may be considered by the President of the United States to be fair and just and in harmony with the economic welfare of the world."[16]

Many officials and scientists in Britain were appalled by America's demands. Yet as Churchill wrote to Lord Cherwell, his scientific adviser, sometime later, he was "absolutely sure" that the British could not have achieved "any better terms . . . than are set forth in my secret agreement with the President." He remained confident that the British association with the United States was permanent and had "no fear that they will maltreat us or cheat us."[17] Cherwell was not so sanguine. At the end of 1944 and the beginning of 1945, as the bomb—and the atomic age—came to the fore, he pressed Churchill to go back to FDR to secure American acquiescence to any effort by the British to conduct independent atomic research after the war.[18] Thus there was another reason, beyond a discussion about the "three kings," for which Churchill made the decision to travel to Alexandria to see FDR a mere four days after he had left the president's side at Yalta.

FDR SPENT THE MORNING OF FEBRUARY 15, 1945, ON THE FLAG DECK of the *Quincy*. Almost immediately after the ship reached its moorings, however, he launched into a series of meetings. The first was with Secretary Stettinius, who came aboard just after 11:00 a.m. in the company of Charles Bohlen and John Winant, the American ambassador to Great Britain. Stettinius had stopped in Alexandria on his way from Moscow to Mexico City to give the president a preliminary report on the discussions in the Russian capital among the three foreign ministers, as well as to bring the president up to date on a number of State Department matters. This included a brief review of Stettinius's coming trip to Mexico City to take part in the Inter-American Conference on the Problems of War and Peace, a conference that FDR insisted Stettinius attend in an effort to solidify Latin American support for the United Nations.[19]

The two men also touched upon a secret and sensitive mission Stettinius was to carry out on his way to Mexico City that was closely linked to the discussions FDR was about to have with Churchill. Stettinius would visit Brazil to meet with President Getúlio Dornelles Vargas, with whom he would arrange an agreement for the US to purchase all of Brazil's production of monazite sands—a mineral rich in thorium, one of the key elements needed for the construction of an atomic bomb. In fact, the secretary of state completed his mission with aplomb, securing access to Brazil's monazite deposits without divulging the reason for the purchase—an outcome that thoroughly pleased FDR.[20]

At approximately 12:35 the shrill sound of the bosun's pipe announced the arrival of Prime Minister Churchill, his daughter Sarah, and the ubiquitous Commander Charles Thompson, Churchill's naval aide-de-camp. While Sarah and Anna enjoyed a few moments on deck, Churchill retired to FDR's quarters where the two men, in the company of Harry Hopkins, discussed what the prime minister referred to as the "Tube Alloys" project.

Churchill began the meeting by reading aloud the memo that Lord Cherwell had prepared for him explaining the British desire to carry out independent research into the potential commercial and industrial uses of atomic energy after the war. FDR reportedly made "no objection of any kind" to Cherwell's arguments. He did say, however, that recent reports indicated new uncertainty about the possibility of atomic power being used for commercial purposes. And, in perhaps an intentional misrepresentation of the timeline reported to him by Stimson at the end of the year, FDR specified September 1945—rather than August—as the likely date for "the first important [military] trials." Churchill was pleased that Roosevelt was not opposed to the British engaging in atomic research after the war. But like many of the other understandings that passed between them, this implied agreement would prove short-lived: just over a year after FDR's death, President Truman would sign the McMahon Act, which brought the wartime atomic collaboration and sharing of information between the two nations to an abrupt halt, eventually leading the British to develop their own atomic arsenal.[21]

At 2:00 p.m. it was time for lunch, where the two leaders and Hopkins were joined by Anna, Sarah, Churchill's son Randolph (who had arrived roughly an hour before), Admiral Leahy, and Ambassador Winant. Given how often Sarah Churchill saw Ambassador Winant, with whom she was having a secret affair, she could not help but be bemused and delighted by his presence. "Yesterday lunch we went on board the President's ship in Alexandria," she carelessly wrote to her mother, "and who do you suppose was there? The Ambassador!! But alas our paths separated right after coffee!"[22] The luncheon was a purely social affair, and a most pleasant one at that. But as Churchill later reflected, FDR seemed placid and frail; it was as if the president possessed "a slender contact with life."[23]

At the close of this convivial gathering, shorn of all of the tensions that had burdened the two leaders at Yalta, something of the old warmth seemed to return. It had been three and a half years since their first fateful wartime meeting, where in far darker circumstances they had created their vision for a better world. Now, they parted affectionately, never to see one another again.

THE *QUINCY* LEFT ITS MOORINGS IN THE ANCIENT HARBOR LESS THAN ten minutes after the prime minister and his party had departed, and arrived in Algiers just before 9:00 a.m. on the morning of Sunday, February 18. The ship's arrival provided Anna a last opportunity to write home. Knowing that her mother would be concerned about her father's health, she wrote first to Eleanor, noting that "father is really fine . . . [and] has been resting for the past two days." Today will be busy, she continued, making reference to the many appointments FDR had scheduled in the hours ahead, "but then we're thru."[24]

Anna offered much the same assessment about FDR's condition in a note she sent to her husband. "OM seems fine, thank goodness," she wrote. But this view was not shared by those who came to see the president on board the *Quincy* that day.

Samuel Rosenman, who had flown from London so that he could assist FDR in drafting the address on Yalta, was deeply disheartened by FDR's appearance. He had never seen the president looking "so tired." FDR appeared to have lost a great deal of weight, and "seemed listless and uninterested in conversation," as he "slowly and silently went through the process of signing some bills and correspondence to be dispatched home by air."[25]

An even less optimistic assessment came from Carmel Ophie, a career diplomat who had traveled to Algiers with the US ambassadors to France and Italy, Jeffrey Caffery and Alexander Kirk, to join the president for lunch.[26] "He looked ghastly, sort of dead and dug up," Ophie observed as he greeted the president and Anna. He was also shocked to see Hopkins "carried off the S.S. *Quincy* on a stretcher," while Pa Watson was "under an oxygen tent" and another aide was "in the sick bay with a bad case of influenza." Nor was Ophie alone in this observation; as Ambassador Kirk said to him, "This is really a ship of death and everyone responsible in encouraging that man [FDR] to go to Yalta has done a disservice to the United States and ought to be shot."[27]

Hopkins, not willing to contemplate a long sea voyage confined to his cabin, had indeed finally made the decision that he had no choice but to leave the *Quincy* and make arrangements to fly back to the United States.[28] FDR had been counting on Hopkins to help him draft his Yalta message to Congress, and the latter's decision to abandon him at this key moment seemed to wound the president. Perhaps out of exhaustion, or hubris, or perhaps overwhelmed by the knowledge that

Watson's health had taken a further turn for the worse, FDR appeared unable or unwilling to recognize the seriousness of Hopkins's condition. He suspected that the real reason Hopkins wanted to leave was to escape the tediousness of the journey. As a result, their parting that afternoon was not a pleasant one. Anna, too, was "furious" over Hopkins's decision to leave. But Hopkins was in fact gravely ill. Within two days of his arrival in Washington, he was flown immediately to the Mayo Clinic, from which he would not emerge until he had to rush back to Washington to attend the president's funeral.[29]

Since Bohlen planned to accompany Hopkins on his return journey, and since Stephen Early was scheduled to depart that day to take up a planned visit to Eisenhower's headquarters in France, Rosenman suddenly found himself tasked with helping the president draft this major address without the assistance of three of the key people who had been at Yalta. Admiral Leahy suggested that Rosenman hold a "hurried conference" with Hopkins, Bohlen, and Early in the hectic hours before their departure. Armed with this "fill-in" information, which was supplemented by a six-page memorandum Bohlen hastily dictated before he left, Rosenman went right to work. He hoped that it might be possible for him and the president to complete a final draft in advance of their arrival at Gibraltar in roughly twenty-four hours, which might allow him to return to London. But it soon became apparent that "the hard voyage to Yalta and the shattering responsibilities of the conference" had sapped the president's strength, and no matter how hard Rosenman tried, he could not get his chief to work on the speech.

THE EXPANSE OF OCEAN BETWEEN ALGIERS ON THE NORTH AFRICAN coast and Newport News, Virginia, runs roughly 4,200 miles. Thus far, Captain Elliott Senn and the other officers of his task force could look back on the president's journey with a high degree of satisfaction. They had run into some fairly high seas and stiff winds in their first traverse of the Atlantic, but they had brought the president to his first destination, Malta, safely, and had not run into any difficulties since their departure from the Great Bitter Lake a few days before.

But as FDR and his party settled down to dinner on the evening of February 18, 1945, Captain Senn was unnerved by a report indicating possible U-boat activity in the region and even more so by the news that two Allied merchant ships had been sunk in the vicinity of Gibraltar the night before. Thus the security screen around the *Quincy* was enhanced considerably. A third destroyer was added to the task force as the president's vessel left the harbor, and within hours of breaking out into the Mediterranean, the group was joined by three more destroyers, so that by 11:00 p.m. that night the *Quincy* was protected by no fewer than seven warships.

At noon the next day, there was much excitement as the now-famous USS *Murphy* approached the Quincy to deliver both the president's mail and Commander Bernard A. Smith's report on the ship's "Mission to Mecca." About an hour later, the *Quincy* and its now eight escort vessels entered the Strait of Gibraltar, steaming ahead at 27 knots. As on the way into the Mediterranean, above them flew two Ventura bombers, a squadron of P-38 fighters, and a K-Class Navy Blimp.[30]

With the famous rock clearly visible seven miles off the starboard bow, the task force increased its speed to 29 knots, passing the Cape Spartel Light shortly after 2:00 p.m. and then, at last, reaching the Atlantic. Roughly three hours later, this most dangerous portion of the return voyage having been completed, four of the eight escorts broke away from the task force, leaving the *Quincy* with the light cruiser USS *Savannah* and the usual complement of three destroyers for the rest of the crossing.

FDR did little over the twenty-four-hour period between the *Quincy*'s departure from Algiers and the ship's safe passage into the Atlantic. Nevertheless, he seemed extremely worn, and as a result, Anna and Drs. Bruenn and McIntire agreed that he should spend the next two days in bed. But on the very morning that Anna intended to put this regime into place, Pa Watson died. Anna had just finished her breakfast when Dr. Bruenn brought her the news, and for a time the two of them talked about what effect this might have on her father. Watson was much more than the president's appointments secretary and aide. He was also a dear friend, and there was no question that his passing would come as a severe blow.[31]

Anna and Dr. Bruenn waited anxiously outside FDR's quarters as Ross McIntire went in to inform the president. Dr. McIntire soon emerged to say that FDR "had taken it in his stride," which, Anna reflected, was "typical of him," although he was prone "to hide much in the way of inside turmoil." Anna then went in to see her father, accompanied by Admiral Brown, and together the three of them discussed the message to send to Frances Watson, the noted concert pianist and the general's spouse of twenty-five years. After determining that it would be best to keep FDR's mind occupied so he would not "be thinking too much about Pa," Anna abandoned the notion that he should spend two days in bed. It would be far better to keep him engaged in his usual routine, and after about fifteen minutes, she suggested he go up on deck to take in the sun.[32]

ANYONE WHO KNEW FRANKLIN D. ROOSEVELT WOULD AGREE THAT he had an ebullient personality. The similarly affable Churchill once compared seeing him to opening a bottle of champagne. Thus his behavior in the days that followed Watson's death suggests that the passing of his old friend and aide threw FDR into a sort of depression.

As Dr. McIntire observed, up to this point the thought of death rarely seemed to enter into FDR's mind. Aside from his "natural buoyancy and sanguine temperament" there was "the immediacy of the tasks that lay before him," which seemed to render him incapable—even after the deaths of many dear associates—of losing faith in his own invulnerability.[33]

But Watson's death was different. Following lunches in his cabin, FDR spent time on the deck "quietly reading, or just smoking and staring off into the horizon." Sometimes Anna, Admiral Leahy, or Judge Rosenman joined him, but more often than not they left him "alone with his book—and his thoughts." When the sun began to sink, the president retired to his cabin for a nap before dinner. Although evening meals were preceded by a "cocktail hour," during which FDR seemed comparatively more animated, he showed no interest in doing any work after dinner in the evenings, which was highly unusual when he was preparing a major address. Instead, he would retire to Admiral Leahy's quarters with the rest of his party to watch a film, followed immediately by bed.[34]

As Rosenman recounted, this somnolent routine continued day after day as the *Quincy* made its way westward. Exasperated at the president's unwillingness to help him draft the Yalta address, Rosenman turned to Anna for help. By the time FDR finally turned his attention to the speech—on February 26, one day before their expected landfall—Anna had more or less churned out two complete drafts of her own.[35]

Once FDR got involved in the drafting of the address, he and Rosenman spent a good deal of time discussing the larger meaning of the Yalta conference. FDR intimated that many challenges lay ahead, not least the task of adhering to the "tough principles contained in the Atlantic Charter," which, he was convinced, would bring to the surface his differences of opinion with Churchill. But like Churchill, FDR believed that Stalin was a man of his word, and that the Soviet leader was interested in maintaining the peace of the world—in part, because peace would allow the Soviets to focus on their recovery from the war. Overall, he remained optimistic that the Yalta conference "had paved the way for the kind of world he had been dreaming, planning and talking about."[36]

As the USS *Quincy* began its final approach to Newport News, FDR drafted another statement, one conveying the sense of loss he felt in the wake of General Watson's death.[37] Taking note of "a great personal sorrow to me," and acutely aware that he would be returning to a White House devoid of the warm presence, good humor, and discerning hand of General Watson, FDR admitted that he "would miss him almost more than I can express." He observed that Watson had been his military aide and, later, his appointments secretary for twelve years, and yet had become such a close friend that "there was never a cloud between us." Then, in an implied reference to the fact that Watson—like FDR—had been advised by his doctors not to undertake this arduous journey, FDR noted how Watson, out of his loyalty to the president and to the country, had insisted on seeing the war through and "on taking this trip with me." This statement, which reflected FDR's emphasis on loyalty and duty, would be repeated almost word for word upon his own death a mere six weeks later.[38]

THE *QUINCY* HAD BEEN BLESSED WITH WHAT ADMIRAL LEAHY described as semi-tropical weather since it left the Mediterranean. But during the final hours of their voyage, the president and his party encountered a stiff headwind and some "very rough seas." In the past, such conditions would not have deterred FDR from going out on deck to take in the sights as the ship made its way through the Chesapeake Channel, past Hampton Roads, and into the harbor. But on this occasion, he remained in his cabin.

At 6:25 p.m., the *Quincy* finally arrived, docking at the same pier from which it had departed more than five weeks before. FDR did not disembark immediately but, rather, stayed on board to have dinner with Captain Senn and a number of other officers. Just over two hours later, the president was wheeled to his waiting railway car, where he would observe the solemn transfer of General Watson's body from the ship to the train, under full military honors; his coffin carried by six officers from the *Quincy* as pallbearers, accompanied by Captain Senn, the ship's chaplain, and the shrill, plaintive piping of the *Quincy's* boatswain.[39] After the general's flag-draped casket was placed on board a special car reserved for that purpose, FDR spent the next thirty minutes on the telephone with various officials in Washington, making sure that all of the necessary arrangements for the burial of his old friend at Arlington the next day were in order. He also spoke to Eleanor and put in a call to Daisy, who was relieved that he was "safely back" but saddened, too, to hear the news about "Pa," the one person "FDR could lean on both figuratively and physically." Unbeknownst to either Eleanor or Daisy, however, FDR also spent five minutes speaking to Lucy Rutherfurd, who expressed similar relief that he had returned safe and sound.[40]

Finally, at 10:15 p.m., the president's train began its slow trek across Virginia, northwest to Richmond and on to Gordonsville, just east of Watson's beloved seventy-five-acre estate at Kenwood, nestled in the rolling hills not far from Monticello. FDR spent many a happy occasion there, first in a cottage that Watson had constructed for the president's use, but more often in the main house, which FDR preferred. It was at Kenwood, in fact, over the course of four anxious days in June 1944, that FDR awaited the long-anticipated invasion of Normandy—an invasion that did so much to seal the fate of the hateful regime that had made his long journey to Yalta a necessity.

Chapter 13

The Last Address

IT WAS JUST BEFORE 9:00 A.M. ON WEDNESDAY, FEBRUARY 28, 1945, that FDR arrived back at the White House. Given that he had been away for a full five weeks, his arrival was met with a good deal of fanfare by the small circle of family, friends, and White House staff who saw the president on a regular basis. One telling aspect of their natural desire to see him was the extent to which one question above all others dominated these encounters: How was his health? Had the long sea voyage and time away from Washington "restored him," as was often the case in the past? Or had the strain of the long journey and conference produced the opposite effect?

His inner circle arrived at mixed conclusions. Eleanor initially thought the trip had done him good. As she wrote to her friend, Joseph Lash, he seemed rested, and in his conversations with her about the journey, FDR averred that "he felt well all the time." But Eleanor's view soon began to change. She found him less and less willing to see people for any length of time. He needed a rest in the middle of the day, and, even though he had been away from Washington for five full weeks, he was soon anxious to get away again.[1]

William Hassett, who went to see FDR as he was having breakfast with Eleanor that first morning, thought that the president "had come home in the pink of condition" and that he hadn't "looked better in a year." Hassett also noted his high spirits. But Grace Tully, who was perhaps the most astute observer of FDR's state of mind and health, due to her almost constant contact with him, was quite alarmed. The "signs of weariness were etched deeply in his thinning face," she thought. More troubling, the sea voyage, which was "usually the best tonic for him in any circumstance, had not brought out the ruddy tan and sparkle of eye which we always expected."[2] Even Dr. McIntire, who always tried to cast FDR's condition in the best light possible, was disturbed, detecting increasing "signs of weariness" as FDR tried to cope with the enormous pile of work that had accumulated on his desk over his long absence.[3]

Perhaps the most revealing comments came from FDR himself. His frequent mentions of his need for rest during the Yalta trip stood in sharp opposition to his claim that "he was really all right." In the two brief and affectionate notes he sent to Tully while he was at sea— one written on the way over and the other upon his return—he confessed that he'd had "[l]ots of sleep & still need more" and, two weeks later, that "[a]ll goes well but again I need sleep."[4]

Nor would there be any let-up in the responsibilities that confronted him. After spending much of his first morning back working on his still-unfinished Yalta speech, which he would deliver the next day to Congress, FDR traveled to Arlington Cemetery with Eleanor, Anna, Anna's husband John Boettiger, and a large contingent of the White House staff for the interment services of General Watson. Owing to a driving rain and sleet, the president remained in his car to look on from an open window, "his face grave and immobile," while Mrs. Watson, Eleanor, and the remainder of the president's party, along with General Marshall, Admiral Leahy, and a number of other top administration officials, stood under the canopy that sheltered the grave.[5]

Following the interment and a quiet lunch with Eleanor, FDR went back to work on his speech, aided by Samuel Rosenman, Anna, and John Boettiger. Together they finished a fourth and then a fifth draft, which was then put into a reading copy. Not satisfied, however, FDR went back to work that evening after dinner, altering the speech by hand to such an extent that it had to be retyped as a sixth draft.[6]

Thus far, the reaction to the Yalta conference had been encouraging—undoubtedly owing to Stephen Early's talent for spin, but also due to the work of James Byrnes, whose job it was to help sell the conference to the Congress and the American public. As a former congressman, senator, and associate justice of the Supreme Court, Byrnes was a highly respected public figure. After leaving Yalta early, he had returned home to give a major press conference in the packed East

Room of the White House on February 13, 1945, only two days after the Crimean summit ended. One purpose underlying this event was to drum up support among the members of Congress for US participation in the proposed world organization.[7]

In keeping with FDR's decision to "frame" Yalta as yet another step in his long-running effort to promote the values articulated in the Four Freedoms and the Atlantic Charter, Byrnes highlighted the Declaration of Liberated Europe as "among the most important specific results of the conference." As Byrnes put it, the declaration meant "the three powers had adopted a policy of acting in concert in liberated areas," in the hope that "political factions that might resort to violence or appeal to some great outside power for support would be deterred." The aim, he went on, "was to cooperate in the support of a provisional government" that would eventually hold "free and fair elections" and lead to the establishment of regimes "truly representative of the people."[8]

Perhaps most significant was Byrnes's insistence that FDR had brought the declaration to the Yalta conference to counter the growing fear "in this country that recent unilateral actions were leading to spheres of influence." Now, thanks to the declaration, the United States would demonstrate that by Washington's assuming "a share of the responsibility for conditions in such countries as Poland, Yugoslavia, [and] Greece," such exclusive spheres of influence were a thing of the past.

Byrnes's "magnificent" handling of the media pleased FDR. But his tendency to present the Declaration of Liberated Europe as a formal agreement rather than as a statement of intent masked many complexities, particularly with respect to Poland. This inclination on Byrnes's part may have been in keeping with FDR's plan to use the declaration to put added pressure on the Soviets to control their behavior in Poland and, in the process, inspire greater confidence among the American public for the Yalta accords. But it was a risky strategy in the event that the Soviets ultimately refused to reshape the Lublin regime along more democratic lines—which is exactly what happened.[9]

At this point, however, with the Soviet Union having signed on to the United Nations, FDR was focused on the need to secure popular support for the world organization. Byrnes's upbeat and optimistic assessment—which may have reflected his genuine view, perhaps because he was not a party to some of the most important discussions that went on at Yalta, especially regarding Poland—certainly helped set the stage for FDR to address Congress. But it also raised public expectations about the extent to which the "Big Three" had achieved a unity of purpose beyond the battlefield. Those expectations would never be far from FDR's mind in the days and weeks following what would prove to be the last major public address of his life.

IN THE MEANTIME, ON THE OTHER SIDE OF THE ATLANTIC, CHURchill was grappling with what he called "a good deal of uneasiness" in the British Parliament over the settlement the three powers had agreed to over Poland. Some of the opposition resulted from the territorial changes that had been agreed to, as one MP put it, without the Poles being consulted as to "how their coat is to be cut." Others were more concerned about the political consequences of the deal for Poland, particularly in light of the skepticism with which the Polish government-in-exile greeted its terms.[10]

Churchill did his best to counter this disquiet in a two-hour address to the House of Commons on February 27. "The impression he brought back from the Crimea," he said, "is that Marshal Stalin and the Soviet leaders wish to live in honorable friendship and equality with the Western democracies." He was confident that Stalin would live up to his promises. Indeed, he knew "of no other government . . . which stands to its obligations more solidly than the Russian Soviet Government."[11] In private, however, Churchill was less sure about the outcome of Yalta, and not only because of potential problems that might emerge from the Kremlin. Soon after the speech, he telegraphed Roosevelt in Washington to inform the president about the mood in Parliament, and to urge that "as many representative Poles as possible should be invited to the consultations in Moscow as soon as possible," all the more so because the London Poles—who had of course been completely locked out of the negotiations at Yalta—were "playing for a breakdown."[12]

Because of the US Constitution's requirement that any formal treaty must be approved by a two-thirds vote in the US Senate, and because of the greater degree of separation between the executive and legislative branches of government in the American system, FDR faced an even more difficult task than Churchill in trying to win congressional approval for the Yalta accords. Keenly aware of Woodrow Wilson's failure to secure Senate ratification for US participation in the League of Nations in 1920, FDR had already begun the process of trying to win Senate approval of the Charter of the United Nations by asking an equal number of Democrats and Republicans to serve on the US delegation to the San Francisco conference, where the final draft of the Charter would be negotiated. In private, the president and senior members of his administration had also explored the idea of launching a constitutional amendment to get rid of the two-thirds vote requirement for ratification of treaties in the Senate. They understood that "this would be a tough . . . amendment to get through," but nevertheless argued that "the fact that it is being pushed would put the Senate on its toes when any treaty came up before it." To bolster this effort, senior administration officials also argued that nongovernmental bodies such as "The Americans United for World Organization" should become part of this effort, doubtless as a means to further pressure the Senate to fall into line and vote to ratify the charter. In addition, FDR invited Senate Majority leader Alben Barkley to the White House for a private briefing on Yalta. There was limited time between the president's return to Washington and his speech to Congress, so the meeting was held early on the morning of March 1—just hours before the president was to make his way to the Capitol.[13]

Barkley found FDR alone in his bathroom, seated in his wheelchair, and preparing to shave. "Sit down," the president said. When Barkley asked where, FDR, "with a whimsical glint in his eyes . . . motioned to a certain functional stool." Barkley complied, and remained there for well over an hour while the two men discussed the world situation in what turned out to be one of the most unusual talks the senator ever had with Franklin Roosevelt. "Every time the President would start to shave," he later recalled, "he would become so absorbed in telling me the details of his conversation with Stalin that the lather would dry on his face and he would have to start all over again."[14]

Barkley came away from the encounter convinced that the president had not underestimated Stalin—that he had not been "taken in by him at Yalta." Nor did he feel there was "any diminution in his mental alertness," though it was clear that he was beginning to fail physically." His mind, however, "was keen," and while in retrospect

FDR—like Churchill—"may have overestimated Stalin's good faith," in Barkley's view this was "perfectly natural" for any member of the wartime alliance.[15]

After seeing the Senate Majority leader off, FDR retired to his Oval Study, to prepare for his noontime address to Congress. As in the past, the president entered the building through a private entrance in the east wing and made his way to Speaker Sam Rayburn's office on the second floor, before making his entrance to the House Chamber. As he was about to be wheeled into Rayburn's office, Benjamin West, a young press aide who was in a desperate rush to retrieve printed copies of the president's address, nearly toppled the president over as he bolted out of an adjacent elevator. West smashed his head on a cast-iron wall cabinet as he flung himself sideways to avoid running into the president and the Secret Service agent who was accompanying him. A bemused FDR said, "Are you all right, young man?" To which the stunned and embarrassed West replied, "Yes, sir, I think so." FDR reached out his hand to the young aide, who would go on to become the superintendent of the House Press Gallery over two decades later. West never forgot the president's kind gesture, nor his sallow features. "He looked terribly bad that day."[16]

ACCORDING TO THE METICULOUS NAVAL LOGS OF FDR'S JOURNEY TO Yalta, the president had traveled 13,842 miles in the previous five weeks. It was an extraordinary expedition, particularly for a man confined to a wheelchair who could manage "to walk" a short distance only with the help of rigid steel braces, a cane, and the strong arm of one of his sons or close aides. FDR had developed this technique after years of convalescence in Warm Springs, Georgia, out of a sheer determination to never be viewed by the public as a "cripple" but instead to be seen as a man who had largely recovered the use of his legs. The first sign that he had succeeded in this effort came at the Democratic Convention in 1928, when he was asked to place the name of Al Smith in nomination for president of the United States. At the same event in 1924—his first public appearance since the onset of his disease—he had made his way from the back of the stage to the podium using crutches as a crowd of more than sixteen thousand looked on in hushed silence, and then burst into rapturous applause as he grabbed the podium, threw back his head, and flashed that famous smile.[17]

Now, four years later, after countless hours of strenuous effort and practice, FDR made his way to the podium during the 1928 convention using the gait the public soon became so familiar with—swinging each braced leg forward one at a time, steadied by a cane and the arm of his son, head up, smiling and laughing as if he were out for a leisurely afternoon stroll.

The truth, of course, was that this exercise in "walking" took tremendous effort and concentration, and was also highly nerve-racking, as an unexpected fall could have shattered the entire illusion—and perhaps his political career along with it. But as the *Washington Post* reported that day in 1928, FDR was "now sufficiently recovered from his physical disability to walk," making his way to the podium "in a perfect thunder of cheering . . . supported only by the arm of his tall, slender son Elliott."[18]

Having convinced the press and public that he had regained the use of his legs, and was no longer "a paraplegic" as the *Chicago Daily Tribune* described him in 1924, FDR went on with his career as if this was in fact true. He rarely discussed his disability, even with those closest to him, and he used his wheelchair only to get from one point to another and refused to be photographed in it. He also seems to have spent much of his life believing that somehow, someway, he might still regain the ability to stand on his own. FDR never thought of himself as disabled, and—despite his association with efforts to eradicate polio, including the famous "March of Dimes"—almost never mentioned his own encounter with the disease in public.[19]

For all of these reasons, perhaps the most remarkable odyssey the president took in the spring of 1945 was not his trip to Yalta but his journey down the center aisle of the US House of Representatives on the morning of March 1, where, in full view of the packed and wildly cheering chamber, he made his way in his wheelchair.[20] No longer willing to use the painful and cumbersome braces that made it possible for him "to stand" at the Speaker's Podium, FDR decided instead to deliver his speech from the Well of the House, on the actual floor, in front of the Rostrum, using a small table and chair placed there for this purpose.

Watching this remarkable scene from the gallery above, as her husband was slowly wheeled forward from the back of the House while the crowd, now standing on its feet, continued to applaud, Eleanor could not help but reflect on the many long years FDR had struggled to regain the full use of his legs: his willingness to try any number of therapies, the endless exercise and attempts to swim his way back to health, and his absolute refusal to give up hope. Now, it was as if he had finally come to accept "a certain degree of invalidism." He was not, as he told a 1928 campaign audience, a man who had come "down with infantile paralysis," and who, thanks to the "very best kind of care," was now back on his feet. Instead, he was someone who had triumphed over his disability in ways that had nothing to do with the fact that he could not—and never would be able to—walk or stand on his own.[21]

After maneuvering himself out of his wheelchair and into the upholstered chair behind a table packed with microphones (again, in full view of the assembled), FDR asked his audience to "pardon me for this unusual posture of sitting down during the presentation of what it is I want to say." He then made only the second direct public reference to his disability since 1928: "But I know that you will realize that it makes it a lot easier for me in not having to carry about ten pounds of steel around on the bottom of my legs; and also because of the fact that I have just completed a fourteen-thousand-mile trip." Frances Perkins found this "casual, debonair" reference to his disability, "made with-out self-pity or strain," deeply moving. Choking up, she, like Eleanor, realized that what FDR was admitting—not only to the audience but to himself—was "You see, I am a crippled man."[22]

To further applause, FDR said "that it was good to be home," and went on to explain why he had gone to Yalta and why he had made the unprecedented decision to give a "personal report" to the members of Congress and also to the American people. There were two main pur-poses behind the Crimea conference: first, to bring about the defeat of Germany "with the greatest possible speed" and, second, to build "an international accord" that would bring order and security to the world after the chaos of war and "some assurance of a lasting peace among the nations of the world." He reviewed many of the issues that had been touched upon at Yalta, stressing, as Byrnes did, the postwar treatment of "liberated areas." This included areas where "political confusion and unrest—as in Greece or in Poland or in Yugoslavia"—had led the world's powers toward creating "spheres of influence" that he regarded as "incompatible with the basic principles of international collaboration."

FDR addressing Congress on the Yalta accords from a seated position, after being pushed to the front of the House of Representatives in his wheelchair, March 1, 1945. (Getty Images)

FDR refused to "place the blame" for this development on any one nation, claiming it was almost inevitable—"unless the major powers of the world continue to work together." It was in part to secure such collaboration and "settle the matter of liberated areas" that the Big Three met in Crimea. As FDR put it, thanks to this effort the Allies now agreed that the political and economic problems of the territories freed from Nazi conquest are a "joint responsibility."

FDR held up Poland as the prime example of how "joint action . . . by the three powers" in a liberated area should work—clearly linking the settlement over Poland to the principles articulated in the broader declaration. He acknowledged that coming to a final decision about a given territory required compromise. "We shall not always have ideal answers or solutions to complicated international problems, even though we are determined continuously to strive toward that ideal." But he insisted that the three powers' objectives regarding Poland were "to help create a strong, independent and prosperous nation." He reiterated this point by issuing what amounted to both a warning to Russia and a reassurance to the Polish-American community. "That is the thing we must always remember," he said, "those words, agreed to by Russia, by Britain and by the United States: the objective of making Poland a strong, independent, and prosperous nation, with a government ultimately to be selected by the Polish people themselves."

FDR then moved on to the United Nations and the upcoming San Francisco conference, stressing the need to establish what he referred to as "the structure of world peace." This, he insisted, "cannot be the work of one man, or one party, or one Nation." Nor, as he had cautioned in his January State of the Union address, was it likely to be "a structure of complete perfection at first." But, he went on, "it can be a peace—and it will be a peace—based on the sound and just principles of the Atlantic Charter—on the concept of the dignity of the human being—and on the guarantees of tolerance and freedom of religious worship."

To achieve this goal, FDR urged the American people to recognize that the world was now much smaller and that "responsibility for political conditions thousands of miles away can no longer be avoided by this great Nation." The public and Congress had the chance to embrace this new world through their support for the establishment of the United Nations. In this sense Yalta was a turning point, but only if the United States continued to work toward the goals that FDR had expressed there. "There can be no middle ground here," he cautioned. "We shall have to take the responsibility for world collaboration, or we shall have to bear the responsibility for another world conflict."

FDR closed on a note of both caution and hope. "Twenty-five years ago," he said, "American fighting men looked to the statesmen of the world to finish the work of peace for which they fought and suffered. We failed them then. We cannot fail them again, and expect the world again to survive."

At the very end of the speech he made a plea to the American people to commit themselves to "the beginnings of a permanent structure of peace upon which we can begin to build, under God, that better world in which our children and grandchildren—yours and mine, the children and grandchildren of the whole world—must live, and can live."[23]

FDR's use of the word *beginnings* is telling, for it shows that FDR did not see Yalta—as later generations still do—as a final settlement for Poland and other parts of Europe. Instead, he viewed it as a starting point, as a time when the American people in collaboration—not confrontation—with their wartime Allies would inaugurate the work toward that permanent structure of peace upon which, he believed, the fate of the world now rested. To FDR, the most critical moment had not passed, but lay in the future.

SAMUEL ROSENMAN, WHO TRAVELED WITH FDR BACK TO THE WHITE House, was of course pleased with the content of the speech. But he was less pleased with FDR's "halting, ineffective manner of delivery," and even more upset over the many extemporaneous remarks the president had inserted into the address. "It was quite obvious that the great fighting eloquence and oratory that had distinguished him in his campaign only four months before were lacking," he later reflected. Indeed, he could not help but feel that "the crushing effect of twelve years of the Presidency was beginning to be more and more evident."[24]

Nor was Rosenman the only person to observe FDR's fatigue. In an article titled "Armchair Speech Stirs Comment on Roosevelt's Health," the *Chicago Daily Tribune* reported that "for the first time since he became President, Mr. Roosevelt permitted himself to be wheeled into the house to address the joint session." The article also quoted one senator's approval of the president's decision to deliver the speech while seated: he "means so much to the nation that he ought to conserve his strength anyway he can." But others present remarked that the president seemed "noticeably tired" and that his voice "did not seem to have the resilience it once did."[25]

In fact, rumors about FDR's health had begun to circulate before his return from abroad. On February 24, the semi-official Vatican News Service reported that the president had "hurriedly left" the summit meeting "due to the fact that the condition of his health is not too good." Other sources reported that the president was fine, but in need of a rest. To counter all of the talk, Dr. McIntire and the White House Press Office once again went on the offensive. In an article published on the same morning that FDR gave his speech, the *New York Times* wrote that companions of the president on his trip "were unanimous . . . in the view that except for a slight cold on his outward journey, his health was excellent." Dr. McIntire was quoted as saying that "in spite of long sessions of hard work the President stood up well under the strain," while FDR's newly appointed press secretary, Jonathan Daniels, swore that the president was in "great shape."[26]

Not everyone within the Roosevelt administration was adhering to the party line. Harold Ickes informed John Boettiger that James Byrnes, perhaps still angry that he had not been chosen to serve as FDR's running mate in the 1944 election, had been spreading the word that "the President's health is bad, or at least not good." This comment led the president's son-in-law to remark to Ickes—in keeping with Anna's instructions—that he had received "several letters from Anna" that spoke "of her father being in good health."[27] FDR himself got into the act, mentioning, in one of his ad-libbed remarks during the Yalta address, that he had returned from his trip "refreshed and inspired" and was "not ill for a second"—that is, until he returned to Washington where he heard "all of the rumors" that had spread in his absence.

His speech over, FDR headed back to the Oval Office. In addition to the enormous backlog of paperwork, there were many visitors all pressing to see him. In the absence of General Watson, the task of setting FDR's appointments calendar now fell to William Hassett, assisted by Jonathan Daniels, and especially Anna, who, shortly after FDR's return, pulled Daniels aside to inform him that Dr. Bruenn was insisting that her father "greatly restrict his activities." Anna asserted that "the President should see very few people" and suggested that Daniels should talk to those who wished to see FDR, and then pass on any relevant messages to Anna and her husband for decision. They hoped not to burden the president "with anything but the greatest matters."[28]

An experienced Washington insider, Daniels was highly skeptical of Anna's "plan," which in his view amounted to something akin to the "regency" that Mrs. Wilson and Dr. Cary Grayson had assumed after President Wilson's debilitating stroke in 1918. But it was a strong indication that the president's health was far more precarious than many people had previously thought. Nor did the plan work. As FDR reported to Daisy in a telephone call on Saturday, March 3, "he has had and is having, an exhausting time seeing people"—fixing things that have gotten out of hand during his absence, with everyone waiting around "for him to lead & guide." Worse still, he had not been able to slip away to Hyde Park the night before as he had originally planned. He was now scheduled to leave on an overnight train later that evening.[29]

Given his love for his home on the Hudson, and the schedule he had maintained over the last two days—including a press conference and a cabinet meeting; separate conferences with acting Secretary of State Joseph Grew, Henry Stimson, Harold Ickes, Bernard Baruch, and James Byrnes; a luncheon with Eleanor and Colonel Harold Hoskins to review FDR's discussions with Ibn Saud over Palestine; and a dinner with Crown Prince Olav and Crown Princess Martha of Norway—FDR could hardly wait to get away. His departure that Saturday night would place him in Hyde Park on the morning of Sunday, March 4, 1945, exactly twelve years to the day since he had first taken the oath of office.

Chapter 14

March Days

IT WAS A COLD AND CRISP MORNING WHEN THE CAR THAT WOULD take Franklin and Eleanor Roosevelt from the train station at Highland, New York, crossed the Mid-Hudson Bridge. Standing majestically 135 feet above the Hudson River, with its elegant granite spires and stunning views of the valley that FDR loved, this magnificent structure was at the time the sixth-longest suspension bridge in the world. Casting an eye in the late winter light upon this all-important waterway that had done so much to shape the history of New York and the nation, FDR could see that the Hudson was still frozen. In years past, long before he had lost the use of his legs, he might well have been out on "the river" that day, "flying" across the frozen surface in *the Hawk,* his much-cherished ice-yacht—the Christmas gift his mother had lavished upon him when he was but a nineteen-year-old student at Harvard.[1]

Perhaps too, FDR might have cast his mind back to a warm summer's day twenty-five years before, when FDR, as governor, had joined former Governor Al Smith in a dedication ceremony to open the span that was witnessed by a crowd of twenty-five thousand people. The lead architect-engineer was the much-celebrated Ralph Modjeski, who, as the principal designer of the San Francisco Bay Bridge in California and the Delaware River Bridge in Philadelphia, was known as "America's bridge builder." As a Polish-American immigrant, Modjeski embodied the "smaller world" that FDR had referred to in his speech to Congress. He was born and raised in Krakow, the official "capital" of the Nazis' murderous "General Government"—a city liberated by the

Red Army a mere six weeks earlier. Modjeski was also a close associate of Ignacy Jan Paderewski, the distinguished Polish musician, composer, and diplomat, who played a key role in convincing Woodrow Wilson to call for the creation of a free and independent Polish state in his January 1918 Fourteen Points—the very state whose fate FDR and Churchill were now struggling to secure.[2]

After breakfast in his study, FDR began replying to the mail that had accumulated since well before his departure for Yalta. He planned to use the next three or four days in Hyde Park to rest and put all of this correspondence behind him. This required both morning and afternoon sessions with his principal secretaries, broken up by lunch, an occasional drive to visit local sites and people, and, when time allowed, a late-afternoon rest.

Daisy was of course thrilled to see FDR back in the Hudson Valley. The following morning, March 5, she left her home in Rhinebeck early to make sure she would be at Springwood in time to serve FDR his breakfast. Elated, as she recorded in her diary, that "F looks so much better than anyone could expect," and happy to hear him report that "he was fine throughout the trip—not sick a day," Daisy indicated that she had arranged for FDR to receive another "treatment" from Lenny Setaro (the masseuse she believed could help restore FDR's health) that evening. Daisy also learned, much to her delight, that FDR was already planning a trip to Warm Springs at the end of the month and that he would like her and "Cousin Polly" to accompany him, not only to Georgia but also to the San Francisco conference in late April.[3]

While in Hyde Park, FDR also took the time to meet with the director of the municipal library, which his family had helped found and which was named for his father.[4] By this point, Eleanor had left for her apartment in New York, and, as was often the case, it seemed to take FDR a day or two to fully relax. But in spite of the simple routine and the extra rest, Daisy often found him "tired and listless." Perhaps, she surmised, he was thinking of the "long list of callers" that awaited him in Washington; then there was the endless correspondence as well. By Wednesday, March 7, FDR had made great progress. But then a heavy mail pouch arrived, so heavy that it would require not only work in the morning and early afternoon, but also some additional work late that evening, between Daisy's departure after dinner at 9:00 and the moment FDR's train pulled out of the Highland Station at 11:00 for the slow overnight trip back to the Oval Office.

THE NEXT SIXTEEN DAYS WOULD PROVE TO BE THE LONGEST CONTINU-ous stretch of time FDR spent in the White House during his fourth term. During this period, Allied forces finally and decisively crossed the Rhine, which was of course welcome news, but this was also the time when the careful diplomatic web that FDR had spun at Yalta began to disintegrate.

The first indication that the conference accords might not hold up came in the form of a telegram from Churchill that arrived on March 8, the same day FDR had returned from his short stay in Hyde Park. Churchill had become increasingly alarmed by Soviet behavior in East-ern Europe. Russian activities in Romania, Bulgaria, and Hungary sug-gested that the Soviets were intent on interpreting the Declaration of Liberated Europe in a manner that suited their own purposes. Chur-chill was unhappy with the growing evidence of the Soviets' brutality in their establishing of "friendly" regimes in these states. But due to the understanding he had achieved over these territories via the October 1944 accords—which included Soviet acquiescence to British actions to put down the communist-led rebellion in Greece—he was as yet unwill-ing to openly challenge the Russians over their treatment of the region.

Soviet behavior in Poland was even more disturbing, not least because the fate of the Poles aroused deep feeling in Britain.[5] Churchill had based his defense of the Yalta accords in Parliament in part "on the assumption that the words of the Yalta declaration will be carried out in the letter and the spirit." But, to date, all of the evidence showed that the Soviets were unwilling to offer even the pretense of Great Power consultation over the future of Poland, let alone adherence to any sort of democratic process.[6] The expansion of the Lublin regime that was supposed to take place in Moscow, for example, had quickly degen-erated into what Churchill called "a farce," as all of the non-Lublin candidates put forward by the British and American ambassadors had been rejected by Molotov. From what little information London could retrieve from within Poland, it also appeared that the Soviets were sys-tematically using "liquidations and deportations" to eliminate Polish political opposition to the Lublin government.[7]

Although still cognizant of the need for Great Power cooperation, Churchill felt that the time had come to take a much tougher line with Moscow. But this was a complicated proposition, given the inherent contradictions in London adopting a policy condemning Soviet spheres of influence in Eastern Europe while doing its best to maintain British control over Greece, Yugoslavia, and the Middle East. Churchill thus recognized that the most effective means to pressure the Soviets was through FDR.[8]

Roosevelt shared many of Churchill's concerns about Soviet activities in Poland. As he wrote to Churchill three days later, "I am fully determined, as I know you are, not to let the good decisions we made at Crimea slip through our hands and will certainly do everything I can to hold Stalin to their honest fulfillment." But he was not as yet convinced that they should confront Stalin. As Charles Bohlen explained to Ambassador Edward Halifax in response to Churchill's démarche, the president wanted to avoid using "heavy artillery" at this point and preferred "to give the matter time." Instead, FDR embraced the idea of a "political truce" designed to end the actions taken against the Lublin Poles' political opponents—a less partisan, more even-handed approach that FDR felt would have a greater chance of success.[9]

FDR was also receiving mixed news from the Pacific Theater. On the one hand, the advance of MacArthur's forces on the island of Luzon in the Philippines and the heroic struggle of the Marines to take Iwo Jima were seen as significant developments. But the casualty reports made clear that the struggle to defeat Japan would be costly. Indeed, it would take a full month of bloody fighting—and the deaths of three of the six Marines who had so heroically hoisted the American flag over Mount Suribachi—before the Japanese garrison of twenty-one thousand men on Iwo Jima was finally annihilated.[10]

On the home front, FDR faced a threatened coal strike and was frustrated by the lack of action in Congress over his manpower bill. Even more vexing—and embarrassing, given FDR's repeated pleas for "some men and some power"—was the press's reaction. By this point the press had relabeled "the work or fight bill" as the "work or loaf bill," suspecting, correctly, that Congress was essentially stalling in the hope that the defeat of Germany would render the law unnecessary.

Then there was the bitter and begrudging manner in which Henry Wallace was finally confirmed as secretary of commerce, and the hostility with which the Senate greeted FDR's nomination of Aubrey Williams as director of the Rural Electrification Agency.[11] Not willing to risk a confrontation with Congress on the eve of the San Francisco conference, FDR did his best to remain on good terms with the legislature, largely by being cautions. He did not, for instance, reappoint David Lilienthal, a prominent liberal, as head of the Tennessee Valley Authority. Eleanor Roosevelt considered this move craven, but FDR insisted it was necessary to avoid a showdown with a number of conservative southern senators who remained determined to get rid of Lilienthal no matter how hard FDR tried to protect him.[12]

FDR also had to cope with the loss or absence of some of his most trusted aides. Pa Watson's death had left a significant void, and the determination of Stephen Early (who was still on assignment in Europe) to leave his post as press secretary created a certain degree of "confusion" in the press office at a critical moment in FDR's presidency. And with Harry Hopkins away at the Mayo Clinic, Charles Bohlen became the principal liaison between the White House and the State Department. Visiting the White House every morning to confer with Admiral Leahy and to check on what telegrams had come into the Map Room, Bohlen found himself "continually worried" by the president's appearance. "His hand shook so," Bohlen recalled, "that he had difficulty holding a telegram." He was clearly a sick man. Yet despite his "weariness and general lassitude," FDR seemed to be able "to call on reserves of strength" whenever he had to meet with congressional leaders or other public figures.[13]

One notable instance took place when a group of visiting French journalists dropped in on one of the president's regularly scheduled news conferences. Seeming to enjoy the presence of the French delegation, which included Jean-Paul Sartre, FDR invited them to stay for a time after the conference so that he could speak to them in his "Roosevelt French."

"Roosevelt does not look at all like his photos," Sartre later reflected. "What is most striking is the profoundly human charm of his long face, at once sensitive and strong." He smiled "and talked to us in his deep slow voice," Sartre wrote, and exhibited such "bright-eyed intelligence" that Sartre came away from the encounter believing that the meeting with Roosevelt made the entire trip to the United States worthwhile.[14]

After the meeting with the French journalists, FDR convened a session of his cabinet. This might have been a fairly routine affair, save that it began with a stark reminder that no American was immune from the costs of the ongoing war. At the very moment the meeting was taking place, Marine Second Lieutenant Raymond Ickes was lying gravely wounded in a hospital tent on the still-contested island of Iwo Jima, having been shot through the lungs while making his way man-to-man through a murderous barrage in an effort to rally his platoon. "Harold, I understand that your boy has been hit," said the president as he entered the Oval Office. To which the grave-faced Secretary Ickes responded in the affirmative, while his colleagues looked on. "Do you know how bad it is?" FDR continued. Ickes had no answer.[15]

Numerous general expressions of sympathy followed, but then it was time to get on with the business at hand. As Secretary of the Navy, James Forrestal recorded, Ickes himself opened the discussion with a rather discouraging assessment of the status of the current negotiations between the United Mine Workers and the mine operators, along with an equally gloomy forecast of the supply of coal for the coming year. Frances Perkins broke in to insist that she was far more optimistic about the state of the negotiations. Reflecting later, Ickes acknowledged that Labor Secretary Perkins had a point about the state of the labor talks, but given the news that Ickes had received from the Pacific, he found himself "not too much interested in what went on at Cabinet." Ickes was just going through the motions while he anxiously awaited word on whether or not his son would pull through, or whether, like Harry Hopkins and thousands of other Americans, he would find himself grieving for the loss of a loved one in battle.[16]

WHILE BACK IN THE WHITE HOUSE, FDR AGAIN LARGELY ABANDONED the "regime" Drs. Bruenn and McIntire had previously prescribed for him. He often missed his afternoon rest; turned his lunches, which were supposed to be quiet affairs, into conferences; and worked far into the night. The more he worked, the more he seemed to crave relief. Indeed, the reason he worked so hard and crammed his schedule so full of meetings was to free up time to see the few people in his life with whom he could relax.

One of these intimates was Canadian Prime Minister Mackenzie King, who spent the weekend of March 10 and 11 in the White House, followed by a second shorter visit on Tuesday, March 13. FDR was a student at Harvard when he first met King. Over the years, while the two men pursued their political careers, they kept in touch, and their friendship deepened as they both tried to meet the challenges of economic depression and war as the leaders of their respective countries. King's scheduled arrival was set for 5:00 p.m. on Friday, March 9. Due to FDR's hectic agenda, King would spend the first half hour having tea alone with Eleanor. Perhaps anticipating the prime minister's first question, Eleanor began the conversation by noting the president's weariness. She also spoke about his being "pretty thin," almost as if she were preparing King, who was seven years older than FDR, for the shock of his appearance. It was obvious, King noted, that Mrs. Roosevelt "was pretty anxious" about her husband, and when the president wheeled himself in, King immediately understood the reason. As soon as he saw his old friend, he was seized by a sense of deep compassion. "He looked much older," he recorded in his diary, and, as Eleanor had cautioned, much thinner—particularly his face, which King noted had taken on a striking resemblance to Woodrow Wilson.[17]

Over the next two days FDR regaled King with accounts of his meetings with Haile Selassie and Ibn Saud, his impressions of Churchill and Stalin, and his expectations for the San Francisco conference. The two men returned to the topic of fatigue, which FDR admitted was "one of the hardest things to overcome." His doctors "kept advising him to take a rest before dinner," but he found it hard to leave the office at that particular time—to which Anna, who was listening, interjected that this was her father's "great trouble."[18]

FDR also found time for Lucy Rutherfurd. They met on the evening of Tuesday, March 13, when FDR, after devoting much of the afternoon involved in an intense discussion of German occupation policy, retired to his family quarters to enjoy a "quiet family meal" with Anna and her husband; Prime Minister King, whom FDR had invited back to the White House was also there; and, as King recorded in his diary, "another relative" with whom he was unfamiliar, a certain "Mrs. Rutherfurd."[19]

Anna had made the dinner arrangements that evening; with her mother out of town for three days on a speaking engagement in North Carolina, she understood that her father might want to seize the occasion to see his dear friend Lucy.[20] As Anna would later assert, there was nothing actually "clandestine" about these visits. She welcomed them, particularly during the hectic period at the end of 1944 and the beginning of 1945, "because they were light-hearted and gay, affording a few hours of much needed relaxation for a loved father and world leader in a time of crises."[21] This overly sanguine view does not account for FDR's persistent need to see Lucy. Eleanor had departed on Sunday, March 11, and the next day FDR skipped his late-afternoon rest and his usual visit to the doctor's office and instead motored over to Georgetown to pick Lucy up from her sister's apartment. After a short drive, the two returned to the White House for dinner in his study that evening with Anna and her husband. FDR and Lucy saw each other again not only on Tuesday but on Wednesday as well.

Prime Minister King found Mrs. Rutherfurd "a lovely woman of great charm." The five of them "dined in the little hall" on the second floor of the White House and had a wonderful time that Tuesday evening, reminiscing about the visit of the King and Queen in 1939, the President's recent trip, and other happy occasions. After dinner, Anna and John delighted in opening a number of the gifts presented to the President and his party during his visit to the Middle East. It really was "a delightful family affair," King reflected, one he thoroughly enjoyed. So too did FDR; and as King made to leave, the President asked him if he wouldn't like to stay the night. When King begged off, saying he had to get the overnight train back to New York, FDR implored his friend to remember that he was always welcome at the White House, at Warm Springs, or in Hyde Park.[22]

With the promise that they would see each other soon in San Francisco, the two friends parted. Anna and her husband walked the prime minister downstairs and out to the front entrance of the White House. Anna asked King again if he might like to stay. Her father, she said, thought of him as family and was sad to see him go. He "missed his old friends," she confessed, and "felt the loss of McIntyre, Miss Lehand, General Watson, [and] Capt. Callaghan—all of whom had been with him in the earlier part of his life." But still, King thought it necessary to be on his way.[23]

As Drew Pearson observed in the *Washington Post*, there was much for the president to do to get "squared away for the toughest six months in his twelve long years" in office. Indeed, many vital matters were pending: establishing peace terms with Germany; devising the best way "to convert a two-front war into a one-front war"; determining how to secure the full employment to which FDR had alluded in his State of the Union Address; and, most important, preparing for the San Francisco conference and the coming peace.[24]

The excitement generated by the upcoming gathering of delegations from around the world to craft the UN charter led to an unprecedented number of requests—often channeled through Eleanor—from organizations and individuals who wished to be included in the American delegation or otherwise represented at the conference. FDR remained adamant, however, that the delegation should remain small, and not be expanded beyond the eight representatives he had chosen.[25]

The president also had to ensure the bipartisan makeup of the delegation. Many of the key Republican nominees, including such leading figures as Senator Arthur Vandenberg, had initially withheld their agreement to serve. As Vandenberg wrote to John Foster Dulles shortly after receiving the president's invitation, he could "not go to this conference as a stooge," and if his instructions were to bind him to the Dumbarton Oaks proposals "as is," he would have preferred not to have been named at all.[26]

Most alarming to Vandenberg was the Polish settlement achieved at Yalta, which he assumed was only temporary and would be subject to review once the world body had been established. Given his skepticism over the agreement on Poland, Vandenberg wanted to know "what specific commitments, if any," would be implicit in his acceptance of the president's invitation. "May I understand that it will not violate your commission," he wrote to the president in late February, "if I feel free to present my own views to my American colleagues . . . and if I reserve my final right of judgment upon the ultimate results?"[27] FDR assured Vandenberg that he expected the senator to express his views freely not only to his fellow delegates but also to the American people—indeed, he was counting on Vandenberg to do so. Having secured his "right to free action," as the senator put it in a statement issued to the press on March 5, he accepted the president's invitation.

But by the time Vandenberg arrived at the White House on March 13 for his first meeting with the president to discuss the conference, he had already begun to have second thoughts. The senator had taken FDR at his word concerning his right to express his views freely and, in response to the mounting criticism of Soviet behavior in Eastern

Europe emanating from London and elsewhere, had warned the Senate that there was "no escaping the fact that the treatment accorded Poland . . . will have a large effect upon the success of our ultimate plans for collective security and organized peace."

Vandenberg's comments brought a sharp rebuke from Moscow, and fearing that he had now become a target for Soviet propaganda, the senator told the president that he would be quite willing to resign from the delegation if FDR felt it would be better for him to do so. "We are going to have to deal with Russia," the senator said, "and I don't want to make it difficult. I can conveniently arrange to break a leg—if you wish." To that FDR replied, in a revealing comment, "Just between us, Arthur, I am coming to know Russia better and if I could name only one delegate to the San Francisco Conference, you would be that delegate."[28]

Indeed, by this point the Anglo-Americans' difficulties with Stalin were becoming more and more frequent. Poland remained an issue of deep concern, and FDR had still not received a satisfactory answer to another item of tension with Moscow: his repeated requests for permission to extract liberated American POWs from behind Red Army lines in Poland. Moreover, it was around this time that a new, highly confidential matter arose, one that would ultimately lead to the most heated exchange between Roosevelt and Stalin in the entire war.

At issue was a report from Allen Dulles, the OSS station chief in Bern, Switzerland, indicating that General Karl Wolff, the ranking SS officer in Italy, had sent a message to the Supreme Allied Commander in the Mediterranean, Field Marshal Harold Alexander, stating that he wanted to go to Switzerland to negotiate the possible capitulation of German forces operating in that theater. Both Admiral Leahy and Secretary Stimson had arranged to see the president to inform him about this potential breakthrough. FDR fully approved of moving forward with Wolff, but as he regarded the negotiations as a purely military affair to be handled by the Combined Chiefs of Staff and the military authorities on the ground, he saw no reason to involve the Russians. The American Chiefs of Staff concurred, as they felt strongly that any Russian involvement, particularly in the delicate early stage of the talks, would bring the whole process to an immediate halt. The United States decided—backed by both the British Chiefs of Staff and Ambassador Harriman in Moscow—to inform the Kremlin merely that the

negotiations were taking place. Churchill, however, felt it was important not only to inform the Russians but also to seek their approval and,
without notifying FDR, overruled his own military commanders and
on March 11 sent a cable to Moscow seeking the Kremlin's assent.[29]

As Roosevelt explained to Mackenzie King on Tuesday, March 13,
1945, Churchill's precipitous move elicited a predictable demand from
Moscow: that the Allies include three Russian generals in the negotiations. FDR found this notion unacceptable. "Russia really had nothing
to do with the campaign in Italy," FDR observed, and so had no right
to intervene. "Winston," he feared "had made the situation very difficult," which left the president quite anxious lest this chance to save
American lives may be lost.[30] Indeed, tensions over what was called
the "Bern incident" would soon escalate into a full-blown diplomatic
row that came very close to leading to an outright break between the
Kremlin and Washington.

Equally distressing was that there still had been no improvement in Russia's heavy-handed conduct in Poland and across the rest
of Eastern Europe. Indeed, the tensions that emerged in mid-March
1945 bore out FDR's prescient comment that "the nearer we come to
vanquishing our enemies, the more we inevitably become conscious
of differences among the victors." But in spite of frustrations with the
Soviets, FDR's military advisers continued to argue that "the maintenance of Allied unity in the prosecution of the war must remain the
cardinal and over-riding objective of our politico-military policy with
Russia." Indeed, the Chiefs suggested that "the instances of Russian
refusal to cooperate . . . while irritating and difficult to understand if
considered as isolated events are of relatively minor moment." They
would only assume real importance "if their occurrence should cause
our government to adopt retaliatory measures in kind, and these in
turn should be followed by further Russian measures, and thus lead to
a break in Allied unity."[31]

FDR shared this view and thus was disturbed by Churchill's
repeated attempts over the past two weeks to push him in the direction
of a more confrontational approach toward the Kremlin. As he told
the members of his cabinet at their regularly scheduled meeting on the
afternoon of Friday, March 16, he was having considerable difficulty
with the British, who seemed "perfectly willing for the United States
to have a war with Russia at any time." This would certainly be the end

result, he said, in an oblique reference to Churchill, of any decision to follow what he referred to as "the British program."[32]

ANOTHER IMPORTANT ISSUE THAT FDR FACED INVOLVED THE PROGRESS of the Manhattan Project. An increasing number of officials and scientists involved in it began to have serious concerns about the moral implications of an atomic weapon. For much of the war, many of those who knew about "the bomb" assumed it would be simply a larger and more effective version of the conventional weapons the United States already used. But as the science involved in developing the atomic bomb progressed, many experts began to realize that the weapon would completely change warfare, and that when nuclear weapons spread to other countries, as they inevitably would, no war would ever again be "winnable."[33] These concerns led to calls for the international control of the bomb.

Perhaps the greatest advocate for international control was the Nobel Prize–winning Danish physicist Niels Bohr. Profoundly disturbed by the likely consequences of the development of nuclear weapons, including the possibility of a nuclear arms race, Bohr had reached out to Felix Frankfurter, a sitting Supreme Court justice and close friend of FDR, while on a visit to the United States in the spring of 1944 in the hope that Frankfurter would convey his concerns to the president. Sharing Bohr's profound trepidations about this weapon of "unparalleled power," Frankfurter not only delivered a detailed memorandum from Bohr but also spoke to FDR himself. As Frankfurter later recorded, FDR was in agreement with Frankfurter's observation that "a solution to the atomic bomb might be more important than all the plans for a world organization." FDR authorized his friend to tell Bohr, who was soon heading to England, that he might inform "our friends in London that the President was most anxious [and] most eager to explore the proper safeguards in relation to X."[34]

What followed was a series of meetings, first with Churchill in May 1944, who dismissed Bohr's concerns out of hand, and then with FDR, who agreed to meet the physicist when the latter next visited the United States, in August. Unlike Churchill, FDR took Bohr's views seriously, and seemed to imply in the meeting that he concurred with Bohr's argument that the time had come to inform the Russians about the project—a key goal of those in favor of international control.

Churchill, however, remained adamantly opposed to sharing of the nuclear secret, and was so disturbed by Bohr's activities that he even suggested it was time to have Bohr arrested for his "mortal crimes."[35]

Churchill's unequivocal opposition resulted in the crafting of a second Anglo-American agreement on the development of nuclear weapons. Referred to as the "Hyde Park Memorandum," and signed in September 1944 while Churchill was on a visit to Springwood, it categorically stated that the "suggestion that the world should be informed regarding tube alloys, with a view to an international agreement regarding its control and use, is not accepted." On the contrary, this "matter should continue to be regarded as one of utmost secrecy." The document also registered Churchill's and Roosevelt's concurrence that the bomb "might perhaps" be used against the Japanese "after mature consideration."[36]

Churchill had consistently opposed any sharing of the atomic secret, and remained convinced that the new weapon was simply a bigger bomb that involved "no difference in the principles of war." Thus his reasons for signing the Hyde Park Memorandum appear to be clear. But why Roosevelt should suddenly have decided to draft and sign a document that seemingly rejected Bohr's concerns is not readily apparent.[37] It may have been that the memorandum's language—such as the notion "that when a 'bomb' is finally available, it might *perhaps, after mature consideration, be used against the Japanese*"—was vague enough to satisfy FDR that he would in all likelihood revisit this question later. FDR had certainly hinted at this possibility when he intimated in a conversation with Churchill, shortly before the two men signed the memorandum, that one alternative to the bomb's use on a civilian target was to offer a demonstration of its power coupled with a warning to the Japanese.[38] But there was still no proof that the effort to build an atomic bomb would be successful, and the president had many other pressing matters in front of him so the discussion ended there.[39]

In the six months since the two leaders had signed the agreement, the atomic project had progressed to the point that the new weapon would almost certainly be ready by mid-summer. Officials involved in the Manhattan Project began to argue that the moment to engage in the "mature consideration" called for in the Hyde Park Memorandum had arrived. Many had come to the same conclusions as Bohr about the inherent risks in maintaining the Anglo-American atomic monopoly. Convinced that it would be impossible to keep the technology secret for long, and that a dangerous arms race might be the result, two of FDR's top scientific advisers, Vannevar Bush and James Conant, favored handing over control of atomic energy to an international agency associated with the Allied nations. By March 1945 they had even raised the possibility that such a provision might be written into the Charter of the United Nations.[40]

Unable to bring the matter to the president's full attention amid the heavy demands on his time in the waning months of 1944, Bush and Conant held a series of meetings with Secretary Stimson between December 1944 and March 1945, pressing to have these important questions put before the president. Stimson was finally able to arrange a meeting with FDR on March 15. He opened by dismissing some concerns about the Manhattan Project that had recently been raised by James Dunn in the State Department. In a memo sent to FDR a few days earlier, which echoed a letter sent to FDR by James Byrnes on March 3, Dunn, much to Stimson's ire, wondered whether Bush and Conant had sold the president "a lemon." Given the huge sums that had been expended on the project, this would prove disastrous if true. Dunn recommended that the president bring in a body of "outside scientists" to review the effort—a notion that Stimson dismissed as "silly," since practically every physicist of any standing, including four Nobel Laureates, was already engaged in the project.[41]

Stimson then arrived at the more important question of international control. After saying that the bomb was on schedule, he explained that there were essentially two schools of thought on the future control of atomic power: "one being the secret closed-in control of the project by those who control it now, and the other being international control based upon freedom both of science and of access." Stimson stressed that the question had to be settled before the first use of a bomb and that the president should be ready with a statement on it "just as soon as it was done."[42] In his diary, Stimson characterized his conversation with the president that day as "on the whole, highly successful."

But there is no indication whether the two men broached the critical questions at the heart of Bush and Conant's push for the internationalization of the atomic secret: how and whether the bomb should be used in the first place. Should a demonstration of the bomb's explosive force over either US or Japanese territory be attempted? Or should the United States make full use of the weapon on the Japanese? In other words, just how and when did the president intend to engage in the "mature consideration" called for in the Hyde Park Memorandum?

In the meantime, halfway across the country, in the halls of the University of Chicago, yet another top scientist was beginning to have doubts about the entire endeavor. Leo Szílard's concerns over German advances in nuclear physics inspired the famous letter that Albert Einstein sent to FDR in the fall of 1939—the letter that sparked the Manhattan Project. Now that it looked as if the atomic bomb would become a reality, Szílard was suddenly unable to sleep at night. Knowing that he would never be able to reach FDR on his own, he turned once again to Einstein, asking his friend to send a letter to the president on his behalf. Szílard hoped to secure an appointment with FDR to discuss his great worry "about the lack of adequate contact between scientists who are doing this work, and those members of your Cabinet, who are responsible for formulating policy."[43]

And so it happened, in one of the ironies of World War II, that Einstein delivered a second letter to the White House, dated March 25, 1945. Although for security reasons the letter made no direct mention of Szílard's fears, the motives behind this communication were quite unlike those that had inspired Szílard to reach out to Einstein in the summer of 1939. Now, the man whose discoveries laid the foundation "upon which all the present work on uranium is based," as Einstein described Szílard, wanted to implore the president not to take this last step into the unknown. "The nation," Szílard later reflected, "which sets the precedent of using these newly liberated forces of nature for the purposes of destruction may have to bear the responsibility of opening the door to an era of devastation of unimaginable scale."[44]

To ensure that the president saw the letter in a timely manner, Szílard requested that Einstein deliver a copy to Eleanor Roosevelt, who soon replied that she was able to find a time for Szílard to meet FDR. But we will never know how Franklin Roosevelt may have responded to Szílard's passionate appeals. The meeting was scheduled for early May, and the letter containing Eleanor's welcome news was delivered to Szílard on April 12, 1945.[45]

Chapter 15

The Architect

IN SHARP CONTRAST TO THE WEATHER IN HYDE PARK A FEW WEEKS before, Saturday, March 17, 1945, was the hottest recorded St. Patrick's Day in Washington, DC. With the temperature climbing to 86 degrees Fahrenheit, the signs of spring were everywhere—in the dogwood and magnolia blossoms that brightened so much of the city, and in the full bloom of the lavender wisteria that graced the south portico of the White House.[1] St. Patrick's Day held special meaning for Franklin and Eleanor. Forty years earlier, in a small and simple ceremony held on the Upper East Side of Manhattan, in what must have seemed like an era long since vanished, the two distant cousins were married. As Eleanor had lost her mother to diphtheria in 1892 and her much-loved father to the consequences of severe alcoholism two years later, the bride was given away by her uncle, Theodore Roosevelt, then president of the United States, who, shortly after the ceremony was over, slapped his young nephew-in-law on the back and said, "Nothing like keeping the name in the family, Franklin!"

FDR woke in a jaunty mood that March morning in 1945. There was much jesting between him and his staff—including Secret Service agent Charlie Fredericks, who had been part of Theodore Roosevelt's presidential detail forty years before—about how things had changed since that happy day in 1905 when the bride and groom were all but overshadowed by the ebullient TR.

FDR was looking forward to celebrating his anniversary, particularly as this year they would be joined by Princess Juliana of the Netherlands. In an effort "to relieve the heavy pressures of callers" for the next week, which included a two-and-a-half-day visit by the governor-general of Canada and his wife, FDR decided to squeeze in two additional senatorial appointments that morning before enjoying a quiet anniversary lunch with Eleanor and the rest of the family.

He then used a relatively tranquil afternoon in his study to work on his mail before receiving Princess Juliana and a small delegation from the Dutch Embassy at 5:00, followed by the usual "children's hour" and then a formal anniversary dinner for eighteen held in the State Dining Room of the White House. Among the other guests were Dutch Ambassador Dr. Alexander Loudon and Mrs. Betty Loudon as well as Justice Robert Jackson and his wife, Irene.

FDR first met Jackson, who would go on to gain fame at the Nuremberg trials after the war, in Albany, New York, when Jackson was a young law student and FDR was a freshman senator in the New York State Legislature. Thanks to Jackson's intense interest in Democratic politics, he made sure to stay in touch with the rising political star, and when FDR became president, Jackson was quite eager to accept FDR's appointment in 1934 as general counsel in the Treasury Department's Bureau of Revenue (the forerunner of the IRS). A series of further high-profile appointments within the Justice Department followed, and in July 1941 FDR nominated Jackson as an associate justice of the Supreme Court.[2]

The president, according to Jackson, seemed in fine spirits that evening. "He mixed some martinis," Jackson recalled, and seemed cheerful and pleased at the progress of the war. He also retained his sense of humor. As the president was being wheeled into the State Dining Room from the Red Room, where drinks were served, one of his three dogs was lying in his path. Unable to move forward, FDR jocularly quipped, "Somebody move the dog—but not by air!" This remark brought a roar of laughter from all who heard it, owing to the recent (and erroneous) press allegations that his son Elliott had used his status to have his dog Blaze flown across the country on a military aircraft.[3]

Seated at a table covered with St. Patrick's baubles—pipes, green hats, shamrocks, and potatoes stuck with small Irish flags—the president and his guests passed a pleasant evening. There was much teasing about FDR's diplomatic faux pas at entertaining the House of Orange with Irish decorations in front of the Dutch princess. After dinner, the group watched a movie and viewed color-film footage taken during the president's trip to Yalta and the Middle East with some commentary from FDR on the experience. At about 10:30 p.m., the Jacksons took their leave, but the president, despite the admonitions of his doctors to avoid late nights, continued to converse with Juliana, the Dutch ambassador, and a few of the other guests until 1:00 a.m.

In the meantime, as Justice Jackson drove home that evening his wife Irene suddenly said, "I don't think we will ever see the President alive again." "That's damn nonsense," Jackson replied; the president may have appeared weary at times, but Jackson did not think "he was in any danger." Still, his wife—in a pattern that would repeat itself as FDR encountered friends and aides who had not seen him for some time—insisted that from where she was sitting, in full view of his face, she could see that he looked "awfully bad."[4]

SUNDAY, MARCH 18, WAS PERHAPS THE QUIETEST DAY FDR SPENT IN Washington during this period in the Oval Office. He held no appointments, aside from his duties as host of a luncheon in honor of Princess Juliana and fifteen other guests. After that, he and the princess set off on a leisurely afternoon drive in the Virginia countryside. In their initial light conversation, FDR—always proud of his Dutch heritage—inquired after Juliana's daughter, and FDR's godchild, Princess Margriet, as well as after Juliana's parents, Queen Wilhelmina and her husband Prince Henry. He also intimated that at Churchill's invitation, he and Eleanor hoped to make a trip to England in June. But it was impossible to keep the war at bay. Part of the reason that Juliana was so anxious to visit the White House, in fact, was to pass directly into the president's hands an eight-page memorandum written by her mother describing the desperate situation in the areas of the Netherlands still under occupation. Not mincing any words, the memorandum detailed the horrific conditions under which the people of Amsterdam, The Hague, Rotterdam, Utrecht, and many other Dutch cities were living, devoid of fuel for the winter and reduced to a diet of one loaf of bread and five potatoes per person, per week.

FDR had already received information about the crisis in the Netherlands from earlier correspondence with the queen, the Dutch foreign minister, and Stanley Hornbeck, the newly appointed American ambassador to the Dutch government-in-exile in London. Indeed, in a February letter Hornbeck warned FDR that unless food could be sent into Western Holland "not only soon, but more than soon . . . the Dutch nation . . . is in danger of being decimated."[5]

In response, FDR proposed a reduction in the domestic rations of certain commodities, a move that brought strong protests from Congress on the charge that the Roosevelt administration was "depriving Americans of necessary nourishment to feed the world."[6] But in the press conference that FDR held the day before his anniversary, he scoffed at such a notion, insisting that "he could not bring himself to believe" that the American people had suffered very greatly in this war when compared to other countries—"for instance . . . Holland, which is a very bad case."[7]

A 10 percent reduction in Americans' consumption of certain items, FDR went on, could save the lives of large numbers of starving people, a trade-off he believed the vast majority of Americans would support as a matter of "national decency."[8] FDR also sent a personal letter to Queen Wilhelmina, thanking her for a telegram of congratulations she had sent on his anniversary and expressing his conviction to do everything he could to alleviate the food crisis. "You can be certain," he assured her, that "I shall not forget the country of my origin."[9]

Two weeks earlier, the queen—whom Winston Churchill once described as "the only real man among the Governments-in-Exile in London"—had made her first visit to Dutch soil, to the southern province of Zeeland, after nearly five years of exile in London. In his letter, FDR expressed the wish that he could have been there that day. He could not have known that later genealogical studies would determine that the Roosevelt family had in fact immigrated to America from the tiny hamlet of Tholen in the same province.

Zeeland was also one of the most devastated regions in the Netherlands, owing in part to the Allied decision in the fall of 1944 to bomb the dikes and flood the island of Walcheren in an attempt to dislodge the heavily fortified German positions that lined the north shore of the river Scheldt. During her visit, the queen spent six hours traversing nearly fifty miles of the island in an amphibious "duck boat," taking in miles of forlorn and dying farmland as the sun glinted off the salt water. In the medieval capital city of Middelburg, "disfigured by enemy bombing and now besieged by sea water," she spent a few moments talking to members of the resistance, while hundreds of Dutch men, women, and children greeted her, crying and singing the Dutch National Anthem as they waved tricolor flags topped by orange streamers.[10]

Juliana left the White House early on Monday, March 19. Before doing so, she elicited a promise from FDR that he and Eleanor would visit The Hague during their planned visit to Europe in June—even if it was necessary for them to camp there in a tent! She also promised to adhere to FDR's admonition that she not return to Holland with her children too soon. "It must be an absolutely safe date," FDR told her, preferably timed to the next major military offensive; even so, she and her family should take great care.[11]

Perhaps it was the warm spring weather, but as March wore on, the mood in Washington and in much of the rest of the country improved. As *New York Times* columnist Anne O'Hare McCormick wrote, there was something special about the approach of Holy Week 1945. The American people's long-standing "belief in victory" had shifted to "a feeling of victory," as Allied triumph on the European battlefield was becoming "an emotional reality." Still, she was careful to point out that the end of war is not necessarily peace. The crucial question now was whether or not the partnership among the Big Three—a partnership that had made the victory possible—would continue after the war.[12]

With something similar in mind, FDR had scheduled a rather unusual meeting at the start of his final full week in the White House. The caller was not a statesman, politician, military officer, or even one of the president's many "personal envoys" sent out to report back to him on the domestic or international scene. Instead, this visitor was portrait artist Douglas Chandor, for whom FDR had a very specific and important task in mind.

Born and raised in England, Chandor had moved to the United States in the mid-1920s. After a successful debut in New York in 1927, he received an invitation to paint President Herbert Hoover and a number of his cabinet members. Chandor's portrait of Hoover, combined with his earlier works depicting various members of the British ruling elite, established his reputation as a painter of the world's political leaders.

Chandor had indicated an interest in doing FDR's portrait, and the president felt it was time to grant his wish. During the early afternoon of March 19, 1945, Chandor spent a full two hours or more with FDR in his study. As Chandor sketched and FDR talked, he described an idea for a painting depicting the "Big Three" at Yalta, which could be hung in the nation's Capitol to mark for posterity this all-important moment in history. FDR did not want a posed portrait but, rather, a work that depicted the three leaders at the discussion table, supported by their aides, working together to create the "structure of peace" that FDR felt was so vital to establish as the war drew to a close.

FDR thought it would be a good idea to have two copies made, "one for London and one for Moscow," and since Chandor refused to paint solely from photographs, the president agreed to send a message to Ambassador Harriman the following day to ask Marshal Stalin to sit for Chandor himself. FDR planned to send a similar message to Churchill once the arrangements with Stalin had been made.[13]

As Franklin D. Roosevelt Jr. reflected two years later, his father was keen on this project and would have ensured its completion had he lived. He felt the work would have immense symbolic value that would "graphically portray the unity of the war . . . which must extend through the years to come if we are to maintain peace."[14]

In keeping with FDR's wishes, the initial study that Chandor painted in March 1945 included a full portrait of FDR and, in the lower-left corner, a smaller sketch of the three leaders at the conference table, surrounded by a series of depictions of FDR's hands—one of which holds a pen in the process of writing "O.K., FDR." In the upper-right corner, the artist left a small inscription in Latin: *Ad familium gentium comem contendit*, "Toward a friendly family of nations."

Optimistic about the future of the world organization, FDR also took the time that week to meet with Joseph Proskauer and Jacob Blaustein, two leading members of the American Jewish Committee to discuss the introduction of an international bill of human rights at the coming San Francisco conference.

According to Proskauer, the president was fully supportive of the American Jewish Committee's intention to introduce a draft international bill of human rights to the delegates at San Francisco.[15] The submission of such a program would help secure "world recognition of human rights for everyone, regardless of race or religion."[16] Moreover,

Portrait of FDR by Douglas Chandor completed in the White House on March 16, 1945. To the left, below the president's right elbow, is the sketch of the painting of the Yalta conference that FDR hoped might one day hang in Washington, London, and Moscow. Underneath the sketch, Chandor depicts FDR in the process of writing his classic sign of approval: "O.K., FDR." In the upper-right corner is the Latin inscription rendered by the artist, *Ad familium gentium comem contendit,* "Toward a friendly family of nations"—a motto similar to the one that FDR would assign to the United Nations stamp that was released on the opening day of the San Francisco conference, April 26, 1945. (*Franklin D. Roosevelt,* by Douglas Granville Chandor, oil on canvas, 1945. National Portrait Gallery, Smithsonian Institution)

even though FDR urged the two men to continue to press for liberal Jewish immigration into Palestine (despite the British government's intransigence), his recent experience in the Middle East had led him to conclude that the establishment of a Jewish state was not possible under the present conditions—and in fact might plunge the world into another major war. Accordingly, FDR felt that the introduction of an international bill of human rights under the auspices of the world organization would be "of exceptional interest to the Jews," who should press for recognition of their rights across the world.

Interestingly, the American Jewish Committee's proposals centered on the establishment of three principal permanent commissions to be included in the world organization, which, in many respects, foreshadowed the process that Eleanor Roosevelt helped orchestrate in 1948: the first "to frame a world decision on human rights," the second to deal with the migrations of peoples that will no doubt occur as a result of the war, and the third to focus on the problem of statelessness and the human rights of those who have no national status—a critical issue for the survivors of the Holocaust.[17]

ALTHOUGH FDR WAS CONFIDENT THAT THE AGREEMENTS STRUCK AT Yalta would lead inevitably to the establishment of a United Nations Organization, not everyone was so optimistic. US signals intelligence had already picked up some dissatisfaction among leadership of the lesser powers over the voting procedure agreed at Yalta, and just one day prior to FDR's appointment with Chandor, a reporter for the *New York Times* observed that "no one expects the United Nations Security Conference that opens April 25 in San Francisco to reach final accord on the new international organization without difficulties." It was hard enough, the *Times* reporter argued, to win acceptance of the charter outline framed at Dumbarton Oaks among the three big powers, "and when forty-three nations with delegates and advisors numbering more than 2,000 persons are assembled . . . there is certain to be widespread grounds for differences of opinion."[18]

The *Times* article identified at least four "main storm centers" including voting power in the Security Council, an issue FDR regarded as all but settled; the operation of regional arrangements, which could threaten the universal structure of the organization; the establishment of trusteeships for certain territories; and an expected effort by some of the smaller powers to obtain guarantees of their sovereignty and territorial borders.[19]

The article did not mention the agreement reached at Yalta to grant the USSR's request for three seats in the General Assembly. In one of his rare political miscalculations, FDR had decided to keep this part of the accords absolutely secret, perhaps in the hope that he could persuade the Soviets to withdraw the request in the weeks between Yalta and the start of the UN conference. Apprehensive about how this decision might be received at San Francisco, both FDR and Stettinius would have preferred that the matter not come up at all and entertained thoughts about trying to find "some way to get around it." By March 19, Stettinius recommended to the president that he take the members of the US delegation into his confidence and solicit their advice on "how to handle the Soviets on this question."[20]

Both Stettinius and Undersecretary of State Grew were also concerned about the possibility that the story might become public, which the latter feared would prove damaging if the delegates to the conference had not been informed beforehand. Grew put these concerns in a memo he sent to the White House on March 22. FDR concurred with his recommendation to inform the members of the US delegation about the decision, and a meeting for the delegation with the president was arranged for the following morning, Friday, March 23.[21]

In the meantime, news from Poland indicated that the work of the tripartite commission had essentially stalled over the Kremlin's insistence that the Lublin Poles had the right to veto any candidate nominated to serve in the reorganized regime, as called for in the Yalta accords. In an effort to revive the negotiations, FDR approved the issuance of a joint Anglo-American memorandum, to be presented to Molotov, pointing out that there had been no agreement at Yalta sanctioning a veto on the matter either for the Warsaw Provisional Government or for the Soviet Union.[22]

Another issue that FDR had to deal with during this final full week in the White House concerned the treatment of postwar Germany. Owing to the opposition put forward by Hull and Stimson in the wake of the promulgation of the Morgenthau plan in September 1944, US policy toward defeated Germany was still in flux. In an intense luncheon meeting with FDR held on Tuesday, March 20, Morgenthau reiterated his earlier call to see Germany broken up and deindustrialized after the war. He soon found his ability to convince the president of the merits of his ideas undermined by the presence of John Boettiger, who was brought along to the meeting by FDR's daughter, Anna. Furious at Boettiger's interference, and at Anna's tendency to back up her husband, Morgenthau expressed his dismay at the whole encounter to Undersecretary of the Treasury Harry Dexter White shortly after he left the White House.[23]

By this point, in fact, Washington was full of rumors that control of access to the president had passed to Anna. As *Life* magazine reported in early March, the first indications that this was the case emanated from the photos and press releases from Malta and Yalta. And although the White House insisted that Anna had no office, official standing, or salary, and was merely there to be "a comfort to her father," Washington insiders understood that this was a vast understatement. Anna may not have been able to fully implement the scheme she suggested to a somewhat shocked Jonathan Daniels shortly after the president's return from Yalta, but as the meeting between Morgenthau and FDR demonstrated, Anna and her husband could and did interject themselves "in discussions of high policy."[24]

Less than five minutes after finishing this acrimonious luncheon, FDR headed back to his office for his scheduled 3:00 p.m. news conference. There, he fielded questions on a host of pressing issues, mercifully none of which involved the treatment of postwar Germany. FDR then left the frenzied confines of the White House to visit former Secretary of State Cordell Hull, who was still convalescing in the quiet confines of the Bethesda Naval Hospital.

FDR took special pride in the Bethesda medical facility, as it was one of the many structures in Washington, Hyde Park, and Warm Springs for which he had sketched the original design. Modeled after the Nebraska State House that FDR had dedicated in 1936, the Bethesda Naval Hospital was made up of a 250-foot tower that rose above the surrounding rural countryside—not unlike, in FDR's view, an English manor house. FDR had always fancied himself as something of an architect, and given his fondness for the structure and the surrounding countryside, the trip to see Hull in the warm afternoon sun was a welcome change—and a sign of the respect FDR still held for Hull. As an influential southern Democrat, Hull played an important part in securing FDR's nomination for president in 1932—something

FDR never forgot—and even though FDR frequently bypassed the State Department in his execution of American foreign policy, it was Hull's persistent focus on postwar planning that laid the foundations not only for the United Nations but also for the multilateral trading regime that helped spur the globalization of the world's economy in the decades to follow.[25]

A highly principled and somewhat vain man, whose frustrations over FDR's insistence on being his own secretary of state frequently drove him to distraction—and to outbursts of colorful Tennessee expletives—Hull was nevertheless deeply moved by the president's visit.[26] The two old colleagues talked a good while, and when FDR admitted to the bedridden Hull that "I ought to be there where you are," the seventy-three-year-old former secretary of state admonished him about his activity level, saying that he should take more rest. Promising to heed Hull's advice, FDR took his leave to enjoy a late-afternoon drive through the Maryland countryside in the company of Lucy Rutherfurd—their fourth encounter in the past ten days. They would see each other again the next day, Wednesday, March 21, over a long lunch in the White House. It is also likely that Lucy stayed on for dinner, as Eleanor would not return from her second March trip to North Carolina until the following morning.[27]

AFTER A RELATIVELY RESTFUL START TO THE WEEK, FDR'S SCHEDULE on Thursday and Friday bordered on the suicidal. On Thursday, March 22, after his usual staff review in bed, the president went on to engage in a full day of back-to-back meetings on a host of difficult issues before he and Eleanor left to meet the governor-general of Canada—the Earl of Athlone, and his wife, Princess Alice, as they arrived at Union Station at 4:00 p.m. Then it was back to the White House for formal welcoming ceremonies conducted on the South Lawn, and tea served in the diplomatic reception room, with FDR, seated between Eleanor and Princess Alice, greeting each guest as they arrived.[28] At roughly 5:45, FDR managed to slip away to the Map Room and White House doctor's office for forty minutes or so, but then it was time to get dressed and rush off to the annual White House Correspondents' Dinner with the Earl of Athlone and his private secretary in tow.

Initiated in 1920, the White House Correspondents' Dinner has become something of an annual ritual that nearly every president has endured or enjoyed, largely depending on his relationship with the press. For FDR, who thoroughly delighted in the company of reporters, these gatherings were usually lighthearted affairs. On previous occasions, as was customary, FDR had avoided making any significant public comments at the dinner. But in March 1941, with freedom of speech and expression facing extinction in Europe and Asia, FDR decided to break with this tradition and deliver a powerful address in defense of democracy.

In the speech, he warned his guests that Nazi forces were not seeking "mere modifications in colonial maps or in minor European boundaries," but the "destruction of all elective systems of government on every continent—including our own." In answer to Hitler's proclamation that he had established a "new order" in Europe, FDR defiantly declared as he stood at the lectern, with his braces locked, and his left hand gripping the podium:

> Yes, these men and their hypnotized followers call this a new order.
>
> It is not new—and it is not order.
>
> For order among Nations presupposes something enduring—some system of justice under which individuals, over a long period of time, are willing to live. Humanity will never permanently accept a system imposed by conquest and based on slavery.[29]

FDR then called upon his fellow citizens to shield the "great flame of democracy from the blackout of barbarism," so that the Four Freedoms would not be superseded by tyranny.

By the time FDR arrived at the Presidential Room of the Statler Hotel in March 1945, however, the contrast between the man who had so boldly defied the forces of hate on the eve of the American entry into the war and the one who was about to address the White House correspondents on the eve of victory could not have been greater. There were about two hundred guests present. At 7:30 p.m., precisely on time, a Marine Band launched into "Hail to the Chief," and as the audience rose, FDR was rolled into the room "leaning forward in his wheelchair, looking old and thin and scrawny-necked." Unlike past occasions, he seemed to pay no attention to the audience as they stood and applauded, not even when he reached his seat. While FDR continued to stare blankly ahead, as Allen Drury observed, "[w]e might not have been there at all, and for the moment it gave one the uneasy feeling that, perhaps preoccupied beyond all such social graces, he did not know we were."[30]

It was only after the president had been formally introduced that "he noticed, snapped out of it, [and] waved and laughed a little in a deprecating way" as if to imply that all of the attention was not really necessary. Something of the old FDR then seemed to return. The president laughed at the jokes being told and genuinely seemed to enjoy himself as he ate his meal, sipped his wine, and smoked steadily throughout the evening. Watching him closely, Drury later reflected, "there came again that strange wonderment," that "puzzled question implicit in the attitude of every audience he meets in this city that knows him better than any other—yet knows him not at all. 'What manner of man is this?' men seem to ask, and they never find the answer."[31]

At the close of the evening FDR opted not to deliver a speech but, rather, gave the assembled press "a story" from his seated position at the table. "But first," the president said, with a hint of humor in his voice, "I want to give you a word, the word Humanity. We all love Humanity," he went on, "you love Humanity, I love Humanity. Humanity's with me all the time. I go to bed and I dream of Humanity, I eat breakfast and there's Humanity, Humanity follows me around all day. So with that in mind, with that word, Humanity, here's your headline and here's your story—in the name of Humanity, I am calling off the press conference for tomorrow morning!"[32]

And with that, and while the crowd rose to its feet and roared with laughter, FDR shifted back into his wheelchair to depart. Now, as he was being wheeled out of the room, he acknowledged the applause and attention, so that the last image many saw of FDR that evening was with his head thrown back, a bright smile on his face, waving his right hand in the friendly, reassuring manner they had all seen countless times before.[33]

THE PRESIDENT'S MEETING WITH THE US DELEGATION ABOUT THE Soviet request for three seats in the General Assembly was set for 10:30 a.m. Friday morning. But thanks to another late night spent conversing with Lord Athlone and Princess Alice after returning to the White House from the correspondents' dinner, FDR was already running an hour behind schedule by the time the delegates had gathered around his desk.

The president laid out in colorful but misleading terms what had transpired at Yalta on the Soviet request for extra seats. He downplayed the firmness of his agreement with Stalin and Churchill on this question, and in words reminiscent of his equivocal backing of Henry Wallace in 1944 said, "If he were a delegate at San Francisco he personally would favor the Soviet proposal."[34]

The delegates were stunned, and Senator Vandenberg was incredulous. As he later wrote, "Why was this news held back when presumably the country was told all about the 'Yalta compromise' on voting (but not a word about this)?"[35] The more he thought about it, the more convinced he became that "[t]his will raise hell."[36] Adding to the tension was the possibility that "the deal" FDR had struck with Churchill and Stalin would be leaked to the press, before some sort of solution could be found, further dampening public and congressional enthusiasm for the world organization.[37]

Seeking to head off this possible outcome, FDR had arranged to spend the next hour in a far-ranging interview with *New York Times* columnist Anne O'Hare McCormick.[38] Although McCormick found him gaunt and tired, she also noted that his normally discursive mind was uncommonly focused on one issue: the world organization. As McCormick listened and later reported, the president presented his arguments in favor of the organization "with a clarity and vigor that belied his look of weariness" and convinced his listener "that all his hopes of success in life and immortality in history were set on getting an international security organization in motion."[39]

Reflecting on his years in office, FDR said he was now looking to the future, beyond the present destruction and chaos, and seeing himself as the "chief architect of a new structure rising out of the wreckage."[40]

When McCormick asked if it might not have been better to allow more time to prepare for the conference, FDR replied that in fact he regretted that the conference could not have been held in March, because a shorter interval between Yalta and San Francisco might have prevented many misunderstandings. "Delay was the dangerous element in enterprises that were launched at the moment of high tide in the affairs of men," he said. "I am not afraid of being too early for the rendezvous, I am afraid that the appointed moment will roll by and we shall be too late."

Fully aware of Americans' alarm over Soviet behavior in Eastern Europe, FDR admitted that the necessity to ensure Soviet support for the world organization was the principal reason he had journeyed to Yalta. It was also one of the main reasons he was so impatient to get to San Francisco. It was the German attack on Russia that "drew the Soviets into the military coalition," he said, and ever since the American entry into the war his administration had made "a consistent effort to overcome the Soviet Union's deep-seated suspicions and draw it into a full political partnership." Maintaining that cooperation may have made it necessary to "ignore rebuffs" or engage in compromises that he did not always like, but these had to be weighed against the simple fact that without Russian cooperation there could be no international security, and "every lesser consideration had to be subordinated to that essential aim."

The second reason FDR was in a hurry was that he could not count on domestic support. Concerned that differences over war settlements "might cause a recession of popular sentiment," and convinced that American public enthusiasm for the world organization was at as high a level as it ever would be, he insisted it was crucial to move ahead quickly. "We must strike while the iron is hot," FDR said. "We can't afford to let disappointment over specific solutions pull us back again from the course we have to take, however hard it is. If we all go our own ways, there will be no guarantee of peace or justice for any nation."[41]

FDR FOLLOWED UP THIS EXTRAORDINARY INTERVIEW WITH A QUIET luncheon with Anna. He then convened what would be his last cabinet meeting. With Stimson on vacation in Florida, and Stettinius at his country estate in Virginia resting in advance of the San Francisco conference, there was not much discussion of the war, other than to mark the happy news of the Allied forces' progress in Europe and the steady recovery of Harold Ickes's son. With the possibility of a coal strike still looming, FDR speculated that it might be necessary to order a government takeover of the mines, and since he would soon be heading out of town for a rest, he suggested that Ickes draft the required authorization that he could sign before he departed.[42]

As was his habit when he was planning to leave Washington for an extended period, FDR met with each of his cabinet members privately for a few minutes to check up on matters particular to them. The last cabinet member to see him—as always, based on rank—was Frances Perkins. Unlike her worrisome encounter with him the day before his inauguration in January, this time she found the president in a happy and expansive mood, "lively and full of pep" in anticipation of his departure for Hyde Park and Warm Springs. She later remembered her last conversation with him.

"All I am going to do while I'm there," FDR said in reference to his trip south, "is work on my speech for the United Nations. Then I'm going to fly out there and make that speech—but I'm not going to stay, Frances, I'm not going to stay. I am going to make the speech, . . . meet all the delegates, and then I am going to come right back."

"But why not stay a while?" Perkins asked.

"No, I want this thing done without me," FDR said. "It's all fixed, it's all arranged and it will be much better," he continued, if "I did not take part in it and sort of bully it through." Then the president paused for a moment, and suddenly said, "I'm going to tell you something, Frances. Eleanor and I are going to England!"

With anticipation and pleasure, FDR reflected to a somewhat astonished Perkins on how long he had wanted "to see the British people for himself," how Eleanor's wartime visit had been such a great success, and how the two of them owed it to the English to make a return visit. "I want to go," he continued, "and this seems the best time." He had even asked Eleanor "to order her clothes and get some fine ones so that she will make a really handsome appearance."

"But, the war!" Perkins protested. "I don't think you ought to go, it's terribly dangerous! Why, the minute [the Germans] know you are at sea they'll send every submarine they own to get you." At which point FDR put his right hand to the side of his mouth and whispered, "The war in Europe will be over by the end of May."

"Are you sure?" Perkins asked. "Yes," came the firm reply. "The war will be over. We are going to make a state visit to England."

Then, leaning back in his chair, and clearly in the mood to talk, he said:

"You know, Frances, when the war's over and everything's all settled and the United Nations is operating, I would like to go out to Saudi Arabia and the Near East. I think if Eleanor and I went out there we could do a magnificent job."

"We could bring some engineers with us. There's water beneath the desert. You just have to bore for it . . . and you will get water to irrigate. There's a wonderful opportunity for that country. The people . . . live dreadfully," he went on. "They live without the necessities of life. All they need is water. I talked to old Ibn Saud about it, and he wasn't interested at all. But I would like to go out to the Near East, and I would like to get the water up and irrigate it and start a new way of life there. We could do wonders."

Listening, Perkins could not help but think that FDR "was looking to the next chapter of his life. He was thinking of the war as over. . . . He'd fought the good fight. He'd done his chore. He'd launched the United Nations. He was going to make his state visit to England, see his friends, and then go to the Near East."[43]

DISTURBED BY THE PRESIDENT'S SCHEDULE AND BY HIS CONTINUED weight loss, which was exacerbated by the fact that he insisted he "could no longer taste his food," both Drs. McIntire and Bruenn again urged him to cut back on his relentless activity. To help him regain his appetite, and recover from what Dr. Bruenn now described as FDR's "anorexia," they suspended his daily dose of digitalis and repeatedly implored him to eat.[44]

There was no indication that his heart condition had worsened, and his blood pressure was more or less stable, but his color was poor and he continued to look tired. Because FDR was unwilling to heed their advice, the two physicians more or less ordered him "to take a period of complete rest" during his time away from the White House and, if possible, to stay away from the Oval Office for a full month— much as they had advised the previous spring, when FDR spent a full four weeks convalescing at "Hobcaw," the vast North Carolina estate of Bernard Baruch.

By this point, rumors about the president's decline had begun to cross the ocean. That very morning, the *New York Times* reported that many Soviet leaders had begun to express "interest in President Roosevelt's health" as well as concern over reports that he was "suffering from strain." The *Times* also reported that the Kremlin was interested "to know Vice President Truman's views."[45]

Churchill was even more concerned. In a highly personal telegram he had sent to FDR a few days before, the prime minister, bothered by the lack of communication between the two of them of late, expressed the hope that the numerous cables he had sent "on so many of our difficulties and intertwined affairs are not becoming a bore to you. Our friendship," he continued, "is the rock on which I build for the future of the world." And, perhaps longing for an earlier time, he wrote: "I always think of those tremendous days when you devised lend-lease, when we met at Argentia, when you decided with my heartfelt agreement to launch the invasion of North Africa, and . . . comforted me for the loss of Tobruk." Indeed, now that the two leaders were finally nearing their first military goal, he could not help but remember "the part our personal relations have played in advance of the world cause."[46]

"The formal naval person" would wait in vain for a response to this warm message, but in the meantime and unbeknownst to Churchill or Stalin, and perhaps even to FDR, the Secret Service had decided it could no longer ignore the obvious and assigned a twenty-four-hour guard to Vice President Truman.[47]

Chapter 16

Hudson Requiem

SATURDAY, MARCH 24, 1945—THE LAST FULL DAY THAT FRANKLIN Roosevelt would spend in the White House—proved to be a day of exhilaration and exhaustion for the president. The newspaper headlines that screamed across the country that morning brought the thrilling announcement that General George Patton's Third Army had stormed over the Rhine and established "a solid and expanding bridgehead on the direct road to Berlin—265 miles away." This was of course welcome news to FDR, who was also looking forward to his impending departure later that evening for a brief four-day visit to Hyde Park, followed by a short layover in Washington, and then on to Warm Springs, Georgia, where he would spend two and a half weeks "resting up," as his doctors had ordered, before heading out to San Francisco.[1]

With victory in Europe now a foregone conclusion, and the Office of War Mobilization and Reconversion focusing on its postwar plans, Secretary Byrnes decided it was time to give up his position as the director of the agency and resign. The president confessed to being "knocked off his feet" by Byrnes's decision to resign before "V-E Day." And even though the two men did not always see eye to eye and Byrnes's departure could not have been entirely unexpected, his parting further diminished the circle of experienced aides the president could turn to.

On the same day, FDR announced that Stephen Early—who had been with him since the beginning of his presidency—had also decided to resign. Unlike Byrnes, however, Early agreed to stay on temporarily to fill the void left by the death of Pa Watson as appointments secretary; Jonathan Daniels, who had been serving as acting press secretary during Early's absence in Europe and the Crimea, would now assume that position permanently.[2]

Between Byrnes's resignation, Watson's death, Early's determination to leave, and Perkins's willingness to stay on only after FDR refused her written resignation—not to mention Hull's and Hopkins's hospitalization—it was clear that running a global war and rescuing the nation from the Great Depression were taking their toll not just on FDR but also on many of his key advisers. Indeed, FDR's slow but steady decline symbolized that of his entire administration. His death would signal the death of an era.

FDR's OFFICIAL DUTIES THAT SATURDAY BEGAN WITH HIS TRYING TO work his way through the "voluminous mail" that always seemed to flood in whenever word got out that the president was about to leave for Hyde Park. FDR then held separate meetings with Patrick Hurley and Bernard Baruch to discuss US policy in China and Baruch's planned visit to London, respectively, before retiring to the third-floor Sun Parlor for a luncheon with Anna Rosenberg. Rosenberg, who had known FDR since his days as governor and had served in his administration in various capacities in the 1930s and '40s, was the regional director of the War Manpower Commission.[3] FDR had invited her to the White House to discuss how best to deal with the millions of American GIs who would be returning from the war. This included the possibility of establishing a guaranteed annual wage for American workers, an idea FDR had been contemplating for quite some time.[4] They also resumed the discussion they began in January about the need for more psychiatrists to deal with the problem of psychological rehabilitation of the many sailors, soldiers, and airmen who would soon be entering civilian life.[5] FDR always enjoyed Rosenberg's company, and was delighted to see her. But the convivial atmosphere of their luncheon was suddenly interrupted when the president was handed a highly disturbing message from Marshal Stalin.

Tensions between FDR and Stalin had been building for some time over three issues: Stalin's consistent rejection of FDR's repeated requests for the Soviets to grant US aircrews the right to fly into Poland to extract American POWs; Soviet suspicions that the American decision to allow the secret "Bern talks" between General Wolff and the Anglo-American high command in Italy to proceed without

Soviet participation might involve not just the possible surrender of German forces in Italy but the entire Western Front; and the failure of the negotiations among W. Averell Harriman, Archibald Clark Kerr, and Vyacheslav Molotov in Moscow to produce the reorganized Lublin regime called for in the Yalta agreement on Poland.

By the time Rosenberg arrived at the White House, FDR had already learned that his latest attempt to convince Stalin to allow American aircrews into Poland—which included the argument that such a move was needed above all else to get the "considerable number of sick and injured" out as soon as possible—had been rejected. FDR was also aware that Ambassador Harriman was in receipt of a highly inflammatory message from Molotov that accused the Western Allies of carrying on the so-called Bern negotiations behind the backs of the Soviet government. More distressing still was what the Bern incident meant for Soviet participation in the San Francisco conference. Claiming that the Soviets had been wronged, Molotov decided he could not lead the Soviet delegation, as he was needed in Moscow to attend "a budget meeting of the Supreme Soviet." Apparently Molotov had come down with the Soviet equivalent of a "diplomatic cold." At the same time, he demanded that representatives from the Lublin Poles be allowed to participate—even though the Moscow talks that were supposed to facilitate the planned reorganization of the Lublin regime had deadlocked over Moscow's insistence that the Lublin government had the right to veto any of the potential candidates brought forward by the three powers.[6]

The joint Anglo-American memorandum that FDR and Churchill had presented to Stalin less than a week earlier—reminding him that no such veto was agreed to at Yalta—was supposed to correct that. It was the telegram indicating Stalin's rejection of this assertion that finally set Roosevelt off.[7] A stunned Anna Rosenberg looked on as FDR, unable to contain his rage, "became quite angry, banged his fists on the arms of his chair," and said, "Averell is right; we can't do business with Stalin. He has broken every one of his promises at Yalta."[8]

Clearly distressed, FDR devoted much of the rest of that afternoon editing two messages, drafted by Leahy, that went off to Stalin that evening. The first expressed his deep disappointment over Foreign Minister Molotov's withdrawal from the San Francisco conference. FDR feared this decision "will be construed all over the world as a lack of comparable interest on the part of the Soviet Government in the great objectives of this conference."[9]

The second message attempted to assuage Soviet fears over the nature of the "discussions" that had taken place in Switzerland, which FDR insisted were launched "to ascertain the accuracy" of a report that "some German officers" were considering the possible surrender of German forces in Italy. He also insisted (disingenuously, as FDR was well aware that a meeting between Wolff and Dulles had already taken place) that all attempts to arrange a meeting with German officers have "met with no success up to the present time." Confident that Stalin, as a military man, would understand the need for prompt action, the president maintained that the efforts in Italy, which had the potential to save American lives, must proceed apace. But, he went on, "I cannot agree to suspend investigation of the possibility because of objection on the part of Mr. Molotov for some reason completely beyond my understanding."[10]

FDR refrained, however, from sending Stalin an immediate response to the latter's refusal to agree that the Lublin Poles—in concert with the Soviets—had any right to obstruct the three powers' efforts to reconstitute the existing provisional government. Given that the last message FDR sent to Stalin on this matter had been in the form of a joint communiqué from both the president and the prime minister, FDR concluded that it would be best to consult with Churchill before doing so.

With the afternoon wearing on into evening, FDR went back to work on his still-unfinished correspondence in a strenuous effort to clear his desk before his departure for Hyde Park. Much to William Hassett's regret, this task kept a weary FDR in his office until well past 6:00 p.m. Then it was time for what would be his last dinner in the White House. The guests on this occasion included Crown Prince Olaf and Crown Princess Martha of Norway—the third time in a week that FDR and Eleanor had entertained royalty.[11]

We do not know if FDR and his guests discussed the Norwegian resistance's recent move—reported as "one of the greatest single acts of sabotage" of the war—to cut the rail lines leading out of their country, so that the 200,000 German troops still occupying Norway would be unable to leave in time to bolster Hitler's final bloody defense of the Reich. Nor do we know if they discussed Norway's upcoming participation in the United Nations conference, another likely topic of conversation. But FDR's decision to host the royal couple kept him occupied until the moment it was time for him to leave for the train that was waiting for him at the Bureau of Engraving and the chance for a well-deserved rest at Springwood, away from the confines of the White House and the pressures of the war.[12]

PALM SUNDAY, MARCH 25, 1945, BROKE SUNNY AND WARM IN HYDE Park, the sort of spring morning that might draw more than just the faithful to St. James, the small, white stucco church that stands beneath the tall pines gracing the Albany Post Road as it winds its way north of the village. Across the road, just to the west of the church and high above the Hudson, the magnificent sculpted grounds that surround the Vanderbilt Mansion offer striking views of the river, as it flows from the north past the Catskills, rising in the distance.

The Reverend George Anthony, rector of St. James, welcomed the throng of worshipers who had gathered outside the church for this morning's service. But FDR, who still served as both vestryman and senior warden for the parish, was not among them. The Secret Service, as a wartime security measure, had ordered the president to keep his visits to public buildings to a minimum, and even though FDR tended to ignore this requirement when he was in Hyde Park, he had nevertheless decided to forego church that morning.

FDR, who had once described his personal philosophy by saying "I am a Christian and a democrat," was proud of his family's long-standing relationship with St. James. Frances Perkins saw FDR in similar terms, characterizing FDR to Eleanor as "a very simple Christian." He had little, if any, understanding of the doctrinal basis of his religion, Perkins later wrote. "To him, man's relation to God seemed based on nature, and the idea that religion was important to man stuck with him always." She believed his attachment to freedom of religion arose out of this uncomplicated personal faith, in that he was able to associate himself without conflict with all expressions of religious worship. "Catholic, Protestant and Jew alike were comprehensible to him and their religious aspirations seemed natural and much the same as his own."[13]

FDR also felt strongly that one's faith was a private matter. "I can do everything in the 'Goldfish Bowl' of the President's life," he once said to Perkins, "but I'll be hanged if I can say my prayers in it." It bothered him "to feel like something in a zoo" when he went to church in Washington, a fact that was compounded by "his affliction," which, as Perkins later reflected, "made him doubly conspicuous and doubly a point of curiosity."[14]

It was for this reason that FDR rarely attended church services in the nation's capital, and why on most occasions when he did, it was never announced in the press. Still, there were times when his public duties required him to go, as on one occasion in 1933 when the bishop of Washington asked the president to participate in a special service of intercession at the National Cathedral. After the service, FDR paused to offer a brief word of thanks to the bishop, who took advantage of this rare opportunity to speak with the president about an issue that was "dear to his heart." He wondered if FDR, like President Wilson and Ambassador Kellogg before him, might not want to be buried in a crypt underneath the Cathedral. The bishop even suggested that perhaps the president should immediately draw up a memorandum indicating this wish.

Horrified, FDR repeatedly referred to the bishop under his breath on his way back to the White House as "the old body snatcher." That evening he dictated a memorandum directing that under no circumstances should his body be buried in the National Cathedral or any other cathedral but, rather, should lie peacefully at the center of the Rose Garden in the grounds at Hyde Park.[15]

"That's where I'm going to be buried, Frances," he later said to Perkins during one of her many visits to Springwood. "Right there— when I am dead. Don't you ever let anybody try to bury me in any cathedral."[16]

THE OSTENSIBLE REASON FDR HAD TRAVELED TO HYDE PARK AT THE start of Holy Week was to select a number of items and artifacts from his Presidential Library for use in a War Exhibition at the National Archives, to take place after V-E Day.

A more pressing aim was to regain his strength. In spite of his best efforts to clear his desk the day before, FDR had no choice but to spend part of that morning working on his correspondence, before he and Eleanor headed north along the River Road to take tea with Daisy at her home in Rhinebeck. Daisy found FDR so tired that "every word" seemed "to be an effort." Even more unnerving, they stayed only three quarters of an hour before Eleanor insisted that it was time for them to go home for an engagement at 6:00. "More people for dinner," Daisy worried. "He just can't stand this strain indefinitely."[17]

The next morning William Hassett, like Daisy, found FDR quite fatigued as he and Dorothy Brady worked through his papers from 9:00 a.m. until noon. But as the warm spring weather continued, FDR's spirits improved. He was in a much better frame of mind on Tuesday, and had enough energy to spend the afternoon with Daisy in the Library, picking out items from his vast collection of artifacts for the exhibition. By this point Eleanor had already left Hyde Park for her Greenwich Village apartment, and on Wednesday, March 28, she was back in Washington, in the company of her old friend Margaret Fayerweather.

Fayerweather arrived at the White House at 2:30 p.m., and the two women soon got to talking about FDR's health. Their conversation is one of the fullest on the subject that survives, and it not only belies the notion that Franklin and Eleanor failed to acknowledge the fragility of his condition but also reveals a good deal about the nature of their relationship.

Eleanor confessed that the "most painful thing is to watch the tremor in his hands" and the noticeable "loss of muscular control. He no longer wants to drive his own car at Hyde Park," she said, but "lets me drive, which he never did before, and [he] lets me mix cocktails if Col. Boettiger is not present." While she felt sure that "the long years of smoking" had contributed to the rapid decline in his health, "it is only a wonder that it has not come sooner, seeing how impossible it is for him, in the drive of official duties, to keep his body in shape."

In rare acknowledgment of the frailty of a man in FDR's condition, and of the ramifications of his fateful decision to run for reelection in 1940, let alone 1944, she said: "I think he faced the fact, five years ago, that if he had to go on in office, to accomplish his work, it must shorten his life—and he made that choice. If he can set out to accomplish what he set out to do, and then dies, it will have been worth it. I agree with him."[18]

On the other hand, Eleanor did note that FDR's heart and blood pressure were much better than last year, with his "smoking having been cut so down." She also recounted a recent conversation with him that touched on what had become a common and half-serious refrain—namely, his expressed desire "to go and live" in the Near East. And when Eleanor demurred, and asked him somewhat mockingly "Can't you think of anything harder to do?" FDR answered in all seriousness, "Well yes, it's going to be awfully hard to straighten out Asia, what with India and China and Thailand and Indochina. I'd like to get into that."

"Does that sound tired to you, Margaret?" she asked, turning toward her friend. "I'm all ready to sit back, and he's looking forward to more work!"[19]

FDR ARRIVED IN WASHINGTON ON THURSDAY MORNING FOR HIS BRIEF layover as planned, "looking worn and gray," but in time to take breakfast with Eleanor and her houseguest and to spend a last frantic eight hours in the White House before departing for Warm Springs at 4:00 that afternoon. Daisy and "Cousin Polly" were also present, but since FDR would be seeing them in Warm Springs, Eleanor insisted that Fayerweather sit next to the president at breakfast so the two might have the chance to talk.

FDR was soon entertaining her with recollections of his trip to the Crimea. They also discussed a letter Fayerweather had recently received from a friend concerned about the fate of World War I cemeteries in France. This raised the subject of death and burial. After a brief exchange about the merits of burial versus cremation, FDR was seized by one of his "impish creative impulses."

"You know, Margaret," he said suddenly. "You could make a lot of money out of death! You could buy a block somewhere on 7th Avenue near the Pennsylvania Station, and build a 40 story building, [with] tiers of sorts of safe deposit boxes."

"A Roman Columbarium up-to-date," Fayerweather interposed.

"That's it," he chuckled. "Why, people would just love it! Solve the whole problem, and you'd make a fortune!"

"Well, you carry out your terrible idea, if you like," Fayerweather responded. "I think it's a grizzly. Burial is much simpler." Turning more serious, FDR then reiterated what he had said to Perkins about the spot in the Rose Garden where he wanted to be laid to rest—the very place where, "to his certain knowledge, have been buried an old mule, two horses, and a dozen or so of the family dogs."[20]

FDR HAD HOPED TO USE THOSE EIGHT HOURS IN THE WHITE HOUSE to tie up various loose ends. But he was thrown off course by the news that broke that day about his "secret plan" to support the Soviet request for three votes in the General Assembly of the United Nations Organization. As Senator Vandenberg had predicted, the revelation did indeed "raise Hell." It also provoked widespread suspicion, as *New York Times* columnist Arthur Krock reported on April 1, "that a great deal lurks in the dark behind what has been revealed" at Yalta.[21]

The press was also reporting that FDR's manpower bill was very much "in doubt," in spite of FDR's efforts to lobby Congress, and much as Ickes had feared, on March 28, the United Mine Workers had overwhelmingly voted in favor of giving John L. Lewis the authority to call a strike.[22] In the meantime, behind the scenes, and unbeknownst to the public, FDR's relationship with Stalin was continuing to deteriorate.

Perhaps this is why James Byrnes found the president "extremely nervous" that Thursday morning, speaking rapidly and hardly allowing Byrnes to get a word in edgewise. Byrnes was there to introduce the president to General Lucius Clay, whom—after months of wrangling over the merits of appointing a civilian versus a military officer—FDR had finally agreed to send to Europe to serve as Eisenhower's deputy in charge of civil affairs for occupied Germany.[23] As Clay stepped out of the room, and Stephen Early rushed in to remind the president that he was behind schedule and needed to turn his attention to his next meeting, FDR took a few private moments with Byrnes. He thanked Byrnes once again for his service and told the soon-to-be-retiring director that he would call Fred Vinson later that day to inform him that he would be Byrnes's successor—a promise that FDR promptly forgot in the rush of activities of that "touch and go day."[24]

Next in line to see the president was Secretary Stettinius, who had sped back to Washington from a vacation at his Virginia farm to help the president craft a response to the news about the General Assembly. Joining him were Undersecretary of State Grew, along with Assistant Secretaries James Dunn and William Clayton, Charles Bohlen, Admiral William Leahy, and Archibald MacLeish, who had recently left his post at the Office of War Information to join the State Department as assistant secretary of state for public affairs.[25]

Their first order of business was the position the administration should take regarding the furor over the news about the General

Assembly. Stettinius was under tremendous pressure to answer a host of questions that had emerged in the wake of the revelation—pressure not only from the press but also from members of the US delegation who wanted to know whether "the President had agreed at Yalta that the delegates at San Francisco should unquestionably support the Russian claim."[26]

FDR made it clear to Stettinius that he had "committed the US Government, but not the delegates." In light of the controversy, however, all agreed that the White House should issue a statement clarifying what had transpired at Yalta; Jonathan Daniels and Archibald MacLeish were instructed to do so at once. In the meantime, Senator Vandenberg, for his part, had already issued a press release saying he would "deeply disagree with any voting proposal . . . which would destroy the sovereign equality of nations."[27]

Also problematic was how to answer Stalin's unacceptable response (communicated through Molotov) to the joint démarche that Churchill and FDR had sent to the foreign minister on March 19. It was this message that had so upset FDR during his luncheon with Anna Rosenberg. Churchill had already expressed to FDR his fear that the British and American governments were being "defrauded by Russia." He was now convinced that the only alternative to confessing total failure was "to stand by our interpretation of the Yalta declaration."[28] FDR concurred, and, with the help of Leahy and Bohlen and the other members of the State Department staff who were present at the White House, crafted a message for Stalin that was sent to Churchill for his reaction. The prime minister, who had been trying unsuccessfully for weeks to get FDR to take a harder line with Stalin, was quite pleased at this development. While Churchill and his aides were impressed by the "grave and weighty" content of the message FDR proposed to send to Stalin, Churchill still thought it could be strengthened by adding a sentence that explicitly addressed the need "to get rid of Molotov's veto." Churchill also wanted the two of them to make clear that the British and American governments would not enter into any arrangements with the "Lublinites" before the arrival of the other candidates. FDR agreed, and the amended message went off to Stalin on March 31.[29]

The exchange of cables with London regarding Poland marked an end to the lull in serious communication that had so distressed

Churchill earlier that month, a change the prime minister erroneously attributed to FDR's improved health. But this was not the view shared by Lord Halifax, FDR's next visitor to the White House, who was there with Oliver Lyttelton to discuss British supply problems now that the war in Europe was drawing to a close. Halifax found FDR in a cheerful frame of mind, but, in sharp contrast to Churchill's false assumptions, "far from well." The president's health had undergone "[q]uite a change," he thought, in the three weeks since he had last seen him.[30]

His scheduled duties finished, FDR left the Oval Office for lunch in the Sun Parlor with Anna, his grandson Curtis, and cousins Daisy and Polly. He also called Grace Tully on the White House telephone to inform her that he would like her to meet him in his study at 3:00 to tackle some mail, and to make some last-minute preparations before their departure for Warm Springs at 4:00. In the meantime, while the president was at lunch, Tully received word from Jonathan Daniels that he had to see the president before his departure. Daniels wanted to go over the statement that he and Archibald MacLeish had drafted clarifying the White House position on Stalin's request for three seats in the General Assembly. Tully suggested that the two men meet her in the president's study at the hour she had agreed to see him.

Knowing how exhausted the president was, Tully had greeted him with some trepidation that morning after his return from Hyde Park. She could tell that the four days of rest had not erased the fatigue from his face, but nothing prepared her for what she saw at 3:00 that afternoon. As she later recalled, the president's appearance as he was wheeled into his study so startled her that she almost burst into tears. In two hours he seemed "to have failed dangerously," with his cheeks "drawn gauntly" across his "ashen face, highlighted by the darkening shadows under his eyes."[31]

Both Daniels and MacLeish, who had joined Tully by this point, were similarly struck. To Daniels, the president looked "almost torpid" as he carefully read the draft statement, made a few changes, and handed it back to them.[32] After Daniels and MacLeish left, Tully did her best to dissuade FDR from going through his mail. She suggested instead that he simply gather the usual leisure material he liked to bring with him on his travels: his stamp collection and catalogue, and a collection of books he wanted to sort through and sign for deposit in his Library in Hyde Park, at Top Cottage, and at the "Big House."

To transport these books to Warm Springs the president had arranged for a long wooden box that he invariably referred to after his arrival in Georgia as the "coffin."[33]

The only other task that Tully thought the president should undertake that afternoon was to sign each of the three bound copies of his D-Day Prayer, which she felt would make good birthday presents for Anna's children. But in the end, she decided to present him with just a single copy to sign for "little Johnnie," whose birthday was coming up soon. Happy to comply with this request, FDR opened the volume and, with a shaking hand, wrote a short note and signed his name in the flyleaf.

Chapter 17

Easter in Warm Springs

THE TINY HAMLET OF WARM SPRINGS, GEORGIA—WITH A POPULATION of just over six hundred people—was certainly an unusual destination for the president of the United States. Yet thanks to FDR's long association with the community, and with Georgia, where Theodore Roosevelt's mother, Martha Stewart Bulloch, spent her childhood and married the father of the future president, FDR always regarded Warm Springs as his second home. It was late on the afternoon of March 30, 1945, when FDR's train finally pulled into the small railway station at the center of the village. There, the "usual crowd" of people from the surrounding area had gathered to welcome him. It fell to Secret Service agent Michael Reilly to help transfer FDR to his waiting car. He usually accomplished this task without too much exertion, as the president, after "walking" or being wheeled to his vehicle, would turn his back to the car, grip both sides of the rear door, and, as Reilly remembered, "surge out of your arms and into the jump seat." Then "he'd reach back, and pull himself into the rear seat . . . with such speed and grace" that the thousands of people who had seen the president accomplish this maneuver "at ball games, rallies and inaugurations, never suspected his condition."[1]

On this occasion, however, it took all of the strength that Reilly could muster to make the transfer. The president "was absolutely dead weight," as the tall, strong Reilly struggled to move him into position. Reilly was worried; he could recall experiencing this on only one previous occasion, when the president became so ill with a dental infection while fishing off the coast of Florida that he had to be rushed back to Washington for treatment. Reilly immediately reported his findings to Dr. Bruenn and the rest of FDR's security detail, notifying them that the president "was heavy."

With FDR safely in the vehicle, the small party made its way out of the village and up the hill toward the "Little White House." On the way they slowly passed Georgia Hall, the building that FDR had had constructed in 1933 to serve as the headquarters of the Georgia Warm Springs Foundation, which, as he noted in the dedication address he made later that year, FDR had founded to help restore "the confidence, self-reliance and cheerfulness" of the many disabled children and adults who had traveled to Warm Springs "seeking to walk again."[2]

As was the case at the village train station that Good Friday afternoon, another crowd greeted the president in front of Georgia Hall. But here, most of the people happily waving and smiling at FDR, while he warmly returned their gesture, sat in a row of wheelchairs. It was a scene that had been repeated every time FDR made his way to what he called his beloved "other home." But it was always deeply moving to this man who, for all his fame, remained a fellow patient and understood, as perhaps no other, their passionate desire "to lead a normal life."[3]

Waiting for the president in the doorway of the modest six-room cottage was Daisy Bonner, the African American cook who had worked for the president at Warm Springs for more than twenty years. Like the rest of the staff at his Georgia retreat, Daisy always looked forward to the arrival of "President Roosevelt," and had already made sure that she had what she needed to prepare some of the president's favorites: Brunswick Stew, Black Nut Cake, and, of course, Country Captain, the dish of southern fried chicken that the president seemed to relish above all else.[4]

Happy to have finally arrived, and having greeted Daisy warmly, FDR took to his favorite chair in the small living room–dining room. It wasn't long before cousins Daisy and Laura began to unpack a set of glasses and tumblers and other items that had been given to FDR for his birthday two months before, doing their best to add "a woman's touch" to the humble abode, while FDR sat quietly reading a book and the "other Daisy" set about preparing a simple evening meal.

As had so often been the case when FDR took time away from Washington, what all of his aides, relatives, and friends in both the White House and Warm Springs most hoped for was that he would get

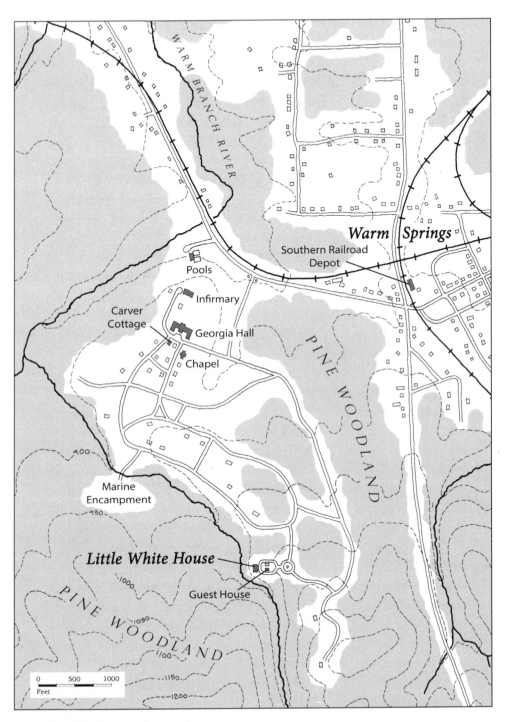

Warm Springs campus

enough rest to somehow "bounce back." Warm Springs seemed particularly well suited for this task, in large part because its isolation rendered the arrival of unexpected visitors much less likely.

There was one individual among the president's party at Warm Springs, however, who could no longer bring himself to entertain the fiction that FDR would somehow be able to recover his health. Standing in front of Georgia Hall that evening, William Hassett did his best to draw out the facts from Dr. Bruenn. After remarking that the president was "slipping away from us and no earthly power can keep him here," Hassett reminded Bruenn of a conversation the two of them had had last December. Hassett, on that occasion, had pressed the physician to reveal the truth about FDR's health.

"I know you do not want to make this admission and I have talked with no one else save one," Hassett observed. "To all the staff, to the family, and to the boss himself, I have maintained the bluff; but I am convinced that there is no help for him."

Suddenly becoming very serious, Bruenn asked how long Hassett had harbored such doubts.

"About a year," Hassett replied, after reluctantly confirming that the person he had confided in was Basil O'Connor. What convinced the two of them was "the Boss's indifference after the Chicago convention—[he] didn't act like a man who cared a damn about the election." Now Hassett could not help but notice FDR's increasing weariness, especially at Springwood, where there was less and less talk about all manner of things, from local stories to politics, books, and pictures. The "old zest" was fading. Then, too, there was "the feebleness of his signature—the . . . boldness of stroke and liberal use of ink—gone."[5]

In response, Bruenn admitted that the president was in "a precarious condition." But perhaps unable to face the truth, he insisted that his situation was not hopeless. He could be saved "if measures were adopted to rescue him from certain mental strains and emotional influences." But as Hassett knew full well, meeting these conditions was impossible, all of which "confirmed his conviction," he later recorded, "that the Boss is leaving us."[6]

It had been just over a year since Lieutenant Commander Bruenn had been assigned the "temporary additional duty" of caring for the president of the United States. Widely regarded as a man of "superior intellect and integrity," he was not given to dramatic displays of emotion. Yet, less than twenty-four hours after his talk with Hassett, the thirty-nine-year-old cardiologist expressed his concerns and frustrations in a second conversation about the president's health—this time with Daisy.

"Miss Suckley," Bruenn declared, "to begin with, you realize that like all people who work with this man—I love him. If he told me to jump out of the window, I would do it without hesitation." But managing FDR had proved nearly impossible. Drs. Bruenn and McIntire had repeatedly worked out a program designed to keep him from getting overtired, and he would "stick to it for three or four days and then abandoned it completely."

Not knowing whether she was justified in offering her opinion, Daisy proposed that he, or Dr. McIntire, or *someone* should put things very plainly to FDR. It was obvious, she said, that his "one really great wish is to get this international organization for peace started," and that "nothing else counts, next to that." This ambition might represent the best leverage they had to make him stick to the prescribed regimen. "You want to carry out the United Nations plan?" Well, "without your health you will not be able to do it. Therefore—take care of yourself."

On one level her conversation with Bruenn came as a relief to Daisy, as his depth of feeling for FDR impressed her. On the other hand, it was now clear, even though Bruenn had not said so directly, that "if he is to live through these trying days"—and she now felt it had come to that—he "must reduce his hours of work & not break the new schedule."[7]

Over the course of FDR's first two days in Georgia, the prospects for some measure of recovery did not look good. On Saturday, March 31, FDR had to cope with an incredible quantity of correspondence that arrived in the overnight pouch from Washington, and although he "seemed all right" in the morning, Hassett found him "worn, weary, [and] exhausted" later that afternoon. Worse still, FDR himself uncharacteristically admitted that he had "no strength, no appetite," and seemed to tire far too easily, all of which a discouraged Hassett dutifully reported to Dr. Bruenn.[8]

Daisy, too, noticed that FDR looked "depressed, both physically and mentally," late that day. She was pleased when he said he wanted to take a drive shortly after lunch, but he let his chauffeur, Monty Snyder, drive the "big car," as FDR, who had taken such pride in driving

FDR working on his correspondence inside the Little White House, April 1945.
(Courtesy of the Franklin D. Roosevelt Presidential Library)

himself around, no longer seemed up to it. Nor did he seem much interested in his dinner. And even though Basil O'Connor had joined them, it was obvious to Daisy that FDR had had enough of talking, in part because he was having a hard time concentrating. Attentive as she was to his every wish and whim, she found it difficult to see him struggle this way, and so was relieved when he suddenly announced he would go to bed at 9:15.[9]

THE GEORGIA SPRING THAT FDR SO LOOKED FORWARD TO WAS EXCEP-tionally beautiful in April 1945. Perhaps the cause was the unusually mild weather, which not only prompted the azaleas and dogwoods that dotted the woods surrounding the Little White House to erupt in a riot of color but also brought about an early blossoming of the peach trees, already covered in fruit.

Easter Sunday, like Thanksgiving, had special meaning for the residents of Warm Springs, with its connotations of rebirth and renewal, and the promise, however distant, of new life. Easter was also a day many of the residents associated with Franklin Roosevelt, who not only frequently celebrated the holiday in the presence of his fellow polio patients but had been instrumental in establishing the small, nonsectarian chapel that stood near the center of the campus where, on this Easter morning, a large percentage of the residents gathered to worship.

Despite the beautiful weather, there was little indication of whether FDR intended to join them. As on most mornings in the Little White House, FDR took his breakfast at 9:00 and remained in bed while Dr. Bruenn checked his overall condition and Hassett started in on his mail. Given the concern the president's fatigue had aroused over the past day or two, it is not surprising that by the time FDR had finished these initial tasks, a kind of conspiracy had developed that morning among virtually his entire retinue—including Daisy, Polly Delano, Hassett, Dr. Bruenn, and Charlie Fredericks—all of whom thought it would be best for the president to stay quietly at home, while Polly and Daisy went to the 11:00 a.m. service.

FDR did not disagree but, somewhat to Daisy's surprise, emerged from his bedroom at five minutes before 11:00 "looking spic & span in a light grey suit," with two periwinkles pinned to his lapel—and with every intention of going to church.[10] Of course, attending church in Warm Springs was far different from doing so in Washington or Hyde Park. The chapel in Warm Springs, like so many of the other buildings located at the facility, was specially designed for disabled worshipers, with a large open area in front of the pulpit that extended into the transept. Here, atop a floor of Georgia pine, there was room for both wheelchairs and gurneys, but space for only a limited number of pews behind. As the *New York Times* reported at the time of its dedication in 1938, "this is a place of worship for those who cannot kneel—a fact that was immediately apparent as FDR wheeled himself down the center aisle ahead of Daisy, Polly, and Hassett to transfer himself without assistance to the third pew on the left, just behind the packed cluster of patients and nurses. The chapel at Warm Springs was unusual in yet another respect: whenever FDR entered, he insisted he was doing so as a private citizen and made it a point never to speak or officially take part in the service while there, as he wanted to remain "just one of the worshipers."[11]

Taking it all in, Hassett found himself consumed by an "overwhelming sense of last things," and couldn't help but recall the Easter Day [they] had spent in Warm Springs in April 1939, just after Hitler

had marched into Czechoslovakia. FDR had attended the Easter service on that occasion as well, where he heard the Presbyterian minister
pray "that all things that obstruct peace be cast out of the world." This
was also the occasion when, upon leaving that evening, FDR famously
remarked to the well-wishers who had gathered at the station to see him
off that he would be back in the fall—if the world "was not at war."[12]

"Alas, for the misery of the years since," Hassett reflected, and with
good reason. April 1, 1945, was also the day on which the first wave of
the more than 500,000 US soldiers and marines landed on the Japanese Island of Okinawa, supported by over 1,200 warships—a military
operation second only to the Normandy landings in size and scope.
Before the battle was over in early June, more than 12,500 Americans
would lay dead, and nearly 40,000 would be wounded, many of them
sailors, casualties of the roughly 3,000 terrifying kamikaze missions
that sank 36 US warships and damaged nearly 400. Thousands of eth-
nic Okinawans also lost their lives, as well as all but 7,000 of the 77,000
Japanese soldiers who had vowed to defend the island to the death.[13]

It was just as well, then, that after the service FDR, Daisy, and
Polly took a drive through the Georgia woods on this balmy day before
returning to the cottage, for lunch, a nap, and a quiet evening, where
the man who had led his nation into war and was determined to see it
through to the end enthralled his guests with stories of a youth spent
in another century and another time.

In the days following Easter, FDR's health and frame of mind
seemed to improve. Although he was frequently tired in the afternoons, Hassett noticed that he was more cheerful and energetic in
the mornings. He appeared to regain his appetite, too. This certainly
pleased Anna, who, owing to her son Johnny's illness, had not been
able to accompany her father to Warm Springs, but phoned in every
day to see how he was getting on.[14]

In the first few days of April, FDR made a number of important decisions. On Monday, April 2, he received a memo from Secretary Stettinius outlining the reasons why he and senior members of
the State Department had become convinced that the United States
should abandon the idea of trying to achieve parity with the Soviet
Union in the General Assembly through the addition of two American states. Stettinius was now firmly opposed to this notion and had

even concluded that the American government would be in a much stronger position going into the San Francisco conference by dropping the claim altogether, even if the United States supported the Soviet request.[15] As Stettinius learned later that day, FDR agreed, and the secretary released a statement to that effect.

FDR also had to respond to the dispatches from Churchill and Stalin he received each day. Indeed, over the course of the fourteen days that he was in Georgia, at least twenty cables arrived from Churchill alone, many of them requiring an immediate response. One issue of great import to Churchill concerned General Eisenhower's decision to focus his forces not on the capture of Berlin but on the destruction of the German army. As Churchill cabled FDR on April 1, this contradicted the British understanding of the plan articulated in February by General George Marshall at the Combined Chiefs of Staff meeting on Malta. Based on these talks, Churchill and his Chiefs assumed that Marshall's emphasis on a drive into Germany, as part of "a broad front in the northwest," included the capture of the German capital.

But Eisenhower had long since concluded that Berlin, heavily damaged by Allied bombing, and devoid of many government ministries, "had lost much of its former military importance." Moreover, with over a million Russian troops poised on the Oder River just to the east of the city, Eisenhower was plagued by a nagging fear that a simultaneous thrust by both the Allied and Soviet forces on Berlin might lead to deadly encounters between the wartime partners; accordingly, he much preferred to drive toward Leipzig in the southeast. Not only might this make it possible for the Allies to split Germany in two, by linking up with Soviet forces in a much more advantageous location than Berlin, it might also prevent the widely reported possibility that the Germans would try to establish an enclave in the south.[16]

Churchill, who was thinking more in political than in military terms, did not agree. What is more, he and his Chiefs were upset that Eisenhower had taken the unprecedented step of communicating his intentions directly to Stalin. Indeed, when the subject of direct communication between Eisenhower's headquarters and the Soviet High Command came up at Yalta, the British rejected the idea, insisting that the liaison should continue to be directed through the offices of the Combined Chiefs of Staff. Churchill also regarded Eisenhower's "shift in axis to the southeast" as "a change in strategy" that was detrimental to General Bernard Montgomery's forces. He felt strongly, as he wrote to FDR, that this move should be put to "our two Chiefs of Staff Committees before any final commitment involving the Russians is entered into." Furthermore, Churchill could not help but wonder what it would mean if the Russians were to take both Berlin and Vienna, the latter of which they were soon to enter. Might that not create the impression that they "have been the overwhelming contributor to our common victory?"[17]

Neither Roosevelt nor his Chiefs of Staff were swayed by these arguments. In a message sent to Churchill on Wednesday, April 4, most likely drafted by Marshall but approved by FDR, the president indicated (in an echo of a comment that Churchill had made previously) that he, too, deplored "any misunderstandings between us . . . particularly at a time of great victories by our Armies." But "he failed to get the point" of the British objections. Leipzig was not that far removed from Berlin, and "is well within the center of the combined effort." At the same time, the British army is pursuing "what seems to me to be very logical objectives on the northern flank." FDR regretted that the wording Eisenhower had used to describe the Allied position on the ground—which seemed to imply a lack of drive among Montgomery's forces—so upset the British prime minister. But he remained convinced that "under Eisenhower's present plans the great German army will in the very near future be completely broken up into separate resistance groups," rendering Allied forces in a position to destroy it.[18]

However sharp the exchanges were between FDR and Churchill over Eisenhower's decision not to take Berlin, they paled in comparison to the communication that passed between FDR and Stalin over the Bern affair. In his previous correspondence with Stalin regarding this incident, which involved the possible surrender of German forces in Italy, FDR had rejected any possible Russian participation in the preliminary stages of these talks out of the conviction that to involve the Russians was to court failure. Hence, in his initial communication with Stalin on this matter, FDR did his best to push off any possible Soviet involvement, which Stalin had demanded, by repeatedly insisting that the initial discussions between representatives of the Allies and the Germans that had occurred in Switzerland had been strictly exploratory—merely focused on establishing the proper contacts between the two sides. Thus there was no need as yet for Soviet participation, which would become necessary only if and when the conversations reached the level of actual negotiations for surrender. This had been the thrust of the message that FDR had sent to Stalin on March 24, 1945, and again in the one sent on March 29, shortly after his arrival in Warm Springs.[19]

Stalin, however, thought otherwise, and in a series of escalating messages sent to FDR that ran between March 29 and April 7, 1945, he continued to maintain that surrender talks were in fact under way, and that these should involve Russian representatives. Stalin justified this argument by indicating that he was not against the idea of negations per se, but only if these talks "will not make the situation for the enemy easier." Thanks to what was going on in Switzerland, the Germans, he claimed, had already felt free to transfer three divisions from Italy to the Eastern Front.[20]

FDR immediately denied that any German troop movements had come about as a consequence of the talks in Switzerland, asserting that Stalin's information about the timing of the German troop transfers was in error. In addition, he reiterated his previous claim that "no negotiations for surrender have been entered into" and expressed disappointment that "an atmosphere of regrettable apprehension and mistrust" had crept into the matter. The president also reminded Stalin that "this entire episode" had arisen through the initiative of a German SS officer reputedly close to Himmler. Accordingly, he and Stalin should recognize that "there is a strong possibility that General Wolff's sole purpose is to create suspicion and distrust between the Allies." FDR could see no reason "why we should permit him to succeed in that aim," and he hoped that his "categorical statement" regarding both his intentions and the state of the talks in Switzerland would "allay the apprehensions" that Stalin had expressed in his previous communications.[21]

FDR was wrong. Stalin's stunning response, in what was undoubtedly the most belligerent message he ever sent to FDR, made it quite clear that the so-called Bern affair had reawakened his suspicions about the possibility that the Anglo-Americans would negotiate a separate peace with the Germans. Indeed, his inflamed reply, delivered to FDR on April 3, all but accused the president of lying. Stalin acknowledged that the episode had led to "an atmosphere of fear and mistrust" but insisted that it was the president who was misinformed—and not just about the movement of troops. According to the best information that Stalin's military officers had acquired, there was "no doubt that negotiations have taken place." Not only that, these same advisers had determined that the talks "have ended in an agreement with the Germans" whereby Field Marshal Albert Kesselring agreed to open the Western Front and permit Anglo-American troops to advance to the east in exchange for a promise "to ease for the Germans the peace terms." How else could one explain the rapid advance of the British and American forces in the west while the Russians faced fanatical resistance in the east?

Stalin also wondered why London had remained silent throughout the whole incident, and why it had allowed the president "to correspond with me on this unpleasant matter" when "it is known that the initiative in this whole affair . . . belongs to the British." He closed by maintaining that "the Germans had ceased the war against England and the United States," while continuing the war against Russia, a situation that, whatever momentary advantage, "in no way serves the cause . . . of the strengthening of trust between our countries."[22]

After reading this message with incredulity, an outraged Roosevelt authorized Leahy, assisted by Marshall and Bohlen, to craft an indignant reply. "I have received with astonishment your message of April 3," the message began, with its "allegation" that arrangements were made between Field Marshals Alexander and Kesselring at Bern that would permit Anglo-American troops to advance east in exchange for an Anglo-American promise "to ease for the Germans peace terms." FDR vehemently rejected this and reiterated the points he had insisted upon earlier: that "no negotiations had taken place," that the preliminary meeting had "no political implications whatever," that in any German capitulation there could be no violation of "the principle of unconditional surrender," and that "Soviet officers would be welcome at any meeting" where an actual surrender might be discussed.

FDR also stood by the credibility of his information. He was "certain that there were no negotiations in Bern at any time" and, for this reason, suspected that Stalin must have learned otherwise "from German sources" as part of their "persistent efforts to create dissension between us" and in an effort to escape responsibility for their war crimes. "If that was Wolff's purpose in Bern," FDR went on, then "your message proves that he has had some success." FDR concluded by writing: "Frankly, I cannot avoid a feeling of bitter disappointment towards your informers, whoever they are, for such vile misrepresentations of my actions or those of my trusted subordinates."[23]

FDR's insistence that no negotiations had taken place is perhaps best described as a half-truth, but Stalin, somewhat paradoxically, was reassured by the strenuousness of FDR's reply, assuring him in response that "I never doubted your honesty and dependability, as well as the honesty and dependability of Mr. Churchill." The conciliatory tone of this response and Stalin's stated reasoning that the Anglo-Americans "think differently" than the Russians were enough to mollify Roosevelt, although Stalin continued to stand by the basic facts as he saw them.[24]

FDR sent copies of this exchange to Churchill, who replied almost immediately to say that he was astounded that Stalin had sent a message "so insulting" to the honor of the United States and that of Great Britain as well. Churchill accounted for Stalin's letter by presuming that Russian leadership was "surprised and disconcerted" by the rapid advance of the Allied armies in the west. And he seized on the contretemps as another opportunity to remind FDR of his stated desire to "join hands with the Russian armies as far to the east as possible, and if circumstances allow, enter Berlin."[25]

Churchill also sent his own message to Stalin, detailing the history of the whole episode from the British perspective. He made it clear that he did not take kindly to Stalin's allegations, writing that "with regard to the charges which you have made in your message to the President of April 3rd, which also asperse His Majesty's Government, I associate myself and my colleagues with the last sentence of the President's reply."[26]

Stalin replied to Churchill two days later, enclosing a copy of his semi-conciliatory message to FDR insisting that the Russian point of view on the Bern question was correct, and informing Churchill that it was his practice to speak his mind clearly and frankly. "This is the advantage of confidential communication," he said, but "if," he went on, "you are going to regard every frank statement of mine as offensive, it will make this kind of communication very difficult. I can assure you that I have no intention of offending anyone."[27]

As was their practice, Churchill forwarded this message to FDR, saying "I have a feeling that this is about the best we are going to get out of them [the Russians], and certainly as near as they can get to an apology." Churchill also indicated that he planned to respond, but would wait until he had heard how FDR wanted to handle the matter, "so that we may keep in line together."[28]

Like so much of what occurred in the last 100 days of FDR's life, this flare-up was rich with irony. Stalin was undoubtedly correct, for example, when he claimed that negotiations had taken place between German officers and representatives of the Allies. FDR may have conveniently regarded these negotiations as "exploratory," but given that he failed to mention the much more substantive second round of talks that took place in Zurich on March 19, it seems clear that—as he mentioned to Mackenzie King—he regarded the Bern talks as strictly an Anglo-American matter. It was this conviction that stood at the heart of FDR's unwillingness "to answer Stalin's main question—why were the Soviets excluded from the Bern talks?"[29]

If the facts were not totally on FDR's side in this respect, they certainly were in another, more serious way. As we now know, what Office of Strategic Services (OSS) chief Allen Dulles had dubbed "Operation Sunrise" was indeed part of a larger German plot to split the Allies—known as "Operation Wool." Conceived in Verona, Italy, in November 1944 by a group of German SS and security officials, and tentatively approved by SS Intelligence Headquarters in Berlin shortly thereafter, the project was given final approval by Hitler himself in a meeting General Wolff held with Himmler and the Fuhrer on February 4, 1945—the first day of the Yalta conference.[30] FDR had been correct all along.

We do not know, however, how seriously Hitler took Operation Wool, and given the mixture of personal and strategic motives involved—many of the SS officials associated with the project, including General Wolff, were just as interested in securing lenient treatment for themselves from the Allies once the war was over as they were in carrying out the actual plot—it hardly seems surprising that the whole endeavor began to fall apart shortly after Wolff's March 19 meeting with General Alexander's representatives.[31]

But the tensions that the episode aroused were real, and in many respects helped inaugurate the growing sense of mutual mistrust that would later find full expression in the Cold War. As Admiral Leahy recounted at the time, the disturbing communications from Stalin laid out in the open "the long-festering suspicion and fear of the Russians that the United States and Great Britain might make a separate peace with Germany." These messages showed clearly the Soviet distrust of Allied motives and promises, and represented "another ill-omen for any successful cooperative agreement at the approaching United Nations political conference at San Francisco for which the President entertained such high hopes."[32]

Chapter 18

Off the Record

As had been the case during their visit to the Little White House in December 1944, Daisy slept in Eleanor's bedroom, which was adjacent to FDR's. Because the walls of the cottage were thin, Daisy had a pretty good idea about how FDR was getting on at night. She noticed a few days after their arrival in Georgia that he had a strong coughing spell at about 5:00 a.m., which concerned her. But Dr. Bruenn assured Daisy this was nothing to worry about, just the clearing of accumulated mucus that often occurs in the early hours.[1]

To help FDR gain weight, Daisy and Polly had taken it upon themselves to bring him "a cup of gruel" most evenings, after Arthur Prettyman had undressed the president and gotten him safely into bed. On more than one occasion, in fact, Daisy would spoon-feed FDR, while she sat devotedly on one side of his bed, and Polly sat on the other. FDR seemed to love this arrangement, as it allowed him "to be able to turn away from his world problems and behave like a complete nut for a few moments, with an appreciative audience laughing with him & at him, both!"[2]

That Daisy loved him there can be no doubt, but Daisy's love was not much different from that of a devoted spouse or nurse who had taken it upon themselves to care for an invalid husband or relative. The propriety the two of them observed was almost surely never broken.

Yet because Daisy was unmarried, there was always the chance that their relationship would be misunderstood. As she admitted, she had on occasion "argued" with herself and "with members of the family as to whether whatever gossip about us there may be, is justified."

But she had long ago made up her mind that "only those who wish to find evil in our friendship will do so."[3]

What made Daisy unique was her ability, as John Boettiger once observed, to allow FDR to relax and "think of completely different things." Nor was Boettiger the only member of FDR's inner circle who noticed as much. Eleanor, too, was aware of her talents, and in fact was pleased when she learned that Daisy and Polly would accompany her husband to Warm Springs. She knew "they would not bother him as I should by discussing questions of state; he would get a real rest and yet would have companionship—and that is what I felt he most needed."[4]

As Anna and others, including Eleanor, had also observed, FDR's patience seemed to have worn thin in the last months of his life. He was less and less interested in discussing issues or policy when he and Eleanor were together, the kinds of conversations that in the past served as the greatest bond between them. Now and then, FDR hinted at a latent desire to draw closer to Eleanor—as he expressed to Elliott over the Christmas holidays, or as he implied when he spoke fondly of making the trip to England with her—but it was more often the case that what he wanted and needed most from her at this point was perhaps the one thing that she herself admitted she was incapable of providing: simple companionship.

FDR's first cousin, Laura "Polly" Delano, another member of the entourage that accompanied him to Warm Springs, was the daughter of Warren and Jennie Walters Delano—FDR's aunt and uncle who, like Daisy, lived up the Hudson River in Rhinebeck. Six years FDR's junior, Polly was not unlike Daisy in that she was unmarried and represented "good company." In virtually all other respects, however, Polly was the polar opposite of Daisy. She was flamboyant, high-spirited, and unpredictable. She also delighted in gossip, though sometimes to the point of recklessness. As one member of the Delano family once put it, Polly "was a law unto herself." For all of these reasons, Eleanor was less comfortable with Polly than she was with the demure and discreet Daisy, and although FDR certainly found Polly entertaining, he was much less apt to confide in her than he was with Daisy.[5]

The one other person in FDR's inner circle, of course, was Lucy Rutherfurd. Like Daisy, Lucy was a person with whom the president could relax, but there was a second dimension to their relationship, a hint of past passion that, although largely left unspoken, was there all the same. Ironically, Daisy was the one person Lucy seems to have confided all of this to. As Lucy noted in a cryptic letter she sent to Daisy shortly after FDR had left for the Crimea, she found it hard to write, as "there seems to be so much to be decided—What is right and what is wrong for so many people & I feel myself incapable of judging anything. Yes—it is difficult when we must speak in riddles but we have spoken to one another very frankly—and it must rest there—One cannot *discuss* something that is sacred—and even simple relationships of friendship and affection are sacred & personal."[6]

The fact that FDR went to great lengths to see Lucy in the final six weeks of his life suggests that he felt a strong need to be near her, though he characteristically never revealed his inner thoughts to anyone—save perhaps Lucy—about the nature of their relationship. The closest he came to admitting that there was a special bond between himself and Lucy was, again somewhat ironically, in a conversation he had with Daisy during that final trip to Warm Springs. Sitting alone together in a quiet moment, FDR admitted that Lucy "had no other person like him—a friend of such long standing to whom to go for the kind of sympathetic understanding which he always gives." Having lost her husband just over a year earlier, Lucy faced an uncertain future—and also was "rather alone" now that her one daughter soon planned to marry. Whatever his reasons, on Wednesday, April 4, FDR decided that he would invite Lucy to join him in Warm Springs for the coming week.

FIRST, THOUGH, ANOTHER VISITOR ARRIVED. PRESIDENT SERGIO Osmena of the Philippines had been trying to arrange a meeting with FDR for quite some time to discuss a host of issues facing the islands now that their complete liberation was close at hand. Osmena was in Florida for medical reasons in late March, and so FDR decided to take advantage of his relatively close proximity to invite him to Warm Springs.[7]

Osmena arrived at the Little White House on April 4 at 11:00 a.m., precisely on time. Over the next three hours the two men reviewed the concerns that Osmena had listed in a memo that he had forwarded to FDR in advance. Osmena could also not help but note the contrast between the beauty and tranquility of the Georgia landscape and the

wholesale destruction in Manila that he had witnessed in his homeland roughly a month earlier. Indeed, by the time the Philippine president met with FDR that morning, the Manila he loved, "once proud
and beautiful," had ceased to exist.[8] As lunchtime approached, FDR
suddenly called in a somewhat embarrassed Daisy, who always did
her best to vanish whenever an official visitor arrived, to telephone
"Hacky," FDR's telephone operator. FDR wanted Hassett and the three
press pool reporters who had accompanied the presidential party to
Warm Springs to be at the cottage at 2:00 for what would be FDR's
998th press conference.

Just why the president should decide without any advance warning
to his staff that he wanted to hold a press conference was a complete
mystery, even to Hassett. But FDR's motives soon became apparent,
and indicated he had not lost his political acumen. What FDR recognized was that Osmena's presence provided him with a perfect opportunity to highlight a number of major issues: that the war in the Pacific
was far from over, that the United States needed to do all it could to
help the people of the Philippines recover from the horrors of the conflict, and that he remained determined to see the Philippines achieve
independence once the Japanese had been driven out of the islands.

During the press conference, FDR also delved into the tricky question of just how the United States might maintain a strong military
presence in the Pacific without violating his preference for the establishment of trusteeships—as opposed to colonies—after the war. In
answer to a question about whether the United States would take over
the "Japanese mandates," FDR alluded to the solution he had expressed
some weeks earlier to his cabinet, when he told his colleagues that these
territories would belong to the United Nations but would be defended
by the United States on behalf of "world security."

In addition, FDR did his best to dismiss the controversy over
Stalin's request for three votes in the General Assembly by offering a
brief review of how the idea arose at Yalta; by insisting that Ukraine
and Byelorussia had earned the right to a vote in the General Assembly given that millions of their citizens had been killed during the
war; and by reminding the three reporters present that the General
Assembly is an investigatory body only and it was "the little fellow"
that needed the votes there, not the United States. In view of these
considerations, he had decided to drop the idea that the United States

would request the same number of seats as the USSR. "I told Stettinius to forget it," he said, "as this business about votes in the General Assembly does not make a great deal of difference."

As FDR closed the conference, he reminded the three reporters that he did not want this material released until he had returned to Washington, in perhaps seven to ten days' time. Then, in classic FDR fashion, he uttered the last words he would ever issue to the press: "By the way, this is all off the record."[9]

THE NEXT THREE DAYS TURNED OUT TO BE THE QUIETEST PERIOD FDR enjoyed during his stay in Warm Springs. The weather had turned "cold and raw," keeping FDR indoors next to the fire, where he worked on his stamps and the "coffin" of books he had brought down.

Having settled into this quiet routine, and with encouraging news about the war in Europe arriving every day, FDR began to reflect once again about his future. In a private conversation he had with Daisy and Polly on the evening of April 5, he said he thought he should be able to retire by next year, "after he gets the peace organization started." As Daisy recalled, this was not the first time he had mentioned the idea of retirement, which initially elicited the same emphatic response from both Daisy and Polly: "that he couldn't do such a thing—[that] it had never been done [before]." But then Daisy said, "No one had ever before had a fourth term, either!"

Indeed, the more Daisy thought about it, the more she realized "that if he cannot physically carry on, he will *have* to resign. There is no sense in his killing himself by slow degrees . . . while not filling his job." It would be far better "to hand it over, and avoid the period of his possible illness, when he wouldn't be able to function."

As she concluded, "From a personal point of view—he can then take care of himself and have perhaps years of useful, happy life, when his influence for good can continue—perhaps on the Peace Organization."[10]

FDR brought up the subject again the next night, as he lay in bed smoking a cigarette, before finishing the gruel that Daisy and Polly had brought him. He spoke "seriously about the San Francisco Conference, and his part in World Peace," and reiterated the idea that "he can probably resign sometime next year, when the peace organization—the United Nations—is well started."[11]

By this point, FDR had been at Warm Springs for a full week, and thanks to his dedicated staff's efforts, his well-being seemed to have improved day by day. The two Daisys and Dr. Bruenn noticed that FDR's appetite was better. He seemed to enjoy his meals and occasionally even asked for second helpings. His face also seemed fuller and had a better color, and although he had not been weighed, Dr. Bruenn thought he may have put on a few pounds.[12] His blood pressure, however, still varied widely, from a range of 170/88 to 240/130—readings that led to continued efforts to reduce the stress on the president as much as possible.

It couldn't have hurt that Churchill, realizing he was not going to convince FDR to endorse his call for the Western Allies to take Berlin, finally conceded defeat in a brief note on April 6. Churchill admitted that he still "thought it was a pity" that Eisenhower had sent his plans to Stalin without anything being said to the British Chiefs, but the prime minister also acknowledged that "the changes in the main plan have turned out to be very much less than we first supposed." Given all of this, Churchill said that he now regarded "the matter as closed," and "to prove my sincerity," he went on, "I will use one of my very few Latin quotations, '*Anmantium irae amoris integration est*,'" which the State Department translated in a handwritten note at the bottom of the cable as "Lovers' quarrels always go with true love."[13]

On the home front, however, the situation was not as promising. Earlier in the week, the US Senate had handed FDR one of the most stinging defeats of his career when it rejected his manpower legislation by a vote of 46 to 29. Since FDR had made numerous appeals on behalf of the act, the *Washington Post* argued that the defeat "portended something more than the death of a bill and a major war policy." After all, the demise of the current legislation followed a "flat refusal to consider anything approaching national service, weeks of bickering over the confirmation of Henry Wallace, [and] a deliberate thumbs down on another Roosevelt nominee—Aubrey Williams." Overall, this "legislative trend," unless dramatically reversed, could mean that "Franklin Roosevelt is losing control of his Congress, much as Woodrow Wilson lost it with the approach of victory."[14] Eleanor was also having difficulties with the press, as a result of a statement she purportedly made indicating that "she saw no reason why the United States should be expected to feed Europe" when there were other nations "that can and should help"—a remark she vehemently denied ever having uttered. Exasperated after a week of public functions, she had escaped to Hyde Park for the weekend of April 7–8. After retiring early on Saturday night, she was perhaps somewhat surprised when she was aroused by a call from FDR.

Apologizing for being "half asleep," Eleanor made no mention of her spat with the press. Instead, the two of them spoke of more routine matters, including the unpacking of new china and other items at "the big house," an illness Johnny had come down with, and FDR's time in Warm Springs. It was a relatively short call, but Eleanor found herself encouraged by her husband's demeanor. He seemed much better than during the first conversation they'd had at the start of his visit, when FDR sounded so weary she found herself praying that "he may be able to carry on till we have peace."[15]

As she wrote in a letter to FDR the next day, the last she ever sent him, she was pleased at his excitement over the coming trip to the United Nations conference. "Give my love to Laura and Margaret," she wrote. "I'm glad they'll be along on the trip to San Francisco. Much love to you, dear. I'm so glad you are going. You sounded cheerful for the first time last night & I hope you will weigh 170 lbs. when you return."[16]

Unbeknownst to Eleanor, FDR had placed another call that Saturday evening, this one to Lucy Rutherfurd, most likely to confirm the plans for her expected arrival on Monday. Lucy had already worked out the details of her visit with Grace Tully, to whom she had written on April 5.[17] Lucy planned to bring the Ukrainian-born artist Madame Elizabeth Shoumatoff with her so that her friend, unsatisfied with an earlier work she had completed of FDR, could use the occasion to paint a second portrait of the president. As always, Lucy very much appreciated Grace's help in making the arrangements for her visit. But the manner in which she closed her letter clearly indicates that she, too, was well aware of the precariousness of FDR's health. "With many thanks again," she wrote to Grace, "for being so very understanding and thoughtful. If you should change your mind & think it would be better for me not to come—call me up. I really am terribly worried—as I imagine you all are."[18]

Lucy was not alone in thinking her visit might add to the strain that FDR was under. Though always happy to see Lucy, Daisy recognized that it was "another interruption in the routine we are trying to keep." Still, Daisy found herself quite excited by the prospect of Lucy's arrival, and she and Polly spent much of Sunday gathering flowers and fixing up the guesthouse where Lucy would stay, so that things would look attractive when she arrived.[19]

MONDAY MORNINGS WERE ALWAYS SOMEWHAT SPECIAL TO WILLIAM Hassett. Owing to the fact that there was no overnight pouch on this one day of the week, Mondays, as Daisy put it, were "as near to a 'do not work Sunday' as F ever gets to."[20] Blissfully devoid of any pressing matters, Hassett took advantage of this relatively quiet moment to talk to "the boss" about his collection of books, which, like stamp collecting, was one of FDR's lifelong passions. As it turns out, Hassett was also a bibliophile, and in addition to his duties as Secretary to the President, Hassett became something of a purveyor for the president's book collection, keeping an eye out for rare or interesting volumes that might come on the market. A somewhat discerning collector, FDR was not always interested in the works Hassett discovered, as was the case when Hassett asked FDR that morning if he might want to purchase a copy of Amasa Delano's *Voyages and Travels,* which the president declined.[21]

"Amasa was one of the 'Maine Delano's,' a distant cousin of my grandfather," FDR explained, "but grandpa had never met him," so FDR decided against the purchase. Nor was he interested in purchasing a copy of Edward Hyde's *The History of the Rebellion and Civil Wars in England,* another rare book that came up during their stay in Warm Springs, even though Hyde Park was named after the author. "Feeling the pinch of poverty," FDR insisted he could not afford the $17.50 purchase price. Still, by the time he died, FDR's book collection numbered over 22,000 volumes—a collection of which he was enormously proud and one of the reasons he insisted on building the nation's first "Presidential Library."[22]

FDR spent the remainder of the afternoon resting in the warm sun, which had come back out from behind the clouds, before he and Daisy headed off for a drive in the direction of Macon, Georgia, in the hope that they might run into Lucy and Madame Shoumatoff as the two women made their way in the opposite direction. After many fruitless miles of driving, the two parties eventually managed to meet up not far from Warm Springs. Given her artist's eye, Madame Shoumatoff could not help but notice the expression of joy on FDR's face upon seeing Lucy. But she also could not fail to notice the striking change in his appearance since the last time she painted him in 1943. Regarding him carefully, she reflected on a question that had now become commonplace: "How can I paint such a sick man? His face was gray and he looked to me much like President Wilson in his last years."[23]

Tuesday, April 10, proved another relatively restful day. FDR accepted an invitation to attend a barbeque on Thursday organized by Frank Allcorn, the mayor of Warm Springs, and Ruth Stevens, the manager of the Warm Springs Hotel. As in Hyde Park, FDR enjoyed getting to know his "neighbors," and was particularly fond of Mrs. Stevens. It was "Ruthie," reputed to be something of a "character," who had decided it would be a good idea to host a barbeque for the president—in part because, as she had announced a few nights earlier at her hotel, "she had just bought a goddamned pig that weighed three hundred pounds!"[24]

At noon, FDR took a few moments to sit for Madame Shoumatoff and Mr. Robbins, the photographer she had brought along as an assistant. The rest of the afternoon proceeded at a languorous pace. Daisy and Polly took a walk with the dogs, and after Madame Shoumatoff and Mr. Robbins had worked sketching and photographing FDR for an hour or so, they all took a break for lunch, joined by Leighton McCarthy, the former Canadian ambassador to Washington who was also one of FDR's oldest friends. Surrounded as he was by such convivial company, FDR seemed quite happy and relaxed. He spoke of his trip to the Crimea, said the war in Europe "might end at any time," and, smiling at Ambassador McCarthy (perhaps knowingly, as Canada was deeply involved in the Manhattan Project), surprised his guests when he predicted that once Germany was defeated, "Japan will collapse almost immediately."[25]

FDR brought the day to a close by taking a drive alone with Lucy through the Georgia woods to Dowdell's Knob, a rocky outcrop at the crest of Pine Mountain that stood roughly 1,400 feet above the low-lying country that lay between the Chattouchee and Flint Rivers far below. Of all the locations in Georgia, this place unquestionably held the greatest meaning for FDR. It was to this spot, during the difficult early years of his "recovery" from the disease that had robbed him of his ability to walk, that he would often venture, to sit alone, lost in thought, as he watched the sun set slowly in the west.[26]

THE RESPITE FROM THE WAR THAT FDR SEEMED TO ENJOY OVER THE past few days could not last, of course, and it was not long before a number of key issues crowded in around him at Warm Springs. Of these, the most serious was the seemingly never-ending problem of Poland. It had now been more than eight weeks since he and Churchill had departed the Crimea in such high spirits. Since then, however, there had been virtually no progress on the establishment of the expanded regime called for by the Yalta accords. The principal obstacle remained the Soviet insistence that the existing members of the Lublin/Warsaw government had the right to veto any of the proposed candidates put forward by London or Washington—the result of which was to bring the whole process of attempting to set up a new interim government to a crashing halt. Churchill and FDR had tried to rectify this situation first by issuing a joint démarche that challenged the Soviet interpretation of the Yalta understandings on March 19, followed roughly ten days later by a second message sent by FDR that in essence called Stalin's bluff by insisting that "any solution that would result in the continuance of the present Warsaw regime would be unacceptable, and would cause the people of the United States to regard the Yalta agreement as having failed."[27]

Stalin's negative reply, which FDR did not receive until April 10, did nothing to alleviate the situation. On the contrary, as Stalin admitted frankly, "matters on the Polish question had . . . reached a dead end." The most Stalin could offer was to use what "influence" he had with the Polish Provisional Government to convince it to withdraw its objection to Stanislaw Mikolajczyk's taking part in the deliberations in Moscow, so long as Mikolajczyk issued a public statement accepting the Yalta decisions and declaring his desire for friendly relations with the Soviet Union. Given that Lublin Poles were in fact controlled by Moscow, Stalin's offer of help was viewed with a good deal of skepticism in London and Washington. Nevertheless, Churchill saw a possible opening in Stalin's démarche, which, "if seriously intended," he wrote to FDR on Wednesday, April 11, "could be important."[28]

Churchill also informed FDR in the same message that he was scheduled to make a statement on the "Polish question" in the House of Commons the following Thursday. In keeping with the two leaders' efforts to stay on the same page when it came to Poland, he requested the president's views "as to how we should answer Stalin as soon as possible." "I have the feeling," he continued, "that they [the Russians] do not want to quarrel with us, and your telegram about CROSS-WORD [the British code word for the Bern talks] may have seriously and deservedly perturbed them."[29]

The prime minister might have been correct in his speculation that FDR's recent, strongly worded telegram to Stalin regarding the Bern incident may have perturbed the Russians, but the tensions this incident caused also alarmed FDR, who was now determined to put the matter behind him. A break with the Soviet Union at this delicate time, exactly two weeks to the day before the start of the San Francisco conference, was simply out of the question. His response to Churchill's request for his views on how the prime minister should answer Stalin in the Commons is entirely consistent with this view.

"I would minimize the Soviet problem as much as possible," FDR said, "because these problems, in one form or another, seem to arise every day and most of them straighten out as in the case of the Bern meeting."[30]

"We must be firm, however, and our course thus far is correct."[31]

This communication, which represents the last word FDR sent to Churchill on Poland, is significant not only because he drafted it entirely himself but also because it is frequently perceived as a broad, overarching statement of how the Anglo-Americans should manage their relationship with Stalin. To a certain extent this observation is correct, but we must remember that the telegram was sent in answer to the specific question Churchill raised about what he should say in the House of Commons regarding Stalin's intransigence on Poland. Accordingly, FDR's reference to "[minimizing] the Soviet problem as much as possible" should be regarded less as an overall statement of policy than as advice about how the prime minister should frame the statement he was about to make on a specific issue.

In fact, there can be little doubt that the message was intended to manage Churchill as much as it was to placate Stalin. The last thing FDR wanted at this stage was another public explosion of Anglo-American differences with the Kremlin—better to downplay current issues in the hope that a more opportune moment to address them would present itself in the future.

That FDR was determined to avoid any major rupture with Stalin in the closing weeks of the war is also evident in the final exchange of the more than 3,100 messages Churchill and Roosevelt sent to each other during the war. At issue, interestingly enough, was Churchill's concern over the dreadful conditions in the heavily populated areas of the Netherlands still under German occupation. Anxious about that country's plight, and despite his own nation's distress, Churchill suggested that he and the president issue an ultimatum to the German commander in Holland demanding that the International Red Cross be allowed to bring relief supplies into the country as soon as possible. Churchill also suggested that if this entreaty failed, the German command in the Netherlands should be branded murderers and held "responsible with their lives."[32]

Roosevelt, whose profound interest in the plight of the Dutch exceeded that of the prime minister's, agreed to this idea in principle. But in view of Stalin's recent allegations regarding the Bern affair, the president replied that he and the prime minister should not send the ultimatum without first obtaining Stalin's consent as to the exact wording of the document. He did not want to engage in any activity with the German government that the Kremlin might construe as "negotiations."[33]

To cap his efforts to close the door on the Bern incident, FDR also took the time that Wednesday to send a succinct reply to the last message he had received from Stalin on the matter:

Thank you for your frank explanation of the Soviet point of view of the Bern incident, which now appears to have faded into the past without having accomplished any useful purpose.

There must not, in any event, be mutual mistrust and minor misunderstandings of this character should not arise in the future. I feel sure that when our armies make contact in Germany and join in a fully coordinated offensive, the Nazi Armies will disintegrate.[34]

As usual, FDR's work on these communications was coordinated with Hassett in the president's bedroom during their regular morning session on Wednesday, April 11, 1945. After finishing this work, FDR emerged from his room about noon, dressed once again in his light-gray suit and crimson tie in preparation for a formal photograph that Madame Shoumatoff had asked Mr. Robbins to take of FDR in advance of her final work on his portrait. At the request of

Photograph of Lucy Rutherfurd, by Nicholas Robbins, April 11, 1945. (Courtesy of the Franklin D. Roosevelt Presidential Library)

the president, Mr. Robbins also took a formal photo of Lucy. He then retired to the sun deck to clear up some additional mail and dictate to Dorothy Brady the first draft of the Jefferson Day speech he had agreed to deliver over the radio on April 13. This was followed by lunch, more work with Brady, a rest, and then a two-hour drive with Lucy, Daisy, and Polly, before the arrival of FDR's old friend and Hudson Valley neighbor, Henry Morgenthau.[35]

MORGENTHAU'S VISIT TO WARM SPRINGS CAME ABOUT AS A CONSEquence of a short trip the treasury secretary had made to Florida,

Photograph of FDR, by Nicholas Robbins, April 11, 1945. (Courtesy of the Franklin D. Roosevelt Presidential Library)

which provided Morgenthau with a convenient opportunity to stop by and see FDR on his return journey to Washington. As planned, Morgenthau arrived at the Little White House just in time for cocktails. He found the president sitting with his feet resting on a large footstool, mixing drinks over a card table that was drawn up over his legs. Like so many of FDR's visitors during these last weeks, Morgenthau was shocked at his appearance. The president seemed very haggard, and when he offered his old friend a drink, "his hands shook so that he started to knock the glasses over"; Morgenthau had to hold each glass as FDR poured. Nor had Morgenthau ever before seen the president experience such difficulty transferring himself from his wheelchair to a regular chair when it was time for dinner. In his diary, Morgenthau described this moment as an agony to watch.[36]

Lucy, Daisy, Polly, and Madame Shoumatoff made up the rest of the dinner party. For about an hour, they engaged in pleasant conversation. FDR gave Morgenthau a rough outline of his schedule over the coming two weeks, including his trip to San Francisco, which in turn included his plan "to appear in his wheelchair," make his speech, and then leave.[37]

After dinner, the four women left FDR and Morgenthau alone so that they could discuss Morgenthau's intention to write a book on postwar German policy. The treasury secretary made it plain that he did not want to continue pursuing the book project "if it wasn't agreeable" to the president. Still, he wanted his friend and boss to know that he was going to continue to fight to weaken Germany, because that meant the country would "not be able to start another war."

At this point, and most likely by design, Polly entered the room to ask if the "two gentlemen were through talking." And if not, would "another five minutes be enough?"

Having received an affirmative reply, the women returned; a short while later, Morgenthau left, but not before saying good-bye to FDR, who was now sitting in front of the fireplace, looking relaxed and happy as he laughed and chatted with his company.

Something about the atmosphere that evening inspired Madame Shoumatoff to regale the party with a Russian ghost story. Just as she had finished, Dr. Bruenn arrived to check on the president and urge him to go to bed. At first, FDR demurred, asking the physician if he could stay up a bit longer; but sensing the latter's disapproval, he consented to retire for the evening.[38] Saying goodnight to Lucy and Madame Shoumatoff, FDR assured them that he would be ready to sit for the painting tomorrow. Then, in what had become a routine procedure, Arthur Prettyman came to wheel the president into his room and get him into bed while Dr. Bruenn took his vital signs.

Soon the cottage was quiet, at which point Daisy slipped into FDR's room once again to feed him his gruel, and to hear him lament that even though it had been a most enjoyable day, he was very tired.[39]

Chapter 19

The Last Day

THURSDAY, APRIL 12, 1945, PROMISED TO BE A HOT DAY IN WARM Springs, so hot that it already seemed to many of the locals as if summer had already arrived. There was a certain excitement in the air that morning. Not far from the Little White House, Mayor Allcorn and Ruth Stevens were already busy preparing for the late-afternoon barbeque in the president's honor that they had arranged to host at the mayor's cottage.

Georgia Hall was no less busy. There Hazel Stephens, a physical therapist and the Georgia Warm Springs Foundation's recreational director, and her assistant Betty Brown were getting ready for a minstrel show—a relatively common thing in Georgia in the 1940s—to be performed by the patients. Mrs. Stephens had been working on the production and costumes for the past two weeks and was pleased that Graham Jackson, a gifted African American musician of whom FDR was fond, had agreed to serve as the accompanist. The show was scheduled for Friday, April 13, but the president, always interested in the patients' activities, asked if they could put on a special performance for him on Thursday at 5:30 p.m., just after the barbeque.[1]

Mrs. Stephens was delighted to accommodate this request, and as she and Betty Brown got to work setting up the stage that Thursday morning, Michael Reilly came by the Foundation's playhouse to check on the placement of the chair that the president was to sit in for the show. Reilly also let Mrs. Stephens know that the Secret Service was going to park a radio car in front of the hall so that when the president left the barbeque, the agents with him would be able to alert her of the president's impending arrival.[2]

In the meantime, back at the Little White House, FDR sat resting in bed and reading yesterday's papers. (The pouch from Washington had been delayed by bad weather.) Because he had woken up with a stiff neck that morning, Dr. Bruenn had ordered a hot-water bottle and spent a few minutes massaging him before Bruenn left to take a swim in the pool. Daisy was also present, sitting off to one corner reading, while "Sister," Polly's Irish setter, slept under the president's small desk and Charlie Fredericks repaired the venetian blinds in the living room.[3]

At about 10:30 a.m., Daisy left the cottage to deliver the morning "bulletin" to Lucy. The pouch was not expected until well past 11:00, so it was determined that FDR would get dressed earlier than usual; thus he was expected to be ready by noon for Madame Shoumatoff to start painting.

The only other major item on the agenda for April 12 besides his correspondence was the speech for the United Nations conference. Since Dorothy Brady, Grace Tully's assistant, had taken dictation from the president the day before, it was Grace's turn to do so today. On most occasions, she or Dorothy would start working with the president in the hour or so before lunch. But because everything was delayed, it was decided that Grace would not start with the president until after he had finished his midday meal, which was invariably served at 1:00 p.m.[4]

Free until mid-afternoon, Grace decided to join Dorothy, "Hacky" (Louise Hachmeister), and Toinette "Toi" Bachelder, another Warm Springs regular, for a refreshing morning swim. Visiting the pool was one of the favorite activities of the president's staff when they were in Georgia, especially for Toi. Stricken with polio as a child, she was one of the Foundation's first "test patients," only fourteen years old when she arrived at the facility in 1925. In the social activities arranged for her first night, to help make her feel comfortable in her new surroundings, she unexpectedly found herself playing bridge with FDR, who developed an immediate attachment to her. From that point on, FDR kept track of her progress from year to year, and in 1933 invited her to join his White House staff as secretary to Marvin McIntyre. She accepted, and became one of the first disabled employees in the federal government.

While Toi, Grace, and the others enjoyed their swim, FDR was wheeled out of his bedroom at noon, dressed once again in his gray suit and crimson tie, ready to sit for the artist who was busily setting up her easel in front of him. Knowing that the president had a full schedule that day, and somewhat anxious and distracted by the fact that her brother had just suffered a mild heart attack, Madame Shoumatoff offered to postpone the sitting until the next day. But FDR insisted that they proceed.[5]

Daisy and Polly helped place FDR in his favorite chair, which they had turned to face toward the windows at exactly the angle that would allow the best light. Just as Madame Shoumatoff was starting her work, William Hassett entered the cottage with a very "heavy pouch."

Hassett had found the president in good spirits earlier that morning when he dropped by to tell him the mail would be late. Perhaps he was encouraged by the laugh that FDR had shared at breakfast with White House maid Lizzie McDuffie, an African American woman of well over two hundred pounds. The subject of reincarnation came up in their conversation about the previous evening's ghost stories, and McDuffie told the president, when asked, that if reincarnated, she would like to come back as a canary, which left them both in stitches.[6]

Still, in spite of FDR's good humor, Hassett thought the president's color was poor and his mien weary. Finding the president looking even more fatigued when he finally arrived with the pouch, Hassett suggested that since they were so late with the mail, perhaps the president "might want to leave it until after lunch."

"No," FDR replied, "let's get started at once."

And so the two men yet again plunged into the task, while Daisy and Polly sat crocheting on the couch and Lucy looked on admiringly. As Hassett and the president worked their way through FDR's correspondence, the secretary increasingly found Madame Shoumatoff "entirely too aggressive." She interrupted their paperwork constantly, took facial measurements, and moved the president "this way and that," prompting Hassett to resolve that once they were through he would speak to Dr. Bruenn and ask him "to put an end to this unnecessary hounding of a sick man."[7]

Yet the president had enough verve to laugh and make an occasional wisecrack. When it came time to sign a measure to extend the Commodity Credit Corporation, for example, he turned to Polly and said, "Here's where I make a law," at which point he wrote "approved" at the bottom of the bill along with his name and date. As Hassett later recorded, this anodyne law turned out to be the last bill FDR ever signed.[8]

Back in Washington, Admiral Leahy was busy preparing a draft response to a cable that had reached the White House's Map Room in the early hours of the morning. The cable was from Ambassador Harriman in Moscow, who was not happy with the message on the Bern affair that the president had sent him the day before for delivery to Marshal Stalin. Harriman disagreed with the president's characterization of the matter as a "minor incident" that had "faded into the past." Before forwarding the message to Stalin, the ambassador respectfully suggested that the word *minor* be deleted because, as Harriman put it, "the misunderstanding appears to me to be of a major character." He also wanted to delay the message long enough to give Churchill the chance to weigh in.[9]

Convinced that the president would not agree with Harriman's suggestions, Leahy drafted an appropriate reply, which he sent to Warm Springs for the president's consideration as "MR-OUT-411" at 10:50 a.m. But given that Hassett and FDR had started working later than usual, it was well past noon before the president saw Leahy's draft, which, first, articulated that Churchill was fully briefed and hence there was no need to delay the message to Stalin and, second, informed Harriman that "I do not wish to delete the word minor as it is my desire to consider the Bern misunderstanding a minor incident."[10] Leahy was correct in his conviction that the president wanted to do everything he could to minimize and move beyond the Bern affair. FDR read the text carefully, O.K.'d it, and passed it back to Hassett.

It was now close to one o'clock, and having finished with his correspondence for the day, FDR turned to other matters. He asked Hassett if he might pick up Leighton McCarthy in his car and give him a ride to the barbeque, where the president would meet them at 4:30; after this, he and McCarthy would attend the minstrel show being put on at Georgia Hall. And then, as Hassett turned to leave, carrying with him the various dispatches, the president gave him what turned out to be his last official directive: to inform Frank Walker, the postmaster general, that the president would indeed, as Walker had suggested, purchase the first stamp of the special issue commemorating the opening of the United Nations conference in San Francisco. As FDR had said to

Daisy a few days before, what better way to remind the American people of the significance of the conference than to issue the very stamp whose design he had selected the prior evening, with its laurel branch etched on a blue background, below the simple phrase "Towards a United Nations, April 25, 1945."[11]

HASSETT MADE HIS WAY DOWN PINE HILL TO CARVER COTTAGE BY 1:00 p.m. His first order of business was to see that the necessary orders and dispatches the president had signed went out. Included among these, of course, was the message that Admiral Leahy was waiting for in the White House. It wasn't long before the teletype in the Map Room clicked into life and, at precisely 1:06 p.m. Warm Springs time, spit out the words Leahy expected: "Reference MR-OUT-411 Approved." Thus the last message to go out of the Map Room under FDR's name concerned Joseph Stalin.[12]

Back at the Little White House, FDR remained sitting in his chair and reading while Madame Shoumatoff went on sketching. Arthur Prettyman brought in the president's midday gruel, placing it, and a small pitcher of cream that Daisy Bonner reserved for FDR, carefully on a table to the president's right. A few minutes later, while FDR kept reading between spoonfuls of gruel, Joe Esperancilla came in to set the table for lunch, which prompted FDR to announce to the small party around him that they had fifteen minutes more to work.[13]

As Daisy looked up from her crocheting, she noticed that FDR seemed to be looking for something, at which point she got up and walked over to his chair.

"Have you dropped your cigarette?" Daisy asked, leaning forward and looking into his face as she did so.

FDR did not reply immediately, but stared at Daisy for a moment with his brow furrowed in pain; then he put his left hand to the back of his neck and said in a low but distinct voice, "I have a terrific pain in the back of my head." Startled, Daisy tried to tell him to rest his head on the back of his chair, but at that moment, the president suddenly slumped forward, unconscious, while Madame Shoumatoff cried out, "Lucy, Lucy! Something has happened!"

As Polly rushed in from her bedroom and Lucy sprang to her feet, a frantic Daisy tried to tilt the president's chair back to an angle that might return him to an upright position so he could breathe properly.

It took all three of the women to accomplish the task. Then Daisy grabbed the phone and said to the operator, "Please get in touch with Dr. Bruenn and tell him to come to the President's cottage!"

At roughly the same time, Madame Shoumatoff rushed outside and cried out to Jim Beary, the lone Secret Service agent on duty, "The President is sick, call the doctor." For a moment Beary just stared at her incredulously, so she repeated her plea "to please call the doctor!"[14] By this point Arthur Prettyman and Joe Esperancilla had hurried into the room and, seeing that the president was unconscious, did their best to pick him up and carry him into his bedroom. But with the president limp in their arms, they had to ask Polly to grab his feet in order to lift him properly.

With Daisy's help, the two men and Polly managed to get the president onto his bed. They could not quite maneuver him into the middle; so Daisy, after she had opened his collar and tie, supported him by lifting up the left side of his pillow while holding the president's right hand. Polly stood on the other side of the bed, with one hand on his heart and the other fanning him. As Daisy and Polly stared at FDR in desperation, he rolled his head from one side to the other, opening his eyes as he did so. Polly thought that her cousin had tried to look at each of them in turn, but Daisy "could see no sign of recognition in those eyes."[15] Twice, FDR drew up the left side of his face in pain, but then he seemed to fall into a deeper stupor, breathing heavily. Lucy dashed into the room at this moment with some camphor that she passed back and forth beneath his nostrils. But the president was unresponsive.

Back at the pool, Grace, Hacky, and Toi were heading to the Georgia Hall cafeteria for lunch, but as they neared their cottage Hacky said she wanted to check her switchboard and speak with the Foundation's operator. As soon as she got on the line, the operator asked her if she knew "the whereabouts of Dr. Bruenn."

"Who wants him?" Hacky asked. "We just left him at the Pool."

"The Little White House."

Hacky put down the phone and plugged in to the president's cottage.

Daisy Bonner answered. "Yes," she said, "they were looking for the doctor."

"Does the President want him for lunch?" Hacky asked.

"No, no," Daisy said, "he's sick, the President is sick."

"I'll get him right away," Hacky replied.

"Dr. Bruenn," Hacky said, her normally calm voice somewhat elevated. "The President is sick. They want you right way at the Cottage."

At Dr. Bruenn's instructions, she switched over to George Fox's line.

"George, the President is sick," Hacky said. "Dr. Bruenn wants you to grab his bag and meet him as soon as possible at the Little White House."[16]

By this point, Jim Beary's call to the Secret Service station at Carver Cottage had alerted Guy Spaman, the agent in charge, that Bruenn was needed at the president's cottage. Wasting no time, Spaman tore off in the direction of the pool, a distance of roughly two miles, to find the doctor. Bruenn—who was in the dressing room at the time, taking the call from Hacky—was soon dashing back to the Little White House.

Michael Reilly, who was off duty and actually in the pool, had a quick word with Spaman as he went to retrieve Bruenn; but not knowing who was ill, Reilly decided not to rush off, lest he disturb or alarm the many patients who were there. He asked Spaman to come back to retrieve him right after he had delivered Dr. Bruenn to the cottage.[17] While Spaman drove the cardiologist to the Little White House, William Hassett, who was now back at Carver Cottage after his lunch at the Foundation cafeteria, overheard the request for George Fox to proceed immediately to the president's cottage. This message was followed a few minutes later by a call from Reilly telling Hassett to head to the Little White House immediately.[18]

DR. BRUENN ENTERED FDR'S BEDROOM AT APPROXIMATELY 1:30 P.M., roughly fifteen minutes after the president had collapsed. Finding the president "pale, cold and sweating profusely," Bruenn immediately asked everyone to leave the room so that he and Commander Fox could check the president's vital signs and get him into dry pajamas—he had voided involuntarily—and under clean bedding as soon as possible. The president was completely unconscious. His lungs were clear, and his heart sounds were excellent, but his blood pressure had spiked to 300/190 and his heart was beating at a rate of 96 times per minute.[19]

Blankets and hot-water bottles were brought in to warm the president, and Dr. Bruenn, suspecting a cerebral hemorrhage, injected him with two vasodilators. Shortly thereafter, he left the room to call Dr. McIntire on the president's private line to inform him "of the catastrophe."[20]

"He appeared quite well, this morning," Bruenn said in answer to McIntire's question, "except that he complained of neck pain"—an ominous sign, of course.[21]

Dr. McIntire said he would call Dr. James Paullin, the noted Atlanta internist who was part of the team that had examined the president the year before, asking that he leave immediately for Warm Springs.[22] Polly got on the line to phone Eleanor, who was in a meeting with Charles Taussig about trusteeships. Eleanor had just offered to call the president when Polly's call came through. "We are worried about Franklin," she said. "He has had a fainting spell. Dr. Bruenn will call you back."[23]

Not wanting to reveal the news to her guest, Eleanor did not ask Polly any questions. But she ended the interview with Taussig and, instead of waiting for a call from Bruenn, summoned Dr. McIntire. The doctor told her he was unsure what the problem was—hardly a forthright answer given that Bruenn had already indicated that he suspected a stroke. McIntire and Eleanor made plans to fly down to Warm Springs that evening. So as not to tip off the press, McIntire urged Mrs. Roosevelt to keep her speaking engagement at the Sulgrave Club in Washington that afternoon, which she did.[24]

Anna was also at the White House when the initial call came in from Dr. Bruenn. She was just about to leave for Bethesda Naval Hospital to visit Johnny, recently hospitalized with a staph infection, when Dr. McIntire caught up with her. With Anna he was more direct, telling her that her father had had a seizure. But he insisted that she should not be overly concerned and should still go visit her son. McIntire then decided to track down Stephen Early, whose crisis experience—including the sudden death of President Warren Harding—could prove invaluable in the coming hours.[25]

By this point, William Hassett had arrived at the Little White House. As soon as he entered he heard heavy breathing through the thin walls, and worried that the president "was mortally stricken." For a time Hassett sat in the living room in silence with Daisy, Polly, and Charlie Fredericks.[26]

As the four of them kept vigil, Lucy decided that she and her friend must leave. Madame Shoumatoff had already removed her easel and painting materials from the cottage, and soon she and Lucy were hastily packing their suitcases in the guesthouse. As the Secret Service men carried their bags out to Madame Shoumatoff's car, Daisy and Grace Tully came out to say a tearful good-bye. The two women, joined by Mr. Robbins, left Warm Springs, heading east toward Macon along the same route they had traveled a mere three days before, uncertain of the president's fate and with his unfinished portrait safely stowed in the trunk of the car.[27]

Unable to bear the thought of FDR dying, Hassett summoned up the courage to go into the president's bedroom. The "Boss's" eyes were closed and his mouth open as he continued the "awful" breathing. In addition to Bruenn and George Fox, Arthur Prettyman and Joe E. Esperancilla were also in the room, but no one spoke as Hassett looked down at FDR's noble forehead. Believing this was the last time he would ever see Franklin Roosevelt, Hassett glanced at his watch; it was 2:12 p.m. Then he left to rejoin Daisy and the others in the living room, where they continued to sit in silence, joined now by Grace Tully, whose lips were moving in prayer.[28]

At 2:45, Dr. Bruenn recorded an improvement in FDR's blood pressure resulting from the medications he had administered. The president's heart rate was still strong and steady, and his color good, but his breathing had become irregular.[29] Bruenn telephoned Dr. McIntire with another update, telling him that it might be necessary for them "to be prepared for a long siege." Then he slipped out to the porch to "speak in whispers" to Hassett, explaining that the president had felt no pain after the first shock. It was evident, Bruenn admitted quietly, and out of earshot of the others, that the president had suffered a massive cerebral hemorrhage in the fluid area of the brain. Suddenly, they heard a change in the president's breathing, and Bruenn ran back into the bedroom.[30]

It was now 3:15. The president's blood pressure was down to 210/190 and his heart rate was still 96 beats per minute, but there was a marked slowing in his respiration and his right pupil remained widely dilated.[31] A few minutes later, a frantic Dr. Paullin arrived at the guard hut at the entrance to the Warm Springs campus. Impressed by the speed at which Paullin had driven the eighty-five miles from Atlanta, John Gorham, the Secret Service agent who had been alerted to the doctor's impending arrival, quickly escorted him to the president's cottage.

Dr. Bruenn was on the phone for the third time with McIntire when Paullin appeared in the cottage and rushed into the president's bedroom. It was 3:30 p.m. and the president was, as recorded later, *in extremis*, "near death"—ash gray, in a cold sweat, and breathing with difficulty.[32]

While Daisy looked on, a voice called out for Dr. Bruenn, who handed the still-open line to Polly as he went back into the bedroom to find the president gasping for breath, his pulse barely perceptible. Then it disappeared completely. Dr. Bruenn hurriedly started artificial respiration, while Dr. Paullin gave the president an intracardiac dose of adrenalin. But it was no use; FDR's heart beat two or three more times, and then stopped.[33]

ANXIOUSLY REMAINING ON THE OTHER END OF THE STILL-OPEN TELEphone line, Dr. McIntire, the physician whose ultimate responsibility it was to care for the president of the United States, stood in disbelief as he waited for Dr. Bruenn. Stephen Early, who was with him by this point, soon heard the tear-choked voice of a woman—Polly Delano—crackle through the receiver, telling Dr. McIntire that the president was dead.[34] Then Bruenn came on, to confirm the news.

It was fortunate for Admiral McIntire and the other, much less experienced members of the dwindling White House staff that Early had decided not to leave immediately, but to stay on for a few more months once he had informed FDR of his decision to resign. Early had known the president for decades, of course, and considered him one of his closest friends, but he could not yet ponder his personal loss; the world had to be informed that its most powerful man had just died, amid an ongoing global war.[35]

Early immediately took charge, ordering both McIntire and Hassett (in Warm Springs) to tell no one about the president's death until he'd had the chance to inform Mrs. Roosevelt. He and Hassett would then coordinate their efforts to disseminate the news to the press. Early also informed Hassett that he, Eleanor, and Dr. McIntire would fly to Warm Springs that evening once they had completed the most urgent tasks at the White House.

BACK IN THE SMALL COTTAGE, NOW FILLING WITH LIGHT AS THE SUN began to move toward the horizon, Daisy found it impossible to put her grief into words. What FDR's death might mean for her, she thought, and for all those who knew the president personally, was simply incomprehensible. There seemed to be nothing to do—and everything to do. Dazed, she and Polly packed their things and moved into the guest house, where they finally gave way to their grief and wept in the arms of Daisy Bonner and Lizzie McDuffie.[36]

Like Daisy, Grace Tully found herself momentarily incapable of emotion—as if "her whole mind and sense of feeling had been swept away." The death of the president was simply "outside belief." Without a word or a glance at the others present, Grace walked into the bedroom and kissed FDR on the forehead. Then she went out to the porch, where suddenly a rush of memories drawn from "seventeen years of acquaintance, close association and reverent admiration" came flooding in. She remembered that the Boss always shunned displays of emotion, and so she did her best to remain composed.[37]

IN THE MEANTIME, UP ON PINE MOUNTAIN, "RUTHIE" AND MAYOR Allcorn had finished preparations for their barbeque for the president. At 4:00 p.m. the first few guests started arriving and the country fiddlers began to play. Ten minutes later, Major De Witt Greer, the head of the White House Signals Corps, arrived to make a quick check on the short-wave radio units his men had installed for the Secret Service. Among the guests awaiting the president's arrival was A. Merriman Smith, one of the three press pool reporters who had been invited to accompany FDR to Georgia. At about twenty minutes past four, Smith noticed that none of the president's advance team had arrived, and there had been no communication whatsoever from the Little White House.

Smith walked over to the Signal Corps sergeant sitting next to his short-wave radio and asked the sergeant to check in with the Secret Service Desk at Carver Cottage. Impatient, Smith himself took the microphone once the corpsman had gotten through and found himself speaking to Howard Anderson, the agent on duty.

"Andy, this is Smitty. What the hell is going on down there?"

"I honestly don't know. No cars have arrived. There's just nothing doing," came the reply.

"But the President is supposed to be here in a few minutes," a puzzled Smith replied.

When Anderson offered to make further inquiries, Smith told him not to bother; he would try to find out by phoning the main switchboard.

"Hacky, this is Smitty," Smith said as soon as he had gotten through on the mayor's phone.

"Why aren't you people on the way?" he went on. "What's holding things up?"

"I don't know," she replied in a panicked voice, "but Mr. Hassett wants to see you. Get the other two boys and go to his cottage as fast as you can."

"Hacky, for Christ's sake, what's going on?"

"Smitty, I can't say anymore. Just get down here as fast as you can."[38]

Smith put down the phone and ran out to collect the other two reporters, Robert Nixon and Harry Oliver. Within minutes, the three of them were racing down the narrow, twisting mountain road in Major Greer's car, convinced that "the big break" they were about to receive was news of the capitulation of Germany. But when the three reporters entered the cottage, they found Hassett standing in front of the fireplace with a mournful expression on his face, flanked by a quietly tearful Grace Tully and Dorothy Brady. They could not possibly be crying about the end of the war, Smith thought.

"Gentlemen," Hassett said carefully, "it is my sad duty to inform you that President Roosevelt died at 3:35 this afternoon."

Hassett went on to fill in some of the further details, but then broke off, as Dr. Bruenn came in to provide a more complete picture.

"It was just like a bolt of lightning or getting hit by a train," the exhausted cardiologist said, wiping his damp face with a handkerchief.

"One minute he was alive, and laughing. . . . [T]he next minute, wham!"

"Did you see this coming?" one of the reporters asked.

"This wasn't the sort of thing you could forecast," Dr. Bruenn said. "It doesn't happen that way. . . . He was awfully tired when we first came down here," Bruenn admitted, but then asked, "Wasn't he in fine spirits" when "the three of you saw him" during his last press conference?

Smith agreed there was some truth to this observation. Smith had been out riding two days earlier when the president's car nearly ran him down. Smith was on a rather nasty little horse, and as he reined in the animal to let the president's slowing car pass, FDR bowed to him majestically and called out in his wonderfully deep and resonant voice, "Heigh-O Silver!"[39]

Now Smith and the other reporters were scrambling to get on phones to their national headquarters to bellow the flash news at 4:47 p.m. Central War Time (CWT) that Franklin D. Roosevelt was dead.

A. Merriman Smith and the guests at the barbeque were not the only people wondering what had happened to the president that afternoon. Glancing out into the main floor of the playhouse as she put the final touches of makeup on one of the members of the cast, Hazel Stephens, the Foundation's recreational director, could see that the venue was full. The only empty seat for the minstrel show, in fact, was the stout leather chair that Agent Reilly had placed in the middle of the aisle earlier in the day, now surrounded by an excited audience made up of children patients, the children of Foundation members, and those adult patients and a few special guests who had never seen the president.

As Stephens continued to work on the cast's makeup, Graham Jackson appeared and came running across the stage, tears streaming down his face.

"Mrs. Stephens," he said in a hoarse whisper, "he's dead, the President is dead. It's on the radio!"[40]

In disbelief, Mrs. Stephens went to the nearest radio to get confirmation; having done so, she then faced the task of making the announcement to the large audience of patients and staff before her. What made this doubly hard was the thought of all the children, whom she had specifically invited to this special performance, waiting

Graham Jackson playing Dvorak's "Going Home," with patients saying good-
bye for the last time, Warm Springs, April 13, 1945. (Edward Clark, TIME/LIFE)

anxiously in their wheelchairs to greet the man whom most Americans referred to as president of the United States, but whom they personally thought of as a special friend, and one of them.

Remembering that there was a Methodist minister, Reverend Benjamin Mize, in the audience, Stephens quietly summoned him back-
stage. Then she gathered the cast to give them the news and, after
asking the minister if he would lead a prayer, mustered all of the courage she had and walked out to center stage.

"It is with a great deal of sympathy and regret on the part of the
cast and the entire Foundation family, that I make the announcement,"
she said, her voice quaking, "that the President of the United States is
dead. He died at 3:35 this afternoon. If you will all stand we will have a
minute of silent prayer, which the Reverend Mize will close."[41]

The audience, most of whom already had tears in their eyes,
brought their hands together to pray. Those who could, stood up on
their braces, or leaned on canes, but many more, confined as they were
to wheelchairs, simply bowed their heads.

ELEANOR ROOSEVELT WAS STILL AT THE EVENT AT THE SULGRAVE Club when she was called to the telephone. Stephen Early found it difficult on this occasion to hide his emotions as he requested that the First Lady return to the White House immediately. Eleanor did not ask why, but given Early's tone and the unexpected call, she suspected something dreadful had happened.

Eleanor went back to the benefit to say her good-byes and express her regret that she could not stay any longer, "because something had come up at home" that made it impossible for her to remain.[42] As the car took her back to the White House, she sat silently with clenched fists. Later on, she remembered that she knew in her heart what had happened, but as she wrote, "One does not actually formulate these terrible thoughts until they are spoken." Upon arrival, she went into her sitting room and waited. Stephen Early and Dr. McIntire came in to tell her "the President had slipped away." They gave her details, including Bruenn's initial report of a hemorrhage.[43]

It was widely reported in the press at the time that Eleanor's first words were "I am more sorry for the people of this country and of the world than I am for ourselves." Eleanor later admitted that she could not recall making this statement, and in fact doubted that she had. Most likely it came from the savvy press wrangler Early. But even if Eleanor had not said those words, the sentiment they expressed were certainly consistent with her thoughts—and with the actions she took after her husband's death.

Her first step was to send at once for Vice President Truman. She then composed a somber, straightforward message for her four sons, who were scattered all over the world by the demands of war.

DARLINGS, PA SLIPPED AWAY THIS AFTERNOON. HE DID HIS JOB TO THE END, AS HE WOULD WANT YOU TO DO. BLESS YOU. ALL OUR LOVE. MOTHER[44]

VICE PRESIDENT TRUMAN HAD SPENT THE AFTERNOON PRESIDING over the institution he loved above all others, the US Senate. With the day's official business through, he headed for the private hideaway that House Speaker Sam Rayburn ran on the ground floor of the Capitol, where it was Truman's custom to enjoy a "libation" and talk business or simply relax with those members who had achieved a certain status in Rayburn's eyes.

Just after 5:00 p.m. Eastern War Time (4:00 p.m. in Warm Springs) Truman entered "room number 9," where he greeted the man who was now second in line for the presidency.

"Steve Early wants you to call him right away," Rayburn said, mentioning that he had just heard from the White House.

Truman mixed himself a drink and then dialed the White House line.

"This is the V.P.," he said.

"Please come to the White House as quickly and quietly as you can," Early said, in a voice that Truman thought sounded strange, "and make sure you enter through the main entrance on Pennsylvania Avenue."

"Jesus Christ and General Jackson," said an alarmed Truman as he put down the phone.

"They want me at the White House right away," he told Rayburn and the two other guests in the room, but "you are to say nothing about it."[45]

It took ten minutes for the vice president's car to reach the White House. "I thought I was going down there to meet the President," Truman later explained, imagining that perhaps FDR had returned early from Warm Springs. Two ushers met Truman at the door. The vice president was escorted to Mrs. Roosevelt's private quarters on the second floor. Waiting there with her were Anna and her husband, along with Early. As soon as Truman entered the room, Eleanor Roosevelt rose, put her hand gently on his shoulder, and said,

"Harry, the President is dead."

Truman stared at her for a moment, then said gravely, "Is there anything I can do for you?"

To which Eleanor replied, in a remark that became famous,

"Is there anything *we* can do for *you,* for you are the one in trouble now."[46]

NINE THOUSAND MILES AWAY, JAMES ROOSEVELT SAT ALONE IN HIS room at Marine Headquarters in Manila, staring at the message he had just been handed from his mother. Rereading the cable, he thought about how the burden of World War II had weighed on his father, much like the Civil War had aged Abraham Lincoln and World War I had laid low Woodrow Wilson. It seemed to him that his father was just as much a victim of the war as any soldier killed in battle.

Reflecting on the time he had spent with his father, James was especially grateful for the years he spent working in the White House just before the war. He was seized by a strong desire to see his father one more time. He thought about the brief hours they had shared at the last inauguration, their discussion of his father's will, and his desire to have all thirteen grandchildren present at the ceremony, which all seemed to make sense now in retrospect. He had always deeply admired his father, but felt that he did not realize until this moment how much he loved him.[47]

James's commanding officer, Admiral Ralph Davis, asked if there was anything he could do, and when James expressed his wish to fly back to Washington for the funeral, the admiral said he would see what could be arranged. Within hours James was on a plane, for the first leg of what would turn out to be a grueling sixty-hour trip back to New York. He arrived an hour and a half too late to join the burial services.[48]

WHEN LUCY AND MADAME SHOUMATOFF REACHED MACON, GEORgia, they stopped at one of the city's major hotels to use the phone, in the hopes of learning about FDR's condition. After Lucy had tried in vain to get through the jammed lines a number of times, Madame Shoumatoff suggested she go upstairs to the main switchboard of the hotel to ask one of the operators to make a special call for them.

When Madame Shoumatoff reached the telephone office, however, she found the two operators weeping and exclaiming "the President is dead!" Even though Madame Shoumatoff had just come from the president's side, the statement jolted her. For a moment she stood staring at the two women. Then she went downstairs to tell Lucy, who, having heard the news from passersby, sat motionless in the lobby. She remained unable to speak as they returned to the car for the long drive back to their homes in Aiken, South Carolina.[49]

THE VICE PRESIDENT REMAINED WITH ELEANOR IN HER SITTING ROOM while Stephen Early returned to his office to place the official White House call to the wire services—an act he had already coordinated with Hassett in Warm Springs and which seemed eerily reminiscent of the call he made four years ago about the bombing of Pearl Harbor. By this point he had also asked Hassett and Dr. Bruenn to select a casket for the president that was in keeping with the First Lady's wishes, and to work with Admiral Leahy and others on making the arrangements to return the president's body to Washington the next day.[50]

At 6:00 p.m. Eastern War Time, Early and Dr. McIntire held a joint press conference. Still unwilling or unable to acknowledge the precariousness of the president's health in the previous months, McIntire insisted that right up to the end FDR was in reasonable shape for a man of his age and that the hemorrhage "came out of the clear sky."[51]

It was 7:00 p.m. by the time a distraught Secretary Stettinius had managed to summon the cabinet together for a solemn swearing-in ceremony in the Cabinet Room. All of the members were present, with the exception of Frank Walker, who was ill. Eleanor had also decided to stay away, so the only women present were the vice president's wife and daughter and Frances Perkins.

After receiving the oath at 7:09 p.m., Truman convened a brief cabinet meeting, and as he rose to speak, Perkins thought he looked frightened at the challenges he now faced. Truman stated that he did not feel worthy or strong enough to carry this load, but "with the help of God, he would do it, and would do it as well as he could."[52]

A few minutes later, Eleanor, McIntire, and Early left for their flight to Columbus, Georgia, about thirty-five miles southwest of War Springs. As Eleanor, "tall and erect" and dressed in black, made her way to the waiting White House limousine, one newspaper reporter could not help but notice her composure, quietly remarking that she was "a trouper to the last."[53]

ELEANOR MAINTAINED THE SAME DEMEANOR WHEN SHE ARRIVED IN Warm Springs about 11:00 p.m. that evening. Entering the Little White House, she embraced Daisy, Polly, and Grace Tully. Grace immediately remarked how deeply sorry she was for Eleanor and the children. "Tully, dear," Eleanor replied, "I am so very sorry for all of you."[54] Then Eleanor sat down on the sofa and asked Daisy and Polly to tell her exactly what happened. After they had spoken to her for some time, she turned to Grace and asked if she too had been present, which led

Grace to recount her own experiences that day, including that she had been in the house when FDR died.

At this point, Polly, perhaps convinced that Eleanor was bound to find out one way or another, or perhaps free to give sway to a long-suspected antipathy for Eleanor now that FDR was gone, revealed that Lucy Rutherfurd and Madame Shoumatoff had been in Warm Springs for the past three days.[55] Somehow, Eleanor managed to maintain her self-control when she learned that the woman her husband had promised never to see again was with him just moments before he died. After asking a few penetrating questions about the nature of their meetings, and who arranged them, Eleanor walked into FDR's bedroom and closed the door.

Eleanor never revealed what she thought or felt in the five minutes or so that she remained alone with her husband, but when she reemerged, as Grace Tully observed, "her eyes were dry, her face grave but composed."[56] Then the First Lady sent them all off to bed.

Heading to the guest cottage, Daisy reflected that Eleanor loved FDR "more than she knows herself, and his feeling for her was deep and lasting. The fact that they could not relax together . . . is the tragedy of their joint lives."[57]

Over time, Eleanor Roosevelt would come to appreciate what Daisy saw all too well—to recognize, as she later wrote, that men and women who live together for decades not only get to know each other's failings "but also come to know what is worthy of respect and admiration in those they live with and in themselves."[58] Eleanor also understood, as she finally retired for the night, that though her husband's passing was a terrible blow, it was impossible to think of it solely in terms of a personal tragedy.

All through that evening, in small towns, hamlets, along railway sidings, and in front of the White House, Americans gathered to express their grief and uncertainty about the future. As James Roosevelt later recalled, "Our lives had gone down one road for so long that we knew no other way. Now our lives would be altered to follow another course." His father, he realized, had been the glue that held his disparate family together, but James might just as well have been speaking about the wartime alliance and the "family of nations" that FDR had so ardently hoped would set the world on the path to peace.[59]

As dawn broke on April 12, 1945, it seemed impossible for the generation who had lived through the two most profound crises of the twentieth century to imagine a world without Franklin Roosevelt. But the leader who had launched a new era with a hundred days of frenetic action in 1933—when, as he put it, "this nation was asking for action and action now"—was no more. It would now be up to others to don his mantle and carry his causes forward—to finish the work he had started twelve long years before, when a paralyzed nation and a troubled world looked to a man who could not stand without the help of others to lift a suffering humanity toward the promise of a new day.

Epilogue

Looking Beyond Victory

IT WAS A BRIGHT SUNDAY MORNING WHEN THE PRESIDENTIAL TRAIN carrying Franklin D. Roosevelt made its way up the Hudson River Valley for the last time. Waiting patiently at the special railway siding adjacent to the river at Springwood stood a contingent of soldiers, sailors, and airmen. It would soon be their task to lift the president's flag-draped coffin onto a caisson, which a team of six US Army horses would then pull up the narrow farm road to the burial site at the crest of the ridge high above. The tulip poplar and oak that FDR had planted years ago had not yet broken out in leaves, and in the deep recesses of the woods, one could still see patches of snow on the ground, but the abundance of skunk cabbage shooting up from the soil was a sure sign that spring had arrived. Inside the rectangular Rose Garden, surrounded by the century-old hemlock hedge that FDR had wanted to see replanted that spring, an enormous bank of flowers lay next to the open grave, which had been prepared by William Plog, the faithful superintendent of the Roosevelt estate who had been hired by FDR's father nearly fifty years before. By the time the president's train arrived at just before 9:00 a.m., nearly two hundred dignitaries, high officials, members of Congress, and senior military officers had already gathered, speaking in hushed tones as they lingered about the gravesite. Accompanying the casket as it made its way northward from Washington were Eleanor, Anna and Elliott and their spouses, and other members of the Roosevelt family. President and Mrs. Truman were also on board, along with their daughter Margaret, as well as all nine justices of the Supreme Court and virtually the entire Roosevelt cabinet, including Frances Perkins and Henry Wallace, both of whom

FDR being laid to rest in the center of the Rose Garden, in the presence of Eleanor, Anna, and other members of the Roosevelt family, Hyde Park, New York, April 15, 1945. (Courtesy of the Franklin D. Roosevelt Presidential Library)

understood that the cord that had bound the cabinet together "had snapped."[1]

At 10:00 a.m. the first loud crack of a twenty-one gun salute echoed through the valley to mark the official start of the interment service, followed by the sound of muffled drums and the slow cadence of Chopin's funeral dirge played by the West Point Army Band, who marched ahead of the president's coffin as it was slowly brought up from the river. Once the procession had reached the entrance to the garden, it halted, and six noncommissioned officers carried the bronze and mahogany casket bearing the president's body to his final resting place, not more than 250 yards from the small second-floor bedroom of the home where he was born.

Left unsaid that morning was how the world was going to cope with the loss of Franklin Roosevelt. Indeed, the only precedent for the outpouring of grief occasioned by his sudden passing was the reaction

A forlorn-looking Winston Churchill leaving St. Paul's Cathedral with his daughter Sarah, following the memorial service for Franklin D. Roosevelt, April 17, 1945. (Getty Images)

to the death of Abraham Lincoln eighty years before. Millions of Americans felt a profound sense of uncertainty about the future. To many, especially those in uniform, it seemed as if they had lost their own father. Nor were these sentiments confined to the United States. In London, more than two thousand people thronged St. Paul's Cathedral for a memorial service called in honor of the late president, while several hundreds more, many of them weeping, gathered outside to listen to the service on loudspeakers. In Moscow, FDR was honored with front-page coverage in the official Soviet press, memorial broadcasts, and black-bordered flags flying above the Kremlin. Many ordinary Russians expressed their sorrow openly, wiping away tears as they spoke of their own personal sense of loss at the American president's demise.[2]

By all accounts, both Churchill and Stalin, even though they had noticed the decline in the president's health at Yalta, were stunned by the news. Near midnight on April 12, 1945, Churchill, working late as usual, had just finished writing out a telegram to Clementine, who was in Leningrad on an official tour for the Red Cross, when he learned that FDR had died. Quickly adding a line saying that he had just received the "grievous news of President Roosevelt's death," he appeared distressed and distracted as he handed the telegram to his assistants. "I am much weakened in every way by his loss," he commented some moments later, before writing out a personal note of condolence to both Eleanor Roosevelt and Harry Hopkins, as well as a letter forwarding the news to King George VI, to whom he lamented that "ties have been shorn asunder which years had woven."[3]

The same alarm and incredulity was evident at the Kremlin some hours later, when Ambassador Harriman called on Marshal Stalin to offer his personal reassurance about the continuation of American foreign policy in the wake of the president's death. Stalin greeted the ambassador in silence, and stood holding Harriman's hand without saying a word for perhaps thirty seconds before he asked him to sit down. Like Churchill, Stalin appeared distressed as he questioned Harriman closely about the circumstances of FDR's death. He also insisted, as Harriman recounted the importance of US–Soviet relations, that "President Roosevelt has died but his cause must live on." Then, in what was perhaps an indication of his sincerity, he agreed to reverse his earlier decision and allow Foreign Minister Molotov to travel to San Francisco to represent the Soviet Union at the United Nations conference.[4]

Stalin was not alone in expressing the view that President Roosevelt's "cause must live on." Countless editorials, press pieces, and radio commentaries made the same argument. As Anne O'Hare McCormick wrote ten days after the president died in an article titled "His 'Unfinished Business'—and Ours" that was based on the remarkable interview she held with FDR on March 23, FDR "may not be present at the conclave he called, but in the most literal sense he will be conspicuous by his absence. His voice will be the loudest there . . . [his] vacant seat will overshadow all of the occupied chairs. It may well be," she concluded, "that the speech he does not deliver—the speech his mind was full of when he fell—will be far more effective in carrying his dream toward reality than anything he could say in person."[5]

In the emotional tribute Churchill delivered to the House of Commons a few days earlier, he arrived at a similar insight: the timing and circumstances of FDR's death may well have contributed to the fulfillment of his legacy. While the president's passing represented a "bitter loss to humanity," he had died what Churchill considered "an enviable death." He had brought his country "through the worst of its perils and the heaviest of it toils" and had "died in harness . . . battle harness, like his soldiers, sailors and airmen," at the very moment when "victory had cast its sure and steady beam upon him."[6]

In many respects Churchill's and McCormick's observations were accurate. FDR had died at an opportune moment, and had not, as he himself feared he might, lingered on to fight the battle over the creation of the United Nations and the establishment of the peace in an incapacitated state, as had Woodrow Wilson decades earlier.[7] The former "Brains Truster" and long-standing Roosevelt associate Benjamin Cohen certainly would have agreed with this assessment. Of all the officials within the Roosevelt administration, Cohen was the one individual who had the wisdom—or temerity—to argue in the spring of 1944 that FDR's running for a fourth term would be a mistake. It would, Cohen feared, lead to a kind of apathy or intellectual and political fatigue among the American public that risked leaving "Rooseveltian ideas, like Wilsonian ideas . . . discredited for a considerable period, not because they are basically unsound but because political conditions will not permit them to be accepted or even understood." If, on the other hand, FDR were to end his career in 1944 on what could only be described as a high point, the influence of his ideas "may be greater," as the people will always remember that at no moment and in no crisis did Roosevelt ever let them down. Thus, whoever succeeds FDR will be under great pressure to follow his example in fighting for and watching out for the common people's interests.[8]

Viewed from a short-term—and even a long-term—political perspective, Cohen's reasoning, much like Churchill and McCormick's, certainly carries a good deal of weight. Yet we should not let these observations about the timing and circumstances of FDR's death overshadow the very real and long-lasting consequence his leadership had on the history of the twentieth—and twenty-first—centuries. The first and most dramatic manifestation of this impact can be seen in the transformative nature of his presidency. The America that huddled around radios or gathered on the Washington Mall to listen to FDR proclaim March 4, 1933, "a day of national consecration" was nothing like the America he left behind twelve years later. FDR took "watching out for the common people" very seriously, and in focusing the efforts of his administration on providing for the social and economic well-being of the average American, through Social Security, unemployment insurance, workers' rights, and the regulation of the financial sector, not to mention a massive investment in infrastructure, he fundamentally altered the relationship between the American people and their government.

With Eleanor's help, FDR also helped usher in an America that was far more inclusive of racial and religious minorities. This is not to say that he rid the country of racism, anti-Semitism, or other forms of bigotry and religious intolerance, but FDR's habit—as a "Protestant Patrician in a Catholic Party"—of "including the excluded" and paying attention to the needs of the marginalized helped lay the foundation for the all-important civil rights movement that followed. As Mary McLeod Bethune once noted, the Roosevelt years represented "the first time in the history" that African Americans felt that they could communicate their grievances to their government with the "expectancy of sympathetic understanding and interpretation." By 1936, over 90 percent of African American voters—most of whom had supported the Republican Party in the past—were voting for Roosevelt and the Democrats.[9]

Roosevelt's leadership had an equally strong impact on the relationship between the United States and the rest of the world. Once again, the most transformative aspect of this change came about in the minds of the American people, who by the time of Roosevelt's death—and despite his lingering fears to the contrary—had largely accepted the idea that the so-called isolationism of the 1930s, or what might better be defined as unilateralism, was a failed policy. To a large extent this conviction stemmed from the lessons FDR and his contemporaries gleaned from the experience of the Great Depression, which included stark recognition of the link between the global economic crisis of the 1930s and the concomitant rise of fascism in Europe and parts of Asia. Commenting on this in his famous Economic Bill of Rights speech in January 1944, FDR said, "We have come to a clear realization of the fact that true individual freedom cannot exist without economic security and independence. 'Necessitous men are not free men.' People who are hungry and out of a job are the stuff with which dictatorships are made."[10]

In light of this, FDR firmly believed that the security and well-being of people on distant continents was directly linked to the security and well-being of the people of the United States.[11] To rid the world of the economic hardships that created the conditions that led to the rise of these anti-democratic regimes—and hence the war—FDR set his administration to work on creating a new postwar *multilateral* order that rejected the economic nationalism and unilateralist tenets of such organizations as the "America First" movement. In place of high tariffs and restrictive trade practices, FDR embraced the free movement of capital and freer trade. By the summer of 1944, the Roosevelt administration had tackled the first of these two major requirements—the free movement of capital—through the successful negotiation of the Bretton Woods agreements that led to the creation of the World Bank and the International Monetary Fund. Three years later, the successful negotiation of the General Agreement on Tariff and Trade (GATT) brought about much of the second requirement. Taken together, these two measures represented a profound change in the structure of the global economy that forms the basis for what we now call globalization.[12]

In keeping with America's expanding role in the world—perhaps best captured in FDR's October 1944 comment to Stalin "that in this global war there is literally no question, military or political, in which the United States is not interested"—FDR not only helped craft the grand alliance that went on to defeat the Axis but also managed the largest buildup of military and industrial capacity the world had ever seen. By 1945, American industry, to take but one example, had produced over 300,000 military aircraft, a significant portion of which went to our Allies via the Lend Lease program, another Roosevelt invention, while the total number of American men and women in uniform—and not working in American industry—had climbed from a paltry 186,000 in 1938 to roughly 16 million. FDR also initiated the Manhattan Project, which brought about the dawn of the nuclear age.

What makes these accomplishments all the more remarkable is that very little of this happened by accident. Much of it, in fact, was the product of Franklin Roosevelt's highly furtive and creative mind. Indeed, FDR's capacity for what we might refer to as Machiavellian reasoning—his ability to stay just far enough ahead of the public to subtly lay the groundwork for future policy directives—is perhaps his most remarkable quality. In this sense, Anthony Eden was surely correct when he remarked that "Roosevelt, was, above all else, a consummate politician. Few men could see more clearly their immediate objective, or show greater artistry in obtaining it."[13]

FDR's penchant for secrecy had its downside, of course. It made the president difficult to read—and, when coupled with his ebullient personality, left him open to the charge, by some, that he lacked depth and was essentially a superficial character, and, by others, that he was a crypto-socialist, fascist, authoritarian, or dictator.[14] It also left Vice President Truman in a state of profound ignorance about the details of many of FDR's policies. The most serious aspect of FDR's proclivity for hiding his innermost thoughts and feelings was his tendency to downplay or cover up—not the extent of his disability, which in 1930s and '40s America was surely a political necessity—but, rather, the far more serious decline in his health that took place in the spring of 1944 and continued in his last 100 days. Benjamin Cohen, in this sense, was right in arguing that FDR should not have run for office again in 1944, but for reasons that even this relatively close confidant failed to recognize.

And yet, given the frank admission that Eleanor Roosevelt made to Margaret Fayerweather about her husband's health just a few weeks before his death, and FDR's own premonitions about the possibility that he might not be around for much longer as he took his fourth oath of office, it seems clear that part of what drove FDR's determination to press on was in fact his own sense of mortality. He knew, as he admitted to James Farley in July 1940—long before the diagnosis of heart disease that Dr. Bruenn made in the spring of 1944—that a man in his condition could "have a breakup at any time." But with the world at war and in desperate need of American support, FDR nevertheless made the decision to break with tradition and run for an unprecedented third term, even if, as Eleanor remarked, "it must shorten his life." FDR's response to Cohen's recommendation that he not run in 1944 reinforces this view. "This is a most interesting analysis," FDR observed, "and I think a very just one. You have only left out one matter—the matter of my own feelings!"[15]

FDR may have suffered from declining physical and mental energy in the final 100 days of his life, but his determination to secure what has rightfully been called "a New Deal for the World" had not waned. His decision to bring Edward Flynn to Yalta, followed by the latter's trip to Rome to orchestrate a possible rapprochement between the

Vatican and the Kremlin, was one example of this phenomenon. A second can be found in his interest in and support for the organization of a world conservation conference as one of the first major international gatherings established under the auspices of the newly formed United Nations. At home, his decision to form a committee to look into the establishment of a guaranteed annual wage as a means to help the nation make the transition "from a war economy to a peace economy" was yet another, as was his support for the inclusion of a possible drafting of an "International Bill of Human Rights" at the San Francisco conference. Finally, his efforts to effect a rapprochement between the Arabs and the Jews in the Middle East as a means to facilitate the establishment of a Jewish homeland in Palestine, though unsuccessful and highly frustrating, in a very real sense marked the beginning of the leading role that FDR expected the United States to play in the world once the war was over.[16]

But none of these lofty goals would be possible without the continuing cooperation of the great powers, which FDR regarded as essential to the preservation of world peace. This made it necessary not only to work with the British but also to recognize that the most important element of postwar security and stability lay in cooperation with the Soviet Union, which, in FDR's mind, could be accomplished only by securing Soviet participation in the United Nations. It was this goal, above all others, that FDR pursued in his last 100 days, and that determined many of the policy decisions he made during the Yalta conference and in the weeks and months that followed.

FDR's critics would later assert that he was too old and ill to stand up to Stalin—that during his last 100 days he sold out Poland and much of the rest of the region to the Russians. But FDR was not alone in thinking that cooperation with the Soviet Union was necessary; the US Joint Chiefs of Staff certainly shared this view and, as late as the spring of 1945, continued to insist that "the maintenance of Allied unity . . . must remain the cardinal and over-riding objective of our politico-military policy with Russia."[17] Moreover, when we consider the array of issues that FDR was attempting to reconcile as the war in Europe drew to a close—the tensions between his belief in fundamental human rights and the realities of geopolitics, his responsibility to guard American interests while promoting international understanding and cooperation, his aspiration to foster a world community of neighborliness and shared values in the face of the potent and often pernicious forces of nationalism—his policies at Yalta become much more understandable.[18]

FDR understood that there were contradictions in his drive to establish a "family of nations." In the same way, FDR knew that the United Nations would not be without its faults—especially given the imbalance between the powers accorded the four (and later, five) "policemen," on the one hand, and the rest of the states that made up the international body, on the other. He never imagined that he could will a perfectly formed world government into being. His aim was to make the exclusive authority enjoyed by the Big Three during the war less exclusive after the war—the first step in what he called "the democratic organization of the world." It was this overarching goal that he saw as the key to the prevention of another, even more cataclysmic war. If the achievement of that objective required him to temporarily compromise some of his principles, so be it; there would be time enough in the future for him, or his successors, to correct any shortcomings.

The UN Charter that passed on June 26, 1945, stands as the purest expression of FDR's cause. Its emphasis on human rights and on the establishment of a human rights commission would eventually lead—under the skillful leadership of Eleanor Roosevelt—to the adoption of the Universal Declaration of Human Rights in 1948. Its call for the establishment of "international machinery for the promotion of the economic and social advancement of all peoples" echoes FDR's 1941 call for "Freedom from Want" in his Four Freedoms address, and closely mirrors the Atlantic Charter's appeal for the "fullest collaboration between all nations in the economic field with the object of securing, for all, improved labor standards, economic advancement and social security." The new world body's emphasis on social and economic progress would ultimately lead to the founding of UNICEF in 1946, the World Health Organization in 1948, and the World Food Program in 1961.

The creation of the Trusteeship Council called for in the UN Charter stands as another reflection of a cause close to FDR's heart—and of the issue that divided him and Churchill. The Council was established "to supervise the administration of Trust Territories and to ensure that Governments responsible for their administration took adequate steps to prepare them for the achievement of the Charter's goals," the latter of which included "the right to equal rights and self-determination." Much as FDR had anticipated, the end of the war set in motion the decolonization of the world. On November 1, 1994, one month after the independence of Palau (the last remaining United Nations Trust Territory), the Trusteeship Council suspended its operations.

The legacy of FDR's globalism—which, in addition to the Bretton Woods agreements and the promotion of freer trade, includes the American-led multilateral security system that has helped prevent the outbreak of another global conflagration—also endures. While he could not have predicted every outcome of his policies, FDR was always a far-sighted politician, especially in his waning days. As Anne O'Hare McCormick noted after her March 23rd interview with the president, FDR was "looking beyond victory" toward the San Francisco conference, when the United States and the world would "project into the picture of victory the design for peace."[19]

AS HE SAT IN THE WARM GEORGIA SUN THE DAY BEFORE HE DIED, FDR was at work on his Jefferson Day radio address. Contemplating the work of the nation's third chief executive, he was struck by the fact that Jefferson, himself a distinguished scientist, once spoke of "the brotherly spirit of Science that had brought into one family all its votaries of whatever grade, and however widely dispersed throughout the different quarters of the globe." There was a lesson in this observation, FDR thought, for "today we are faced with the preeminent fact that, if civilization is to survive, we must cultivate the science of human relationships—the ability of all peoples, of all kinds, to live together and work together, in the same world, at peace."[20]

Knowing that millions of people the world over shared his resolve, FDR remained confident that a lasting peace could be achieved—that it would be possible to move "against the terrible scourge of war." To all those who were ready to dedicate themselves to this purpose, he then wrote out in his frail hand the last words he would ever craft for the public: "The only limit to our realization of tomorrow will be our doubts of today. Let us move forward with strong and active faith."[21]

Unfortunately, FDR's unbounded optimism and faith in his own ability to carry on despite his utter exhaustion after years of toil could not revive his frail body. His final tribute to Jefferson was never delivered; there would be no address from his wheelchair to the opening of the United Nations conference; his chance to return to his beloved home upon the Hudson to live out his years in tranquility and peace, denied. But his spirit and vision endure in the institutions he helped create and in the determination of people the world over to continue to build that "permanent structure of peace" that he worked so hard to establish during his time in office, and at no time more urgently than in his last 100 days.

IN THE CENTER OF THE SMALL TOWN OF HYDE PARK, ABOUT A MILE from the Rose Garden, stands a bronze plaque that lists the names of all those from the community who served in World War II. At the top of the plaque, a separate smaller list denotes the names of those "who gave the supreme sacrifice," among which is included, in alphabetical order, Franklin D. Roosevelt. Over the last few months of his life FDR often referred to those who had made "the supreme sacrifice" and, in reference to the United Nations, frequently insisted, as he did in his final State of the Union address, that "this organization must be the fulfillment of the promise for which men have fought and died in this war. It must be the justification of all the sacrifices that have been made—of all the dreadful misery that this world has endured."[22] He also cautioned the American people not to forget that "in our disillusionment after the last war, we preferred international anarchy to international cooperation with Nations which did not see and think exactly as we did. We gave up the hope of gradually achieving a better peace because we had not the courage to fulfill our responsibilities in an admittedly imperfect world. We must not let that happen again," he said, "or we shall follow the same tragic road again—the road to a third world war."

The world we live in today is certainly not perfect. But as the American people retreat into xenophobia and nationalism and demonstrate less willingness to engage with other nations and peoples, we should reflect on the price that Franklin Roosevelt and so many hundreds of thousands of other Americans paid to secure global peace. We should remember FDR's vision, faith, and idealism—his conviction that the world's problems are America's problems—and ask ourselves if, in the face of the challenges confronting us today, we will exhibit the same courage to live up to our responsibilities.

Acknowledgments

As any historian worth his or her salt will readily admit, getting to know Franklin Roosevelt is not easy. It takes years of patient prodding to peel away the many outer layers of his personality before the essence of the man starts to emerge—and even then, one is never quite sure. This task becomes all the more daunting for the biographer—a fact in which the mysterious and inscrutable FDR would no doubt take delight. Given FDR's complex nature, it is impossible for me to conceive how I might have been able to complete this work without the help and support of a number of friends and colleagues who have also sought to fathom the depths of this multifaceted "juggler." Sharing ideas and friendship with them has enriched me and this book.

Much of the inspiration for this work stems from a series of conversations held with Richard Aldous and Mark Lytle, of Bard College, whose friendship, astute analysis, and deep fascination for the enigmatic FDR helped shape the contours of this project from day one. For their willingness to listen to—and critique—my ideas, as well as read and evaluate the first draft of the manuscript, I remain profoundly grateful. I owe an equal debt of gratitude to David Reynolds of Christ's College, Cambridge—another friend, colleague, and mentor, whose fascination for the man he frequently refers to as "the wheelchair president" also helped shape the contours of this work. David's willingness to take time to review the entire manuscript and engage in a number of spirited electronic conversations about its strengths and weaknesses is deeply appreciated. William Leuchtenburg—the dean of American historians, a Roosevelt biographer, and one of the kindest and most generous people I have ever chanced to meet—also read the entire work and offered the type of sage advice and criticism that could only come from a man who lived through these tumultuous years. My thanks also go to Warren Kimball, another great friend and teacher, for his input on the work, as well as to Richard Breitman, Geoffrey Ward, and John B. Hattendorff, all of whom took the time to read and discuss various aspects of the manuscript. I would like to thank David Douglas and Joan Murray for providing me with access to the unpublished version of the diary of Henry A. Wallace; Vladimir Petchatnov for his help in obtaining documentary material from the Foreign Ministry Archives in Moscow; Norman J. W. Goda for pointing me toward an important new source concerning FDR's visit to the Great Bitter Lake; Richard Grinnell for his poetic counsel; Natalia Garrity for some last-minute Russian translation; Kenneth Moody for some long-distance research; and the late Curtis Roosevelt for his willingness to allow me to interview him about his memories of his grandparents. Special thanks also go to Jonathan Alter and Robert Dallek for the important advice and encouragement they provided at the inception of this effort. I want to thank my friend Peter Shaw, the cartographer, for his excellent illustrations, as well as Neil and Annie Mozer for their kind hospitality during my many research trips to Washington.

I am also grateful for the support I received from a number of institutions and archives. First and foremost, I want to extend my appreciation to Marist College, especially to Dr. Dennis Murray, the visionary who served as president of Marist for nearly forty years, and who today, as president emeritus, continues to strive to make Marist one of the foremost educational institutions in the United States. It was thanks to a chance meeting on the steps of St. John's Episcopal Church across the street from the White House on the first of May 1997 that Dr. Murray and I began the conversation that would eventually lead to my employment at Marist and residence in Rhinebeck, New York, less than ten miles up the Albany Post Road from Hyde Park. I also owe a heartfelt thanks to my fast friends and colleagues in the History Department at Marist, especially chairs Nicholas Marshall, Robyn Rosen, and Sally Dwyer-McNulty, for their unwavering support and for their patience with all of my various endeavors over the years.

It was the presentation of the Four Freedoms Awards and unveiling of the FDR Memorial that brought me to Washington in May 1997, and for this and for my subsequent involvement in the Franklin and Eleanor Roosevelt Institute I would like to thank William J. vanden Heuvel, John F. Sears, and Frederica Goodman, the three individuals who, along with Verne Newton, first introduced me to the organization. My thanks also go to Anne Roosevelt, the chair of the Roosevelt Institute's board of directors; to my friend and colleague-at-arms Christopher Breiseth, former president and CEO of the Institute and an astute scholar on the life and times of Frances Perkins; and to the Institute's current president, Felicia Wong, whose leadership and dedication to progressive causes has helped shape today's US political landscape.

None of this would have been possible, of course, without the resources of the Franklin D. Roosevelt Presidential Library and Museum. It has been my privilege to work in close association with the FDR Library for the past two decades and I owe much to the entire staff, especially Supervisory Archivist Kirsten Carter and her colleagues Sarah Navins, Matt Hanson, and Virginia Lewick, for their help and especially their tolerance of my all-too-frequent habit of rushing into the reading room at the last minute to request assistance in finding a particular document. I would like to thank FDR Library director Paul Sparrow for his support and encouragement and extend my appreciation as well to the former director, Lynn Bassanese, for the steady leadership she provided the Library over the years, and to former Senior Archivist Robert Clark for his help and willingness to discuss the merits of this project when I first began.

In addition to the FDR Library, the Churchill Archives Center, at Churchill College, Cambridge, proved vitally important. For all of their cheerful assistance, I would like to thank the Center's entire archival staff, especially its director, Allen Packwood, for facilitating my visits and always making me feel so welcome in Cambridge. My thanks also go out to the Roosevelt Study Center (RSC), in Middelburg, the Netherlands, and to its former director, Cornelius van Minnen, whose thirty-plus years of leadership turned the RSC—now reorganized into the Roosevelt Institute for American Studies—into one of the most important archives for the study of twentieth-century American history in Europe. I would be remiss if I did not also thank the RSC's former assistant director, Hans Krabbendan, as well as Darrio Fazzi, Giles Scott-Smith and especially Leontien Joosse, who was never too busy to help me with whatever difficulty I might bring to her attention.

A good share of the writing and a fair amount of the research for this book took place at the RSC. This would not have been possible without the support I received from University College Roosevelt

(UCR), also located in Middelburg, which granted me a Roosevelt Fellowship in the spring of 2016. This allowed me to spend five months working in and around the twelfth-century abbey at the center of this charming capital city of the Dutch province of Zeeland. Middelburg proved an ideal place to write, and my stay there—complete with frequent forays into the Dutch countryside by bicycle—was made all the more enjoyable by the friendship and support I received from my colleagues at UCR, especially Barbara Oomen, Anya Luscombe, and Sophie Krier, whose observations on Eleanor Roosevelt and the centrality of human rights helped inform my thinking. My thanks also go to Alexei Karas, whose knowledge of the Russian language and skill as an economist proved an ideal combination as I struggled to interpret various Soviet texts and decipher a number of equally perplexing economic questions. The welcome I received from the members of the Roosevelt Foundation, especially its chair and the King's Commissioner for Zeeland, Han Polman, and his chief of cabinet, Pieter Jan Mersie, also enhanced my sojourn in Holland.

My ability to stay focused on the writing of this work has been facilitated by the support I have received from University College Dublin (UCD), where I was awarded the Mary Ball Washington Chair in American History for the 2016–2017 academic year. I have benefited greatly from the support and friendship of a number of colleagues in UCD's Department of History and Archives, especially Professors Maurice Bric and Tadhg O Hannrachain. My conversations about the turbulent nature of the first half of the twentieth century with Robert Gerwath, the director of UCD's Centre for War Studies, have also proven most helpful. I first became involved in UCD through a conference on American progressivism that I helped organize with Liam Kennedy, the director of the Clinton Institute for American Studies, whose ongoing friendship and interest in my work are much appreciated. My thanks also go to Kate Breslin and Sarah Feehnan for all that they have done to make my stay in Dublin a success.

The research for this book has taken me to a host of other archives and I am thankful to the staff of all of them. In the United States these include the National Archives and Records Administration; the Library of Congress; the Albert and Shirley Small Special Collections Library at the University of Virginia; the Special Collections and Archives of Clemson University; the Seeley G. Mudd Manuscript

Library at Princeton University; the Sterling Memorial Library at Yale University; the Special Collections and Archives of the Nimitz Library at the United States Naval Academy; the Manuscript Division of the Milton S. Eisenhower Library of Johns Hopkins University; the Columbia Center for Oral History at Columbia University; the Arthur and Elizabeth Schlesinger Library on the History of Women in America, at the Radcliff Institute for Advanced Study; the Houghton Library of Harvard; the Archives of the Archdiocese of New York; the Center of Jewish History at the American Jewish Historical Society of New York; and the Manuscripts and Archives Division of the New York Public Library. In the United Kingdom, in addition to the Churchill Archives, my research took me to the National Archives, Kew; the Cadbury Research/Special Collections Library of the University of Birmingham; the Special Collections of the Cambridge University Library; and the Archives and Manuscript Collections of the Wellcome Library in London. I also wish to thank the National Archives of Canada, as well as the National Archives, the National Library, and the National War Museum of Malta.

I am fortunate in having such a dedicated and astute editor in Daniel Gerstle, whose discerning eye, patience, deep love of history, and gentle prodding not only vastly improved this book but also greatly enhanced the whole experience of bringing this work to fruition. I've been equally fortunate to have John Wright as my literary agent. His years of experience, wise counsel, and unflagging encouragement not only led me to the ideal publisher but also helped frame the scope of the narrative. The two of them, in short, were a wonderful team to work with.

My final thanks go to my family, for whom I owe the greatest debt of all. None of this would have been remotely possible without the support and encouragement of my wife, Meliza, whose patience, real-world observations, and faith in my abilities have been a constant source of strength and inspiration. My deep appreciation also goes out to our three daughters, Maia, Leah, and Clara, not only for their willingness to reciprocate their father's habit of critiquing their writing (and in Clara's case, scanning hundreds of pages of historical material) but also for the joyful diversions they continue to bring to our lives.

It was always my intention to dedicate this work to my father—the one person whom I have always looked up to and tried to emulate in this journey we call life. His endless curiosity, love of the English language, dedication to his wife and children, and quiet compassion for those around him never faltered for a single moment throughout his remarkable 102 years. We spoke a number of times about this book, and when we both became aware that the end was near, I thankfully told him of my intention to dedicate it to him. He died one week later—at almost exactly the same time that I was putting the final touches on the last sentence of the last paragraph. I dedicate this work now to his memory.

DAVID B. WOOLNER
Dublin and Rhinebeck, Spring 2017

Notes

Preface

1. On FDR's response to the Great Depression, see David M. Kennedy, *Freedom from Fear: The American People in Depression and War, 1929–1945* (New York: Oxford University Press, 2001); William E. Leuchtenburg, *Franklin D. Roosevelt and the New Deal, 1932–1940* (New York: Harper Perennial, 2009); and Arthur Schlesinger Jr., *The Coming of the New Deal 1933–1935* (New York: Mariner Books, 2009).

2. On FDR's first 100 days as president, see Anthony Badger, *FDR: The First Hundred Days* (New York: Farrar, Strauss and Giroux, 2009); Adam Cohen, *Nothing to Fear: FDR's Inner Circle and the Hundred Days That Created Modern America* (New York: Penguin, 2009); and Jonathan Alter, *The Defining Moment: FDR's Hundred Days and the Triumph of Hope* (New York: Simon & Schuster, 2007).

3. For more on the impact of the fall of France, see David Reynolds, "1940: Fulcrum of the Twentieth Century," *International Affairs* 66, no. 2 (April 1990): 325–350.

4. On FDR's war leadership, see Eric Larrabee, *Commander-in-Chief: Franklin D. Roosevelt, His Lieutenants, and Their War* (New York: Bluejacket Books, 2004); Nigel Hamilton, *The Mantle of Command: FDR at War 1941–1942* (New York: Houghton Mifflin, 2014) and *Commander in Chief: FDR's Battle with Churchill, 1943* (New York: Houghton Mifflin Harcourt, 2016); and David Kaiser, *No End Save Victory: How FDR Led the Nation into War* (New York: Basic Books, 2014).

5. Frances Perkins, *The Roosevelt I Knew* (New York: Harper Collins, 1946), 381.

6. See Geoffrey C. Ward, *Before the Trumpet: Young Franklin Roosevelt, 1882–1905* (New York: Harper Collins, 1985), and Geoffrey C. Ward and Ken Burns, *The Roosevelts: An Intimate History* (New York: Knopf, 2014).

7. "The Presidency: Prelude to History," *Time*, no. 24 (June 10, 1940), 17–19.

8. For more on FDR's health, see Robert H. Ferrell, *The Dying President: Franklin D. Roosevelt, 1944–1945* (Columbia, MO: University of Missouri Press, 1998); Steven Lomazow, MD, and Eric Fettmann, *FDR's Deadly Secret* (New York: Public Affairs, 2009); and W. Bruce Fye, "President Roosevelt's Secret Hypertensive Heart Disease," in Fye's *Caring for the Heart: Mayo Clinic and the Rise of Specialization* (New York: Oxford University Press, 2015), 127–157. Two additional works that discuss FDR's health and cover the last year of life of FDR's life include James Bishop's *FDR's Last Year: April 1944–April 1945* (New York: Pocket Books, 1975), and Joseph Lelyveld's recent fine work, *His Final Battle: The Last Moments of Franklin Roosevelt* (New York: Knopf, 2016).

Prologue: The Last Christmas

1. Anthony Beevor, *Ardennes 1944: The Battle of the Bulge* (New York: Viking, 2015), 81; Hanson W. Baldwin, "Enemy Offensive Alters War on Western Front," *New York Times*, December 24, 1944, 49.

2. "74,788 Lost on Western Front in December," *Washington Post*, January 19, 1945, 1; "Germans Drive to Point Within 4 Miles from Meuse," *New York Times*, December 27, 1944, 1 (in fact, Robert Sherwood, one of FDR's speechwriters, thought the war might be over by the time of the

election); Robert Sherwood to Samuel Rosenman, July 3, 1944, Samuel Rosenman Papers, Box 4, Franklin D. Roosevelt Presidential Library (hereafter cited as FDRL), Hyde Park, New York.

3. Lansing Warren, "Hatch and Ball See Danger in United Nations' Disunity," *New York Times,* December 24, 1944, 1; Franklin D. Roosevelt Calendar, December 23, 1944, FDRL.

4. Ben W. Gilbert, "Charter only a Combined Press Release: President Reveals Atlantic Document Never Existed as Formal State Paper," *Washington Post,* December 20, 1944, 1.

5. "'People Fooled' About Charter, View in Capital," *Chicago Daily Tribune,* December 21, 1944, 4; "Atlantic Charter: History Repeats," *Washington Post,* December 22, 1944, 8; Robert Sherwood, *Roosevelt and Hopkins: An Intimate History* (New York: Harper & Brothers, 1948), 838; "U.S. Opposes the British on Italy, Bars Intervening in Freed Lands . . . ," *New York Times,* December 6, 1944, 1. For more on the difference between London and Washington over governance in Italy, see Andrew Buchanan, *American Grand Strategy in the Mediterranean During World War II* (New York: Cambridge University Press, 2014); for a discussion of the outbreak of fighting in Greece in December 1944, see Procopis Papastratis, *British Policy Towards Greece During the Second World War, 1941–1944* (Cambridge: Cambridge University Press, 1984).

6. "Atlantic Charter Never Signed, Says President," *Los Angeles Times,* December 20, 1944, 1; Franklin D. Roosevelt Press Conferences, December 19 and 22, 1944, The Complete Press Conferences of President Franklin D. Roosevelt, 1933–1945, Series 1, Transcripts, Franklin D. Roosevelt Presidential Library and Museum Website, version 2016 (hereafter cited as Complete Press Conferences), FDRL.

7. Sherwood, *Roosevelt and Hopkins,* 843–845; Samuel Rosenman, *Working with Roosevelt* (New York: Harper & Brothers, 1952), 509. The Allied Control Commission was the organization established by the European Advisory Commission to govern Germany during the period of occupation.

8. "Tighter Rationing," *New York Times,* December 27, 1944, 18.

9. Vice Admiral (Dr.) Ross T. McIntire, *White House Physician* (New York: Putnam & Sons, 1948), 183–187; Clinical Notes on the Illness of the President, Dr. Howard G. Bruenn Papers, 1944–1946, FDRL.

10. Drs. James Paullin and Frank Lahey also served as "Honorary Navy Medical Consultants"; see interview with Dr. Howard G. Bruenn conducted by Jan K. Herman, Bureau of Medicine and Surgery, Riverdale, New York, January 31, 1990.

11. Ibid.; Oral History, The Medical Heritage Library, US Navy Bureau of Medicine and Surgery, Office of Medical History Collection, Bethesda, Maryland; Howard G. Bruenn, M.D., "Clinical Notes on the Illness and Death of President Franklin D. Roosevelt," *Annals of Internal Medicine* 72 (April 1970): 579–591; Clinical Notes, March 28, 1944, Howard G. Bruenn Papers, FDRL.

12. Ross T. McIntire, medical notes, March 30, 1944, Ross T. McIntire Papers, Box 2, FDRL; Franklin D. Roosevelt, Medical Information, 3/27/44–4/12/45, Howard Bruenn Papers, 1944–1946, FDRL

13. Memorandum by Dr. Frank Lahey, July 10, 1944, Lahey Clinic, Burlington, MA, as cited in Steven Lomazow, MD, and Eric Fettmann, *FDR's Deadly Secret* (New York: Public Affairs, 2009), 119–121. Lahey's reference to Russia in the memo refers to FDR's meeting with Stalin and Churchill at Tehran in late 1943. For more on the medical questions surrounding FDR's health and cause of death, see Robert H. Ferrell, *The Dying President: Franklin D. Roosevelt, 1944–1945* (Columbia, MO: University of Missouri Press, 1998), and Lomazow and Fettmann, *FDR's Deadly Secret.* Lomazow and Fettmann assert that FDR most likely suffered from a malignant melanoma (a virulent form of skin cancer) that metastasized to his brain, and that this is what brought on the cerebral hemorrhage that was the immediate cause of his death. They admit, however, that absent an autopsy or objective confirmation from FDR's still-missing medical records, they cannot be incontrovertibly certain of their diagnosis.

14. Memorandum by Dr. Frank Lahey, July 11, 1944; Bruenn, "Clinical Notes on the Illness and Death of President Roosevelt," *Annals,* April 1970; Dr. McIntire, Press Conference, June 8, 1944; transcript of interview with *US News and World Report,* March 13, 1951, McIntire Papers, Box 9, FDRL.

15. Margaret ("Daisy") Suckley Diary, May 5, 1944, Reel 2, FDRL; "President's Heath," *Chicago Daily Tribune,* October 17, 1944, 14; "A Vote for F.D.R. May be a Vote for Truman," *Chicago Daily Tribune,* October 28, 1944, 10; "The President's Health Not a Private Matter," *Los Angeles Times,* October 25, 1944, A4.

16. Eleanor Roosevelt, *The Autobiography of Eleanor Roosevelt* (New York: Da Capo Press, 1992), 272–273; Franklin D. Roosevelt Press Conference, July 11, 1944, Complete Press Conferences, FDRL.

17. Editorial, *Chicago Daily Tribune*, July 12, 1944.

18. Franklin D. Roosevelt to Frederick B. Adams, September 4, 1944, President's Personal File (PPF), FDRL.

19. William Hassett Diary, December 23, 1944, Box 22, FDRL.

20. Ibid., December 25, 1944.

21. Margaret (Daisy) Suckley Diary, December 26, 1944, FDRL. See also *Closest Companion: The Unknown Story of the Intimate Friendship Between Franklin Roosevelt and Margaret Suckley*, edited and annotated by Geoffrey C. Ward (New York: Houghton Mifflin, 1995), xv–xvii.

22. "7,000 Planes Batter German's Winter Offensive," *Washington Post*, December 25, 1944, 2.

23. Elliott Roosevelt, *As He Saw It* (New York: Duell, Sloan and Pearce, 1946), 226; Grace Tully to Marguerite "Missy" LeHand, November 4, 1943, Grace Tully Papers, Box 2, FDRL; Margaret (Daisy) Suckley Diary, December 29, 1944.

24. Ibid.

1. An Uncertain New Year

1. "Slick Streets Hospitalize Score, Injure Others Here," *Washington Post*, December 31, 1944, M1; "New Year Greeting with Hope and Joy by City's Millions," *New York Times*, January 1, 1945, 1.

2. Vice Admiral (Dr.) Ross T. McIntire, *White House Physician* (New York: Putnam & Sons, 1946). The Declaration by United Nations was drawn up on January 1, 1942, under the direction of FDR. It committed the signatories to employ a maximum war effort and not to sign a separate peace with the Axis. The term *United Nations* would thus become the official name of the anti-Axis alliance, and by the end of 1943 FDR had decided to call the international body that he hoped would emerge after the war *the United Nations Organization*.

3. Lord Edward Halifax, *The Wartime Diaries of Lord Halifax*, diary entry dated January 4, 1945, The University of York Digital Library (hereafter cited as Halifax Diary); Gifford Pinchot to Franklin D. Roosevelt, January 4, 1945, and to General Edwin ("Pa") Watson, January 8, 1945, PPF, 299–300, FDRL; Anna Rosenberg to Franklin D. Roosevelt, January 15, 1945, Anna Rosenberg Hoffman Papers, Container 3, Arthur and Elizabeth Schlesinger Library on the History of Women in America (hereafter cited as Schlesinger Library), Harvard University, Cambridge, Massachusetts.

4. "Roosevelt Hints That Allies Differ, But Hints at Big 3 Talk 'Anon,'" *New York Times*, January 3, 1945, 1; "Congress Gathers in Solemn Mood for Opening Today," *New York Times*, January 3, 1945, 1; "New Congress in Clash at First Session," *Chicago Daily Tribune*, January 4, 1945, 1; "Lublin Poles Ask Wide Recognition," *New York Times*, January 3, 1945, 9. As expected, the Soviet Union extended formal recognition to the Lublin Poles two days later, on January 5, 1945.

5. Samuel Rosenman, *Working with Roosevelt* (New York: Harper & Brothers, 1952), 510.

6. "Draft of Textual Material for Possible Inclusion in the President's Address to Congress on the State of the Nation," December 27, 1944, Folder 28, Box 81, George C. Marshall Papers (hereafter cited as GCM papers), George C. Marshall Research Library, Lexington, Virginia; Marshall to Stimson, January 5 and January 11, 1945, Folder 23, GCM papers, Marshall Research Library, Lexington, Virginia.

7. Franklin D. Roosevelt, State of the Union Address, January 6, 1945, Presidential Speech File, FDRL (emphasis added).

8. Ibid.

9. Ibid.

10. "Roosevelt Demands a National Service Act, Draft of Nurses, and 4Fs Postwar Training," *New York Times*, January 7, 1945, 1; "President Calls for Total Draft, *Los Angeles Times*, January 7, 1945, 1; "President Asks Full Use of Manpower," *Washington Post*, January 7, 1945, 1; "Draft War Deserters," *Chicago Daily Tribune*, January 7, 1945, 1; Arthur Vandenberg Diary, January 11, 1945, in *The Private Papers of Arthur Vandenberg* (Greenwich, CT: Greenwood, 1974), 147.

11. Edward R. Stettinius Diary, January 11, 1945, Box 243, Albert and Shirley Small Special Collections Library, University of Virginia, Charlottesville, Virginia.

12. Diary of Henry Stimson, January 11, 1945, Sterling Library, Yale University, Hartford, Connecticut; Unpublished Diary of Henry Wallace, January 11, 1945, in possession of the Wallace family.

13. Unpublished Diary of Henry Wallace, January 11, 1945; Frances Perkins, *The Roosevelt I Knew* (New York: Penguin Classics, 2011), 390–391; Frances Perkins Oral History, Columbia University Library.

14. Curtis Roosevelt, in discussion with the author, May 2, 2015; Margaret (Daisy) Suckley Diary, January 6, 1945, FDRL; Anna Roosevelt Halsted interview with Bernard Absell, in *Mother and Daughter: The Letters of Eleanor and Anna Roosevelt* (New York: Penguin, 1982), 177.

15. Anna Roosevelt Halsted, Oral History, Columbia University.

16. See, for example, the letters from FDR to Mrs. Winthrop (Lucy) Rutherfurd dated September 15, 1927, and May 18, 1928, Lucy Mercer Rutherfurd Papers, Box 1, FDRL, as well as Reminiscences of Anna Roosevelt Halsted, Papers of Anna Roosevelt Halsted, FDRL.

17. Margaret (Daisy) Suckley Diary, January 12, 1945.

18. William Hassett Diary, January 13, 1945.

19. Geoffrey Ward, *Closest Companion: The Intimate Friendship Between Franklin Roosevelt and Margaret Suckley* (New York: Simon & Schuster, 2009), 383;Testamentary Instructions, 1945, Grace Tully Papers, Box 12, FDRL.

20. Gifford Pinchot to Franklin D. Roosevelt, August 29, 1944, "Conference on Conservation and Natural Resources, 1944–1945," Official File, 5637, FDRL; Franklin D. Roosevelt to Gifford Pinchot, October 24, 1944, Box 397, Gifford Pinchot Papers, Library of Congress; FDR Memorandum for Under-Secretary of State, November 22, 1944, and Franklin D. Roosevelt to Gifford Pinchot, January 16, 1945, "Conference on Conservation and Natural Resources, 1944–1945," Official File 5637, FDRL; Gifford Pinchot to Franklin D. Roosevelt, January 21, 1945, and Gifford Pinchot to Anna Boettiger, January 21 and January 22, 1945, Box 397, Gifford Pinchot Diary, January 22, 1945, Gifford Pinchot Papers, Library of Congress.

21. Franklin D. Roosevelt Press Conference, January 19, 1945, FDRL.

22. Unpublished Diary of Henry Wallace, January 19, 1945.

23. Ibid.

24. Ibid.

25. Ibid.

26. *The Roosevelt I Knew*, 391–392; Harold Ickes, The Diary of Harold Ickes (hereafter cited as Harold Ickes Diary), Harold Ickes Papers, Box 21, Library of Congress, Washington, DC.

27. Frances Perkins Oral History, Columbia University Library; Perkins, *The Roosevelt I Knew*, 393–394.

28. Margaret (Daisy) Suckley Diary, January 19, 1945.

29. Statement of the Joint Congressional Inaugural Committee, Edith B. Helm Papers, Box 28, Library of Congress; "Shivering Thousands Stamp in the Snow at Inauguration," *New York Times,* January 21, 1945, 1; Margaret (Daisy) Suckley Diary, January 20, 1945; author's interview with Curtis Roosevelt, May 2, 2015.

30. Margaret (Daisy) Suckley Diary, January 20, 1945; "Shivering Thousands Stamp in the Snow at Inauguration," *New York Times,* January 21, 1945, 1.

31. Franklin D. Roosevelt, Fourth Inaugural Address, January 20, 1945, Presidential Speech File, FDRL.

32. Unpublished Diary of Henry Wallace, January 20, 1945.

33. Joseph P. Lash, *Eleanor and Franklin* (New York: W. W. Norton, 2014), 715.

34. James Roosevelt Papers, FDRL; James Roosevelt, *My Parents: A Differing View* (New York: Playboy Press, 1976), 283–284.

35. Author's interview with Curtis Roosevelt, May 2, 2015.

36. James Roosevelt, *My Parents,* 284. For more on the important role that Missy Lehand played in FDR's life see Kathryn Smith, *The Gatekeeper: Missy Lehand, FDR, and the Untold Story of the Partnership That Defined a Presidency* (New York: Touchstone, 2016).

37. See Roosevelt Family Papers, Boxes 20–21, FDRL; James Roosevelt, *My Parents,* 281–284; Harold Ickes Diary, January 27, 1945; Anna Roosevelt Halsted Diary, February 1, 1945, Box 84, FDRL.

38. Harold Ickes Diary, January 27, 1945.

39. "The President's and Jones' Letters," *New York Times,* January 22, 1945, 30; John C. Culver and John Hyde, *American Dreamer: A Life of Henry Wallace* (New York: W. W. Norton, 2009), 384.

40. Margaret (Daisy) Suckley Diary, January 20, 1945.

2. Atlantic Sojourn

1. Franklin D. Roosevelt, Address to the University of Virginia, Charlottesville, Virginia, June 10, 1940, Master Speech File, FDRL.

2. Robert Sherwood, *Roosevelt and Hopkins: An Intimate History* (New York: Harper & Brothers, 1948), 827; Thomas M. Campbell, "The Resurgence of Isolationism at the End of World War II," *American Diplomatic History Issues and Methods* (June 1974), 41–56.

3. Charles Bohlen, *Witness to History, 1929–1969* (New York: W. W. Norton, 1973), 177; "An Appreciation of Anglo-American Relations," by Mr. Stephenson, British Security Coordination, New York, December 14, 1944, FO371/44559, The National Archives, Kew.

4. William Hassett Diary, January 22, 1945, Box 22, FDRL.

5. Eleanor Roosevelt, *The Autobiography of Eleanor Roosevelt* (New York: Da Capo Press, 1992), 273; interview with Dr. Howard G. Bruenn conducted by Jan K. Herman, Bureau of Medicine and Surgery, Riverdale, New York, January 31, 1990, 14; Margaret (Daisy) Suckley Diary, January 22, 1945, FDRL.

6. Conferences at Malta and Crimea, Official Log, Box 29, Map Room Files, FDRL; Edward I. Bloom, "FDR and the Potomac Stewards," *Potomac Currents* (Spring Edition, 2011), 3; Anna Roosevelt Halsted Diary, January 23, 1945, Box 84, FDRL.

7. Anna Roosevelt Halsted Columbia Oral History, 1970–1975, Box 12, FDRL; Curtis Roosevelt, *Too Close to the Sun* (New York: Public Affairs, 2009), 282–283; Joseph P. Lash, *Eleanor and Franklin* (New York: W. W. Norton, 2014), 699–700, 716; author's interview with Curtis Roosevelt, May 2, 2009.

8. Anna Roosevelt Halsted Diary, January, 23, 1945.

9. The President's Conferences at the Crimea and the Great Bitter Lake, Official Log, Map Room Files FDRL.

10. William Leahy, *I Was There* (New York: Whittlesey House, 1950), 296–297; James F. Byrnes, *Speaking Frankly* (New York: Harper & Brothers, 1947), 22.

11. Official Log, January 24, 1945, FDRL.

12. Brynes, *Speaking Frankly,* 22.

13. Ibid.

14. Edward J. Flynn, *You're the Boss: The Practice of American Politics* (Viking Press: New York, 1947), 186–188.

15. Edward J. Flynn to Helen Flynn, January 30, 1945, Edward J. Flynn Papers, Box 25, FDRL.

16. Flynn, *You're the Boss,* 185; Peter C. Kent, "Toward the Reconstitution of Christian Europe: The War Aims of the Papacy, 1938–1945," in David B. Woolner and Richard Kurial, eds., *FDR, the Vatican and the Roman Catholic Church in America, 1933–1945* (New York: Palgrave, 2003), 171–172.

17. Flynn, *You're the Boss,* 186; Anna Roosevelt Halsted Diary, January 24, 1945; Edward J. Flynn to Helen Flynn, February 9, 1945, Edward J. Flynn Papers, Box 25, FDRL.

18. Anna Roosevelt Halsted Diary, January 24, 1945.

19. Anna Roosevelt Halsted Diary, January 25, 1945.

20. Hopkins to Roosevelt, and Churchill to Roosevelt, January 24, 1945, Cab 120/170, The National Archives, Kew.

21. Churchill to Roosevelt, January 26, 1945, Cab 120/170, The National Archives, Kew.

22. "Four Presidents as I Saw Them," unpublished memoir by Vice Admiral Wilson Brown, Wilson Brown Papers, Special Collections and Archives, Nimitz Library, United States Naval Academy, Annapolis, Maryland.

23. Franklin D. Roosevelt Diary, July 15–18, 1918, Papers of Assistant Secretary of the Navy, Personal Files, Box 33, FDRL; The William Lyons Mackenzie King Diary (hereafter cited as Mackenzie King Diary), March 11, 1945, National Archives, Canada.

24. Memorandum by Vice Admiral Wilson Brown, "Normal Schedule at Sea," January 24, 1945; William Rigdon Papers, 1942–1945, FDRL; William D. Leahy Diary, January 29, 1945, Library of Congress.

25. William D. Leahy Diary, January 30, 1930; Roosevelt to Rosenman, February 1, 1945, Official File 5430, Box 2, FDRL.

26. Anna Roosevelt to John Boettiger, January 30, 1945, John Boettiger Papers, Box 6, FDRL.

27. Brown, "Four Presidents as I Saw Them."

28. Ibid.

29. Ibid.

30. Ibid.; Stephen Early Papers, Box 37, FDRL; "De Gaulle Sees High Official: Hint It's Hopkins," *Chicago Daily Tribune,* January 29, 1945, 2.

31. Brown, "Four Presidents as I Saw Them"; Ship's Log, Conferences at Malta and Crimea, January 31, 1945, FDRL.

32. Ibid.; Brown, "Four Presidents as I Saw Them."

33. Ship's Log, Conferences at Malta and Crimea, January 31, 1945; Anna Roosevelt Halsted Diary, January 31, 1945.

34. Ship's Log, Conferences at Malta and Crimea, February 1, 1945; Anna Roosevelt Halsted Diary, February 1, 1945; Margaret (Daisy) Suckley Diary, February 9, 1945.

3. Interlude at Malta

1. Roger Crowley, *Empires of the Sea: The Siege of Malta, the Battle of Lepanto, and the Contest for the Center of the World* (New York: Random House, 2009), xvii; National War Museum, Valletta, Malta.

2. James Holland, *Fortress Malta: An Island Under Siege, 1940–1943;* "Islands Under Siege," *Malta Times,* April 16, 1942, the National Library, Valletta, Malta; Ashley Jackson, *The British Empire in the Second World War* (London: Bloomsbury Academic, 2006), 122–131; *The Oxford Companion to World War II,* edited by I.C.B. Dear and M.R.D. Foot (New York: Oxford University Press, 2002), 558.

3. Andrew Buchanan, *American Grand Strategy in the Mediterranean in World War II* (New York: Cambridge University Press, 2014), 40.

4. Franklin D. Roosevelt, speech at Malta, December 8, 1943, Master Speech File, Box 76, FDRL.

5. Ibid.

6. Presidential Proclamation, "To the People of Malta," December 8, 1943, Master Speech File, Box 76, FDRL, Hyde Park, New York.

7. Edward R. Stettinius, *Roosevelt and the Russians* (New York: Doubleday, 1949), 60.

8. Stettinius, *Roosevelt and the Russians,* 60; Robert Meiklejohn Diary, February 2, 1945, Box 211; also see Harriman Papers, Library of Congress.

9. Edward R. Stettinius Calendar Notes, February 2, 1945, Edward R. Stettinius Papers, Box 278, University of Virginia Library.

10. Edward J. Flynn to Helen Flynn, February 4, 1945, "Yalta Trip: Letters to Family," Box 25, FDRL; Ship's Log, February 2, 1945, Grace Tully Papers, FDRL; Anthony Eden, *The Memoirs of Anthony Eden: The Reckoning* (London: Houghton Mifflin, 1965), 511.

11. Churchill to Roosevelt, January 4, 1945, Map Room Files, FDRL.

12. "Weekly Strategy Resume," January 23, 1943, ABC 334.4, Policy Committee, Records of the Joint Chiefs of Staff, RG 218, National Archives and Records Administration (hereafter cited as NARA).

13. David Reynolds, *Summits: Six Meetings that Shaped the Twentieth Century* (London: Allen Lane, 2007), 98.

14. Ibid.; David Reynolds, *From World War to Cold War: Churchill, Roosevelt, and the International History of the 1940s* (New York: Oxford, 2006), 122–125; Michael Howard, *The Mediterranean Strategy in the Second World War* (New York: Greenwood, 1993), 36–40.

15. Warren F. Kimball, *Forged in War: Churchill, Roosevelt and the Second World War* (London: Harper Collins, 1997), 237–238.

16. Churchill to Roosevelt, January 8, 1945, Map Room Files, FDRL.

17. Roosevelt to Churchill, January 9, 1945, Map Room Files, FDRL; Churchill to Roosevelt, January 10, 1945, Map Room Files, FDRL.

18. General Albert C. Weydemeyer to George Marshall, October 8, 1944, Weydemeyer Papers, Hover Institution, Stanford University; Mark Stoler, *Allies and Adversaries: The Joint Chiefs of Staff, the Grand Alliance, and U.S. Strategy in World War II* (Chapel Hill: University of North Carolina Press, 2000), 223.

19. Kimball, *Forged in War,* 285–286.

20. Roosevelt to Stalin, October 4, 1944, Map Room Files, FDRL; Roosevelt to Harriman, October 4, 1944, Map Room Files, FDRL.

21. Robert E. Sherwood, *The White House Papers of Harry L. Hopkins, Vol. II: January 1942–July 1945* (London: Eyre & Spottiswoode, 1949), 840; W. Averell Harriman and Elie Abel, *Special Envoy to Churchill and Stalin, 1941–1946* (New York: Random House, 1975), 355–358.

22. Edward R. Stettinius Calendar Notes, February 2, 1945.

23. Cordell Hull, *The Memoirs of Cordell Hull,* Vol. II (New York: Macmillan, 1955), 1663.

24. Memorandum of Conversation at the White House, Questions Left Unsettled at the Dumbarton Oaks Conference, November 15, 1944; State Department Memorandum of Conversation, Preparations for the Yalta Conference, January, 8, 1945, Leo Pasvolsky Papers, Box 5, Library of Congress.

25. Edward R. Stettinius Calendar Notes, September 8, 1944; Andrei Gromyko, *Memoirs* (New York: Doubleday, 1990), 116; Roosevelt to Stalin, September 8, 1945, Map Room Files, FDRL.

26. Edward R. Stettinius, telephone message for the president, September 18, 1944, Harry Hopkins Papers, Yalta, Box 337, FDRL; Leo Pasvolsky to Secretary of State Cordell Hull, Progress Report on Dumbarton Oaks, September 18, 1944, Pasvolsky Papers, Box 5, Library of Congress.

27. Ruth Russell, *A History of the United Nations Charter* (Washington, DC: Brookings Institution, 1958), 148; Stephen Schlesinger, *Act of Creation: The Founding of the United Nations* (New York: Basic Books, 2003), 55–56; Robert C. Hilderbrand, *Dumbarton Oaks: The Origins of the United Nations and the Search for Postwar Security* (Chapel Hill: University of North Carolina Press, 1990), 249–250.

28. Edward R. Stettinius Calendar Notes, February 1–2, 1945; Stettinius, *Roosevelt and the Russians,* 69.

29. Edward R. Stettinius Calendar Notes, February 2, 1945; Anthony Eden Diary, February 2, 1945, Cadbury Research Library, Birmingham University, Birmingham, United Kingdom.

30. Anna Roosevelt Halsted Diary, February 2, 1945.

31. Archives of Malta to Franklin Roosevelt, December 9, 1943, William Rigdon Papers, 1942–1945, FDRL; Report for Combined Chiefs of Staff from Bedell Smith, January 30, 1945, Chiefs of Staff Record, CAB 120/178, the National Archives, Kew.

32. Stephen W. Stathis, "Malta: Prelude to Yalta, *Presidential Studies Quarterly* 9, no. 4 (Fall 1979): 469–482; Marshall to Eisenhower, January 11, 1945, W 90175, as cited in *The Papers of Dwight David Eisenhower: The War Years: IV* ((Baltimore: Johns Hopkins University Press, 1970), 2423 (n. 1); Chester Wilmont, *The Struggle for Europe* (New York: Harper & Row, 1963), 665.

33. Stoler, *Allies and Adversaries,* 123.

34. Maurice Matloff, "The 90-Division Gamble," in Kent Roberts Greenfield, ed., *Command Decisions* (Washington, DC: US Government Printing Office, 1960), 367.

35. Forrest C. Pogue, *George C. Marshall: Organizer of Victory, 1943–1945* (New York: Viking, 1999), 516–517; Wilmont, *The Struggle for Europe,* 666.

36. Pogue, *George C. Marshall: Organizer of Victory,* 517–518; Foreign Relations of the United States (FRUS), Diplomatic Papers, *The Conferences at Malta and Yalta, 1945* (Washington, DC: US Government Printing Office, 1955), 543.

37. FRUS, Diplomatic Papers, *The Conferences at Malta and Yalta, 1945,* 544–546; John Davis Memo, November 15, 1943, Office of Strategic Services (OSS), E190, Box 573, Record Group (RG) 226, NARA, as cited in Stoler, *Allies and Adversaries,* 117.

38. Edward R. Stettinius Calendar Notes, January 2, 1945.

39. See Fredrik Logevall, *Embers of War: The Fall of an Empire and the Making of America's Vietnam* (New York: Random House, 2014), 48–66.

40. Joint Chiefs of Staff (JCS), 713, Strategy in the Pacific, February 16, 1944, ABC 384 Pacific, RG 165, NARA; Stoler, *Allies and Adversaries*, 224–225; Logevall, *Embers of War*, 54–55.

41. Stoler, *Allies and Adversaries*, 224.

42. FRUS, Diplomatic Papers, *The Conferences at Malta and Yalta, 1945*, 546; Anthony Eden Diary, February 2, 1945.

43. Anthony Eden Diary, February 2, 1945.

44. Anna Roosevelt Halsted Diary, February 2, 1945.

4. On to the Crimea

1. Robert Meiklejohn Diary, February 3, 1945, W. Averell Harriman Papers, Library of Congress.

2. William Leahy, *I Was There* (New York: Whittlesey House, 1950), 296; William D. Leahy Diary, February 2, 1945, Library of Congress; Official Log, Conferences at Malta and Yalta, FDRL.

3. Anna Roosevelt Halsted Diary, February 2, 1945, Box 84, FDRL; FDR, Official Log, Conferences at Malta and Yalta; Robert Meiklejohn, "To Malta in the President's Plane," Meiklejohn Diary, January 27, 1945, Library of Congress; Leahy, *I Was There*, 295–296.

4. Anna Roosevelt Halsted Diary, February 2, 1945, FDRL; Sarah Churchill to Clementine Churchill, February 4, 1945, Sarah Churchill Papers (SCHL) 1/1/8, Churchill Archives, Cambridge; Alanbrooke Diary, February 2, 1945, War Diaries, 1939–1945; Alex Danchev and Daniel Todman, eds., *Field Marshal Lord Alanbrooke* (London: Phoenix Press, 2002).

5. Interview with Dr. Howard G. Bruenn, conducted by Jan K. Herman, Bureau of Medicine and Surgery, Riverdale, New York, January 31, 1990, Oral History, The Medical Heritage Library, US Navy Bureau of Medicine and Surgery, Office of Medical History Collection, Bethesda, Maryland.

6. Anna Roosevelt Halsted Diary, February, 3, 1945.

7. Martin Gilbert, *Winston S. Churchill, Vol. VII: Road to Victory, 1942–1945* (New York: Houghton Mifflin, 1986), 1171; Lord Moran Papers, PP/cmw/Q1/S, Wellcome Library, London.

8. Anna Roosevelt Halstead Diary, February 3, 1945; Alexander Cadogan Diary, February 3, 1945, ACAD 148, Churchill Archives, Cambridge.

9. Ibid.

10. Wilson Brown Papers, Special Collections and Archives, Nimitz Library, United States Naval Academy, Annapolis, Maryland.

11. Robert Meikeljohn Diary, February 3, 1945; Sarah Churchill to Clementine Churchill, February 4, 1945, SCHL 1/1/8, Sarah Churchill Papers, Churchill Archives.

12. Robert Meikeljohn Diary, February 3, 1945; Alexander Cadogan Diary, February 4, 1945.

13. Anna Roosevelt Halsted Diary, February 3, 1945.

14. Official Log, Conferences at Malta and Yalta, FDRL; Edward R. Stettinius Calendar Notes, February 3, 1945, Edward R. Stettinius Papers, Box 278, University of Virginia Library.

15. Kathleen Harriman to Pamela Harriman, February 1, 1945; Box 176; W. Averell Harriman Papers, Library of Congress; A. H. Birse, *Memoirs of an Interpreter* (New York: Coward-McCann, 1967), 178.

16. J. K. Herman, "Cleaning Up Yalta," *Navy Medicine* 81, no. 2 (March–April 1990): 14–16; Original Diaries and Notes of Lord Moran, February 4, 1945, PP/CMW/Q1/5, Wellcome Library, London; Vice Admiral (Dr.) Ross T. McIntire, *White House Physician* (New York: Putnam & Sons, 1946), 215.

17. Lord Moran Diary, February 4, 1945, in Lord Moran, *Churchill Taken from the Diaries of Lord Moran* (New York: Houghton Mifflin, 1966); McIntire, *White House Physician*, 215.

18. Lady Onslow Papers, February 5, 1945, Churchill Archives, Cambridge.

19. S. M. Plokhy, *Yalta: The Price of Peace* (New York: Viking, 2010), 233–234.

20. Anna Roosevelt Halsted Diary, February 3, 1945; Kathleen Harriman to Mary Marshall, February 4–10, 1945, W. Averell Harriman Papers, Library of Congress.

21. Ibid.; Edward R. Stettinius Calendar Notes, February 3, 1945.

22. Memorial to Harry Hopkins, written by John Steinbeck, May 22, 1946, Hopkins Papers, Grinnell College Archives, cited in June Hopkins, *Harry Hopkins: Sudden Hero, Brash Reformer* (New York: Palgrave Macmillan, 1999), 2; Robert Sherwood, *Roosevelt and Hopkins: An Intimate History* (New York: Harper & Brothers, 1948), 2.

23. Anna Roosevelt Halsted Diary, February 3, 1933; James A. Halsted, "Severe Malnutrition of a Public Servant in World War II: The Medical History of Harry Hopkins," Clinical Nutrition Program, Division of Gastroenterology, Department of Medicine, Albany Medical College, Albany, New York, 1975.

5. Sunrise over Yalta

1. Franklin D. Roosevelt, Fireside Chat Address to the Nation, February 2, 1942, Master Speech File, FDRL.

2. Edouard Mark, "Revolution by Degrees: Stalin's National Front Strategy for Europe, 1941–1947," Cold War History Project, Working Paper No. 31, February 2001, Woodrow Wilson Center; Dennis J. Dunn, *Caught Between Roosevelt and Stalin* (Lexington: University Press of Kentucky, 1998), 159–160; Lloyd C. Gardner, "FDR and Cooperation with the Soviet Union," in *Franklin D. Roosevelt and the World Crisis, 1937-1945* (New York: D. C. Health, 1973), 135–158; Franklin D. Roosevelt, Memo to General Watson, May 26, 1941, President's Secretary's Files (PSF), FDRL.

3. Fraser J. Harbutt, *Yalta 1945: Europe and America at the Crossroads* (New York: Cambridge University Press, 2010), 214–216, 277–279, 285.

4. Anna Roosevelt Halsted Diary, February 4, 1945, Box 84, FDRL.

5. Edward R. Stettinius, *Roosevelt and the Russians* (New York: Doubleday, 1949), 85–87; Minutes of Meetings of FDR with Joint Chiefs of Staff, 1942–1945, Map Room Files, Box 29, FDRL.

6. Anna Roosevelt Halsted Diary, February 5, 1945.

7. S. M. Plokhy, *Yalta: The Price of Peace* (New York: Viking, 2010), 56–57; Geoffrey Roberts, *Molotov: Stalin's Cold Warrior* (Dulles, VA: Potomac Books, 2012), 52. See also W. Averell Harriman, *Special Envoy to Churchill and Stalin, 1941-1946* (New York: Random House, 1975), 535–536.

8. "Harriman, *Special Envoy,* 80–105; "Prime Minister Declares Moscow an Ally of Britain; Past Fade Out, He Says, Before Sole Aim—Victory," *Washington Post,* June 23, 1941, 1; "Our Policy Stated: Welles Says Defeat of Hitler Conquest Plans, Is Greatest Task," *New York Times,* June 24, 1941, 1.

9. Stalin to Churchill, November 8, 1941, cited in Sir Llewellyn Woodward, *British Foreign Policy in the Second World War,* Vol. II (London: Her Majesty's Stationery Office, 1971), 48–49; Ivan Maisky, *Memoirs of a Soviet Ambassador, The War: 1939–1943* (London: Hutchison & Co., 1967), 200–201; Anthony Eden Diary, February 2, 1945, Birmingham University Library.

10. Diary of Georgi Dimitrov, January 28, 1945, *The Diary of Georgi Dimitrov, 1933–1949,* edited by Ivo Banac (New Haven: Yale University Press, 2003); Roberts, *Molotov,* 78–81; see also p. 83.

11. Charles Bohlen, *Witness to History, 1929-1969* (New York: W. W. Norton, 1973), 180.

12. Foreign Relations of the United States (FRUS), Diplomatic Papers, *The Conferences at Malta and Yalta, 1945* (Washington, DC: US Government Printing Office, 1955), 571; Anna Roosevelt Halsted Diary, February 3, 1945.

13. FRUS, Diplomatic Papers, *The Conferences at Malta and Yalta,* 572–573.

14. Plokhy, *Yalta,* 72.

15. FRUS, Diplomatic Papers, *The Conferences at Malta and Yalta,* 574.

16. William Rigdon, *Sailor in the White House* (New York: Doubleday, 1962), 136; Brian Lavery, *Churchill Goes to War* (Annapolis, MD: Naval Institute Press, 2007); "Summitry and Modern Diplomacy," *Satows Diplomatic Practice, Sixth Edition,* edited by Sir Ivor Roberts (London: Oxford, 2009), 18–22. For more on summit meetings as a form of diplomacy, see David Reynolds, *Summits: Six Meetings That Shaped the Twentieth Century* (New York: Basic Books, 2007).

17. Roberts, *Molotov,* 86.

18. Alistair Horne, *Macmillan, 1894-1956, Volume I of the Official Biography* (London: Macmillan, 1988), 165; Warren F. Kimball, *The Juggler: Franklin Roosevelt as Wartime Statesman* (Princeton: Princeton University Press, 1991), 92–93.

19. Donald E. Shepardson, "The Fall of Berlin and the Rise of a Myth," *Journal of Military History* 62 (January 1998): 138; John Erikson, *The Road to Berlin: Stalin's War with Germany*, Vol. II (London: Castle Books, 1983); Harbutt, *Yalta 1945*, 290.

20. Plokky, *Yalta*, 85.

21. Stettinius, *Roosevelt and the Russians*, 110–111; Diane Shaver Clemens, *Yalta* (Oxford: Oxford University Press, 1970), 135; Plokhy, *Yalta*, 89.

22. Anna Roosevelt Halsted Diary, February 4, 1945.

23. Ibid.

24. Ibid.; Harriman, *Special Envoy*, 395.

25. Anna Roosevelt Halsted Diary, February 4, 1945.

26. Ibid.; FRUS, Diplomatic Papers, *The Conferences at Malta and Yalta*, 589; Bohlen, *Witness to History*, 181.

27. Stettinius, *Roosevelt and the Russians*, 112–115; Bohlen, *Witness to History*, 181; FRUS, Diplomatic Papers, *The Conferences at Malta and Yalta*, 590–591.

28. Anna Roosevelt Halsted Diary, February 4, 1945.

6. Coming to Grips with "The German Problem"

1. Howard G. Bruenn, "Clinical Notes on the Illness and Death of President Franklin D. Roosevelt," *Annals of Internal Medicine* 72 (April 1970): 579–591; Vice Admiral (Dr.) Ross T. McIntire, *White House Physician* (New York: Putnam & Sons, 1946), 220.

2. Edward R. Stettinius, *Roosevelt and the Russians* (New York: Doubleday, 1949), 117–118.

3. Foreign Relations of the United States (FRUS), Diplomatic Papers, *The Conferences at Malta and Yalta, 1945* (Washington, DC: US Government Printing Office, 1955), 610–611; Charles Bohlen, *Witness to History, 1929–1969* (New York: W. W. Norton, 1973), 184–185.

4. Robin Edmonds, *The Big Three: Churchill, Roosevelt and Stalin in Peace and War* (London: Penguin Books, 1991), 409–410.

5. David Reynolds, *Summits: Six Meetings That Shaped the Twentieth Century* (London: Allen Lane, 2007), 124.

6. David B. Woolner, "Coming to Grips with the 'German Problem': Roosevelt, Churchill and the Morgenthau Plan at the Second Quebec Conference," in David B. Woolner, ed., *The Second Quebec Conference Revisited: Waging War, Formulating Peace: Canada, Great Britain and the United States in 1944–1945* (New York: St. Martin's Press, 1998), 66; Henry Morgenthau, *Germany Is Our Problem* (New York: Harper & Bros., 1945), v–viii; "Suggested Post-Surrender Program for Germany," September 1, 1944, Henry Morgenthau Diary, Book 768, September 1–4, 1944, FDRL.

7. Woolner, "Coming to Grips with the 'German Problem,'" 73–74.

8. Roosevelt to Stimson, August 26, 1944, President's Secretary's Files (PSF), Box 82, FDRL.

9. Ibid.

10. Briefing Notes, Yalta Conference, Harry Hopkins Papers, Box 337, FDRL; "Threats on Reich Said to Spur Nazis," *New York Times*, October 25, 1944, 9; "Morgenthau Nazi Plan Called Costly to US," *Los Angeles Times*, November 1, 1944, 7.

11. FRUS, Diplomatic Papers, *The Conferences at Malta and Yalta*, 611–612.

12. J. S. Dunn, *The Crowe Memorandum: Sir Eyre Crowe and Foreign Office Perceptions of Germany* (Newcastle: Cambridge Scholars, 2013); Woolner, "Coming to Grips with the 'German Problem,'" 85–86.

13. "War Cabinet Memorandum by the Secretary of State for Foreign Affairs (Eden), September 20, 1944, Foreign Office (FO) 371.39080, The National Archives, Kew.

14. Minutes of the Crimean Conference, February 5, 1945, The Crimean Conference, Minutes Prepared by James F. Byrnes, James F. Byrnes Papers, Series 4, Box 19, Clemson University, Special Collections Library, Clemson, South Carolina (hereafter cited as Byrnes Minutes).

15. The Treatment of Germany, January 12, 1945, Political Memoranda for the Yalta Conference, Hopkins Papers, Box 169–171, FDRL.

16. Bohlen, *Witness to History*, 182–183; Anthony Eden, *The Memoirs of Anthony Eden: The Reckoning* (London: Houghton Mifflin, 1965), 513.

17. Byrnes Minutes, February 5, 1945.

18. FRUS, Diplomatic Papers, *The Conferences at Malta and Yalta,* 616–618; Russell D. Buhite, *Decisions at Yalta: An Appraisal of Summit Diplomacy* (New York: Scholarly Resources, 1986), 29.

19. Buhite, *Decisions at Yalta,* 33.

20. Ivan Maisky, "The Ivan Maisky Diaries: Red Ambassador to the Court of St. James's, 1932–1943," in Gabriel Gorodetsky, ed., *The Ivan Maisky Diaries: Red Ambassador to the Court of St. James's, 1932-1943* (New Haven, CT: Yale University Press, 2015), 546–547.

21. Byrnes Minutes, February 5, 1945; FRUS, Diplomatic Papers, *The Conferences at Malta and Yalta,* 621.

22. Records of the Proceedings of the Argonaut Conference, February 5, 1945, Prime Minister's Office Records (PREM) 3/51/4, The National Archives Kew.

7. The Polish Quandary

1. FDR in conversation with Francis Cardinal Spellman, Cardinal Spellman Diary, September 3, 1943, Cardinal Spellman Papers, Archdiocese of New York.

2. Foreign Office Minutes on Poland, January 12, 1945, Foreign Office (FO) 371/47577, The National Archives Kew; Roosevelt to Stalin, December 30, 1945, Map Room Files, FDRL; Recognition of Lublin Committee, Extract from War Cabinet, FO 371/47575, The National Archives Kew; Warren F. Kimball, *Forged in War* (London: Harper Collins, 1997), 307; Oscar Cox to Harry Hopkins, December 19, 1944, Harry Hopkins Papers Kew; Box 335, FDRL.

3. Cordell Hull, *The Memoirs of Cordell Hull,* Vol. II (New York: Macmillan, 1948), 1273; FDR as quoted by British Ambassador Archibald Clark Kerr, the Diary of Lord Halifax, September 18, 1943.

4. Record of Conversation Between Arthur Bliss Lane and Roosevelt, November 30, 1944, Arthur Bliss Lane Papers, Sterling Memorial Library, Yale University, New Haven, Connecticut.

5. Record of Conversation Between Richard Law and Roosevelt, December 22, 1944, FO 371/44595. The National Archives, Kew.

6. Herbert Feis, *Churchill, Roosevelt, Stalin: The War They Waged and the Peace They Sought* (Princeton: Princeton University Press, 1957), 200; W. Averell Harriman, *Special Envoy to Churchill and Stalin, 1941-1946* (New York: Random House, 1975), 245–246, 287–290.

7. Summary of Recommendations, Policy Towards Liberated States: Czechoslovakia, July 18, 1944, Edward R. Stettinius Papers, Box 363, University of Virginia Library; Report on Poland, November 30, 1944, Harry Hopkins Papers, Crisis in Poland, Box 337, and Political Memoranda for Yalta Conference, February 1945, Boxes 169–171, FDRL; Record of Conversation Between Roosevelt and Halifax, January 6, 1945, FO 371/47575, The National Archives, Kew.

8. Feis, *Churchill, Roosevelt, Stalin,* 374.

9. Geoffrey Roberts, *Stalin's Wars: From World War to Cold War, 1939-1953* (New Haven, CT: Yale University Press, 2006), 212–213; Susan Butler, *My Dear Mr. Stalin: The Complete Correspondence Between Franklin D. Roosevelt and Joseph V. Stalin* (New Haven, CT: Yale University Press, 2005), 247.

10. Roberts, *Stalin's Wars,* 216; "Poles Assail Lack of Aid to Warsaw," *New York Times,* September 5, 1944, 9. A good share of the anger that was directed towards the Russians over the Warsaw incident stemmed from the widespread belief that they purposely halted their advance in order ot give the Germans time to destroy the Polish Home Army. Not everyone agreed. As one Foreign Office official put it some months later, he remained convinced that if the Russians could have broken the German line and advanced, they would have done so "with pleasure," but "military considerations, e.g., weakness of communication, lack of supplies, etc....prevented them from striking before the winter. However, nothing will convince the Poles that this was the case." (Minute by M. Nowak, March 15, 1945, FO 371/47577, the National Archives, Kew).

11. Feis, *Churchill, Roosevelt, Stalin,* 518; Foreign Office Minutes, Mr. Mikolajczyk and London, Minutes by Denis Allen, January 8, 1945, FO 371/47575; "War Cabinet Conclusions and Minutes, December 30, 1944," Recognition of Lublin Committee, December 30, 1944–January 5, 1945, FO 371/47575, The National Archives, Kew.

12. Memorandum for the President, Stettinius to Roosevelt, January 16, 1945, PSF Subject Files, State Department, 1945. The American press at that time hailed the Moscow conference, especially

the Four Power Declaration issued at the end of the gathering, as "a great victory for the United Nations, matching any victory yet achieved on the battlefield"; see, for example, "Triumph at Moscow," *New York Times,* November 2, 1943, 24.

13. Record of Conversation Between Andrei Gromyko and Leo Pasvolsky, September 18, 1944, Leo Pasvolsky Papers, Box 5, Library of Congress.

14. Edward R. Stettinius Calendar Notes, February 6, 1945.

15. Anna Roosevelt to John Boettiger, February 7, 1945, John Boettiger Papers, Box 6, FDRL.

16. Alexander Cadogan Diary, February 6, 1945, Churchill Archives; William Rigdon, *Sailor in the White House* (New York: Doubleday, 1962), 150–151.

17. Hamilton Fish Armstrong to Secretary Stettinius, January 30, 1945, Leo Pasvolsky Papers, Box 5, Library of Congress.

18. Foreign Relations of the United States (FRUS), Diplomatic Papers, *The Conferences at Malta and Yalta, 1945* (Washington, DC: US Government Printing Office, 1955), 661; Byrnes Minutes, February 6, 1945.

19. Byrnes Minutes, February 6, 1945.

20. Ibid.; Record of Meeting Held at Livadia Palace, Yalta, February 6, 1945, War Cabinet Memoranda, "Record of the Political Proceedings of the 'Argonaut' Conference Held at Malta and in the Crimea from 1st February to 11th February 1945," Cabinet (hereafter cited as CAB) 66/63, The National Archives Kew.

21. FRUS, Diplomatic Papers, *The Conferences at Malta and Yalta,* 667.

22. James F. Byrnes, *Speaking Frankly* (New York: Harper, 1947), 37.

23. Lord Moran Diary, February 7, 1945, in Lord Moran, *Churchill Taken from the Diaries of Lord Moran* (New York: Houghton Mifflin, 1966), 241–242.

24. FRUS, Diplomatic Papers, *The Conferences at Cairo and Tehran, 1943,* 512, 594, 598–602; Byrnes Minutes, February 6, 1945; Remi A. Nadeau, Stalin, Churchill and Roosevelt Divide Europe (New York: Praeger Press, 1990), 133–134.

25. FRUS, Diplomatic Papers, *The Conferences at Malta and Yalta,* 667.

26. Situation in Poland, January 26, 1945, FO 371/47577; Byrnes Minutes, February 6, 1945.

27. William Leahy, *I Was There* (New York: Whittlesey House, 1950), 305.

28. FRUS, Diplomatic Papers, *The Conferences at Malta and Yalta,* 669–670.

29. Ibid., 686; Charles Bohlen, *Witness to History, 1929–1979* (New York: W.W. Norton, 1973), 188–190.

30. Ibid.

31. Ibid.; Stettinius Calendar Notes, February 7, 1945.

32. Fraser J. Harbutt, *Yalta 1945: Europe and America at the Crossroads* (New York: Cambridge University Press, 2010), 298; Geoffrey Roberts, *Molotov: Stalin's Cold Warrior* (Dulles, VA: Potomac Books, 2012), 241; Anthony Eden, *The Memoirs of Anthony Eden: The Reckoning* (London: Houghton Mifflin, 1965), 514–515.

33. FRUS, Diplomatic Papers, *The Conferences at Malta and Yalta,* 711.

34. Diane Shaver Clemens, *Yalta* (Oxford: Oxford University Press, 1970), 189; Ivan Maisky Diary, as cited in Plohky, *Yalta,* 184.

35. FRUS, Diplomatic Papers, *The Conferences at Malta and Yalta, 1945,* 715–716; Byrnes Minutes, February 7, 1945; Record of the Meeting Held at the Livadia Palace, Yalta, February 7, 1945, CAB 66/63, The National Archives, Kew.

36. Byrnes Minutes, February 7, 1945.

37. FRUS, Diplomatic Papers, *The Conferences at Malta and Yalta, 1945,* 729; Alexander Cadogan Diary, February 7, 1945; Eden, *The Reckoning,* 517.

38. Byrnes Minutes, February 7, 1945; FRUS, Diplomatic Papers, *The Conferences at Malta and Yalta,* 716–717.

39. Stettinius, *Roosevelt and the Russians,* 183–185; Record of Meeting Held at Livadia Palace, Yalta, February 7, 1945, CAB 66/63; Byrnes Minutes, February 7, 1945.

40. Byrnes Minutes, February 7, 1945.

41. Minutes of the first tripartite military meeting, held at the Soviet Headquarters, Yalta, on Monday, February 5, 1945, at 12:00 noon; CAB 120/170, the National Archives, Kew; Minutes of

Second Tripartite Meeting, February 6, 1945, FRUS, Diplomatic Papers, *Conferences held at Malta and Yalta, 1945*, 641–642.

42. Edward R. Stettinius, *Roosevelt and the Russians* (New York: Doubleday, 1949), 186.

43. Anna Roosevelt to John Boettiger, February 7, 1945, John Boettiger Papers, FDRL.

8. The Birth of the United Nations

1. W. Averell Harriman, *Special Envoy to Churchill and Stalin, 1941–1946* (New York: Random House, 1975), 409; Edward R. Stettinius, *Roosevelt and the Russians* (New York: Doubleday, 1949), 187–188; Lord Moran Diary, February 8, 1945, in Lord Moran, *Churchill Taken from the Diaries of Lord Moran* (New York: Houghton Mifflin, 1966), 226–227.

2. Diane Shaver Clemens, *Yalta* (Oxford: Oxford University Press, 1970), 194–195; Foreign Relations of the United States (FRUS), Diplomatic Papers, *The Conferences at Malta and Yalta, 1945* (Washington, DC: US Government Printing Office, 1955), 771–772; Eden to the Foreign Office, February 8, 1945, FO371/47577, the National Archives, Kew.

3. Edward R. Stettinius Calendar Notes, February 8, 1945, University of Virginia Library.

4. Stettinius, *Roosevelt and the Russians,* 189–190; Valentine Lawford, Yalta Diary, February 8, 1945, Valentine Lawford Papers (LWFD) 2/8, Churchill Archives, Cambridge.

5. Harriman to Roosevelt, October 17, 1945, Box 33, Map Room Files, FDRL; Russell D. Buhite, *Decisions at Yalta: An Appraisal of Summit Diplomacy* (New York: Scholarly Resources, 1986), 88–89; Harriman to Roosevelt, December 15, 1944, W. Averell Harriman Papers, Box 174, Library of Congress.

6. FRUS, Diplomatic Papers, *The Conferences at Malta and Yalta,* 766.

7. Political Memoranda for the Yalta Conference, February 1945, Box 169–171, Harry Hopkins Papers, FDRL; Buhite, *Decisions at Yalta,* 93; Michael Schaller, "FDR and the 'China Question,'" in David B. Woolner, Warren F. Kimball, and David Reynolds, eds., *FDR's World: War, Peace, and Legacies* (New York: Palgrave Macmillan, 2008), 166.

8. George Q. Flynn, *American Catholics and the Roosevelt Presidency, 1932–1936* (Nashville: University of Kentucky Press, 1968), 128–129; Peter C. Kent, "The Roman Catholic Church and the Division of Europe," in David B. Woolner, ed., *FDR, the Vatican and the Roman Catholic Church in America* (New York: Palgrave Macmillan, 2003); 174.

9. Edward M. Bennett, *Franklin D. Roosevelt and the Search for Security 1933–1939* (New York: Scholarly Resources, 1985), 23; Yalta Briefing Papers, Political Memoranda for the Yalta Conference, February 1945, The Far East, Harry Hopkins Papers, Group 24, Boxes 169–171, FDRL.

10. FRUS, Diplomatic Papers, *The Conferences at Malta and Yalta,* 770.

11. Fredrik Logevall, *Embers of War: The Fall of an Empire and the Making of America's Vietnam* (New York: Random House, 2014), 64–65; Warren F. Kimball, *The Juggler* (Princeton: Princeton University Press, 1991), 193; Lloyd C. Gardner, "FDR and the Colonial Question," in David B. Woolner, Warren Kimball, and David Reynolds, eds., *FDR's World: War, Peace, and Legacies* (New York: Palgrave Macmillan, 2008), 133.

12. FRUS, Diplomatic Papers, *The Conferences at Malta and Yalta,* 771.

13. Record of Meeting Held at Livadia Palace, February 8, 1945, CAB 66/63, The National Archives.

14. Byrnes Minutes, February 8, 1945.

15. FRUS, Diplomatic Papers, *The Conferences at Malta and Yalta,* 775–776.

16. Byrnes Minutes, February 8, 1945.

17. Ibid.

18. William Leahy, *I Was There* (New York: Whittlesey House, 1950), 309.

19. Sarah Churchill to Clementine Churchill, February 9, 1945, Sarah Churchill Papers, SCHL 1/1/8, Churchill Archives, Cambridge; Kathleen Harriman to Mary Harriman, February 4–10, 1945, W. Averell Harriman Papers, Box 176, Library of Congress.

20. FRUS, Diplomatic Papers, *The Conferences at Malta and Yalta,* 797; A. H. Birse, *Memoirs of an Interpreter* (New York: Coward-McCann, 1967), 184–185.

21. Ibid.

22. FRUS, Diplomatic Papers, *The Conferences at Malta and Yalta*, 798.

23. Stettinius, *Roosevelt and the Russians*, 219; Kathleen Harriman to Mary Harriman, February 4–10, 1945, Box 176, W. Averell Harriman Papers, Library of Congress.

24. Howard G. Bruenn, M.D., "Clinical Notes on the Illness and Death of President Franklin D. Roosevelt," *Annals of Internal Medicine* 72 (April 1970): 579–591 at 589; and Howard Bruenn Papers, 1944–1946, FDRL.

9. The Final Turn

1. Robert Meiklejohn Diary, February 9, 1945, W. Averell Harriman Papers, Box 211, Library of Congress, Washington, DC.

2. Foreign Relations of the United States (FRUS), Diplomatic Papers, *The Conferences at Malta and Yalta, 1945* (Washington, DC: US Government Printing Office, 1955), 842.

3. FRUS, Diplomatic Papers, *The Conferences at Malta and Yalta*, 805–806.

4. William Leahy, *I Was There* (New York: Whittlesey House, 1950), 312; FRUS, Diplomatic Papers, *The Conferences at Malta and Yalta, 1945*, 834.

5. Robert Hopkins, conversation with the author, June 10, 2000.

6. Byrnes Minutes, February 9, 1945, Clemson University Library: "Record of a Meeting Held at the Livadia Palace, February 9, 1945," CAB 66/63, The National Archives.

7. Geoffrey Roberts, *Molotov: Stalin's Cold Warrior* (Dulles, VA: Potomac Books, 2012), 85.

8. Valentine Lawford Diary, February 9, 1945, Lawson Papers, 2/8, Churchill Archives, Cambridge.

9. Edward R. Stettinius Calendar Notes, February 9, 1945, University of Virginia Library; Edward R. Stettinius, *Roosevelt and the Russians* (New York: Doubleday, 1949), 223–224.

10. Record of Meeting Held at Livadia Palace, February 9, 1945, CAB 66/63, The National Archives.

11. Charles Bohlen, *Witness to History, 1929–1969* (New York: W. W. Norton, 1973), 191–192; "Research Material Yalta Conference," Charles Bohlen Papers, Box 28, Library of Congress.

12. Halifax to Foreign Office, Record of Conversation with President Roosevelt, January 6, 1945, FO 371/47575, National Archives, Kew.

13. Hugh Dalton Diary, February 23, 1945, in Hugh Dalton, *The Second World War Diary of Hugh Dalton* (London: Cape, 1986), quoted in David Reynolds, *From World War to Cold War: Churchill, Roosevelt, and the International History of the 1940s* (Oxford: Oxford University Press, 2006), 242.

14. Hugh Dalton Diary, February 23, 1945, in Dalton, *The Second World War Diary of Hugh Dalton*; Reynolds, *From World War to Cold War*, 239–242.

15. David Reynolds, *Summits: Six Meetings That Shaped the Twentieth Century* (New York: Basic Books, 2007), 107.

16. William Leahy, *I Was There* (New York: Whittlesey House, 1950), 315–316 (emphasis added).

17. Byrnes Minutes, February 9, 1945; Foreign Relations of the United States (FRUS), Diplomatic Papers, *The Near East and Africa, 1945*, Vol. III (Washington, DC: US Government Printing Office, 1955), 853–854.

18. Byrnes Minutes, February 9, 1945; Stettinius, *Roosevelt and the Russians*, 252; Edward R. Stettinius Calendar Notes, February 9, 1945, Edward R. Stettinius Papers, University of Virginia Library.

19. Lord Moran Diary, February 9, 1945, in Lord Moran, *Churchill Taken from the Diaries of Lord Moran* (New York: Houghton Mifflin, 1966), 244; FRUS, Diplomatic Papers, *The Conferences at Malta and Yalta*, 849, 854; Byrnes Minutes, February 9, 1945.Mifflin, 1966), 244; FRUS, Diplomatic Papers, *The Conferences at Malta and Yalta*, 849, 854; Byrnes Minutes, February 9, 1945. In a letter sent to Leo Pasvolsky shortly after the conference, Alger Hiss noted that for Churchill "the mere mention of the phrase 'territorial trusteeships' almost gave him an attack of apoplexy" (Alger Hiss to Leo Pasvolsky, February 14, 1945, Box 279 Stettinius Papers).

20. Reynolds, *Summits*, 109–110.

21. FRUS, Diplomatic Papers, *The Conferences at Malta and Yalta*, 906.

22. Mark Lytle, *The Origins of the American-Iranian Alliance, 1941–1953* (New York: Holmes and Meier, 1987), 25.

23. Edward R. Stettinius, Random Notes, Yalta Conference, February 10, 1945, Edward R. Stettinius Papers, University of Virginia Library.

24. Stettinius, *Roosevelt and the Russians*, 266.

25. FRUS, Diplomatic Papers, *The Conferences at Malta and Yalta*, 926; S. M. Plokhy, *Yalta: The Price of Peace* (New York: Viking, 2010), 318.

26. Robert Meiklejohn Diary, February 11, 1945, Yalta Conference, W. Averell Harriman Papers, Box 211, Library of Congress; Linda Lotridge Levin, *The Making of FDR: The Story of Stephen T. Early, America's First Modern Press Secretary* (New York: Prometheus Books, 2008), 408–409.

10. The Last Mission

1. "Crimea Is Cleared: Red Army in Three Days Takes Port That Axis Besieged for Nearly Year," *New York Times*, May 10, 1944, 1; "Sevastopol—A City of Death and Wreckage," *Chicago Daily Tribune*, May 20, 1944, 7.

2. Anna Roosevelt Boettiger to John Boettiger, February 13, 1945, John Boettiger Papers, Box 6, FDRL.

3. Admiral Leahy recorded that the drive along the coast was the most beautiful mountain drive he had ever taken (see William D. Leahy Diary, February 11, 1945); George Stroganoff Oral History, George Stroganoff-Scherbatoff Papers, Columbia University Oral History Project; William Rigdon, *Sailor in the White House* (New York: Doubleday, 1962), 154.

4. Charles Bohlen, *Witness to History, 1929–1969* (New York: W. W. Norton, 1973), 202.

5. Ship's Log, February 12, 1945, Map Room Files, Box 24; FDRL; Rigdon, *Sailor in the White House*, 154–155.

6. James Landis to Franklin D. Roosevelt, January 17, 1945, Foreign Relations of the United States (FRUS), Diplomatic Papers, *The Near East and Africa, 1945*, Vol. VIII (Washington, DC: US Government Printing Office, 1969), 680–682.

7. Lloyd C. Gardner, *Three Kings: The Rise of an American Empire in the Middle East After World War II* (New York: The New Press, 2009), 16–20.

8. Peter Novick, *The Holocaust in American Life* (New York: Houghton Mifflin, 1999), 47–53; Richard Breitman and Allan J. Lichtman, *FDR and the Jews* (Cambridge, MA: Belknap Press, 2013), 1–7, 67–84, 325. Much of the criticism that has been leveled against the Roosevelt administration during the war stems from David S. Wyman's work, *The Abandonment of the Jews: America and the Holocaust, 1941–1945* (New York: New Press, 1984). FDR's most ardent defenders include William D. Rubenstein, *The Myth of Rescue: Why the Democracies Could Not Have Saved More Jews from the Nazis* (New York: Routledge, 1997), and Robert N. Rosen, *Saving the Jews: Franklin D. Roosevelt and the Holocaust* (New York: Thunder Mouth, 2006). For a review of the historical debate over FDR and America's reaction to the Holocaust, see Novick, *The Holocaust in American Life*, 47–48. For a more detailed look at the British government's reaction to the Holocaust, see Bernard Wasserstein, *Britain and the Jews of Europe, 1939–1945* (New York: Oxford University Press, 1979).

9. For more on the British Mandate for Palestine, see "Introduction: Palestine from the Balfour Declaration to the Anglo-American Committee," in James G. McDonald, *To the Gates of Jerusalem: The Diaries and Papers of James G. McDonald*, edited by Norman J. W. Goda, Barbara McDonald Stewart, and Richard Breitman (Bloomington: Indiana University Press, 2014), 1–17.

10. Note of Certain Conversations Held Between President Franklin D. Roosevelt and Colonel Hon. Arthur Murray, at Hyde Park on the Hudson, October 16th to the 24th, 1938, handed to the Prime Minister, December 14, 1938, Correspondence of Arthur C. Murray, Scottish National Archives, Edinburgh, Scotland; Arthur Murray to Franklin D. Roosevelt, December 20, 1938, and Franklin D. Roosevelt to Faith and Arthur Murray, January 19, 1939, President's Secretary's Files (PSF) Box 38, FDRL.

11. British White Paper of 1939, PSF Box 46, Palestine, FDRL.

12. Roosevelt to Hull, May 17, 1939, PSF Box 46, Palestine, FDRL.

13. Breitman and Lichtman, *FDR and the Jews*, 241; Adolf A. Berle Diary, May 26, 1939, as cited in Beatrice Bishop Berle, *Navigating the Rapids, 1918–1971: From the Papers of Adolf A. Berle* (New York: Houghton Mifflin, 1973), 223.

14. Allis Radosh and Ronald Radosh, *A Safe Haven: Harry S. Truman and the Founding of Israel* (New York: Harper Perennial, 2009), 8; "11 Allies Condemn Nazi War on Jews: United Nations Issue Protest on 'Cold-Blooded Extermination,'" *New York Times*, December 18, 1942, 1 (emphasis added). For more on the American Jewish Community's shifting response to the Holocaust, see Thomas Kolsky, *Jews Against Zionism: The American Council of Judaism, 1942–1948* (Philadelphia: Temple University Press, 1990).

15. Henry Morgenthau Diary, December 3, 1942, FDRL; Breitman and Lichtman, *FDR and the Jews*, 246; diary entry, May 23, 1943, in Henry A. Wallace, *The Price of Vision: The Diary of Henry A. Wallace, 1942–1946* (New York: Houghton Mifflin, 1973); Henry Morgenthau Diary, June 15, 1943; Foreign Relations of the United States (FRUS), Diplomatic Papers, *The Near East and Africa, 1943*, Vol. IV (Washington, DC: US Government Printing Office, 1964), 792–794. Churchill, who was Colonial Secretary at the time the British Mandate for Palestine was issued, was of a similar mind to FDR about the right of the Jews to establish a homeland in the Levant. As with FDR, however, his ability to push this idea forward was met with considerable resistance within British government and military circles—a fact that clearly grieved the prime minister as Nazi persecution of the Jews intensified. As Churchill said in a minute issued in January 1944, "I have always considered the White Paper a disastrous policy and a breach of understanding for which I was prominently responsible" (Churchill Memo to the Deputy Prime Minister and Foreign Secretary, January 12, 1944, Prime Minister's Office Records [PREM] 4/52/5, The National Archives, Kew). For more on the British government's response to the Holocaust, see Bernard Wasserstein, *Britain and the Jews of Europe, 1939–1945* (Oxford: Clarendon Press, 1979), and Monty Noam Penkower, *Decision in Palestine Deferred: America, Britain and Wartime Diplomacy, 1939–1945* (New York: Routledge, 2002).

16. Acting Secretary of War Robert Patterson to Secretary of State Cordell Hull, July 27, 1943, forwarded to FDR, July 30, 1943, Samuel Rosenman Papers, Box 13, FDRL; Secretary of War Henry Stimson to Senator Tom Connolly, Chairman of the Senate Foreign Relations Committee, February 5, 1944, Pentagon Office Correspondence, Palestine 1944, Box 78, George C. Marshall Papers, Lexington, Virginia.

17. Henry Morgenthau Diary, March 15, 1944.

18. Report on US Consumption of Oil, 1943, James F. Byrnes Papers, Series 4, Box 13, Clemson University, Special Collections Library, Clemson, South Carolina; Ross Gregory, "The Conference of Franklin D. Roosevelt and King Ibn Saud in February 1945," in J. Gary Clifford and Theodore A. Wilson, eds., *Presidents, Diplomats, and Other Mortals: Essays Honoring Robert H. Ferrell* (New York: Columbia University Press, 2007), 117–118.

19. David Painter, *Oil and the American Century* (Baltimore: Johns Hopkins University Press, 1986), 8.

20. Ibid., 35.

21. Halifax to the Foreign Office, February 19, 1944, No. 846 FO/371/42688, the National Archives, Kew.

22. Ambassador John Gil Winant to Winston Churchill, June 14, 1943, PREM 4/52/5, The National Archives Kew; Hoskins to Hull, August 31, 1943, FRUS, Diplomatic Papers, *The Near East and Africa, 1943*, Vol. IV, 807–810; Breitman and Lichtman, *FDR and the Jews*, 252.

23. Breitman and Lichtman, *FDR and the Jews*, 259; "President Pledges Free Jewish State," *New York Times*, October 16, 1944, 19.

24. Herbert Feis, *The Birth of Israel: The Tousled Diplomatic Bed* (New York: Norton, 1969), 17.

25. Edward R. Stettinius Calendar Notes, January 2, 1945, University of Virginia Library.

26. FRUS, Diplomatic Papers, *The Near East and Africa, 1945*, Vol. VIII, 680–682; Donald A. Ritchie, *James M. Landis: Dean of Regulators* (Cambridge, MA: Harvard University Press, 1980), 130–131.

27. Record of Conversation Between Franklin D. Roosevelt and Rabbi Stephen Wise, March 9, 1944, FO371/40135, The National Archives Kew.

11. Failure at Bitter Lake

1. Foreign Relations of the United States (FRUS), Diplomatic Papers, *The Near East and Africa, 1945*, Vol. VIII (Washington, DC: US Government Printing Office, 1969), 4.

2. "What Franklin Roosevelt Learned from the Italian-Ethiopian War," from the unpublished memoir by Vice Admiral Wilson Brown, Special Collections, Nimitz Library, United States Naval Academy, Annapolis, Maryland.

3. William D. Leahy Diary, February 13, 1945, Library of Congress; William Rigdon, *Sailor in the White House* (New York: Doubleday, 1962), 162.

4. FRUS, Diplomatic Papers, *The Near East and Africa, 1945*, Vol. VIII, 5–6; Edward R. Stettinius, *Roosevelt and the Russians* (New York: Doubleday, 1949), 288, "Selassie Puts Wreath on Roosevelt Grave," *Washington Post*, May 31, 1954, 9.

5. Captain John S. Keating, "Mission to Mecca: The Cruise of the Murphy," *Proceedings Magazine*, US Naval Institute, January 1976, Vol. 102/1/875, 54–55; William A. Eddy, "F.D.R. Meets Ibn Saud," Original Manuscript, 11, William A. Eddy Papers, Box 14, Mudd Library, Princeton.

6. Official Log, President's Trip to Malta and Crimea, FDRL; "Our American Minister to Saudi Arabia," Department of State Publication, William A. Eddy Papers, Box 17, Mudd Library, Princeton.

7. Keating, "Mission to Mecca," 59; William A. Eddy, "F.D.R. Meets Ibn Saud," Original Manuscript, 19–20, William A. Eddy Papers, Box 14, Mudd Library, Princeton.

8. Keating, "Mission to Mecca," 62.

9. Anna Roosevelt to John Boettiger, February 14, 1945, Boettiger Papers, Box 6, FDRL; Michael Reilly and Robert Slocum, *Reilly of the White House* (New York: Simon & Schuster, 1947), 221; Rigdon, *Sailor in the White House*, 164.

10. Reilly and Slocum, *Reilly of the White House*, 222.

11. William A. Eddy, *FDR Meets Ibn Saud*, Original Manuscript, 17–19, Eddy Papers, Box 14, Mudd Library, Princeton

12. FRUS, Diplomatic Papers, *The Near East and Africa*, 1945, Vol. VIII, 7–9.

13. Ibid.

14. Ibid., 2; William A. Eddy, *FDR Meets Ibn Saud*, Original Manuscript, 26, Eddy Papers, Box 14, Mudd Library, Princeton.

15. William A. Eddy, *FDR Meets Ibn Saud*, Original Manuscript, 26–27, Eddy Papers, Box 14, Mudd Library, Princeton.

16. Ibid., 27–28; FRUS, Diplomatic Papers, *The Near East and Africa*, 1945, Vol. VIII, 3.

17. Richard Breitman and Allan J. Lichtman, *FDR and the Jews* (Cambridge, MA: Belknap Press, 2013), 303.

18. Lloyd C. Gardner, *Three Kings: The Rise of an American Empire in the Middle East After World War II* (New York: The New Press, 2009), 20.

19. William D. Leahy Diary, February 14, 1945, Library of Congress.

20. James G. McDonald Diary, December 13–15, 1945, as cited in James G. McDonald, *To the Gates of Jerusalem: The Diaries and Papers of James G. McDonald*, edited by Norman J. W. Goda, Barbara McDonald Stewart, and Richard Breitman (Bloomington: Indiana University Press, 2014).

21. "Visit of Committee to Riyadh," report of the Anglo-American Committee of Inquiry, by Sir John Singleton, March 19, 1946, FO371/ 52514/E3067, The National Archives, Kew.

22. Elliott Roosevelt, *As He Saw It* (New York: Greenwood Press, 1946), 245.

23. Franklin D. Roosevelt, Address to Congress, March 1, 1945, Speech File, FDRL.

24. Breitman and Lichtman, *FDR and the Jews*, 303–304.

25. Memorandum by Joseph Proskauer to the Leadership of the American Jewish Committee, April 1945, Box 31, YIVO Institute for Jewish Research, American Jewish Historical Society, New York; Jacob Blaustein to FDR, March 24, 1945, OF 76C, Box 9, FDRL.

26. Harold Hoskins, Memorandum of Conversation with FDR, March 5, 1945, FRUS, Diplomatic Papers, *Near East and Africa, 1945*, Vol. VIII, 690–691.

27. Ibid.

28. William D. Leahy Diary, February 14, 1945.

29. Record of Conversation with King Abdul Aziz Ibn Saud in the Fayoum, February 17, 1945, FO141/1047, The National Archives Kew.

30. Martin Gilbert, *Winston S. Churchill: Road to Victory, 1941–1945* (Boston: Houghton Mifflin, 1986), 1225.

31. William Eddy to Secretary of State Edward Stettinius, February 22, 1945, in FRUS, Diplomatic Papers, *The Near East and Africa, 1945*, Vol. VIII, 689–690; Stettinius, *Roosevelt and the Russians*, 278; Charles Bohlen, *Witness to History, 1929–1969* (New York: W. W. Norton, 1973), 203.

32. Ibid.; Joseph Grew to FDR, March 10, 1945, President's Secretary's Files (PSF) Box 50, FDRL.

33. Ross Gregory, "The Conference of Franklin D. Roosevelt and King Ibn Saud in February 1945," in J. Gary Clifford and Theodore A. Wilson, eds., *Presidents, Diplomats, and Other Mortals: Essays Honoring Robert H. Ferrell* (New York: Columbia University Press, 2007), 132–133.

34. Joseph Grew to William D. Moreland, March 24, 1945, FRUS, Diplomatic Papers, *The Near East and Africa, 1945*, Vol. VIII, 697; Roosevelt to Ibn Saud, President's Personal File (PPF) 7960, FDRL.

35. "Passover Dinner Held at Two Hotels," *New York Times*, April 1, 1945, 34; "Roosevelt Asks Spiritual Rebirth in Congratulations to Emanu-El: Tells Congregation All Problems Would 'Melt' Before Faith in God—Spellman Also Praises Institution on Its Centenary," *New York Times*, April 6, 1945, 17.

12. Going Home

1. Anna Roosevelt to John Boettiger, February 14, 1945, John Boettiger Papers, Box 6, FDRL.

2. Ibid.

3. Margaret (Daisy) Suckley Diary, February, 19, 1945, FDRL; emphasis in original.

4. Ibid.; Franklin D. Roosevelt to Eleanor Roosevelt, February 12, 1945, in Franklin D. Roosevelt, *His Personal Letters, 1928–1945*, Vol. II, edited by Elliott Roosevelt (New York: Duell, Sloane & Pearce, 1950). The lack of correspondence between Franklin and Eleanor did not go unnoticed both by Anna, who called it a "sad situation," and by her husband John, who in a letter to Anna referred to the fact that Eleanor had received no mail from her husband to this point in his long trip to Yalta as "somewhat tragic" (Anna Roosevelt to John Boettiger, February 7, 1945, and John Boettiger to Anna Roosevelt, February 11, 1945, Boettiger Papers, Box 6, FDRL).

5. William Leahy, *I Was There* (New York: Whittlesey House, 1950), 325.

6. Official Log, Conferences at Malta and Crimea, FDRL.

7. Sarah Churchill to Clementine Churchill, February 12, 1945, Sarah Churchill Papers, 1/1/8, Churchill Archives, Cambridge; Valentine Lawford Diary, February 11, 1945, Churchill Archives, Cambridge.

8. Mary Soames, *The Personal Letters of Winston and Clementine Churchill* (London: Black Swan, 1999), 517; Harold Macmillan Diary, February 14, 1945, in Harold Macmillan, *War Diaries: The Mediterranean, 1943–1945* (London: Papermac, 1984), 693.

9. Diary entry dated June 21, 1942, in *War Diaries: 1939–1945, Field Marshall Lord Alanbrooke*, edited by Alex Danchev and Dan Todman (London: Phoenix Press, 2002), 269; Martin Gilbert, *Winston S. Churchill: Road to Victory, 1941–1945* (Boston: Houghton Mifflin, 1986), 128–129.

10. Notes on the President and the P.M., Lord Moran Papers, PP/CMW/K3/1/2, Wellcome Library, London; Roosevelt to Churchill, March 17, 1942, Map Room Files, FDRL.

11. Albert Einstein to Franklin D. Roosevelt, August 2, 1939, Alexander Sachs Papers, FDRL.

12. Wilson C. Miscamble, C.S.C., *The Most Controversial Decision: Truman, the Atomic Bomb, and the Defeat of Japan* (New York: Cambridge University Press, 2011), 8.

13. Roosevelt to Churchill, October 11, 1941, Map Room Files, FDRL.

14. Robin Edmonds, *The Big Three: Churchill, Roosevelt and Stalin in Peace and War* (London: Penguin Books, 1991), 399–400.

15. Ibid.

16. Quebec Agreement, President's Secretary's Files (PSF) Quebec, Box 25, FDRL.

17. Churchill to Lord Cherwell, May 27, 1944, Prime Minister's Office Records (PREM) 3/139/11A, The National Archives Kew.

18. Cherwell to Churchill, January 26, 1945, PREM 3/139/11A.

19. Edward R. Stettinius Calendar Notes, February 15, 1945, Edward R. Stettinius Papers, Box 279, University of Virginia Library.

20. Edward R. Stettinius Calendar Notes, January 8, 1945; Edward R. Stettinius Calendar Notes, January 23, 1945; Edward R. Stettinius, *The Diaries of Edward R. Stettinius, Jr., 1943–1946*, edited by Thomas Campbell and George C. Herring (New York: New Viewpoints, 1975), 262; Edward R. Stettinius Calendar Notes, January 23, 1945.

21. Prime Minister Personal Minutes, February 16, 1945, PREM 3/139/11A.

22. Sarah Churchill to Clementine Churchill, February 16, 1945, Sarah Churchill Papers, 1/1/8, Churchill Archives, Cambridge.

23. Winston Churchill, *Triumph and Tragedy* (Boston: Houghton Mifflin, 1983), 397.

24. Anna Roosevelt Halsted to Eleanor Roosevelt, February 18, 1945, Anna Roosevelt Halsted Papers, Box 84, FDRL.

25. Samuel Rosenman to Dorothy Rosenman, February 11, 1945, Samuel Rosenman Papers, Box 10, FDRL; Samuel Rosenman, *Working with Roosevelt* (New York: Harper & Brothers, 1952), 522.

26. William D. Leahy Diary, February 18, 1945, Library of Congress.

27. Carmel Offie to William Bullitt, William Bullitt Papers, Sterling Library, Yale; Orville H. Bullitt, *For the President, Personal & Secret: Correspondence Between Franklin D. Roosevelt and William C. Bullitt* (Boston: Houghton Mifflin, 1972), 611.

28. Harry Hopkins to Louise Hopkins, February 15, 1945, Charles Bohlen Papers, Library of Congress.

29. Anna Roosevelt Halsted, Oral History, Columbia Oral History Project, Columbia University Library. For years, the Mayo physicians who treated Hopkins deliberated over what was wrong with him. In an article published in 1948 by Dr. James Halsted, Anna Roosevelt's last husband, Halsted speculated that he had adult celiac disease.

30. Official Log, Conferences at Malta and the Crimea, FDRL.

31. Anna Roosevelt Halsted Diary, February 20, 1945, Box 84, FDRL.

32. Ibid.

33. Vice Admiral (Dr.) Ross T. McIntire, *White House Physician* (New York: Putnam & Sons, 1946), 234.

34. Rosenman, *Working with Roosevelt,* 523.

35. Anna Roosevelt Halsted Papers, Yalta Drafts, Box 84, FDRL.

36. Rosenman, *Working with Roosevelt,* 526.

37. Ibid.

38. Official Log, Conferences at Malta and Yalta, FDRL.

39. "Arlington Burial for General Watson," *New York Times,* March 21, 1945, 21.

40. Margaret (Daisy) Suckley Diary, February 27, 1945, FDRL; White House Telephone Logs, February 27, 1945, President's Personal File (PPF) 1N, Box 81, FDRL.

13. The Last Address

1. Eleanor Roosevelt to Joseph Lash, February 28, 1945, FDRL; Eleanor Roosevelt, *The Autobiography of Eleanor Roosevelt* (New York: Da Capo Press, 1992), 275.

2. William Hassett Diary, February 28, 1945, Box 22, FDRL; Grace Tully, *FDR: My Boss* (Chicago: The People's Book Club, 1949), 354–355.

3. Vice Admiral (Dr.) Ross T. McIntire, *White House Physician* (New York: Putnam & Sons, 1946), 236.

4. Roosevelt to Grace Tully, January 29, 1945, and February 12, 1945, Grace Tully Papers, FDRL.

5. William Hassett Diary, February 28, 1945, Box 22, FDRL; "Arlington Burial for General Watson," *New York Times,* March 1, 1945, 21.

6. Samuel Rosenman, *Working with Roosevelt* (New York: Harper & Brothers, 1952), 527; Tully, *FDR: My Boss,* 355; Jonathan Daniels, *White House Witness* (New York: Doubleday, 1975), 265–266.

7. David Reynolds, *Summits: Six Meetings That Shaped the Twentieth Century* (New York: Basic Books, 2007), 136; Robert L. Messer, *The End of an Alliance: James F. Byrnes, Roosevelt, Truman, and the Origins of the Cold War* (Chapel Hill: University of North Carolina Press, 1982), 62–63;

Fraser J. Harbutt, *Yalta 1945: Europe and America at the Crossroads* (New York: Cambridge University Press, 2010), 321; Lela Stiles Papers, Box 9, FDRL.

8. "Roosevelt Shaped Two Yalta Solutions," *New York Times*, February 14, 1945, 1.

9. Franklin Roosevelt to James Byrnes, February 26, 1945, Box 19, Yalta Conference, James Byrnes Papers, Clemson University Library; Harbutt, *Yalta 1945: Europe and America at the Crossroads*, 320–322.

10. Churchill to Roosevelt, February 28, 1945, Map Room Files, FDRL; *Hansard*, Record of the House of Commons Debates, February 27, 1945, columns 1299–1300.

11. Churchill to the House of Commons, February 19, 1945, in Robert Rhodes James, *Winston Churchill: His Complete Speeches, Volume VII* (London: Chelsea House, 1974).

12. Churchill to Roosevelt, February 28, 1945, Map Room Files, FDRL.

13. Arthur Cox to Harry L. Hopkins, Memorandum: "Majority Ratification of Treaties," January 10, 1945, Arthur Cox Papers, Box 151, FDRL.

14. Alben W. Barkley, *That Reminds Me: The Autobiography of the VEEP* (New York: Doubleday, 1954), 191–192.

15. Ibid.

16. "Benjamin C. West, Oral History Interview," Office of the Historian, US House of Representatives, August 24, 2005.

17. James Roosevelt, *My Parents: A Differing View* (New York: Playboy Press, 1976), 93–94; "Outburst Beats M'Ado's: Smith Demonstration the Loudest Any Convention Ever Heard," *New York Times*, June 27, 1924, 1.

18. "Governor Offered by F. D. Roosevelt," *Washington Post*, June 28, 1928, 1.

19. "Smith Forces Stage Huge Demonstration When He Is Placed in Nomination at New York," *Chicago Daily Tribune*, June 27, 1924, 36.

20. Dean Acheson, *Present at the Creation* (New York: W. W. Norton, 1969), 102; Allen Drury, *A Senate Journal* (New York: McGraw-Hill, 1963), 371–373; "Report on Yalta," *New York Times*, March 2, 1945, Halifax Diary, March 1, 1945.

21. Eleanor Roosevelt, *The Autobiography of Eleanor Roosevelt*, 275; Roosevelt Campaign Speech, Rochester, New York, October 22, 1928, Master Speech File, FDRL.

22. Frances Perkins, Oral History, Columbia University Library Oral History Project.

23. Franklin D. Roosevelt, Address to Congress, March 1, 1945, Master Speech File, FDRL.

24. Rosenman, *Working with Roosevelt*, 528.

25. "Armchair Speech Stirs Comment on Roosevelt's Health," *Chicago Daily Tribune*, March 2, 1945, 9.

26. "Rome Paper Hints at FDR Health Lapse," *Los Angeles Times*, February 25, 1945, 1; "Roosevelt Said to Rest," *New York Times*, February 26, 1945, 5; "President Returns Home in 'Great' Health; 'He Is in Grand Spirits,' Secretary Reports," *New York Times*, March 1, 1945, 13.

27. Harold Ickes Diary, February 25, 1945, Library of Congress.

28. Daniels, *White House Witness*, 266.

29. Ibid.; Margaret (Daisy) Suckley Diary, March 3, 1945, FDRL.

14. March Days

1. Geoff Ward, *Before the Trumpet, Young Franklin Roosevelt: 1882–1905* (New York: Harper Collins, 1885), 234.

2. "25,000 See Opening of Mid-Hudson Span: Gov. Roosevelt and Ex. Gov. Smith Praise Projectors and Engineers of Toll Bridge," *New York Times*, August 26, 1930, 5; "Funeral Today for Modjeski, Famed Bridge Builder," *Los Angeles Times*, June 28, 1940, A12.

3. Margaret (Daisy) Suckley Diary, March 5, 1945, FDRL.

4. Ibid., March 7, 1945; FDRL.

5. Churchill to Roosevelt, March 8, 1945, Map Room Files, FDRL.

6. Ibid.; Warren F. Kimball, *Churchill and Roosevelt: Their Complete Correspondence, Vol. III, Alliance Declining* (Princeton: Princeton University Press, 1984), 546.

7. Churchill to Roosevelt, March 8, 1945, Map Room Files, FDRL.

8. Kimball, *Alliance Declining*, 545–546.

9. Halifax to Eden, March 8, 1945, FO371/50835; Roosevelt to Churchill, March 11, 1945, Map Room Files, FDRL.

10. James McGregor Burns, *FDR: The Soldier of Freedom, 1940–1945* (New York: Harcourt, 1970), 588.

11. "Senate Rejects Williams," *New York Times*, March 24, 1945, 1.

12. Ibid.; Jonathan Daniels, *White House Witness* (New York: Doubleday, 1975), 264–265; Burns, *FDR, Soldier of Freedom*, 594.

13. Linda Lotridge Levin, *The Making of FDR: The Story of Stephen T. Early, America's First Modern Press Secretary* (New York: Prometheus Books, 2008), 417; Charles Bohlen, *Witness to History, 1929–1969* (New York: W. W. Norton, 1973), 206.

14. Jean-Paul Sartre, *"Jean-Paul Sartre en Amérique," Le Figaro*, March 12, 1945.

15. Harold Ickes Diary, March 9, 1945.

16. James Forrestal Diaries, March 9, 1945, Mudd Library, Princeton; Harold Ickes Diary, March 10, 1945.

17. Mackenzie King Diary, March 9, 1945, National Archives, Canada.

18. Ibid., March 10, 1945.

19. Ibid., March 13, 1945.

20. Anna Roosevelt Halsted, Oral History, Columbia University Oral History Project.

21. Misc. Notes, Anna Roosevelt Halsted Papers, Box 84, FDRL.

22. Mackenzie King Diary, March 13, 1945.

23. Ibid.

24. Drew Pearson, "Washington Merry-Go-Round," *Washington Post*, March 18, 1945, 5.

25. Edward R. Stettinius Diary and Calendar Notes, March 12–13, 1945, Edward R. Stettinius Papers, University of Virginia.

26. Vandenberg to J. F. Dulles, February 17, 1945, in Arthur S. Vandenberg, Jr., *The Private Papers of Senator Vandenberg* (Boston: Houghton Mifflin, 1952), 151.

27. Vandenberg to Roosevelt, March 1, 1945, in Vandenberg, *The Private Papers of Senator Vandenberg*, 153.

28. Vandenberg, *The Private Papers of Senator Vandenberg*, 155.

29. Henry Stimson Diary, March 11–12, 1945, Sterling Library, Yale University; OSS memo to FDR, March 10, 1945, Recently Declassified Holdings, FDRL; S. M. Plokhy, *Yalta: The Price of Peace* (New York: Viking, 2010), 361.

30. Mackenzie King Diary, March 13, 1945.

31. Mark Stoler, *Allies and Adversaries: The Joint Chiefs of Staff, the Grand Alliance, and U.S. Strategy in World War II* (Chapel Hill: University of North Carolina Press, 2000), 232.

32. James Forrestal Diaries, March 16, 1945.

33. Godfrey Hodgson, *The Colonel: The Life and Wars of Henry Stimson, 1867–1950* (New York: Knopf, 1990), 306.

34. Felix Frankfurter Papers, February, 25 1945, Library of Congress; Martin J. Sherwin, *A World Destroyed: Hiroshima and Its Legacies* (New York: Random House, 1975), 100.

35. Robin Edmonds, *The Big Three: Churchill, Roosevelt and Stalin in Peace and War* (New York: Norton & Norton, 1991), 404–405; Churchill to Cherwell, September 20, 1944, Prime Minister's Office Records (PREM) 3/139/8A, The National Archives, Kew.

36. Hyde Park Memorandum on Tube Alloys, September 18, 1944, PREM 3/139/11A, The National Archives, Kew.

37. Wilson D. Miscamble, *The Most Controversial Decision: Truman, the Atomic Bomb and the Defeat of Japan* (New York: Cambridge University Press, 2011), 14; Richard Rhodes, *The Making of the Atomic Bomb* (New York: Simon & Schuster, 2012), 530.

38. Hodgson, *The Colonel*, 304 (emphasis added).

39. Ibid.; Hyde Park Memorandum, September 19, 1944, FDRL.

40. Hodgson, *The Colonel*, 310.

41. James G. Hershberg, *James B. Conant: Harvard to Hiroshima and the Making of the Nuclear Age* (Stanford, CA: Stanford University Press, 1993), 221; Diary of Henry Stimson, March 15, 1945.

42. Ibid.

43. Rhodes, *The Making of the Atomic Bomb*, 635–636; Einstein to Roosevelt, March 25, 1945, FDRL.

44. Leo Szílard Memorandum, Atom Bombs and the Postwar Position of the United States in the World, Spring 1945, Memorandum for the President, attached to the Einstein Letter, March 25, 1945, Leo Szílard Papers, University of South Carolina; also in Leo Szílard, *Leo Szílard: His Version of the Facts*, edited by Spencer R. Weart and Gertrud Weiss Szílard (Cambridge, MA: MIT Press, 1978), 196–204, 205–207.

45. Dario Fazzi, *A Voice of Conscience: Eleanor Roosevelt and the Anti-Nuclear Movement* (New York: Palgrave Macmillan, 2016), 43.

15. The Architect

1. "Hottest St. Patrick's Day on Record," *Washington Post,* March 18, 1945, 1.

2. John Q. Barrett, "The Nuremberg Roles of Justice Robert H. Jackson," *Washington University Global Studies Law Review* 6, no. 3 (*Symposium—Judgment at Nuremberg,* 2007).

3. Robert H. Jackson, *That Man: An Insider's Portrait of Franklin D. Roosevelt,* edited by John Q. Barrett (New York: Oxford University Press, 2004), 152.

4. Ibid., 154.

5. Stanley Hornbeck to Roosevelt, February 21, 1945, President's Secretary's Files (PSF) Netherlands, 1944–1945, FDRL.

6. "Tighten Belts and Help Feed the World: F.D.R.," *Chicago Daily Tribune,* March 17, 1945, 1.

7. Franklin D. Roosevelt, Press Conference, March 16, 1945, Complete Press Conferences, FDRL.

8. "FDR Calls for Food Aid," *Chicago Daily Tribune,* March 17, 1945, 1.

9. Franklin D. Roosevelt to Queen Wilhelmina, March 21, 1945, PSF Netherlands, FDRL.

10. Wilhelmina Returns to the Netherlands: To a Joyous and Moving Welcome," *New York Times,* March 21, 1945, 12.

11. Franklin D. Roosevelt to Queen Wilhelmina, March 21, 1945, PSF Netherlands, 1944–1945, FDRL.

12. Anne O'Hare McCormick, "Abroad: The Stone Will Not be Rolled Away by a Miracle," *New York Times,* March 31, 1945, 18.

13. Douglas Chandor to Grace Tully, January 14, 1947, Correspondence, Douglas Chandor, 1947–1954, Grace Tully Papers, FDRL.

14. Ina Hill Chandor to Grace Tully, January 30, 1947, Correspondence, Douglas Chandor, 1947–1954, Grace Tully Papers, FDRL.

15. Jacob Blaustein to Franklin D. Roosevelt, March 24, 1945, OF 76-C, Box 9, Folder 1, FDRL.

16. "International Bill of Rights to Be Offered at World Peace Parley," *New York Times,* March 21, 1945, 13.

17. Ibid.; Joseph Proskauer to Sumner Welles, January 23, 1945, Sumner Welles Papers, Box 197, FDRL.

18. Stephen Schlesinger, *Act of Creation: The Founding of the United Nations* (New York: Westview, 2003) 194; Lansing Warren, "Hurdles for the San Francisco Conference: Agreement on World Security," *New York Times,* March 17, 1945, E3.

19. Ibid.

20. Edward R. Stettinius Calendar Notes, March 12 and March 19, 1945, Edward R. Stettinius Papers, University of Virginia.

21. Edward R. Stettinius Calendar Notes, March 19, 1945; Joseph Grew to Franklin D. Roosevelt, March 22, 1945, in Foreign Relations of the United States (FRUS), Diplomatic Papers, *United Nations, 1945,* Vol. I (Washington, DC: US Government Printing Office, 1967), 144–145.

22. W. Averell Harriman, *Special Envoy to Churchill and Stalin, 1941–1946* (New York: Random House, 1975), 426–428.

23. Henry Morgenthau Diary, March 20, 1945, FDRL.

24. John Chamberlain, "FDR's Daughter," *Life,* March 1945, 96–100, 102–108; Henry Morgenthau Diary, March 20, 1945.

25. Raymond P. Schmidt, "A Tower in Nebraska: How FDR Found Inspiration for the Naval Medical Center in Bethesda, Maryland," *Prologue* 41, no. 4 (Winter 2009), National Archives and Records Administration.

26. Cordell Hull, *The Memoirs of Cordell Hull, Vol. II* (New York: Macmillan, 1948), 1721.

27. Usher's Log, March 12–14, 20, and 21, 1945. FDR also telephoned Lucy at least four times during this period, in conversations that lasted from five to fifteen minutes; see White House Telephone Logs, March 8, 9, 11, and 23, 1945, President's Secretary's Files (PPF) 1N, Box 81, FDRL.

28. Harold Ickes Diary, March 31, 1945, Library of Congress.

29. Franklin D. Roosevelt, Speech to Annual Correspondents' Dinner, March 22, 1941, Master Speech File, FDRL.

30. Allen Drury, *Senate Journal*, March 24, 1945, in Allen Drury, *A Senate Journal, 1943–1945* (New York: McGraw Hill, 1963), 388–390.

31. Harold Ickes Diary, March 22, 1945; Jackson, *That Man*, 154; Drury, *Senate Journal*, March 22, 1945, 389–390.

32. Drury, *Senate Journal*, March 22, 1945, 390.

33. Ibid.

34. Frank Freidel, *Franklin D. Roosevelt: A Rendezvous with Destiny* (Boston: Little Brown, 1990), 602–603.

35. Arthur Vandenberg Diary, March 23, 1945, in *The Private Papers of Arthur Vandenberg* (Boston: Houghton Mifflin, 1952).

36. Arthur Vandenberg Diary, March 27, 1945.

37. Ibid.

38. Notes of Conversation with President, March 23, 1945, Box 40, Anne O'Hare McCormick Papers, New York Public Library.

39. Ibid.; "His 'Unfinished Business'—and Ours: A Final Interview with Franklin Roosevelt," *New York Times*, April 22, 1945, SM3.

40. Ibid.

41. Ibid.

42. Harold Ickes Diary, March 24, 1945.

43. Frances Perkins, Oral History, Columbia University Library.

44. Howard G. Bruenn, M.D., "Clinical Notes on the Illness and Death of President Franklin D. Roosevelt," *Annals of Internal Medicine* 72 (April 1970): 579–591 at 22.

45. "Moscow Stresses Desires for Peace: Leaders Imply Rehabilitation Is Principal Aim—Health of Roosevelt Watched," *New York Times*, March 23, 1945, 3.

46. Churchill to Roosevelt, March 17, 1945, Map Room Files, FDRL.

47. "U.S. at War," *Time*, April 23, 1945, 20.

16. Hudson Requiem

1. "Patton's Men Storm over Rhine," *Los Angeles Times*, March 24, 1945, 1.

2. Jonathan Daniels, *White House Witness* (New York: Doubleday, 1975), 275; "President Transfers Daniels to Press Job," *New York Times*, March 25, 1945, 40; Linda Lotridge Levin, *The Making of FDR: The Story of Stephen T. Early, America's First Modern Press Secretary* (New York: Prometheus Books, 2008), 418.

3. William Hassett Diary, March 24, 1945, FDRL; Anna Kasten Nelson, "Anna M. Rosenberg: 'An Honorary Man,'" *Journal of Military History* 68, no. 1 (January 2004): 133–161.

4. "F.D.R. Orders Study of Guaranteed Annual Pay," *Los Angeles Times*, March 21, 1945, 1.

5. Rosenberg to Roosevelt, January 15, 1945, and Roosevelt to Rosenberg, March 31, 1945, Anna Rosenberg Papers, Schlesinger Library, Harvard.

6. Stalin to Roosevelt, March 22, 1945, Map Room Files, FDRL; Harriman to Secretary of State, March 17, 1945, Foreign Relations of the United States (FRUS), Diplomatic Papers, *European Advisory Commission; Austria; Germany, Vol. III* (Washington, DC: US Government Printing Office, 1968), 732–733; FRUS, Diplomatic Papers, *United Nations, 1945*, Vol. I (Washington, DC: US Government Printing Office, 1967), 151 (n15).

7. Harriman to Roosevelt, March 23, 45, Map Room Files, FDRL.

8. Wilson C. Miscamble, *From Roosevelt to Truman* (New York: Cambridge University Press, 2007), 74.

9. Roosevelt to Stalin, No. 293, March 24, 1945, Map Room Files, FDRL.

10. Roosevelt to Stalin, No. 294, March 24, 1945, Map Room Files, FDRL.

11. William Hassett Diary, March 24, 1945, Box 27, FDRL.

12. "200,000 Germans Trapped in Norway," *New York Times,* March 20, 1945, 4.

13. Frances Perkins, *The Roosevelt I Knew* (New York: Penguin Classics, 2011), 135.

14. Ibid., 138–139.

15. Geoffrey Ward, *Before the Trumpet* (New York: Harper Collins, 1985), 3–4.

16. Frances Perkins, Oral History, Columbia University Library Oral History Project.

17. Margaret (Daisy) Suckley Diary, March 25, 1945, FDRL.

18. Margaret Fayerweather, Diary, March 28, 1945, Eleanor Roosevelt Papers, Box 1559, FDRL.

19. Ibid. FDR's references to development work in these last months hint he might resign as President to become the first Secretary-General of the UN. Benjamin Cohen first suggested this idea to FDR as he was contemplating a fourth term run. See "Memo Concerning a 4th Term," March, 1944, Cohen Papers, Box 12, LOC.

20. Ibid.

21. Arthur Krock, "Secret Yalta Vote Poses Serious Problem," *New York Times,* April 1, 1945, E3.

22. "Roosevelt Urges Senate to Adopt Manpower Truce," *New York Times,* March 29, 1945, 1; "Strike Is Voted by Heavy Margin in Poll of Soft Coal Miners," *New York Times,* March 29, 1945, 1.

23. Jean Edward Smith, "Selection of a Proconsul for Germany: The Appointment of Gen. Lucius D. Clay, 1945," *Military Affairs* 40, no. 3 (October 1976): 123–129.

24. James F. Byrnes, *All in One Lifetime* (Harper & Brothers, 1958), 273; William Hassett Diary, March 29, 1945.

25. Edward R. Stettinius Calendar Notes, March 29, 1945, Edward R. Stettinius Papers, University of Virginia.

26. Ibid.

27. "White House Admits Bow to Russia on League Votes," *Washington Post,* March 30, 1945, 1.

28. Churchill to Roosevelt, March 27, 1945, Map Room Files, FDRL.

29. Churchill to Roosevelt, March 30, 1945, Map Room Files, FDRL; Roosevelt to Stalin, March 31, 1945, Map Room Files, FDRL.

30. Churchill to Roosevelt, March 30, 1945, Map Room Files, FDRL; Halifax Diary, March 29, 1945.

31. Tully, *FDR: My Boss,* 356.

32. Ibid., 357; Daniels, *White House Witness,* 276.

33. Tully, *FDR: My Boss,* 359.

17. Easter in Warm Springs

1. Michael Reilly and Robert Slocum, *Reilly of the White House* (New York: Simon & Schuster, 1947), 226–227; letter from Hazel Stephens to William MacKay Davis, April 15, 1945, reprinted in William Warrens Rogers, Jr., "The Death of a President, April 12, 1945: An Account from Warm Springs," *The Georgia Historical Quarterly* 75, no. 1 (Spring 1991), 112–113.

2. Franklin D. Roosevelt, Address at the Dedication of Warm Springs Hall, November 24, 1933, Master Speech File, FDRL.

3. Ibid.; Warrens, "The Death of a President," 113.

4. Margaret "Daisy" Suckley Diary, March 31, 1945, FDRL; Daisy Bonner Notes on Cooking for FDR, Little White House, Warm Springs, Georgia; Adrian Miller, *The President's Kitchen Cabinet: The Story of the African Americans Who Have Fed Our First Families, from the Washingtons to the Obamas* (Chapel Hill: University of North Carolina Press, 2017), 139.

5. William Hassett Diary, March 30, 1945, FDRL.

6. Ibid.

7. Margaret (Daisy) Suckley Diary, March 31, 1945.

8. William Hassett Diary, March 31, 1945.

9. Margaret (Daisy) Suckley Diary, March 31, 1945.

10. Margaret (Daisy) Suckley Diary, April 1 1945.

11. "Roosevelt Joins Chapel Dedication," *New York Times,* March 28, 1938, 3; Margaret (Daisy) Suckley Diary, April 1, 1945.

12. William Hassett Diary, April 1, 1945; "Roosevelt Hints War Might Upset Plans," *Washington Post,* April 10, 1939, 6.

13. William Hassett Diary, April 1, 1945; David Kennedy, *Freedom from Fear: The American People in Depression and War, 1933-1945* (New York: Oxford University Press, 1999), 832–834; *The Oxford Companion to World War II* (New York: Oxford University Press, 1995), 836.

14. William Hassett Diary, April 2 and 3, 1945; Anna Roosevelt Halsted, Oral History, Columbia University Library.

15. Stephen Schlesinger, *Act of Creation: The Founding of the United Nations* (New York: Westview Press, 2003), 70; Edward R. Stettinius Calendar Notes, April 1, 1945, University of Virginia.

16. Eisenhower to Marshall, April 7, 1945, Dwight D. Eisenhower Papers (Baltimore: Johns Hopkins University Press, 1970), 2401; Warren F. Kimball, *Churchill and Roosevelt: Their Complete Correspondence, Vol. III, Alliance Declining* (Princeton: Princeton University Press, 1984), 602–603.

17. Churchill to Roosevelt, April 1, 1945, Map Room Files, FDRL.

18. Roosevelt to Churchill, April 4, 1945, Map Room Files, FDRL. General Omar Bradley was even more blunt, asking at one point whether casualties as high as one hundred thousand were "not a pretty stiff price to pay for a prestige objective, especially when we've got to fall back and let the other fellow take over" (Eisenhower to Churchill, April 7, 1945, Eisenhower Papers, 2401).

19. Roosevelt to Stalin, March 24 and 29, 1945, Map Room Files, FDRL.

20. Stalin to Roosevelt, March 29, 1945, Map Room Files, FDRL.

21. Roosevelt to Stalin, March 31, 1945, Map Room Files, FDRL.

22. Stalin to Roosevelt, April 3, 1945, Map Room Files, FDRL; correspondence between J. V. Stalin and Franklin Roosevelt in the Years of the Great Patriotic War, Vol. 2, edited by V. O. Pechativov and I. E. Magadeev (Moscow: OLMA Publishing Group, 2015), 478–479.

23. Roosevelt to Stalin, April 4, 1945, Map Room Files, FDRL. Wolff also claimed "joint action by Kesselring himself would have a vital repurcussion on . . . the Western Front, since many Generals are only waiting for someone to take the lead." OSS Memo to the President, March 10, 1945, Declassified Holdings, FDRL.

24. Stalin to Roosevelt, April 7, 1945, Map Room Files, FDRL.

25. Churchill to Roosevelt, April 5, 1945, Map Room Files, FDRL.

26. Churchill to Roosevelt, Text of Message to Stalin, April 5, 1945, Map Room Files, FDRL.

27. Churchill to Roosevelt, April 11, 1945, Text of Message from Stalin, April 7, 1945, Map Room Files, FDRL.

28. Churchill to Roosevelt, April, 11, 1945, Map Room Files, FDRL.

29. Kimball, *Alliance Declining,* 609. Stalin had additional information from other sources in the UK, most likely from Anthony Blunt, a member of the Cambridge Five. For more on this, see S. M. Plokhy, *Yalta: The Price of Peace* (New York: Viking, 2010), 363–364.

30. Plokhy, *Yalta,* 360.

31. Richard Breitman, "U.S. Intelligence and the Nazis," *Journal of American History,* January 30, 2015.

32. William Leahy, *I Was There* (New York: Whittlesey House, 1950), 334.

18. Off the Record

1. Margaret (Daisy) Suckley Diary, April 5, 1945, and April 4, 1945, FDRL.

2. Margaret (Daisy) Suckley Diary, April 4, 1945.

3. Margaret (Daisy) Suckley Diary, January 22, 1945.

4. Eleanor Roosevelt, *This I Remember* (New York: Harper & Brothers, 1949), 343.

5. Doris Kearns Goodwin, *No Ordinary Time: Franklin and Eleanor Roosevelt: The Home Front in World War II* (New York: Simon & Schuster, 1994), 361; Geoffrey C. Ward, ed., *Closet*

Companion: The Unknown Story of the Intimate Friendship Between Franklin Roosevelt and Marga-ret Suckley (New York: Houghton Mifflin, 1995), 20–21.

6. Lucy Rutherfurd to Daisy Suckley, February 9, 1945, Margaret (Daisy) Suckley Papers, FDRL.

7. Osmena to Roosevelt, March 31, 1945, President's Secretary's Files (PSF) Philippines, 1944–1945, FDRL.

8. William Hassett Diary, April 5, 1945; List of Matters to Be Taken up by the President; Osmena to Roosevelt, March 31, 1945, PSF Philippines, 1944–1945.

9. Franklin D. Roosevelt, Press Conference, April 5, 1945, Complete Press Conferences, FDRL.

10. Margaret (Daisy) Suckley Diary, April 6, 1945.

11. Ibid.

12. Interview with Dr. Howard Bruenn conducted by Jan K. Herman, Bureau of Medicine and Surgery, Riverdale, New York, January 31, 1990, 22; Howard G. Bruenn, M.D., "Clinical Notes on the Illness and Death of President Franklin D. Roosevelt," *Annals of Internal Medicine* 72 (April 1970): 579–591.

13. Churchill to Roosevelt, April 5, 1945, Map Room Files, FDRL.

14. "Manpower Action Hints FDR, Like Wilson, May Lose Congress Control," *Washington Post,* April 8, 1945, B5.

15. Eleanor Roosevelt to Maude Gray, April 1, 1945; it was also in this letter that Eleanor alluded to Henry Wallace as the one person able to carry on.

16. Eleanor Roosevelt to Franklin D. Roosevelt, April 8, 1945, Eleanor Roosevelt Papers, FDRL.

17. Lucy Rutherfurd to Grace Tully, April 5, 1945, Grace Tully Papers, FDRL; White House Tele-phone Logs, April 5, 1945, FDRL.

18. Ibid.

19. Margaret (Daisy) Suckley Diary, April 8, 1945.

20. Margaret (Daisy) Suckley Diary, April 9, 1945.

21. William Hassett Diary, April 9, 1945.

22. Ibid.

23. Elizabeth (Madame) Shoumatoff, *FDR's Unfinished Portrait: A Memoir* (Pittsburgh: Pitts-burg University Press, 1991), 101.

24. William Hassett Diary, April 10, 1945.

25. Margaret (Daisy) Suckley Diary, April 10, 1945; Shoumatoff, *FDR's Unfinished Portrait,* 107.

26. Hugh Gallagher, *FDR's Splendid Deception: The Moving Story of Roosevelt's Massive Disabil-ity and the Intense Efforts to Keep It from the Public* (St. Petersburg, FL: Vandamere Press, 1999), 208.

27. Roosevelt to Stalin, March 31, 1945, Map Room Files, FDRL.

28. Churchill to Roosevelt, April 11, 1945, Map Room Files, FDRL.

29. Ibid.

30. Roosevelt to Churchill, April 11, 1945, Map Room Files, FDRL.

31. Ibid.

32. Churchill to Roosevelt, April 9, 1945, Map Room Files, FDRL.

33. Roosevelt to Churchill, April 11, 1945, Map Room Files, FDRL. The president would not live long enough to see how Allied policy with respect to the Netherlands would play out, but in keeping with the assurances he made to Queen Wilhelmina three weeks before, Eisenhower would eventually negotiate a truce with the German Command in Holland that would allow the British, Canadian, and American air forces to drop in the final weeks of the war over 11,000 tons of much-needed food to the anguished Dutch population.

34. Roosevelt to Stalin, April 11, 1945, Map Room Files, FDRL.

35. Margaret (Daisy) Suckley Diary, April 11, 1945; Shoumatoff, *FDR's Unfinished Portrait,* 110.

36. Henry Morgenthau Diary, April 11, 1945, HMD, FDRL.

37. Henry Morgenthau Diary, April 11, 1945.

38. Shoumatoff, *FDR's Unfinished Portrait,* 114.

39. Margaret (Daisy) Suckley Diary, April 12, 1945.

19. The Last Day

1. Margret (Daisy) Suckley Diary, April 5, 1945; letter from Hazel Stephens to William MacKay Davis, April 15, 1945, reprinted in William Warrens Rogers, Jr., "The Death of a President, April 12, 1945: An Account from Warm Springs," *The Georgia Historical Quarterly* 75, no. 1 (Spring 1991), 114–115.

2. Ibid.

3. Margaret (Daisy) Suckley Diary, April 12, 1945, FDRL; Roosevelt Medical Information, Howard Bruenn Papers, 1944–1946, FDRL.

4. Grace Tully, *FDR: My Boss* (Chicago: People's Book Club, 1949), 361.

5. Ibid.; "Toinette Marya Bachelder," Obituary, *Washington Post,* October 5, 1995, B4; Elizabeth Shoumatoff, *FDR's Unfinished Portrait: A Memoir* (Pittsburgh: Pittsburgh University Press, 1991), 117.

6. William Hassett Diary, April 12, 1945, FDRL; Shoumatoff, *FDR's Unfinished Portrait,* 120.

7. William Hassett Diary, April 12, 1945.

8. Ibid.

9. Map Room Files, April 12, 1945, Map Room Files, FDRL.

10. Ibid.

11. William Hassett Diary, April 12, 1945; Margaret (Daisy) Suckley Diary, April 6, 1945.

12. Map Room Log Sheet, April 12, 1945, FDRL.

13. Margaret (Daisy) Suckley Diary, April 12, 1945; Shoumatoff, *FDR's Unfinished Portrait,* 117.

14. Shoumatoff, *FDR's Unfinished Portrait,* 118; Michael Reilly and Robert Slocum, *Reilly of the White House* (New York: Simon & Schuster, 1947), 230.

15. Margaret (Daisy) Suckley Diary, April 12, 1945.

16. Tully, *FDR: My Boss,* 361–362.

17. Reilly and Slocum, *Reilly of the White House,* 231.

18. William Hassett Diary, April 12, 1945.

19. Roosevelt, Medical Information, Howard G. Bruenn Papers, 1944–1946, FDRL.

20. Roosevelt, Medical Information, Howard G. Bruenn Papers, 1944–1946, FDRL; Howard G. Bruenn, M.D., "Clinical Notes on the Illness and Death of President Franklin D. Roosevelt," *Annals of Internal Medicine* 72 (April 1970): 579–591.

21. Shoumatoff, *FDR's Unfinished Portrait,* 118–119.

22. Vice Admiral (Dr.) Ross T. McIntire, *White House Physician* (New York: Putnam & Sons, 1946), 241.

23. Joseph Lash, *Eleanor and Franklin* (New York: W. W. Norton, 1971), 720–721; Margaret (Daisy) Suckley Diary, April 12, 1945.

24. Eleanor Roosevelt, *The Autobiography of Eleanor Roosevelt* (New York: Da Capo Press, 1992).

25. Wilson Brown, "Four Presidents," unpublished manuscript, Wilson Brown Papers, Annapolis, Maryland; Linda Lotridge Levin, *The Making of FDR: The Story of Stephen T. Early, America's First Modern Press Secretary* (New York: Prometheus Books, 2008), 77–78.

26. William Hassett Diary, April 12, 1945.

27. Shoumatoff, *FDR's Unfinished Portrait,* 119.

28. William Hassett Diary, April 12, 1945.

29. Roosevelt Medical Information, Howard G. Bruenn Papers, 1944–1946, FDRL.

30. William Hassett Diary, April 12, 1945.

31. Clinical Notes on the Illness and Death of the President, and Roosevelt Medical Information, Howard G. Bruenn Papers, 1944–1946, FDRL.

32. Dr. James Paullin to Dr. McIntire, June 24, 1946, Box 12, Ross T. McIntire Papers, FDR; McIntire, *White House Physician,* 242–243.

33. Clinical Notes on the Illness and Death of the President, and Roosevelt Medical Information. Howard G. Bruenn Papers, 1944–1946, FDRL.

34. McIntire, *White House Physician,* 275; Margaret (Daisy) Suckley Diary, April 12, 1945.

35. Levin, *The Making of FDR*, 427.

36. Margaret (Daisy) Suckley Diary, April 12, 1945.

37. Tully, *FDR: My Boss*, 362–363.

38. A. Merriman Smith, *Thank You, Mr. President: A White House Notebook* (New York: Da Capo Press, 1976), 220–221.

39. Ibid., 223.

40. Hazel Stephens and Betty Brown to Mr. Mackey, April 15, 1945, in Rogers, "The Death of a President," 115–116.

41. Ibid.

42. Eleanor Roosevelt, *The Autobiography of Eleanor Roosevelt*, 276.

43. Ibid.

44. Eleanor Roosevelt Papers, FDRL.

45. David McCullough, *Truman* (New York: Simon & Schuster, 1992), 340–341.

46. Eleanor Roosevelt, *The Autobiography of Eleanor Roosevelt*, 275.

47. James Roosevelt, *My Parents: A Differing View* (New York: Playboy Press, 1976), 285–286.

48. "James Roosevelt Delayed in Flight," *New York Times*, April 16, 1945, 3.

49. Shoumatoff, *FDR's Unfinished Portrait*, 120.

50. William D. Leahy Diary, April 12, 1945, Library of Congress.

51. Stephen Early Papers, Box 34, FDRL.

52. Ibid.; Kirstin Downey, *The Woman Behind the New Deal* (New York: Anchor Books, 2009), 341.

53. "Mrs. Roosevelt Flies to Georgia; Was at Benefit When News Came: SHE CARRIES BRAVELY ON," *New York Times*, April 13, 1945, 4.

54. Tully, *FDR: My Boss*, 366.

55. Bernard Asbell, *Mother and Daughter: The Letters of Eleanor and Anna Roosevelt* (New York: Fromm International, 1988), 186.

56. Tully, *FDR: My Boss*, 366.

57. Margaret (Daisy) Suckley Diary, April 12, 1945.

58. Eleanor Roosevelt, *Autobiography*, 279.

59. James Roosevelt, *My Parents*, 286.

Epilogue: Looking Beyond Victory

1. Frank L. Kluckhohn, "Grave Is in Garden: As the Nation Paid Homage to Its Departed Commander in Chief," *New York Times*, April 16, 1945, 1; Henry A. Wallace, Unpublished Diary of Henry Wallace, April 15, 1945.

2. David B. Woolner, Warren Kimball, and David Reynolds, eds., *FDR's World: War, Peace, and Legacies* (New York: Palgrave Macmillan, 2008), 227–228; "Two Hemispheres Honor Roosevelt," *Los Angeles Times*, April 22, 1945, 6; "Soviet Flags Show Mourning Border," *New York Times*, April 15, 1945, 4.

3. Martin Gilbert, *Winston S. Churchill: Road to Victory, 1941–1945* (Boston: Houghton Mifflin, 1986), 1291–1292; Churchill to King George VI, April 13, 1945, Winston S. Churchill Papers, CHAR 20/193B/185–186, Churchill Archives, Cambridge.

4. W. Averell Harriman, *Special Envoy to Churchill and Stalin, 1941–1946* (New York: Random House, 1975), 441–442; Foreign Relations of the United States (FRUS), Diplomatic Papers, *Europe, 1945*, Vol. V (Washington, DC: US Government Printing Office, 1967), 826–827; Vladimir Pechatnov, "Stalin and Roosevelt: Allies in War/The Great Victory," in multivolume series, edited by S. Naryshkin and A. Torkunov, Vol. IX, (in Russian), (Moscow: MGIMO-University Publishing: 2013). Stalin was also anxious to know if U.S. foreign policy would remain consistent under President Truman. On April 22, 1945, Ambassador Gromyko telegraphed the Kremlin with word that that there was a great deal of unease in Washington in the days following FDR's death. He also indicated that Truman's speech to Congress on April 16, helped calm things down, although "the address was framed in rather sharp expressions, and there was a lack of original thought that one could see in Roosevelt's speeches." Nevertheless, Gromyko thought it was unlikely that Truman

would return to a policy of isolationism, but would continue on the path of cooperation with the Soviet Union and Great Britain—"at least for the time being." (Archive of Foreign Policy of the Russian Federation, Moscow, fond .059, folder. 15, folder. 46, file. 370, L .23, 218, 17).

5. Anne O'Hare McCormick, "His 'Unfinished Business'—and Ours," *New York Times,* April 22, 1945, SM3.

6. "Churchill Eulogizes Roosevelt As Best U.S. Friend to Britain," *New York Times,* April 18, 1945, 5.

7. One further telling example of this resolve can be found in FDR's reaction to the 1944 film *Wilson,* which he viewed while attending the Second Quebec Conference in September 1944, just a few days following his conversation with Mackenzie King about the election. As recorded by Dr. Bruenn, FDR—while watching the scenes of President Wilson fighting in vain for US participation in the League of Nations, and collapsing from a stroke in the process—muttered under his breath, "By God that's not going to happen to me!" (interview with Dr. Bruenn, conducted by Jan K. Herman, Bureau of Medicine and Surgery, Riverdale, New York, January 31, 1990).

8. Benjamin Cohen, "Confidential Memorandum Concerning a Fourth Term," sent to FDR, March 8, 1944, Benjamin V. Cohen Papers, Box 12, Library of Congress.

9. Michael Barone, "Franklin D. Roosevelt: A Protestant Patrician in a Catholic Party," in David B. Woolner and Richard Kurial, eds., *FDR, the Vatican, and the Roman Catholic Church in America, 1933-1945,* 3-10: Mary McLeod Bethune, quoted in Alan Brinkley and David B. Woolner, "Franklin Roosevelt and the Progressive Tradition," in David B. Woolner and John M. Thompson, eds., *Progressivism in America: Past, Present, and Future* (New York: Oxford University Press, 2016), 21.

10. Franklin D. Roosevelt, State of the Union Address (including Economic Bill of Rights speech), January 11, 1944, Master Speech File, FDRL.

11. For more on this, see Alan K. Henrikson, "FDR and the World-Wide Arena," in David B. Woolner, Warren F. Kimball, and David Reynolds, eds., *FDR's World: War, Peace and Legacies* (New York: Palgrave Macmillan, 2008), 35–62. As FDR remarked to Harry Hopkins when the latter commented that it would be hard to get the American people to be interested in Java as implied by the global scope of FDR's Four Freedoms Address, "I'm afraid they will have to be some day, Harry. The world is getting smaller and even the people of Java are going to be our neighbors, now" (Robert Sherwood, *Roosevelt and Hopkins: An Intimate History* [Boston: Houghton Mifflin, 1948], 231).

12. David B. Woolner, "Epilogue: Reflections on Legacy and Leadership—the View from 2008," in Woolner et al., *FDR's World,* 234–235.

13. Charles Bohlen, *Witness to History, 1929-1969* (New York: W. W. Norton, 1973), 182–183; Anthony Eden, *The Memoirs of Anthony Eden: The Reckoning* (London: Houghton Mifflin, 1965), 513.

14. Franklin Roosevelt, Fireside Chat to the Nation, June 30, 1934, Master Speech Files, FDRL.

15. John C. Culver and John Hyde, *American Dreamer: The Life of Henry Wallace* (New York: W. W. Norton, 2000), 210; Roosevelt to Cohen, March 16, 1944, Box 12, Benjamin Cohen Papers, Library of Congress.

16. Elizabeth Borgwardt, *A New Deal for the World: America's Vision for Human Rights* (New York: Belknap Press, 2005); Woolner et. al., *FDR's World,* 230

17. Mark A. Stoler, *Allies and Adversaries: The Joint Chiefs of Staff, the Grand Alliance, and U.S. Strategy in World War II* (Chapel Hill: University of North Carolina Press, 2000), 232; "Problems and Objectives of United States Policy," April 2, 1945, Marshall Papers, Pentagon Office File, Box 67, George C. Marshall Research Library, Lexington, Virginia.

18. Woolner et al., *FDR's World,* 228.

19. Anne O'Hare McCormick, "His 'Unfinished Business'—and Ours: A Final Interview with Franklin Roosevelt," *New York Times,* April 22, 1945, SM3.

20. Franklin D. Roosevelt, Jefferson Day Address, April 1945, Master Speech File, FDRL.

21. Ibid.

22. Ibid.

Index

David B. Woolner is Senior Fellow and Hyde Park Resident Historian at the Roosevelt Institute, Professor of History at Marist College, and Senior Fellow of the Center for Civic Engagement at Bard College. He is the editor or coeditor of five books, including *Progressivism in America: Past, Present, and Future* and *FDR's World: War, Peace, and Legacies.* He lives in Rhinebeck, New York.

Photograph by Michael Benabib

31901060860782